D1327823

Wrongful Damage to Property in Roman Law

Wrongful Damage to Property in Roman Law

British Perspectives

Edited by Paul J du Plessis

EDINBURGH
University Press

Edinburgh University Press is one of the leading university presses in the UK. We publish academic books and journals in our selected subject areas across the humanities and social sciences, combining cutting-edge scholarship with high editorial and production values to produce academic works of lasting importance. For more information visit our website: edinburghuniversitypress.com

Edinburgh University Press Ltd
The Tun – Holyrood Road
12 (2f) Jackson's Entry
Edinburgh EH8 8PJ

Typeset in 10/12pt Goudy Old Style by
Servis Filmsetting Ltd, Stockport, Cheshire,
printed and bound by CPI Group (UK) Ltd
Croydon, CR0 4YY

A CIP record for this book is available from the British Library

ISBN 978 1 4744 3446 1 (hardback)
ISBN 978 1 4744 3447 8 (webready PDF)
ISBN 978 1 4744 3448 5 (epub)

Contents

Contributors

John W Cairns, Professor of Civil Law, The University of Edinburgh (john.cairns@ed.ac.uk)

Paul J du Plessis, Professor of Roman Law, The University of Edinburgh (p.duplessis@ed.ac.uk)

Robin Evans-Jones, Professor of Jurisprudence, The University of Aberdeen (revansj@abdn.ac.uk)

David Ibbetson, Regius Professor of Civil Law, The University of Cambridge (dj22@cam.ac.uk)

David Johnston QC, Advocate in the Court of Session, Edinburgh and sometime Regius Professor of Civil Law, The University of Cambridge (david.johnston@axiomadvocates.com)

Alberto Lorusso, Associate Professor of Roman Law, The University of Madrid (Alcalá de Henares) (lorussounitn@yahoo.it)

Paul Mitchell, Professor of Laws, University College London (p.mitchell@ucl.ac.uk)

Joe Sampson, David Li Fellow in Law, Selwyn College, Affiliated Lecturer, The University of Cambridge (jws43@cam.ac.uk)

Helen Scott, Tutorial Fellow, Lady Margaret Hall, and Professor of Private Law, The University of Oxford (helen.scott@law.ox.ac.uk)

Benjamin Spagnolo, Fellow and Lecturer in Law, Trinity College, Affiliated Lecturer, The University of Cambridge (benjamin.spagnolo@law.cam.ac.uk)

Giuseppe Valditara, Professor of Roman Law, The University of Turin (beppevaldi@gmail.com)

Preface

Few topics have had a more profound impact on the study of Roman law in Britain than the *lex Aquilia*, a Roman statute enacted c. 287/286 BCE to reform the law on wrongful damage to property. Writing an article on this topic has become a proverbial rite of passage for nearly all British Romanists. A brief survey of modern Roman law literature demonstrates that British Romanists have made a substantial contribution to the study of this topic.[1] The relevant titles[2] in Justinian's compilation have been translated into English more than once and, judging by recent *Festschriften* for Alan Rodger[3] and Boudewijn Sirks,[4] the *lex Aquilia* continues to be studied in great depth by a number of British Romanists. And yet, the British fascination with the *lex Aquilia* is not immediately apparent to anyone outside these circles, nor has it been explored systematically.

The aim of this volume is to investigate the reasons for the peculiarly British fixation with wrongful damage to property in Roman law against the backdrop of the teaching of Roman law in Britain during the last century. This necessarily involves an investigation of certain broader themes. First, the significance of the *lex Aquilia* for the Oxford, Cambridge and Edinburgh legal curricula (as an ever-present topic in the advanced course in Roman law at all these universities) will be assessed. Within this theme, specific topics such as how the subject was taught, what materials were used and what impact the teaching of this topic had on subsequent generations of legal academics who studied at these universities (even if they did not proceed to further study and specialisation in Roman law – since the *lex Aquilia* clearly also had an impact on legal scholars working on modern tort/delict) will be investigated.

In second place, and related to the first (especially the issue of teaching

---

[1] Neil H Andrews, '*Occidere* and the *Lex Aquilia*' (1987) 46 CLJ 315 and Geoffrey MacCormack, 'Juristic Interpretation of the *Lex Aquilia*' in Studi in onore di Cesare Sanfilippo vol 1 (Giuffrè 1982) to name but two of the many contributions.

[2] Eg Charles Henry Monro (ed), *Digest IX. 2 Lex Aquilia* (CUP 1898).

[3] Andrew Burrows, David Johnston and Reinhard Zimmermann (eds), *Judge and Jurist: Essays in Memory of Lord Rodger of Earlsferry* (OUP 2013); Hector MacQueen, 'Lord Rodger: Jurist Then Judge (The UK Supreme Court Annual Review: Commentary and Reflections) (Testimonial)' (2014) 3 Cam J Int and Comp Law 11.

[4] Jan Hallebeek and others (eds), *Inter Cives necnon Peregrinos: Essays in Honour of Boudewijn Sirks* (Vandenhoeck & Rupprecht 2014).

materials), the impact of Frederick Henry Lawson's work on tort liability will be contextualised. This work, first published in 1950 and appearing in a number of subsequent editions, not only contained a thorough exposition of law in subsequent periods of European legal development, but undoubtedly also exercised a significant influence upon the teaching of wrongful damage to property in Roman law in the above-mentioned universities. Finally, the contribution of German émigré lawyers (including their training in Germany) who sought refuge in Britain before and during the Second World War and their subsequent impact on the study of Roman law during the course of the twentieth century will also be addressed. While the collected volume, *Jurists Uprooted*,[5] has done much to uncover the contribution by these scholars to British academic life, it has not examined specific areas of law. This book will therefore build upon the foundational work already done in the aforementioned volume.

But this volume is not an exercise in jingoism. Its aim is not to make any claims about the superiority or dominance of Roman law scholarship on wrongful damage to property in Britain *qua* other European jurisdictions. The study of Roman law is a truly international discipline strongly rooted in the European legal discourse (see, for example, the chapters by Lorusso and Valditara). With that said, within this discourse, it is possible to distinguish distinct national approaches to the study of Roman law (for example, in German or Dutch legal scholarship). Such national 'methods' have not only been formed and influenced by the nature of the legal systems in which they are rooted, but have also generated a specific national 'legal culture' for the study of Roman law in that jurisdiction. The aim of this volume is therefore to establish whether, using the *lex Aquilia* as a test case, a distinctly British approach to the study of Roman law may be identified. In doing so, the study of the *lex Aquilia* in Britain will be placed in context with a view to shedding light on the 'legal culture' of Roman law scholarship in the United Kingdom.

Paul J du Plessis
Alberto Lorusso

---

[5]   Jack Beatson and Reinhard Zimmermann (eds), *Jurists Uprooted: German-Speaking Émigré Lawyers in Twentieth-Century Britain* (OUP 2004).

Part I

Matters of Context

Chapter 1

The Early Historiography of the Lex Aquilia in Britain: Introducing Students to the Digest

John W Cairns*

1. INTRODUCTION

In 1886, Frederick Pollock was working on the first edition of his famous monograph on the law of torts.[1] In the same year he also completed a provisional version of a draft bill on civil wrongs that he was preparing for the government of India.[2] In his role as editor of the newly founded *Law Quarterly Review*, he received, again in 1886, a copy of Erwin Grueber's commentary on the *lex Aquilia*.[3] Pollock commissioned a review of this work from James Muirhead, Professor of Civil Law in the University of Edinburgh. This appeared in the July 1886 issue.[4] The choice of Muirhead was obvious. Educated at Edinburgh and Heidelberg, he was the most notable scholar of Roman law in the United Kingdom in the 1880s. He was certainly the only one who had acquired an international reputation in the field.[5] Furthermore, Pollock and Muirhead were almost certainly already acquainted, as the University of Edinburgh had conferred on Pollock the degree of LLD *honoris causa tantum* in 1880.[6]

Grueber had also presented a copy of his book to Pollock. This presentation copy survives.[7] Given Pollock's current research and writing, the book

* The author is grateful for the generous assistance of Wolfgang Ernst and Paul du Plessis, and expresses his thanks to Edinburgh University Library, Centre for Research Collections.

[1] Frederick Pollock, *The Law of Torts: A Treatise on the Principles of Obligations Arising from Civil Wrongs in the Common Law* (Stevens & Sons Ltd 1887).

[2] Frederick Pollock, *The Law of Torts: A Treatise on the Principles of Obligations Arising from Civil Wrongs in the Common Law: To Which is Added the Draft of a Code of Civil Wrongs Prepared for the Government of India* (2nd edn, Stevens & Sons Ltd 1890) 517.

[3] Erwin Grueber (ed), *The Roman Law of Damage to Property, Being a Commentary on the Title of the Digest Ad Legem Aquiliam (IX. 2), with an Introduction to the Study of the Corpus Iuris Civilis* (Clarendon Press 1886).

[4] James Muirhead, 'Book Review' (1886) 2 LQR 379.

[5] John W Cairns, 'Henry Goudy, Hannis Taylor, and Plagiarism Considered as a Fine Art' (2015) 30 Tul Eur & Civ LF 1, 45–46.

[6] 'University of Edinburgh Graduation Ceremonial' *The Scotsman* (Edinburgh, 22 April 1880) 3.

[7] See Karen Baston and Ernest Metzger (eds), *The Roman Law Library of Alan Ferguson Rodger, Lord Rodger of Earlsferry: with a Bibliography of His Works* (Traditio Iuris Romani 2012) 67.

was of considerable interest to him, and no doubt he had been pleased to receive the complimentary copy. His reading of the work, however, raised some issues that troubled him. He wrote to Muirhead seeking answers and clarification, posing a number of, often technical, questions that the Scots professor answered. Muirhead's letter survives, pasted into Pollock's copy of Grueber's work. Pollock's copy also contains some pencil annotations that he made; these can be linked to his discussion with Muirhead, and indeed with some of his notes in his *Law of Torts*. I have discussed these elsewhere, so there is no need to reflect further on them here.[8]

It would be an obvious – and extraordinary – exaggeration to state that this correspondence in 1886 marked the beginning of the very obvious British fascination with the *lex Aquilia*. But it undoubtedly came at a significant time. It is true, if trite, to say that delict and torts were undergoing very significant development in the nineteenth century because of industrial and commercial growth. All over the industrial worlds of Europe, the Americas, and the Colonies boilers exploded, dams burst, and mines collapsed, leading to significant financial loss caused by injuries to people and property. Booms in construction led to individuals falling into holes dug for foundations. Mechanisation led to the injury of factory workers. Mass circulation of newspapers made it easy to disseminate defamatory material. The development of a consumer society based on industrial production in factories raised all kinds of new delictual problems. This is indeed the background to Pollock's book. The lively, messy complexity of all of this is ably revealed in, for example, some of the work of the late Brian Simpson.[9]

In the Anglo-American world a new intellectual approach to torts developed. Scholars considered torts a specific branch of the discipline of law, a specialised area of study.[10] Pollock thus prefaced his new book with an open letter to Oliver Wendell Holmes, writing:

> I claim [your goodwill] because the purpose of this book is to show that there really is a Law of Torts, not merely a number of rules of law about various kinds of torts – that this is a true living branch of the Common Law, not a collection of heterogeneous instances.

Pollock's presentation copy of Grueber's book was latterly in the Library of Lord Rodger of Earlsferry, from whose estate it was generously gifted to the author.

[8] John W Cairns, 'English Torts and Roman Delicts: The Correspondence of James Muirhead and Frederick Pollock' (2013) 87 Tul L Rev 867, 878–83.

[9] A W Brian Simpson, 'Bursting Reservoirs and Victorian Tort Law: Rylands and Horrocks v. Fletcher (1868)' in A W Brian Simpson, *Leading Cases in the Common Law* (OUP 1996) 195; for a further lively example of the type of issue involved, see George Dargo, 'Steamboats and Tugboats on the Mississippi' in George Dargo, *Colony to Empire: Episodes in American Legal History* (Lawbook Exchange Ltd 2011) 235.

[10] David Ibbetson, *A Historical Introduction to the Law of Obligations* (OUP 1999) 169–87; G Edward White, *Tort Law in America: An Intellectual History* (expanded edn, OUP Inc 2003).

He claimed that 'a complete theory of Torts is yet to seek, for the subject is altogether modern', stressing that the 'really scientific treatment of principles begins only with the decisions of the last fifty years', the development of which 'belongs to that classical period of our jurisprudence which in England came between the Common Law Procedure Act [1852] and the Judicature Act [1873]'.[11]

In Scotland, the law of delict increased in its significance for the same historical reasons;[12] but Scots law's intimate relationship with Roman law and the classificatory schemes developed by its institutional writers under the influence of Roman law and natural law provided an obvious structure into which to insert the modern developments.[13] Nineteenth-century England, on the other hand, had inherited from the middle ages the complex and messy law of torts to which Pollock alluded in his letter to Holmes;[14] but in the eighteenth century ideas of fault had started progressively to develop into 'negligence', a process involving influence from Roman and natural law, the former in particular having a specific impact on legal theorists.[15] Pollock considered the study of Roman law to be of primary importance for the understanding of English law, so that it held the potential to help the new discipline of torts crystallise (to adopt Ibbetson's chemical metaphor) out of the older actions of trespass and case. Pollock's biographer sums up his attitude as based on two justificatory opinions: first, 'Roman law provided a model for the consolidation of the common law into a rational system, so that its development might be understood as a whole'; and second, 'proficiency in Roman law and its attendant scholarship promoted better understanding of common-law doctrines, rescued the common lawyer from insularity, and gave to the student of the common law a comparative perspective'.[16] This will have reinforced his interest in Grueber's book.

It is important to emphasise, however, that the publication of Grueber's book was only one indicator of a general move in the British universities to develop the teaching of Roman law away from what had become a near-exclusive focus on the *Institutes* of Gaius and Justinian. His was not even the first publication with this aim in view, though it was the first on the *lex*

---

[11] Pollock (n 1) vi–vii.
[12] Consider the early cases in which individuals fell into drains and pits linked to new construction: Hector MacQueen and W David H Sellar, 'Negligence' in Kenneth Reid and Reinhard Zimmermann (eds), *A History of Private Law in Scotland: Volume II: Obligations* (OUP 2000) 517, 526–28.
[13] Daniel Visser and Niall Q Whitty, 'The Structure of the Law of Delict in Historical Perspective' in Reid and Zimmermann (n 12) 422.
[14] Ibbetson (n 10) 95–151.
[15] ibid 164–68.
[16] Richard A Cosgrove, 'Pollock, Sir Frederick, Third Baronet (1845–1937)', *Oxford Dictionary of National Biography* (OUP 2004; online edn Jan 2008) <www.oxforddnb.com/view/article/35563> accessed 4 August 2017.

Aquilia. Muirhead remarked in his review of Grueber's work that, though study of the *Institutes* of Gaius and Justinian and of the history of Roman law was valuable in itself, it was also valuable as equipping 'the student for the intelligent appreciation of the master-pieces of practical jurisprudence preserved in the Digest'. He added:

> For the man who reads Roman law as a professional training, rather than in the expectation of having to deal with it as authoritative positive law, the study of the very words of the great jurists of the first two centuries and a half of the empire is likely to prove more profitable than the most careful perusal of the most perfect systematic treatise of a Savigny, a Windscheid, or a Brinz. Be the doctrine there expounded ever so true, precise, and complete a reproduction of that contained in the Roman texts, yet it is doctrine only. It can teach little or nothing of the sur-passing art of the Roman jurists, – the apparently instinctive skill with which they dissected a case, exposed its points, and discovered and applied the rule that was to determine the question to which they gave rise.[17]

This gives us the context for Grueber's book. It was part of a general move-ment in the British universities to deepen study of Roman law through specialist treatment of a title of the Digest. But it was not yet clear that that title was so often to be D.9.2, even though Muirhead commented that it was 'rather a favourite . . . for academical exercitations, and, as it happens, has for the last two years been prescribed for the graduation examination in Edinburgh, along with that *de Rei Vindicatione*'. Though full of interest, it had, for Muirhead, the disadvantage, 'although of considerable length', of wanting 'that diversity of authorship which is met with in many other titles'. Thus, three-quarters of the title was taken from Ulpian, while Papinian had only a few lines.[18]

This chapter will explore this development in the second half of the nine-teenth century, with a glance forward in the conclusion. It deserves more examination than is possible here in the context of a short chapter, which will raise questions that will inevitably be left unanswered. It is evident that this renewal of the teaching of Roman law is part of a general reform in the British universities from 1850 onwards. It is related to the development of professional education in Victorian Britain. Though Grueber's work was published in 1886, it seems that it was only in the twentieth century that the British love affair with the *lex Aquilia* was to flourish. But the later nine-teenth century prepared the way. This love affair grew out of a concern with focusing on the details and practicalities of the law, as revealed through study of a title of the Digest.

---

[17] Muirhead (n 4) 379.
[18] ibid 380.

2. UNIVERSITY REFORMS AND CURRICULA IN EDINBURGH AND OXFORD AND CAMBRIDGE

The publication of Grueber's book was the indirect result of significant reform in university education in Great Britain. Acts of Parliament reformed the universities both north and south of the border after investigation by Royal Commissions. In England, Royal Commissions appointed in 1850 resulted in the Oxford University Act of 1854 and the Cambridge University Act of 1856.[19] In Scotland, the universities were reformed by the Universities (Scotland) Act of 1858, influenced by a Royal Commission set up in 1826 that had reported in 1831.[20] The three Acts, as well as introducing major reforms in governance to these British universities, used the mechanism of appointing Commissioners to provide detailed regulations for the universities in both countries. At the same time, the legal profession in both countries was concerned about the education and training of those seeking admission to its ranks.[21]

In 1872 there was a further Royal Commission appointed to look into the finances of Oxford and Cambridge; by the time it had reported there was a different government, which nonetheless undertook enactment of the Oxford and Cambridge Act 1877, which again appointed Commissioners to effect reforms.[22] In 1876 another Royal Commission with a wide remit was appointed to examine the Scottish universities. This eventually led to an Act of Parliament in 1889 that established Commissioners to implement reforms by Ordinance. There were further reforms to law degrees in the Scottish universities, and also the creation of a Board of Studies in Law and History in Edinburgh, which led to certain LLB courses, notably civil law, becoming courses that could be taken for graduation with the degree of MA; but we need only glance at these here.[23]

---

[19] W Reginald Ward, 'From the Tractarians to the Executive Commission 1845–1854' in Michael G Brock and Mark C Curthoys (eds), *The History of the University of Oxford. Volume VI: Nineteenth-Century Oxford, Part 1* (Clarendon Press 1997) 306; Laurence W Brockliss, *The University of Oxford: A History* (OUP 2016) 347–60; Peter Searby, *A History of the University of Cambridge. Volume III: 1750–1870* (CUP 1997) 507–44.

[20] David B Horn, *A Short History of the University of Edinburgh 1556–1889* (EUP 1967) 170–85.

[21] David B Horn, 'The Universities (Scotland) Act of 1858' (1958) 19 University of Edinburgh Journal 169; Stephen D Girvin, 'Nineteenth-Century Reforms in Scottish Legal Education: The Universities and the Bar' (1993) 14 J Leg Hist 127, 131–36; Christopher W Brooks and Michael Lobban, 'Apprenticeship or Academy? The Idea of a Law University, 1830–1860' in Johnathan A Bush and Alain Wijffels (eds), *Learning the Law: Teaching and Transmission of English Law, 1150–1900* (Hambledon Press 1999) 353.

[22] Christopher N L Brooke, *A History of the University of Cambridge. Volume IV: 1870–1990* (CUP 1993) 82–89; Brockliss (n 19) 363–68; A J Engel, *From Clergyman to Don* (Clarendon Press 1983) 156–201.

[23] James Mackintosh, 'The Faculty of Law' in A Logan Turner (ed), *History of the University of Edinburgh, 1883–1933* (Oliver and Boyd 1933) 83, 85–88.

In England, the University of Oxford Act of 1877 led to major reforms in the Law School in Oxford through the activities of the Commissioners. These are of great importance for the topic of this chapter, and will be discussed because of their impact on the teaching of Roman law. In Scotland, the Commissioners appointed under the 1858 Act created by Ordinance the degree of LLB, to be taken after completion of a first degree in arts. This was a new departure. Prior to this, law students in Edinburgh did not take a degree, though they usually studied law after arts. The curriculum of the new degree required study of civil (or Roman) law, with the Professor of Civil Law teaching in both the winter and summer sessions.[24] Pollock's correspondent Muirhead was appointed to the Chair of Civil Law in 1862, with the aim he should fulfil these requirements.[25]

Developments in Oxford

In Oxford the 1854 Act and the work of the Commissioners under it did not have a significant impact on legal study. An honours school of Law and Modern History had already been established in 1850 for the degree of BA. Study of Roman law was part of this honours school, with an examination on Justinian's *Institutes*. An examination for the degree of Bachelor of Civil Law (BCL) was introduced in 1851. This was based on both Justinian's *Institutes* and the *Syntagma* of J G Heineccius.[26] The latter was a work originally published in 1718 exploring the historical issues that arose in Roman law, following the text of the *Institutes*. There was a modern edition of 1841 that also related it to recent research and discoveries, such as of Gaius' *Institutes*.[27] The 1854 Act and the Commissioners appointed did implement measures that started a tentative focus of legal study in the College of All Souls and the development of an extended professoriate.[28] It is worth noting that a collection of law books accessible to students started to be built up in the Codrington Library in All Souls.[29]

In 1872 Law split from History to become the independent Honour

---

[24] Horn (n 20) 177–78.

[25] John W Cairns, 'James Muirhead, Teacher, Scholar, Book-Collector' in *The Muirhead Collection Catalogue* (C B B B – B C B B 1999 [= (1999) 146 *Bibliographica Belgica*]) 1, 1–2, 8–9.

[26] Frederick Henry Lawson, *The Oxford Law School, 1850–1965* (Clarendon Press 1968) 20–33; Barry Nicholas, 'Jurisprudence' in Michael G Brock and Mark C Curthoys (eds), *The History of the University of Oxford. Volume VI: Nineteenth-Century Oxford, Part 2* (Clarendon Press 2000) 385, 386–88.

[27] Johann Gottlieb Heineccius, *Antiquitatum romanarum jurisprudentiam illustrantium syntagma secundum ordinem Institutionum Justiniani Digestum* (new edn with notes by C G Haubold and C F Mühlenbruch, H L Broenner 1841).

[28] John S G Simmons, 'All Souls' in Brock and Curthoys (n 26) 209, 210–12.

[29] Lawson (n 26) 30–31.

School of Jurisprudence.[30] The success of the implementation of this innovation was disputed before the Commissioners appointed in 1877. For
example, Sir Henry Maine, then Corpus Professor of Jurisprudence, stated
that 'examinations in the Honour School of Jurisprudence were established
before there was an adequate provision for teaching the students who were
to be examined'.[31] T E Holland, the Chichele Professor of International Law,
commented on the rapid growth of legal study in Oxford after 1873.[32] The
general consensus was that more teachers were needed.

Opinions differed as to how the teaching should be organised. Holland
and Sir William R Anson, then Vinerian Reader in English Law, were
examined together by the Commissioners. With minor variations, they
both supported the Board of Law Studies' view that six new professors
were needed, including another Professor of Roman Law in addition to the
Regius Professor.[33] A strongly contrary view was expressed by H A Pottinger
of Worcester College, who thought that the professorial lectures were not
valuable for his students and were too infrequent. He was disparaging: 'The
professors' lectures are so few and so scrappy and they cover such a little
ground that I find it almost impossible to utilise them.' He commented of the
Regius Professor of Civil Law, James Bryce: 'The Regius Professor lectures
occasionally at half-past four o'clock in the afternoon.' It was put to him that
Anson, who was not lecturing that current term, was giving 'informal instruction'. He agreed, adding: 'but I do not think much of that instruction'. He
explained that 'the men do not go'. He further complained that 'non-resident
professors do not give us notice in time, and when the work is settled it is
very often difficult to dovetail things in'. More generally, he thought that in
developing a law school it would be better to 'trust the colleges than to trust
the professoriate'. '[C]ollege tuition is infinitely superior to the professorial
tuition', he commented.[34] John C Wilson, a College Lecturer, who taught
for five colleges, was more moderate. He stated that in the Lent term there
were 255 college lectures to forty professorial. But he noted that the college
lecturers saw 'the professorial lectures as part and parcel of the education
scheme which we have to deal with', and they arranged their lectures accordingly. What comes out of Wilson's evidence is an appearance of duplication.
When asked about the difference between the professorial and the college
lectures, he explained: 'Their subjects, I think, are, with rare exceptions,
very much the same as ours are. They do, I think, generally cover much the

---

[30]   ibid 34–60; Nicholas (n 26) 389–96.
[31]   *University of Oxford Commission. Part I. Minutes of Evidence Taken by the Commissioners,
       Together with an Appendix and Index. Part II. Certain Circulars Addressed by the Commissioners
       to the University and the Colleges, Together with the Answers, or a Digest Thereof 1881* (C 2868)
       370 (5601) [PP 1881 LVI.1].
[32]   ibid 61 (992).
[33]   ibid 61 (992, 998, 1000).
[34]   ibid 265–67 (4252–53, 4256–59, 4263, 4277).

same ground as that which we attempt to cover in very much the same way.' He did not think the professorial lectures were delivered in 'a more scientific method', but he thought that 'in many instances the method is better'.[35]

The evidence reflects the characters as well as the self-interest and sometimes enlightened disinterest of those questioned. What emerged from the work of the Commission was a revitalised School of Law. The thrust of the Commission's work is summed up by F H Lawson's chapter title 'The Age of the Professors'[36] – not that the Board of Studies in Law achieved its wishes of six new professors, but some of its desires were met. Readerships were created. These were university appointments. Also, there was a move to make the professors resident rather than non-resident, which required more money. The income of All Souls was used for this.[37] Developments were no doubt eased by Anson's election as Warden of All Souls in 1881, as the College became in part a centre for research, law, and university professors.[38] New statutes for the university reveal what happened.

The Regius Professor of Civil Law was instructed to 'lecture and give instruction on Roman Law, its principles and history', while he was to be entitled to the 'emoluments now assigned to the Professorship', excepting 'any temporary payment' (this was to cover some provisions made for Bryce) and 'to the additional emoluments which are appropriated to it by the statutes of All Souls' College'.[39] The successors to Bryce in the Regius Professorship were also to be Fellows of All Souls.[40] Another statute revived the Vinerian Chair as an effective teaching institution. Its last holder had been J R Kenyon, who died in 1880; he had already long been superseded, however, by a statute in 1867 providing for a Vinerian Readership, tenable for a three-year period, pending the next appointment to the chair. Held in turn by K E Digby, described by Lawson as 'a man of great ability', by Holland, and then by Anson, the Readership came to an end with Anson's election as Warden of All Souls.[41] The revived Vinerian Chair was now attached to All Souls, which again provided some funding to support it.[42] The Chichele Professorship of International Law (already attached to All

[35] ibid 71–72 (1173, 1178–79).
[36] Lawson (n 26) 61.
[37] Simmons (n 28) 213–15.
[38] H C G Matthew, 'Anson, Sir William Reynell, Third Baronet (1843–1914)', *Oxford Dictionary of National Biography* (OUP 2004; online edn May 2006) <www.oxforddnb.com/view/article/30423> accessed 11 August 2017; Herbert H Henson, *A Memoir of the Right Honourable Sir William Anson* (Clarendon Press 1920) 67–83.
[39] *Statutes Made for the University of Oxford, and for the Colleges and Halls Therein, by the University of Oxford Commissioners Acting in Pursuance of the Universities of Oxford and Cambridge Act, 1877: Approved by the Queen in Council* (Clarendon Press 1882) 60.
[40] ibid 413–14.
[41] Harold G Hanbury, *The Vinerian Chair and Legal Education* (Basil Blackwell 1958) 96–97; Lawson (n 26) 50.
[42] *Statutes, 1877* (n 39) 61–62, 413–14, 422.

Souls) and the Corpus Christi Professorship of Jurisprudence were also given a new foundation in the statutes.[43] The new statute for All Souls allocated £800 to fund two new readerships in the university (in addition to the Readership in Indian Law). The tenure of their holders was to be for a period of five years, though they could be re-elected for further periods of five years.[44]

Another provision in the new All Souls' statutes was to this effect:

> So long as the existing Regius Professor of Civil Law retains his professorship and is not resident within the University, the Warden and Fellows shall pay out of the Revenues of the College a yearly sum of 400 l. for the maintenance of a Readership in Roman Law. The Readership shall, as regards the mode of appointment thereto, its tenure and duties, and in all other respects, be regulated in accordance with a Statute made for the University by the University of Oxford Commissioners, and dated 20th day of March, 1880. If the existing Professor should cease to hold his professorship, the Warden and Fellows may continue this payment for so long afterwards as the circumstances may in their judgment render expedient. So long as this payment is made no appropriation shall be made out of the revenues of the College to the Professorship.[45]

The earlier statute to which this refers states that the Warden and College of All Souls offered to pay £400 per annum 'so long as the Regius Professorship of Civil Law is held upon its present conditions, to be applied by the University to the endowment of a Readership in Roman Law'. The Reader in Roman Law was to 'be appointed from time to time for successive periods of three years'. This was until the Regius Professorship became vacant or the existing professor became, by his own consent, subject to the new regulations. The Reader was to be entitled to his stipend, unless he resigned earlier, to the end of the period of three years for which he had been appointed, although the Regius Professorship may have fallen vacant. He was to be elected by the Regius Professor of Civil Law, the Chichele Professor of International Law, the Corpus Professor of Jurisprudence, the chairman of the Council of Legal Education and a nominee of the Warden and Fellows of All Souls.

Reflecting some of the anxieties expressed to the Commissioners, it was stated that the Reader was 'to reside within the precincts of the University for six months in each year between 10 October and 1 July following'. The Reader was to lecture for seven weeks of each term ('Easter and Trinity Terms being counted as one') at least twice each week on separate days. 'He shall take as the subject of his Lectures Roman Law and the Sources and History thereof.' He was also to be ready 'to give private instruction to the

---

[43] ibid 63–65.
[44] ibid 414.
[45] ibid 422–23.

Students attending his lectures'. Subject to this, he was also to be governed by any further statute concerning all Readers.[46]

The wishes for two Professors of Roman Law were not fulfilled; but a step was thus taken to ensure that the university provided organised, structured classes in Roman law. The potential problems posed by Bryce's position as both a non-resident and a man much involved in public life were thus remedied. Given the centrality of Roman law to legal study in Oxford, university (as distinct from college) classes in Roman law could thus be maintained. But this was clearly an interim measure, intended to supply a need until Bryce resigned or died, and was replaced. The Queen approved this statute by Order in Council on 2 March 1881.

Bryce and Grueber

The current Regius Professor of Civil Law, James Bryce, had been appointed in 1870, and was well known as a historian and Liberal politician.[47] This Professorship was not attached to any college, but was a purely university appointment, though Bryce was independently a Fellow of Oriel College, having been elected in 1862. During his tenure of the Regius Chair, though not formally resident in Oxford, he usually spent his weekends at Oriel College.[48] A politician and practising barrister, Bryce was no specialist in the study of Roman law as the discipline was developing in the later nineteenth century.

Bryce resigned in 1893, but he had not taught in his final year, as he had become a member of Gladstone's Cabinet. Gladstone consulted him on his successor. Bryce favoured Henry Goudy, then Professor of Civil Law in the University of Edinburgh, where he had succeeded Muirhead. Educated at the Universities of Edinburgh and Köningsberg, with a successful career at the Scots bar, Goudy's experience as a teacher attracted Bryce, as no doubt did his support for the Liberal Party.[49] With Goudy's appointment the statute made by the Commissioners under the Act of 1877 came into force. This meant that Goudy was to be a Fellow of All Souls, with the funding allocated to support the Reader in Roman Law now reallocated to support his chair. The Readership, which involved successive three-year appointments, would now come to an end.

Given Bryce's other commitments, and the description we have of his

---

[46] ibid 65–66.

[47] Christopher Harvie, 'Bryce, James, Viscount Bryce (1838–1922), Jurist, Historian, and Politician', *Oxford Dictionary of National Biography* (OUP 2004; online edn Jan 2008) <www.oxforddnb.com/view/article/32141> accessed 10 Aug 2017; Herbert A L Fisher, *James Bryce (Viscount Bryce of Dechmont, O.M.)* vol 1 (Macmillan and Co 1927) 130.

[48] Fisher (n 47) vol 1, 134–35. His Fellowship of Oriel was vacated by his marriage in 1889, but in 1890 he was elected a Professorial Fellow and in 1894 made Honorary Fellow: ibid vol 1, 135 n 1.

[49] Cairns (n 5) 24–28.

lectures, he cannot have had much time to devote to developing classes in Roman law. Thus, until his resignation from the Chair, much of the uni-versity – as distinct from college – teaching will have fallen to the Reader. So it was important to fill this post. In discussing the establishment of the Readership, Lawson states that an attempt was made 'in the first instance to attract Ludwig Mitteis' (1859–1921).[50] He cites no source; but as it was only in 1881 that Mitteis gained his doctorate, he was then an unknown, untested man of twenty-two, which perhaps makes an approach to Mitteis unlikely, if not impossible.

B(ernhard) Erwin Grueber was in post as Reader in Roman Law by August 1881.[51] The committee that appointed him consisted of Bryce, Holland, and Maine, by virtue of their chairs, along with the Chairman of the Council of Legal Education appointed by the Inns of Court in London, and a representative of All Souls.[52] Further information may come to light as to how Grueber came to be selected, and as to why he chose to take the post, but in the meantime it seems fair to assume that the Oxford Faculty consulted contacts in Germany and searched more generally. Whatever the truth about the rumour of approaching Mitteis, one suspects that it reflects a desire to modernise the teaching of Roman law through appointment of a man trained in the latest techniques and intellectual developments centred in Germany. But a major issue must have been language skills. If a German scholar was sought, it would have to be one with a high level of competency in spoken and written English. This may have been Grueber's strong suit. It is important to devote some attention to his life.

Grueber was not only Reader in Roman Law in the University of Oxford, but also a Fellow of Balliol College, and he was further described as 'College Lecturer in Roman Law'.[53] Born in 1846, he was the son of the architect and art historian Bernhard Grueber, who had held a chair at the Fine Art Academy in Prague.[54] Grueber had studied law in Munich, gaining his doctorate in 1874, and his *Habilitation* in 1875, the first with a thesis on D.23.3.9.1,[55] the second with a study of the influence of property actions on legal rights in Rome.[56] He then taught in Munich as a *Privatdozent*, publishing in 1880 a new edition of the *Juristische Encyklopädie und Methodologie* of the

---

[50] Lawson (n 26) 79.

[51] Joseph Foster, *Oxford Men and Their Colleges, Illustrated with Portraits and Views, Together with the Matriculation Register, 1880–92* (James Parker & Co 1893) col 7.

[52] *Statutes, 1877* (n 39) 66.

[53] Foster (n 51) cols 7 and 69.

[54] ibid col 69.

[55] Erwin Grueber, *Versuch einer Erklärung der L. 9. §1. D. de jure dotium: inaugural Dissertation zur Erlangung der juristschen Doctorwürde* (Theodor Ackermann 1874).

[56] Erwin Grueber, *Über den Einfluss der Eigenthumsklage auf die Ersitzung nach römischem Rechte* (Theodor Ackermann 1875).

noted Pandectist scholar, K L Arndts von Arnesberg.[57] Grueber presumably taught *Juristische Encyklopädie und Methodologie*, which he later described as 'intended ... to explain the fundamental legal conceptions, and the leading classifications and subdivisions of law', thereby supplying 'the beginner with a general introduction to all the departments of legal study'.[58] It was from this position that he was recruited to Oxford.

Grueber's teaching in Oxford will be discussed below. But it is important to note that he served in 1892–93 as Deputy Regius Professor of Civil Law. This was because, as mentioned, Bryce had just joined Gladstone's Cabinet, and so could no longer fulfil the duties of the Chair and a replacement was required.[59] This led to Goudy's appointment in 1893,[60] which ended the funding from All Souls for Grueber's Readership. The year 1893–94 was also the final year of one of the triennial periods for payment. This will have led to Grueber's return to Munich, and resignation from Balliol, after his sojourn of twelve years among Arnold's 'dreaming spires'. Perhaps he had even hoped for the Chair, though we know that Bryce had advised Gladstone that he was unsuitable.[61] Grueber then taught in Munich until 1932, shortly before his death in 1933.[62]

Grueber resumed his role of *Privatdozent* in Munich, and was so described in 1895 on the title page of his new edition of the *Juristische Encyklopädie und Methodologie* of Arndts von Arnesberg; he is also described as some-time Professor of Roman Law at Oxford.[63] He had acquired the coveted title of professor by 1898, and he was now designed as 'k[önigliche] Universitätsprofessor in München'.[64] In 1908 he is designated as 'Professor der Rechte an der Universität München, Mitglied von Balliol College und vormals Professor des römischen Rechts an der Universität Oxford'.[65] But he was not the possessor of a university chair as an Ordinarius Professor, as later he was formally described as 'planmäßiger außerordentlicher Professor'. This is presumably the status he had acquired by 1898 in recognition of his work teaching for the Faculty at Munich. Thus, he was

---

[57] Karl Ludwig Arndts von Arnesberg, *Juristische Encyklopädie und Methodologie* (Erwin Grueber ed, 7th edn after the author's death, Cotta 1880).

[58] Erwin Grueber, 'Introduction' in Rudolph Sohm, *The Institutes of Roman Law: A Textbook of the History and System of Roman Private Law* (J C Ledlie tr, 2nd edn, Clarendon Press 1901) xv, xvi.

[59] Foster (n 51) cols 7 and 69.

[60] Cairns (n 5) 25–30.

[61] Lawson (n 26) 219.

[62] L[eopold] Wenger, Obituary (1934) 54 ZSS (RA) 498, 498–99.

[63] K L Arndts von Arnesberg, *Juristische Encyklopädie und Methodologie* (Erwin Grueber ed, 9th edn after the author's death, Cotta 1895).

[64] Erwin Grueber, 'Die Willensmängel der Rechtsgeschäfte nach dem Bürgerlichen Gesetzbuche' (1898) 63 Dr. J. A. Seuffert's Blätter für Rechtsanwendung 445, 461.

[65] Erwin Grueber, *Einführung in die Rechtswissenschaft: Einer juristische Encyklopädie und Methodologie* (D Häring 1908).

an 'extraordinary professor', one without a *Lehrstuhl*, but who had a salary, since he was 'planmäßiger'. This was a relatively lowly position in the hierarchy, above the single *nichtplanmäßiger außerordentlicher Professor* and the *Privatdozenten* in the Munich Law Faculty, but below the *Honorarprofessoren* and the *ordentliche öffentliche Professoren*, who were at the top as the *ordinarii* with public chairs.[66]

Grueber was listed in 1930 as 'Professor für Rechtsenzyklopädie und Rechtsmethodologie sowie für Abhaltung von exegetischen und praktischen Übungen in römischen Zivilrecht'.[67] Thus, in Munich he had resumed teaching classes on the structure and methodological system of the law, as well as providing exegetical and practical exercises (*Übungen*) in Roman civil law. These classes were aimed at students at the start of their studies. This explains his publication of new editions of Arndts' *Juristische Encyklopädie und Methodologie*, of which he produced a final edition in 1908 for Cotta, the famous publishing house.[68] In the same year, he published for his classes his own *Einführung in die Rechtswissenschaft: Einer juristische Enzyklopädie und Methodologie*. This was developed out of the section entitled 'Einführung in die Rechtswissenschaft' (introduction to the science of law) that he had written for the extensive, multi-authored *Encyklopädie der Rechtswissenschaft* of Karl von Birkmayer, first published in 1900 (1901).[69] Birkmayer's *Encyklopädie* was intended to cover the whole system of law in Germany, following the reform of legal study introduced after promulgation in that year of the *Bürgerliches Gesetzbuch* (*BGB*). In 1902 Grueber explained that the new regulations governing teaching after the promulgation of the *BGB* in 1900 required 'an introductory course of lectures, called "Einführung in die Rechstwissenschaft" (Introduction to the Science of Law)'. The aim was 'to serve as a general preparation for all the various branches of legal study'. He explained the subject matter was 'identical with that of the ... [former] lectures on "Encyklopädie" and "Methodologie"'.[70]

Grueber's *Einführung* went through several editions with the last, the seventh, appearing in 1928;[71] in 1922 the full title had become *Einführung in die Rechtswissenschaft: Einer juristische Enzyklopädie und Methodologie mit Einschluß der Grundzüge des bürgerlichen Rechts*.[72] The book had greatly

---

[66] *Personenstand der Ludwig-Maximilians-Universität München. Sommer-Halbjahr 1930* (Universitäts-Buchdruckerei Dr C Wolf & Sohn 1930) 11–12.

[67] ibid 12.

[68] K L Arndts von Arnesberg, *Juristische Encyklopädie und Methodologie* (Erwin Grueber ed, 11th edn after the author's death, Cotta 1908).

[69] See the Foreword in Grueber (n 65) [V].

[70] Grueber (n 58) xix.

[71] Erwin Grueber, *Einführung in die Rechtswissenschaft: Einer juristische Enzyklopädie und Methodologie mit Einschluß der Grundzüge des bürgerlichen Rechts* (7th edn, J Schweitzer 1928) (not seen).

[72] Erwin Grueber, *Einführung in die Rechtswissenschaft: Einer juristische Enzyklopädie und*

developed from its beginnings. Of particular interest are the editions of 1918 and 1919. The First World War had disrupted the education of many university students. This was an issue that troubled Grueber. In May 1917 the professors of the University and Polytechnic at Munich had sent a memorandum on the questions raised to the Reichstag. In 1918 Grueber published a pamphlet entitled *Was können unsere Universitäten und Hochschulen für ihre im Studium gehemmten Kriegsteilnehmer tun?*[73] In these two editions of his *Einführung* he tried to take account of the problems facing soldiers as students. The subtitle of the book had now become 'Zugleich der Wiedereinführung der Kriegsteilnehmer in das Rechtsstudium insbesondere das Bürgerliche Gesetzbuch', in other words he was specially aiming it at returning soldiers to reintroduce them to study, particularly of the civil code.[74] The 1918 edition had been prepared when the war was in its final year; that of 1919 had to take into account the changes caused by the abdication of the Kaiser and the proclamation of a republic.[75]

The impression one gets is that Grueber was a keen teacher concerned for his students and anxious to give them the grounding necessary for successful pursuit of legal studies. The summary of his life by his biographer, Wenger, tends to support this:

> Grueber was an inspired and talented teacher. Numerous, especially North German, students have participated in his lectures and exercises. In the last few decades, the reform and the introduction into the legal sciences have been the tasks to which he devoted himself untiringly.[76]

University education was indeed always a matter of concern for Grueber. Thus, before the Great War he wrote articles on the reform of legal education and law teaching in technical colleges (*Technische Hochschulen*).[77]

Given that we are here concerned with the *lex Aquilia*, it is important to reflect on what Grueber published on Roman law. His thesis and his *Habilitationsschrift* (which were very short by modern standards) were of course on the discipline. After he published the volume on the *lex Aquilia* in

---

Methodologie mit Einschluß der Grundzüge des bürgerlichen Rechts (6th edn, Springer 1922) (not seen).

[73] Erwin Grueber, *Was können unsere Universitäten und Hochschulen für ihre im Studium gehemmten Kriegsteilnehmer tun?* (Beck 1918) (not seen).

[74] Erwin Grueber, *Einführung in die Rechtswissenschaft: . . . Zugleich der Wiedereinführung der Kriegsteilnehmer in das Rechtsstudium insbesondere das Bürgerliche Gesetzbuch* (4th edn, Springer 1918) (not seen).

[75] Erwin Grueber, *Einführung in die Rechtswissenschaft: . . . Zugleich der Wiedereinführung der Kriegsteilnehmer in das Rechtsstudium insbesondere das Bürgerliche Gesetzbuch* (5th edn, Springer 1919) XII.

[76] Wenger (n 62) 499.

[77] Erwin Grueber, 'Zur Reform der deutschen Universitäten' (1911–12) 5 Archiv für Rechts- und Wirtschaftsphilosophie 576; Erwin Grueber, 'Rechtsunterricht und Technische Hochschulen' (1914) 7 Archiv für Rechts- und Wirtschaftsphilosophie 256.

1886, he wrote an article on the *actio legis Aquiliae* in relation to usufruct and pledge.[78] This derived from his work for the book. In 1891, shortly before he left Oxford, he was stimulated by the publication of a new view on the decline of the Roman jurists expressed by Franz Hoffmann of Vienna in a set of essays he dedicated to his colleague Leopold Pfaff. This led to a short article in the *Law Quarterly Review*, in which Grueber essentially agreed with Hoffmann's view.[79] He also touched on Roman law in an article on consideration in English law, analysing two English cases in its light.[80] The only other publication of his that I have traced on Roman law, other than a book review, is the introductory essay that he provided for James Ledlie's translation into English of Rudolph Sohm's *Institutes of Roman Law*, published in 1892. In it he provides an overview of the current understanding of the historical development of the study of Roman law in Europe, with a particular focus on Germany, though he does pay some attention to England.[81] For the second edition of 1901, he focused in his introduction on the recent reforms in legal education in Germany consequent on promulgation of the BGB.[82]

Grueber also addressed the question of legal education in Roman law in his essay in the first edition of Ledlie's translation of Sohm. He noted that the progressive dilution of the influence of Roman law in England had meant that 'English jurists were unable to take part in the great synthetical efforts of modern times'. The revival of the study of Roman law in England in the middle of the century was accordingly focused on commentaries on the text, particularly on the textbooks of Gaius and Justinian, but attempted also to take into account other issues that did not readily present themselves in such a treatment, such as the various *iura in re aliena*. This made mastering the discipline difficult, he thought; but Sohm's 'systematic and historical exposition of the elements of Roman private law' should in these circumstances help the English student. But Grueber stressed that he hoped that the use of Sohm ought not to 'interfere with the present system of instruction', based on study of the Roman sources, which meant that:

> [t]he beginner is thus made familiar with the text itself of the law instead of a mere abstraction from the text. And the text introduces him to the numerous cases which form a constant, living, illustration of the abstract rules of law which he

---

[78] Erwin Grueber, 'Zur Aquilischen Klage des Nießbrauchers und des Pfandgläubigers' (1889) 75 Archiv für die civilistische Praxis 303.

[79] Erwin Grueber, 'The Decline of Roman Jurisprudence' (1891) 7 LQR 70, reflecting on Franz Hoffmann, *Kritische Studien im römische Rechte: Eine Festschrift* (Manz 1885), a series of essays by Hoffmann dedicated to Pfaff.

[80] Erwin Grueber, 'A Difficulty in the Law of Consideration' (1886) 2 LQR 33 (his analysis led to a typically trenchant editorial note by Pollock, essentially disagreeing with his analysis of a case: (1886) 2 LQR 37).

[81] Erwin Grueber, 'Introductory Essay' in Rudolph Sohm, *The Institutes of Roman Law* (J C Ledlie tr, Clarendon Press 1892) [xiii].

[82] Grueber (n 58) xv.

finds in the Institutes. The student is, accordingly, familiarised with, and prepared for, the practical task of his calling: the application, namely of the law to a particular set of circumstances falling under its provisions.

He hoped that the student, already 'acquainted ... with the text of the Institutes', would use Sohm's *Institutes* to 'find himself in possession of a clear survey of the whole subject both in its systematical and historical aspect'.[83]

After achieving the doctorate and *Habilitation*, it was only when at Oxford that Grueber wrote on Roman law. While he obviously had the competencies required of a contemporary scholar in the discipline, and had a knowledge of its literature, it is tempting to conclude that he was not motivated to be a researcher in the field. Indeed, his work on the *lex Aquilia* was intended as a textbook, not as a novel contribution to knowledge on the topic. This makes his appointment interesting. Further research may illuminate matters, but one suspects that the Readership, with its uncertainties and renewable triennial contracts, was not so attractive to most German scholars of Roman law. Moreover, competency in English would have been needed. In 1886 James Muirhead was to remark that Grueber's 'assiduity as Reader in Roman law is on all hands acknowledged to have conduced materially to the attainment of that higher standard in legal education for which Oxford has of late years been distinguished'.[84]

The curriculum in Roman law in Oxford

Bryce's biographer quotes him as stating:

> Till 1870 there was scarcely any teaching in Roman Law and what little did exist in the Colleges was confined to commenting on the solitary book (*The Institutes of Justinian*) set for the examination. No one had lectured on the Digest; no one had treated the history of the subject.[85]

Lawson's account of the classes in Roman law in this era tends to confirm this. The public examination of the School of Law and History from Trinity Term in 1853 demonstrates the relatively elementary nature of the course.[86]

The separate Final Honour School of Jurisprudence had a Board of Studies from 1870 that controlled the exams. Roman law continued to be a major focus. The relevant statute of the university stated that the examination should 'always include ... [s]uch departments of Roman Law ... as may be specified from time to time by the Board'.[87] An examination paper of 1872 shows the elementary and largely dogmatic nature of the learning leav-

---

[83] Grueber (n 81) xxxiv–xxxv.
[84] Muirhead (n 4) 380.
[85] Fisher (n 47) vol 1, 132.
[86] Lawson (n 26) 184–85.
[87] ibid 36.

ened by historical reflection promoted through a study of Gaius.[88] By 1877 the syllabus stated that Roman law was '[t]o be studied in the Institutes of Gaius and Justinian. Candidates [were] expected to be acquainted with the History of Roman legislation and Roman Judicial Institutions'.[89]

The BCL degree (to be taken after that of a BA) also underwent reform, with an extensive examination introduced in 1873. The university hoped that the Council of Legal Education might accept successful achievement of this degree as exempting from some if not all of the bar examinations. This did not happen.[90] The examinations for the degree were regulated by the Board of Studies on 11 June 1877. As regards Roman law, they stated:

> Candidates will be expected to possess a general acquaintance with the principles of Roman private law. They will be required to offer one of the following special subjects:
> 1. The law of family relations.
> 2. Ownership and possession.
> 3. The Theory of Contracts generally.
> 4. The four consensual contracts.
> 5. The history of Roman legislation and Roman judicial institutions.
> No particular books are recommended, but candidates are advised to refer as frequently as they can to Gaius and to the titles of the Digest which bear upon the special subject they have selected.

The regulation goes on to list titles from the Digest as follows for the first special subject: D.1.5, 1.6, 1.7, 14.5 and 23.2; for the second: D.41.1 and 41.2; for the third: D.2.14 and 44.7; for the fourth: D.18.1 and 19.1; and for the fifth: D.1.1, 1.2, 1.3 and 1.4. Because it constituted a difference from what had hitherto been in force, the regulation also specially drew the candidates' attention to the fact that in Roman law it was 'stated that the candidates will be expected to possess a general acquaintance with the principles of Roman private law; and the special subject of the law of family relations is no longer limited by the words "father and child, husband and wife"'.[91] Thus, the Digest was studied for the BCL, but this did not include D.9.2 on the *lex Aquilia*.

It was for these classes that Holland and C L Shadwell started to publish selected titles of the Digest in 1874, collected under the headings 'Introductory Titles', D.1.1–4; 'Family Law', D.1.1–6, 50.16–17, 23.2, 1.7 and 14.5; 'Property Law', D.41.1–3, 39.5, 8.1, 8.6 and 7.1; 'Law of Obligations', D.2.14, 44.7, 12.1, 13.6, 16.3, 13.7 and 45.1; and 'Law of

---

[88] ibid 187–89.
[89] ibid 40.
[90] ibid 42–43.
[91] *University of Oxford Commission. Minutes* (n 31) 394 (Appendix); Lawson (n 26) 196–98. For an earlier examination, see Lawson (n 26) 200–04.

Obligations (continued)': D.18.1, 19.1–2; 17.2, 17.1, 47.2 and 9.2. The selection of titles, and the sequence of their printing, reflect the curriculum for the BCL as revealed in the regulation of 1877. As well as being available separately in five parts, these titles were published in one volume in 1881.[92] The authors describe the headings as reflecting the familiar structure of the *Institutes*. They explained their departure from the structure of the Digest as justified by the almost random structure of the Digest itself, following that of the Edict.[93] The headnote attached to each title provided the student with guidance to parallel passages and to relevant texts of Gaius.[94] It was a book obviously calculated to assist students. The inclusion of D.9.2 made the title readily available for prescription to the students.

Restructuring led to the replacement of the Boards of Studies of the Honour Schools with Faculty Boards in 1883.[95] In 1884 the new Faculty Board of Law reformed the requirements in the teaching of Roman law for undergraduates, by introducing, in addition to the two existing papers on the *Institutes* of Gaius and Justinian, a special paper on D.9.2, *ad legem Aquiliam*, parts of which were compulsory for those who aimed at a first or second class. This was to take effect in 1886.[96] Grueber explained this development as the result of the Board's view that 'a more thorough knowledge of Roman law would be the best means of advancing a scientific understanding and culture of English law'. The Board had accordingly selected the title D.9.2 'for that purpose' because 'it contains, perhaps more fully than any other title in the Digest, the chief materials referring to one particular topic, viz. the Roman law of damage to property'.[97]

Given the current structures and methods of teaching in Oxford, with classes on Roman law given by college lecturers and tutors, as well as lectures by Grueber as Reader in Roman Law and Bryce as Professor of Civil Law, teaching beyond the *Institutes* of Justinian and Gaius presented a problem of organisation. Grueber's textbook was intended to remedy that problem. Its use ensured that all teachers would teach appropriately and relevantly for the exam set by the university on D.9.2 and that students could work successfully on their own. Indeed this very point was made by Muirhead in his review of Grueber's book. He commented that in teaching a course on the Digest 'tutorial instruction would be more advantageous', as

> [the student's] attention can be drawn ever and again to the merits or defects of the
> treatment of particular passages ... and his knowledge can be tested on collateral

---

[92] Thomas E Holland and Charles L Shadwell (eds), *Select Titles from the Digest of Justinian* (Clarendon Press 1881).
[93] ibid [v]–vii.
[94] ibid viii.
[95] Lawson (n 26) 61.
[96] ibid 66, 216–17.
[97] Grueber (n 3) [vii].

points of law, whose apprehension is often necessary to the thorough understanding of the question directly under discussion, but familiarity with which is in most cases presumed by the Roman jurists.

Muirhead pointed out that in Germany, 'although exegetical courses of lectures are not infrequent in the Universities, the best of this sort of work is done in the so-called *privatissima* or in the law seminaries (*Seminarien*)'. This meant that the German press had produced few works similar in nature to that of Grueber; he also knew of few in France. He suggested that this indicated that oral instruction was probably better.[98] In other words, a book such as Grueber's was necessary where a student was working largely on his own, and when direction was not given by a single professor.

Developments in Edinburgh

Circumstances in Edinburgh were simpler, because of the professorial method of instruction and because of the professor's control over his classes. He taught and he examined, though, from 1875, there were also two specially appointed "non-Professorial" Examiners in Law, who had to hold the degree of LLB and who were invariably members of the Faculty of Advocates.[99] But there were no competing teachers. Towards the end of his tenure as Professor of Civil Law, Muirhead had an assistant in James Mackintosh,[100] but Mackintosh was an assistant to the Chair, working in collaboration with the professor, not someone with a potentially different attitude to the syllabus.

The Commissioners appointed under the Act of 1858 stated that the new postgraduate degree of LLB created by their Ordinance of 1862 'should be considered as a mark of academical and not of professional distinction', which entailed that it 'should therefore be subject to such conditions, as would imply a more extended course of legal study, and the possession of higher attainments, than are ordinarily required for mere professional purposes'. The degree was taken over three years, and consisted of courses in civil law, the law of Scotland, conveyancing, public law (which encompassed international law), constitutional law and history, and medical jurisprudence.[101]

---

[98] Muirhead (n 4) 380–81.

[99] Order of Her Majesty in Council, 6 Aug 1874, Ordinance No 75, Edinburgh No 8, in Alan E Clapperton (ed), *The Universities (Scotland) Act, 1858 Together with Ordinances of Commissioners Under Said Act With Relative Notes of Alterations Thereon* (James MacLehose and Sons 1916) 208–09.

[100] 'Edinburgh University – Appointment of Professor of Civil Law' *The Scotsman* (Edinburgh, 29 November 1893) 10.

[101] Scottish Universities Commission, *General Report of the Commissioners under the Universities (Scotland) Act, 1858. With an Appendix, Containing Ordinances, Minutes, Reports on Special Subjects, and Other Documents* (Murray and Gibb for HMSO 1863) xxxv–xxxvi.

In Scotland there was considerable cooperation and coordination on the development of law teaching between the Faculty of Advocates (the Scots bar) and the universities. Those joining the Scots bar had traditionally studied law at the University of Edinburgh (and that of Glasgow in the eighteenth century). The Faculty of Advocates had therefore always paid close attention to developments in the universities and had monopolised appointments to the chairs in Edinburgh, other than those of conveyancing and medical jurisprudence. Indeed, the Faculty had held the patronage of three of the law chairs in Edinburgh since 1722.[102] In 1854 it adopted regulations requiring those seeking admission to possess the degree of MA from a Scottish university (or an equivalent) or to demonstrate the same level of learning in its examinations, and to have studied law for at least two years in a Scottish university, taking civil law, Scots law, conveyancing (or another session of civil law or Scots law) and medical jurisprudence.[103] Its views exercised considerable influence on the Commissioners in drafting their Ordinances for law.[104] After the creation of the degree of LLB, the Faculty, from 1866, required intrants to have attended all the subjects that made up the curriculum for the degree of LLB in Edinburgh; it took the next logical step in late 1874, and accepted possession of the degree of LLB as exempting from the need to sit and pass the Faculty's exams.[105] The Faculty still required a public examination for admission, namely the writing and defence of a thesis written in Latin on a title of Roman law, though this had not needed to be printed since 1853.[106] The Faculty's own examination in civil law was on Justinian's *Institutes*, along with an elementary treatise, and the Digest title *de diversis regulis iuris antiqui* (D.50.17).[107] The *University Calendar* of 1858 in the entry for 'Civil Law' states that 'students intended for the Scotch bar must make themselves acquainted with Warnkönig's *Institutiones Juris Romani Privati* or Mackeldey's *Systema Juris Romani hodie usitati*', thereby indicating the elementary treatises the Faculty had in mind.[108]

[102] John W Cairns, 'History of the Faculty of Advocates to 1900' in Sir Thomas Smith and others (eds), *The Laws of Scotland: Stair Memorial Encyclopædia* vol 13 (Butterworths/Law Society of Scotland 1992) 499, 507–08 (§1239, §1257).

[103] ibid 527–29 (§1279).

[104] Scottish Universities Commission (n 101) xxxv–xxxvi.

[105] Cairns (n 102) 529 (§1279).

[106] ibid 527 (§1278).

[107] ibid.

[108] *The Edinburgh University Calendar for the Session 1858–59, Including Lists of the Graduates and Distinguished Students of the Previous Session* (Thomas Constable and Co 1858); Leopold A Warnkönig, *Institutiones iuris Romani privati: in usum praelectionum academicarum vulgatae cum introductione in universam iurisprudentiam et in studium iuris Romani* (3rd edn, Adolphus Marcus 1834) (there is a 4th edn 1860); Ferdinand Mackeldey, *Systema Juris Romani hodie usitati* (J C Hinrichsius 1847).

The initial curriculum in civil law for the degree of LLB

According to the Ordinance establishing the degree of LLB, there were to be at least eighty lectures on civil law.[109] The lectures were to be given in both the winter and the summer sessions;[110] this meant from November through to the end of March, and May to July. Civil law was also recommended as the first subject to be studied, whether or not a student wished to graduate with the degree.[111]

The curriculum for the class was not further described. The requirements for admission as an advocate inevitably meant that the classes – as a minimum – had to be tailored to meet the Faculty's examinations. Thus, in academic year 1862–63 the *University Calendar* stated:

> [The Lectures hitherto delivered in this Class have comprised the general principles of the Roman law treated very much in the order of Justinian's Institutes. The Books specially recommended were Cumin's Manual of Civil Law, and Sandar's Institutes of Justinian. Students intended for the Scotch Bar must make themselves acquainted with either Warnkoenig's *Institutions Juris Romani Privati*, or Mackeldey's *Systema Juris Romani hodie usitati*.][112]

This is headed by Professor Muirhead's name; but the square brackets and cautious phrasing indicate that this reflected his predecessor's classes; indeed, while Muirhead had been selected for the Chair, he had not yet been admitted to it by the date of the printing of the *Calendar*.[113]

Muirhead's chosen description and curriculum was published the next year. He treated the substantive law within a typical Pandectist structure:

> The Course of Civil Law extends over a Winter and Summer Session.
>
> During the Winter Session the History of the Law of Rome is traced through its various stages. The General Principles of the Law, bearing more or less upon all its departments, are then examined with some minuteness. Next are considered, in detail, the Special Doctrines of the Law of Property and Real Rights. Finally, the Law of Obligations is also examined in detail.
>
> In the Summer Session the course is completed with the examination of the Law of the Family Relationships and the Law of Succession.

---

[109] Scottish Universities Commission (n 101) 98.

[110] ibid 160.

[111] *The Edinburgh University Calendar for the Year 1864–65* (Published for the Senatus Academicus by MacLachlan and Stewart 1864) 51.

[112] *Edinburgh University Calendar, 1862–63. Corrected to October 1862* (Printed by Thomas Constable for the Senatus Academicus 1862) 44.

[113] He was admitted in October 1862: Edinburgh University Archives [hereafter EUA], IN1/GOV/SEN/1, Minutes of the Senatus vol 2, 183–85 (20 Oct 1862). There is a complexity over volume numbering. They are numbered 1–7 to 1855 but then start at 1 again. This is the second sequence of volume numbers.

Examinations are held once a week, and subjects prescribed occasionally for written papers at home.

The course is adapted not only for students intending to enter some branch of the Legal Profession in Scotland, but also for those qualifying for practice in England, or service in India or the Colonies.

The only treatise prescribed as a text-book is Gneist's edition of the Institutes of Gaius and Justinian (*Institutionum et Regularum Juris Romani Syntagma, Lipsiae,* 1858). The *Corpus Juris Civilis*, however, is expected to be in the hands of every student: the edition recommended is that of the Kriegels, Leipzig, 1846. Also recommended are Lord Mackenzie's *Studies in Roman Law*, Puchta's *Institutionen*, and Ortolan's *Explication Historique des Instituts*.[114]

He stated his examination for the degree would 'embrace the External History of the Roman Law in the Ante-Justinianian and the Justinianian Periods; and the Principles of the later law of Property, of Real Rights, and of Obligations, including their application in the Jurisprudence of Scotland and England'. The books prescribed for the examination were 'Warnkönig's Histoire Externe du Droit Romain, the Institutes of Gaius and Justinian, and Lord Mackenzie's Studies in Roman Law'.[115]

I have discussed elsewhere Muirhead's choice of books to recommend to his class,[116] but a few remarks may be helpful here, always bearing in mind that, then as now, teachers' recommendations to their students of what to read may be more aspirational than realistic. Gneist's *Syntagma*, first published in 1858, printed the *Institutes* of Gaius and Justinian in parallel columns, while also including two post-classical works, the *Sententiae Pauli* and *Regulae Ulpiani*.[117] Gneist's notes and comments were accessible to Scottish students as the edition was in Latin. What is interesting in this choice is Muirhead's obvious historical focus. Warnkönig's work was a textbook published in Brussels; a German scholar, Warnkönig had passed a significant part of his career in the Low Countries. It is a remarkably clear account of his topic, well suited for the students for whom it was intended.[118] Ortolan's *Explication historique des instituts* was a very popular work, which went through many editions, and was eventually translated into English.[119]

114　*The Edinburgh University Calendar for the Year 1863–64* (Maclachlan and Stewart … for the Senatus Academicus 1863) 47; see Grueber (n 81) xxvi–xxvii for the various Pandectist stuctures.

115　*Edinburgh University Calendar 1863–64* (n 114) 134.

116　Cairns (n 25) 11–15.

117　Rudolf Gneist, *Institutionum et regularum iuris romani syntagma exhibens Gai et Iustiniani institutionum synopsin Ulpiani librum singularem regularem Pauli sententiarum delectum tabulas systema institutionum iuris romani illustrantes praemissis duodecim tabularum fragmentis* (B G Teubner 1858).

118　Ludwig A Warnkönig, *Histoire externe du droit romain, à l'usage des élèves en droit* (H Tarlier 1836).

119　Joseph-Louis E Ortolan, *Explication historique des instituts de l'empereur Justinien, avec le texte, la*

It would have been very informative for students, with its details and extensive annotations of the actual texts as well as its historical introduction. Warnkönig's work may have been recommended for the examination as shorter and simpler in its focus. It is significant that these two works were in French; this was a language more likely to be known to Edinburgh students than German. One wonders how many students Muirhead expected to read the *Kursus der Institutionen* of the famous Pandectist G F Puchta, though he later himself donated a copy of it to the Law Students Library, and recommended that the University Library acquire the new edition in 1881.[120] His recommendation of an edition of the entire *Corpus Iuris Civilis* suggests a desire that the students should have some acquaintance with it.

With one exception, Muirhead republished this syllabus, with only minor variations, each academic year until that of 1876–77.[121] It is important to discuss the single departure from this practice. In 1864–65, we find the course described as follows:

> During the Winter Term the Professor of Civil Law delivers a course of Lectures on the External History and General Principles of the Law of Rome, as developed in the Institutes of Gaius and Justinian.
>
> During the Summer Term the Lectures are devoted to a more minute exposition of some particular branch of the law, as developed in the Pandects, the Code, and the Novels. In the Summer of 1864 the subject will be the Law of Possession, Property, and Real Rights. In that of 1865 it will probably be the Law of Obligations.[122]

The textbook of Gneist was still recommended, as was the Kriegels' edition of the *Corpus Iuris*; the other works mentioned in the previous year were no longer included among the reading. Over the next few years these were to be the only works recommended as textbooks. The weekly examinations and papers to be written at home are never mentioned again, but we know that Muirhead, as was normal among the Scots professors, will have continued to hold regular examinations or quizzes in class.[123] The examination for graduation was to 'embrace the External History of the Roman Law down to the time of Justinian, as described in any of the Standard modern text-books; the General Principles of the Law as set forth in the *Institutes* of Gaius and Justinian', while the different approach was represented by examination on

traduction en regard, et les explications sous chaque paragraphe, précédée de l'histoire de la législation romaine, depuis son origine jusqu'à la législation moderne, et d'une généralisation du droit romain, d'après les textes anciennement connus, ou plus récemment découverts (6th edn, H Plon 1857).

[120] Cairns (n 25) 11–15.

[121] ibid 9–11.

[122] *The Edinburgh University Calendar for the Year 1864–65* (Maclachlan and Stewart ... for the Senatus Academicus 1864) 51–52.

[123] *Report of the Royal Commissioners Appointed to Inquire into the Universities of Scotland with Evidence and Appendix* vol 2 (Murray and Gibb for HMSO 1878) 399.

> the Doctrines of the Law of Real and Consensual Obligations as explained in
> Molitor's Traité des Obligations; and so much of the Doctrines of the Law
> of Legacies and Mortis Causa Trusts as is set forth in Books xxx-xxxii. of the
> Pandects.[124]

There is no evidence as to what inspired this change. Molitor's treatise was
published in Ghent based on the lectures of the deceased professor.[125]

The next year Muirhead's syllabus reverted to a version of the wording
of 1863–64, but without, as noted, the notice on weekly class examinations
and the restricted reading list. But, in contrast, the examinations thereafter
tended to include specific questions on doctrines found in the Digest, sometimes with suggested reading. Thus the topics in 1865–66 for examination
were stated to be:

> the External History of the Roman Law down to the time of Justinian ... the
> general Principles of the Law of Property and Possession as set forth in the 41st
> Book of the Pandects; and so much of the Law of Obligations as is explained in
> Vernet's Textes Choisis sur la Théorie des Obligations en Droit Romain (Paris
> 1865).[126]

Vernet's collection was for an advanced Roman law course, and included
the relevant texts in Latin and translation into French, along with commentary.[127] The next year the examination was stated to be on, as well as the
external history and the doctrines in the *Institutes* of Gaius and Justinian,
'the doctrines specially dealt with in the 44th, 45th and 46th Books of the
Pandects'.[128] In 1867–68, it was now 'the doctrines specially dealt with in
the 6th, 7th, and 8th Books of the Pandects'.[129]

Another apparent change came in 1868–69. Again the syllabus stayed
the same, but this time the examination was now stated to be on, as well
as the external history and the principles in the *Institutions* of Gaius and
Justinian, 'the doctrines specially dealt with in the titles of the Pandects *De
rei vindicatio* and *De acquirendo rerum dominio*'.[130] Muirhead has now moved

---

[124] *Edinburgh University Calendar 1864–65* (n 122) 155.

[125] Jean P Molitor, *Les obligations en droit romain, avec l'indication des rapports entre la législation romaine et le droit français, cours professé à l'université de Gand et publié sur les manuscrites de l'auteur, après sa mort* (L Hebbelynck 1851). There were several editions.

[126] *The Edinburgh University Calendar for the Year 1865–66* (Maclachlan and Stewart ... for the Senatus Academicus 1865) 139–40. See ibid 62–63 for a syllabus like that of 1863–64.

[127] Prosper Vernet, *Textes choisis sur la théorie des obligations en droit romain: conférence pour le doctorat professée dans le second semestre de l'année scolaire 1863–1864 à la faculté de droit de Paris* (August Durand 1865).

[128] *The Edinburgh University Calendar for the Year 1866–67* (Maclachlan and Stewart ... for the Senatus Academicus 1866) 141.

[129] *The Edinburgh University Calendar for the Year 1867–68* (Maclachlan and Stewart ... for the Senatus Academicus 1867) 144–45.

[130] *The Edinburgh University Calendar 1868–69* (Edmonston and Douglas 1868) 149.

to individual titles of the Digest, rather than books, perhaps suggesting an increasing specialisation. The same two titles were stated to be the object of examination the next year.[131] The following year it was to be 'the titles of the Digest *de Obligationibus et Actionibus* and *de Verborum Obligationibus*, xliv. 7, and xlv. 1'.[132] The next year, however, Muirhead prescribed two books for the examination: 'in detail the doctrines of the Law of Servitudes, as set forth in the 7th and 8th Books of the Digest'.[133] The same books were set in the next four years.[134] It is possible this represents a failure to update the *Calendar* entry; after 1872–73, however, the law examinations for the previous academic year were no longer included in the *University Calendar*, so it is impossible to check for the next few years. But it does seem best to suppose that Muirhead continued to focus on these two books of the Digest on servitudes for a few years as the subject of detailed study.

The degree of BL

While the numbers of those studying law in Edinburgh were relatively large, very few individuals actually took the degree of LLB. In 1868 the Representation of the People (Scotland) Act had created two university constituencies in Scotland, one consisting of Edinburgh and St Andrews, the other of Glasgow and Aberdeen. The electors were members of the General Council of the Universities, that is to say, the graduates.[135] This gave graduation new value. Hitherto, many men intending to join the legal profession, particularly those aiming to become solicitors, law agents or writers, had not graduated. In traditional manner they had just attended those courses they considered as likely to be of value to them, generally while serving an apprenticeship.

In April 1869 the Scots Law Society, a student organisation in Edinburgh, petitioned the Senatus requesting that a new degree in law be created. The petition narrated that those aiming to be solicitors and law agents did not have the time to graduate in arts, which meant that the degree of LLB was not open to them. It further pointed out that this meant that the Faculty of Law would not be fairly represented among the electors. The Senatus remitted the Petition to the Faculty of Law for reflection.[136] The Faculty presented its report on 29 January 1870; the Senatus remitted it to the Faculties of Law

[131] *The Edinburgh University Calendar 1869–70* (Edward Ravenscroft 1869) 163.

[132] *The Edinburgh University Calendar 1870–71* (Edward Ravenscroft 1870) 171.

[133] *The Edinburgh University Calendar 1871–72* (Edward Ravenscroft 1871) 155.

[134] *The Edinburgh University Calendar 1872–73* (James Thin 1872) 160; *The Edinburgh University Calendar 1873–74* (James Thin 1873) 164; *The Edinburgh University Calendar 1874–75* (James Thin 1874) 171; *The Edinburgh University Calendar 1875–76* (James Thin 1875) 174.

[135] Representation of the People (Scotland) Act 1868 ss 9, 27–41.

[136] EUA, IN1/GOV/SEN/1, Minutes of the Senatus vol 4, 19–23 (3 Apr 1869).

and Arts for further consideration.[137] In 1870 the recommendation to the Senatus was to retain graduation in arts as a prerequisite for graduation in law, pending discussions of revival of the degree of BA.[138]

But the tide started to turn. A committee of the General Council, chaired by Professor James Lorimer, made recommendations in line with the Student Law Society's petition, presenting to the Court in 1871 proposals very similar to the scheme eventually adopted.[139] Considering this representation from the General Council, the University Court proposed amendment of the Ordinance on Graduation in Law, through the creation of a new degree of BLS (or Bachelor of the Law of Scotland). Its Resolution stated that the LLB degree would continue to be a postgraduate degree, and 'hold the position of a high scientific degree' with its requirements unchanged. The BLS was 'intended for those persons preparing for the profession of Law, who may not be able to give up the time necessary for obtaining the MA degree, and for attending the full curriculum in Law'. Candidates for the degree of BLS were, however, to have passed an examination in Latin, Greek (or two modern languages) and any two of logic, moral philosophy and mathematics. They were also to have studied for one academic year in a recognised university at least one or more subjects in the arts curriculum. After this the study for the degree was to be for two years, requiring study of civil law, Scots law and conveyancing, and any one of public law, constitutional law and history, or medical jurisprudence.[140] This came before the Senatus and the General Council a few days later.[141]

By July 1872 the Court had received a draft of the alterations to the Ordinance on Graduation in Law. A difficulty in seeking the amendment was that the Ordinance applied to all the Scots universities, not just that of Edinburgh, so their views and agreement were needed. This stalled progress.[142] By the end of the year the Faculty of Law proposed to the Court that since no progress was being made by the other universities, an alteration by Order in Council should be sought that applied only to the University of Edinburgh.[143] This was agreed on 10 February 1873.[144] More rapid progress was now made in refining the proposal, though now involving discussions,

137 EUA, IN1/GOV/SEN/1, Minutes of the Senatus vol 4, 152 (29 Jan 1870).
138 EUA, IN1/GOV/SEN/1, Minutes of the Senatus vol 4, 191 (26 Mar 1870).
139 EUA, IN1/GOV/CRT/MIN/2, Court Minutes (Draft) and Papers, 1872–73, 325–27.
140 EUA, IN1/GOV/CRT/MIN/1, Minutes of the Court vol 2, 58–60 (12 Apr 1872).
141 EUA, IN1/GOV/SEN/1, Minutes of the Senatus vol 4, 458–60 (17 Apr 1872); EUA, IN1/ GOV/CRT/ MIN, Minutes of the Court vol 2, 64 (13 May 1872).
142 EUA, IN1/GOV/CRT/MIN/1, Minutes of the Court vol 2, 68–69 (12 July 1872) 73 (7 Oct 1872).
143 EUA, IN1/GOV/CRT/MIN/1, Minutes of the Court vol 2, 98 (10 Dec 1872); EUA, IN1/ GOV/CRT/ MIN/2, Court Minutes (Draft) and Papers, 1874–75, 219–21.
144 EUA, IN1/GOV/CRT/MIN/1, Minutes of the Court vol 2, 101 (10 Feb 1873).

disagreements and negotiations with the University of Glasgow.[145] In March 1874 the Faculty of Law proposed that the new degree be Bachelor of Law (BL) rather than Bachelor of Scots Law (BSL). This was agreed, and Glasgow also accepted this change.[146] These and further problems were finally resolved and the requisite Order in Council obtained on 6 August 1874, with separate amendments for each of the two universities.[147]

While the focus on practice in this reform is obvious, the new degree had some parallels with the contemporary Oxford BA in its mixture of arts and law. Of course, the contents and blend were different from the BA in Law and History and later from the BA in Jurisprudence, reflecting the different focus in the degrees in arts in the two universities. If one aim was to encourage graduation in law, as well as to extend the franchise for the election of the Parliamentary representative, it also created in Edinburgh a system that had a superficial resemblance to that in Oxford, with the LLB resembling the BCL and the BL the BA. But these are rather rough parallels, and there is no evidence to suggest any mutual influence.

It is possible that it may have been this prolonged debate over the new degree that led Muirhead to stick with the topic of servitudes in his examination, as he reflected on the potentially different needs of those admitted to study for the degree of BL, for the achievement of which a pass in civil law would be necessary. In reality, the degree of BL proved no more attractive than that of LLB to law students, who continued to prefer simply to attend the courses in which they were interested.[148] The regulations for the new degree were first set out in the *Calendar* in 1875.[149]

The first exam in civil law was sat under the new system on 30 June 1875. It was included in the *Calendar* published in 1876. It was organised differently. Instead of one continuous set of questions, as had previously been the norm when we have evidence, Muirhead divided it into sections reflecting the new structure of his course: General History; Persons; Property and Real Rights; Servitudes in Particular; Succession; Obligations; Actions.[150] But it does not seem to mark a significant difference other than in form. And in 1876 the exam reverted to a long list of twenty-five questions, in the same order as in 1875, but without stated subdivisions.

---

[145] EUA, IN1/GOV/CRT/MIN/1, Minutes of the Court vol 2, 105–06 (24 Feb 1872), 107–09 (4 Mar 1873), 111–12 (8 Apr 1873), 116 (28 May 1873), 126 (17 July 1873), 135 (13 Oct 1873).

[146] EUA, IN1/GOV/CRT/MIN/1, Minutes of the Court vol 2, 155–56 (13 Mar 1874), 156–57, 158–59 (21 Apr 1874), 176 (6 July 1874).

[147] Order of Her Majesty in Council, 6 Aug 1874, Ordinance No 75, General No 8 and Edinburgh No 8, in Clapperton (ed) (n 99) 207–09.

[148] Horn (n 20) 178.

[149] *Edinburgh University Calendar 1875–76* (n 134) 172–75.

[150] *The Edinburgh University Calendar 1876–77* (James Thin 1876) 267–69; see below.

Reform in civil law

In 1876–77, Muirhead restructured his course. The *Calendar* entry now read:

> The Course of Lectures on Civil Law extends over a Winter and Summer Term, covered by one entrance fee of £5,5s. The Winter Lectures begin in November, and continue to the end of March; the Summer Lectures are given in May, June, and July.
>
> The subject-matter of the Course is the external and internal history and general and particular doctrines of the Law of Rome, as developed in the Institutes of Gaius and Justinian, supplemented by the other ante-Justinianian and Justinianian texts.
>
> During the Session 1876-77, the Professor proposes to lecture according to the order of Justinian's Institutes.
>
> The Lectures will be equally adapted for Students intending to enter the legal profession in Scotland or England, or qualifying for service in India or the Colonies.
>
> *Text-Books.-* The Institutes of Gaius and Justinian. The edition of the Corpus Juris Civilis recommended is that of the Kriegels, stereotyped at Leipzig.
>
> For preliminary reading, intending Students may consult Ortolan's "History of Roman Law," by Pritchard and Nasmith; Poste's "Gaius;" and Sandar's "Justinian."[151]

Muirhead had now departed from his earlier structure for teaching and had chosen to follow the *Institutes*. This was basically to be the stated syllabus of his course until his death in 1889, with only trivial variations in wording and occasional alteration of the recommended preliminary reading.

This change in the syllabus did not necessitate a change in the content of the examination. The examination was still stated to be 'on the History and Principles of the Law, as contained in the *Institutes* of Gaius and Justinian; and in detail the doctrines of the Law of Servitudes, as set forth in the 7th and 8th books of the Digest'.[152] In 1877 Muirhead made a change and stated that the examination would be 'on the History of the Law of Rome; on its Principles as explained in the Institutes of Gaius and Justinian; and on the 6th and 45th Books of the Digest'.[153] This was now continued until the academic year of 1881–82.[154] In the following academic year, the examination was stated to be 'on the History of the Law of Rome; on its Principles as explained in the Institutes of Gaius and Justinian; and on Book vi., tit.1, Book xli., tits 1 and 2, and Book xlv., tit.1, of the Digest'.[155]

---

[151] ibid 87–88.

[152] ibid 156.

[153] *The Edinburgh University Calendar 1877–78* (James Thin 1877) 155.

[154] *The Edinburgh University Calendar 1878–79* (James Thin 1878) 159; *The Edinburgh University Calendar 1879–80* (James Thin 1879) 137; *The Edinburgh University Calendar 1880–81* (James Thin 1880) 143; *The Edinburgh University Calendar 1881–82* (James Thin 1881) 119.

[155] *The Edinburgh University Calendar 1882–83* (James Thin 1882) 120.

From 1878 Muirhead had started once more to divide his examination paper into sections; in that year, for example: 'History'; 'Institutes of Gaius and Justinian'; 'Book VI. of Digest''; and Book XLV. of Digest'.[156] These last two sections contained more complex questions, involving translation or engagement with the text. The next year, split over two papers, his examination was in three sections: 'History'; 'Institutes of Gaius and Justinian'; 'Digest, Books VI. and XLV.'[157] The following year it was back simply to two papers, but the questions on the Digest were specially indicated. One gets the impression that Muirhead was experimenting. For example, in 1878 he stated of the four questions on History 'at least' three should be attempted; of the fourteen on the *Institutes* 'at least ten' should be attempted; and of the three questions on each of the sections of the Digest, 'at least two' should be answered.[158] This introduction of choice is not repeated.

In 1881 Muirhead made a major change in his style of examination, differentiating for the first time between candidates for the LLB and those for the BL. In the first of the two papers that now constituted the exam, it was stated that candidates for the BL need answer no more than two questions in each of the four groups of questions, while candidates for the LLB had to answer them all: history; Institutes; Institutes; Institutes and Digest, twelve questions in all. The second paper had six questions, of which candidates for the BL did not need to answer more than two and those for the LLB more than four. These questions were on *usucapio*, praetorian testaments, *fideicommissa*, literal obligations, the *lex Aquilia* and the formulary system.[159] None of the other examinations in law differentiated between the candidates for the two different degrees.[160] The same structure was used in 1882.[161]

Muirhead now continued to follow his prescription in 1882 of specific Digest titles for examination. But in 1883 he stated that they would be an object of examination *only* for the candidates for the degree of LLB:

> In Civil Law the examination for both degrees will be on the History of the Law of Rome, and on its Principles as explained in the Institutes of Gaius and Justinian. Candidates for LL.B. will also be examined on Book xii., tit. 1, Book xviii., tit. 1, and Book xliv., tit. 7, of the Digest.[162]

The instructions for the examination based on this now became quite complex. There were five groups of questions. The candidates were instructed as follows:

[156] *Edinburgh University Calendar 1879–80* (n 154) 263–65.
[157] *Edinburgh University Calendar 1880–81* (n 154) 277–79.
[158] *Edinburgh University Calendar 1879–80* (n 154) 263–65.
[159] *Edinburgh University Calendar 1882–83* (n 155) 283–85.
[160] ibid 285–90.
[161] *The Edinburgh University Calendar 1883–84* (James Thin 1883) 293–95.
[162] ibid 124.

Candidates for LL.B. and Competitors for the Forensic Prize must answer all the questions in Groups I. and V., and three questions in each of Groups II., III., and IV. Those candidates for BL who are not competitors for the Forensic Prize must answer all the questions in Group I., and three questions in each of Groups II., III., and IV., but need not answer any in Group V.[163]

Group I had three questions, groups II to IV five each and group V three, each of which was a fragment from the Digest which the candidate had to translate and on which he had also to comment.[164]

Prescription of some specific titles from the Digest for candidates for the degree of LLB now became Muirhead's regular practice, though those study-ing for the BL had also to answer them to be eligible for the Forensic Prize, which was a prize for the 'candidate who shall pass with the greatest distinc-tion the examination in the subjects for a Degree in Law'. First awarded in 1876, and funded by the Forensic Society, this was based on the passing of four subjects, which made those studying for the BL eligible.[165] This meant that the test for these students had to be the same as that for those taking the LLB. Thus, in 1884, the Digest titles prescribed were D.6.1, *de rei vindicatio*, and D.9.2, *ad legem Aquiliam*;[166] these were prescribed once more in 1885 (in this year the competition for the Forensic Prize became for the Vans Dunlop scholarships, eligibility for which required a pass at LLB level).[167] They were duly the objects of examination in the fifth group of questions in 1884 (two on each) and 1885 (two on D.6.1 and one on D.9.2).[168] Muirhead continued this practice of prescribing two titles of the Digest in this fashion for examination in the fifth part of his exam for the rest of his tenure of the Chair, as did his immediate successors, Goudy (Professor 1889–93) and James Mackintosh (1893–1938) (though the latter changed the structure of the exam in the mid-1890s).[169] This section always contained translation and commentary on texts from the prescribed titles.

---

163   *The Edinburgh University Calendar 1884–85* (James Thin 1884) 304–05.
164   ibid.
165   ibid 402–03. There was also an older Forensic Essay prize that was – and is – different.
166   *Edinburgh University Calendar 1884–85* (n 163) 129.
167   *The Edinburgh University Calendar 1885-86* (James Thin 1885) 133.
168   ibid 312–14; *The Edinburgh University Calendar 1886–87* (James Thin 1886) 330–31.
169   ibid 145: D.3.5 and 8.1 (1886); *The Edinburgh University Calendar 1887–88* (James Thin 1887) 260: D.8.2 and D.20.1 (1887); D.27.3 and D.46.2 (1888); *The Edinburgh University Calendar 1888–89* (James Thin 1888) 263: D.19.1 and 23.2 (1889); *The Edinburgh University Calendar 1889–90* (James Thin 1889) 274: D.26.1, 2; D.41.3 (1890); *The Edinburgh University Calendar 1890–91* (James Thin 1890) 301: D.26.1, 2; D.45.1 (1891); *The Edinburgh University Calendar 1891–92* (James Thin 1891) 300: D.18.1; D. 45.1; *The Edinburgh University Calendar 1892–93* (James Thin 1892) 300: D.18.1; D.45.1 (1893); *The Edinburgh University Calendar 1893–94* (James Thin 1893) 352: D.18.1; D.41.1; *The Edinburgh University Calendar 1894–95* (James Thin 1894) 508: D.18.1; D.41.1; *The Edinburgh University Calendar 1895–96* (James Thin 1895) 556: D.18.1; D.19.1; *The Edinburgh University Calendar 1896–97* (James Thin 1896) 519: D.18.1; D.19.1; *The Edinburgh University Calendar 1897–98* (James Thin 1897) 296: D.18.1;

The curriculum stayed the same until the creation of the Board of Studies in Law and History opened civil law as a graduating course in arts in 1893. It is worth setting out the new *Calendar* entries here, first in arts:

> The Course of Lectures qualifying for Graduation in Arts to be delivered by the Professor of Roman Law next Winter Session will extend to eighty-eight meetings of the Class.
>
> The Course will be divided into two distinct parts. The first half of the Course (extending to not less than forty-four meetings of the Class) will be devoted to the History of the Laws of Rome, and in particular –
>
> 1. *The External History* – shewing the growth of the Constitution and the development of the law from the earliest period till the close of the Republic, the matured system in the early empire, and the ultimate decline under the later Emperors; and
>
> 2. *The Internal History* – embracing the sources of the laws and their general effects in relation to the family (such as slavery, marriage, adoption, emancipation, etc.), to property, to succession, to matters of contract and delict, and to actions. This half of the course will terminate at the commencement of the Christmas Vacation, and it qualifies as a half-course for Graduation in Arts.
>
> The second half of the Course will be devoted to a doctrinal exposition, in detail, of the laws relating to persons and the family, and to property and real rights.

Fees were two guineas for the half course and three for the full. There was also a listing of preliminary reading, while the textbooks were stated to be the *Institutes* of Gaius and Justinian.[170] The new entry in the LLB programme read as follows:

> The Course of Lectures on Civil Law extends over a Winter and a Summer Term, covered by one entrance fee of £5, 5s. The Winter lectures usually begin on 15th October, and continue until 20th March; the Summer Lectures usually begin on 12th May, and end on 20th July.
>
> The subject matter of the Course is during the Winter Session the same as that qualifying for Graduation in Arts. ... The Summer Session will be devoted to the doctrines of Succession, Obligations, and Actions.
>
> The Lectures will be equally adapted for students intending to qualify in Scotland or England, or qualifying for service in India or the Colonies.

The entry then referred to the same preliminary reading and textbooks as in the arts programme, while adding that 'The "Muirhead Prize," and the "Forensic Prize," are offered annually for competition'.[171]

D.19.1; *The Edinburgh University Calendar 1898–99* (James Thin 1898) 304: D.18.1; D.19.1; *The Edinburgh University Calendar 1899–1900* (James Thin 1899) 311–12: D.18.1; D.19.1; *The Edinburgh University Calendar 1900–1901* (James Thin 1900) 315: D.18.1; D.19.1.

[170] *Edinburgh University Calendar 1893–94* (n 169) 106–07.
[171] ibid 340–41.

The examination for the degree of LLB remained as before for the time being, with five parts, the last of which was devoted to the titles prescribed from the Digest.[172] The exam for the degree in arts was more straightforward, and organised in two papers, one historical, the other doctrinal, the latter involving translation from an institutional text.[173]

The succession of James Mackintosh led to innovation. In 1894–95, Mackintosh subtly altered the description of the course in the *Calendar*. The summer session was now described as being devoted to 'Succession, Obligations, and Contract'. A new sentence was added: 'The Contract of Sale will be dealt with in detail.'[174] D.18.1, *de contrahenda emptione*, had been one of the (usually two) titles set every year since 1891–92; from 1895 it was joined by D.19.1, *de actionibus empti venditi*.[175] Indeed, Mackintosh appears to have continued his practice of examining both of these titles until 1935, when the *Calendar* stated the examination would only be on D.18.1, a direction which was retained until Mackintosh retired from the Chair of Civil Law in 1938.[176] The reason for favouring these titles is obvious. In 1892, while still assistant in the Chair to Goudy, Mackintosh had published *The Roman Law of Sale with Modern Illustrations: Digest XVIII.1 and XIX.1 Translated with Notes and References to Cases and the Sale of Goods Bill*. The work contained the Latin text with a facing English translation and had very full explanatory and comparative annotations below the text. These contain references to modern cases and writers on Scots and English law, as well as to contemporary or near-contemporary scholars of Roman law. Given the topic, it is no surprise that Pothier is often cited. The notes also discuss textual issues and provide explanations of Latin terminology where relevant.[177] Mackintosh, who was an excellent classicist, produced this work on the prompting of Goudy. It was again intended for students, to make them familiar with the Digest, while drawing on an area of law that the proposed reform of the law on sale of goods made topical, as well as being of intrinsic interest.[178] The continued reliance on Mackintosh's edition and translation in Edinburgh and other universities meant the work proved a success. A second edition was published in 1907; this was reprinted in 1929.[179] The work was well reviewed.[180]

---

[172] ibid 358–59; *Edinburgh University Calendar 1894–95* (n 169) 519–21.

[173] *Edinburgh University Calendar 1893–94* (n 169) 231–32.

[174] *Edinburgh University Calendar 1894–95* (n 169) 494.

[175] See n 169.

[176] I have not checked every *Calendar*.

[177] James Mackintosh, *The Roman Law of Sale with Modern Illustrations: Digest XVIII.1 and XIX.1 Translated with Notes and References to Cases and the Sale of Goods Bill* (T & T Clark 1892).

[178] ibid v–vii; Cairns (n 5) 21–22.

[179] James Mackintosh (ed), *The Roman Law of Sale with Modern Illustrations: Digest XVIII.1 and XIX.1 Translated with Notes and References to Cases and the Sale of Goods Act* (T & T Clark 1907).

In 1891 Mackintosh had done something similar on a much smaller scale, translating and commenting on D.4.9, the edict *nautae caupones stabularii*, and D.47.5, *furti adversus nautas caupones stabularios*, both very short titles.[181] It is tempting to suppose that this arose out of teaching he carried out as assistant to the Chair of Civil Law. Much later, a student recalled him teaching the Edict in class.[182] In 1935 a revised version of the article was published in the *Juridical Review*, because 'it has been found of service to students and in Court'.[183] For example, under Mackintosh's successor in the chair, Matthew Fisher, D.4.9 was one year prescribed for the examination for the degree of LLB, with the book recommended being *The Edict Nautae Caupones Stabularii* by James Mackintosh, listed as published by W Green and Son.[184] This must have been an offprint of this article, made available for students by W Green, who published the *Juridical Review*. I can certainly trace no such actual book.

By 1896 Mackintosh had combined the two separate exams (that for arts students and that for law students) into one and changed the structure. The four-hour examination in civil law was now divided into three parts: the first ('A') was devoted to 'History' and contained eight questions, with all candidates expected to answer six; the second ('B') to 'Institutes' had ten questions, all candidates expected to answer the first (translations and commentary) with MA and BL candidates expected to answer seven and LLB candidates five of the remaining questions; and the third ('C') to D.18.1 and 19.1, to be answered only by LLB candidates, testing skills of translation, analysis and interpretation.[185]

Cambridge parallels

So far this chapter has focused on Oxford and Edinburgh for its details. But it is evident that a parallel development can be traced for Cambridge, a development that awaits greater exploration than is possible here. A few comments may nonetheless be found useful to illuminate the general thesis. Indeed, events in Cambridge may turn out to have a particular importance in the British context.

From the 1850s through to 1869, a law tripos existed at Cambridge. For honours in the degree of LLB, fixed subjects included the *Institutes* of Gaius

---

[180] J Dove Wilson, 'Book Review' (1892) 4 Jur Rev 262; [Anon], 'Review', *The Scotsman* (Edinburgh, 13 June 1892) 2; [Anon], 'Book Review' (1907) 19 Jur Rev 87.

[181] James Mackintosh, 'The Edict *Nautae Caupones Stabularii*' (1891) 3 Jur Rev 306.

[182] Archie H Campbell, 'Memories of the Faculty of Law, 1921–1971' (1977) 28 Univ Edin J 60, 62.

[183] James Mackintosh, '*Nautae Caupones Stabularii*: Special Liabilities of Shipmasters, Innkeepers, and Stablers' (1935) 47 Jur Rev 54, 54 n 1.

[184] *The Edinburgh University Calendar 1956–57* (James Thin 1956) 92.

[185] *Edinburgh University Calendar 1896–97* (n 169) 525–27.

and Justinian and the seventh book of Quintilian, *de Institutione Oratoria*. As well as the fixed books, there were to be 'others selected by the Board of Legal Studies, of which one or more books of the Digest shall always form part'.[186] In 1870 a change came with the creation of the law and history tripos, in some ways reminiscent of the law and history honours school at Oxford.[187] One of the subjects for this tripos was again Roman law. For 1870 the curriculum and examination were described thus:

> Roman Law. – (a) General Subject. Gaii Commentarii, and Justiniani Institutiones. (b) Special Subject. The Roman Theory of Obligatio and the law relating to Obligationes ex delicto, the explanation of which will be found in Mackeldey's Systema Juris Romani, pp. 340-361 and 428-437; and Warnkœnig's Commentarii Juris Romani Privati, Vol. II. Pars prior, Cap. 1, 2, 3, pp. 1-215 and Pars post. Cap. 3, pp. 404-442.[188]

It was stated that there would be a paper on each of these subjects, and that in 'that on Gaius and Justinian questions on the subject matter as well as extracts for translation will be set'.[189] The special subject changed each year. Thus, in 1871 it was:

> The Roman Theory of Rights and Duties as explained in Mackeldey's Systema Juris Romani, Pars Generalis, Sect. IV. pp. 167-224, §§ 158 *b* to 207 *c*. 18, and Linley's Introduction to the Study of Jurisprudence, Part II. Divisions 1 and 3, §§ 182-194 and § 210.[190]

If books of the Digest had been prescribed under the now superseded law tripos, this marked a change. It is certain that during the period of the history and law tripos neither books nor titles of the Digest were prescribed;[191] a particular area of law as a special subject seems to have been substituted instead.

After 1875 there was once more simply a law tripos, still leading either to the degree of BA or LLB.[192] In 1876 the Board of Legal Studies explained that in teaching Roman law, there were two classes of subject:

> 1. Fixed; viz., the Commentaries of Gaius, the Institutes of Justinian, and Lord Mackenzie's 'Roman Law.'
>   Of these the first is peculiar to Candidates for Honours, the third to Candidates for the Ordinary Degree, and the second is common to both.

---

[186] J T Abdy, 'Letter from the Regius Professor of Laws at Cambridge' (1856) 2 Law Mag & L Rev Quart J Juris 269, 270, 273; J R Tanner (ed), *The Historical Register of the University of Cambridge* (CUP 1917) 854–58.

[187] Tanner (n 186) 859–61.

[188] *The Cambridge University Calendar for the Year 1869* (Deighton, Bell, & Co 1869) vi.

[189] ibid.

[190] *The Cambridge University Calendar for the Year 1870* (Deighton, Bell, & Co 1870) [v]–vi.

[191] John T Abdy and Bryan Walker (eds), *The Commentaries of Gaius* (CUP 1870) vi.

[192] Tanner (n 186) 862.

2. Variable: e.g. portions of the works of Ulpian, or of the Digest.

The second Class, together with Jurisprudence, is peculiar to Candidates for Honours.[193]

What this meant in terms of examinations was explained later in discussing the papers for the law tripos examination: 'Passages for Translation, taken from the sources of Roman Law, particularly from Gaius, Ulpian, Justinian, and some specified portion of the Digest'; and 'Questions on Roman Law and its history'. The Roman law component for the Special Examination for the ordinary degree in law was 'Justinian's Institutes in the original Latin, Lord Mackenzie on Roman Law, or the Elements of Hindu and Mohammedan Law'.[194] This practice was maintained through the 1880s, and this approach to Roman law survived the later division of the law tripos into two parts, which took effect from 1889.[195] Reforms in 1922 meant that 'in the case of Roman Law a portion of the Digest will no longer be prescribed, and the amount of the Institutes, both of Gaius and Justinian, in respect of which a knowledge of the Latin text is to be required, is curtailed'.[196]

The practice in Cambridge of prescribing portions of the Digest, as well as the *Institutes*, explains a number of publications. Thus, J T Abdy, the Regius Professor of Civil Law from 1854 to 1872, and Bryan Walker, sometime law student of Trinity Hall, then Fellow of Corpus Christi, before becoming Law Lecturer of St John's College, published a translation of Gaius, *Institutes* in 1870;[197] the second edition of 1874 included the Rules of Ulpian, presumably in deference to the needs of students preparing for the tripos which now required them to study the jurist.[198] It was reissued with a title page of 1876.[199] The same team also published a translation of Justinian's *Institutes* with Cambridge students in mind.[200]

Abdy's successor in the Regius Chair, E C Clark, did no similar work for students. But Abdy's collaborator Walker carried on translating, under the pressure created by the regular prescription of changing titles of the Digest for the tripos in law. In 1879 he published a translation of D.17.1,

---

[193] *Copy of the Report, Dated 27th March 1876, of the Syndicate Appointed 27th May 1875, by the University of Cambridge, to Consider the Requirements of the University in Different Departments of Study, with Appendices* (House of Commons Papers 272) 24 [PP 1876 LIX.35].

[194] ibid 27.

[195] G Glover Alexander, 'Legal Education at Cambridge' (1888) 2 Columbia Law Times 94, 95.

[196] H A Hollond, 'The Revision of the Law Tripos' (1922) 1 CLJ 193, 194.

[197] Abdy and Walker (eds), *Commentaries of Gaius* (n 191).

[198] John T Abdy and Bryan Walker (eds), *The Commentaries of Gaius and Rules of Ulpian* (new 2nd edn, CUP 1874).

[199] John T Abdy and Bryan Walker (eds), *The Commentaries of Gaius and Rules of Ulpian* (new 2nd edn, CUP 1876).

[200] John T Abdy and Bryan Walker (eds), *The Institutes of Justinian* (CUP 1876).

mandati vel contra.[201] He explained that he had been working for some years on translating books of the Digest. He also stated that he published the title on mandate first, as it was ready, and it was 'the selected topic for the Cambridge Law Tripos Examination of 1879'. He hoped that it would therefore 'supply an immediate want' and indicate whether there was a demand by a considerable number of readers to have the Digest translated into English. He added that the title *pro socio* would follow shortly in order to complete book 17.[202] In fact what was next published was a translation of D.41.1 and 2.[203] This was again to meet the needs of the students who had to deal with D.41.1 in the tripos of 1880; D.41.2 was also included to aid understanding. *Pro socio* was again postponed.[204] Walker's translation of it was not to be published, as the next year appeared his translation of D.42.1 and 4–7 and D.43.1–3.[205] No more of his work of translation was published, and he died in 1887.

The continued prescription of specific titles for the tripos stimulated others to translate them to assist the students. C H Monro, Fellow of Gonville and Caius, essentially picked up the mantle let slip by Walker, producing a series of translations of individual titles, published in small volumes still familiar to those who use the Roman law sections of British law libraries. In 1891 Monro published a translation of D.19.2, *locati conducti*; this was followed in 1893 by D.47.2, *de furtis*; in 1898 by D.9.2 *ad legem Aquiliam*; in 1900 by D.41.1, *de acquirendo rerum dominio*; and in 1902 by D.17.2, *pro socio* (promised so long ago by Walker).[206] These were slim volumes, small in format, designed for the convenience of students, with clear translations and helpful notes. Monro was conscious of his intended readers: 'This publication is an attempt to give some assistance to Cambridge students', he wrote in 1893.[207] In 1902 he explained that '[a]t Cambridge, the object of this book is evident'.[208] He explained that he published his own translation of D.41.1, though there was an existing translation by Walker, because the latter did not provide much in the way of notes, and, the notes being new, a new trans-

---

[201] Bryan Walker (ed), *Selected Titles from the Digest: Part I. Mandati vel contra. Digest XVII.I* (CUP 1879).

[202] ibid [v]–vi.

[203] Bryan Walker (ed), *Selected Titles from the Digest: De acquirendo rerum dominio and de acquirenda et amittenda possessione. Digest XLI.I. and II.* (CUP 1880).

[204] ibid [v].

[205] Bryan Walker (ed), *Selected Titles from the Digest: De condictionibus. Digest XII.I. and IV.–VII. and Digest XIII.I–III. Selected and Annotated* (CUP 1881).

[206] Charles Henry Monro (ed), *Digest XIX.2: Locati conducti* (CUP 1891); Charles Henry Monro (ed), *Digest XLVII.2: De furtis* (CUP 1893); Charles Henry Monro (ed), *Digest IX.2: Lex Aquilia* (CUP 1898); Charles Henry Monro (ed), *Digest XLI.1: De adquirendo rerum dominio* (CUP 1900); Charles Henry Monro (ed), *Digest XVII.2: Pro socio* (CUP 1902).

[207] Monro (ed), *Digest XLVII.2* (n 206) preface.

[208] Monro (ed), *Digest XVII.2* (n 206) [v].

lation was thought desirable.[209] Monro and Cambridge University Press had worked out a successful style, structure and size.

Like Walker, Monro had the ambition to produce a complete translation of the Digest, and in 1904 a first volume was published (without a Latin text).[210] He left the task incomplete, though a second volume of the translation appeared in 1909, after Monro's death, edited by W W Buckland.[211]

3. CONCLUSION

In 1892 James Mackintosh wrote:

> In many cases candidates for legal examinations are now very properly required, in showing a general knowledge of the traditional and somewhat tedious textbook, the *Institutes of Justinian*, to profess some special subject as treated in the *Digest*, and are thus introduced to an acquaintance with the most interesting and characteristic monument of the Roman genius for law.[212]

Thus, by 1900, in the British universities, the detailed study of a title of the Digest had become a standard way of advancing students' knowledge of Roman law. Grueber's commentary on the *lex Aquilia*, with which this chapter started, was just one of a number of works to assist the students. It was of course considerably more extensive as a work than the small texts produced by Monro. With its introduction, extensive commentary into which the text of the title was woven and systematic exposition, it was, according to Monro, the longest of the three monographs written on the *lex Aquilia* published in the nineteenth century.[213] But it is clear that Grueber's rather ponderous volume did not become the standard work to introduce students to the Digest.

Two years before Grueber's work appeared, Henry John Roby's *Introduction to the Study of Justinian's Digest Containing an Account of its Composition and of the Jurists Used or Referred to Therein, Together with a Full Commentary on One Title (de usufructu)* was published.[214] It was even more

---

[209] Monro (ed), *Digest XLI.1* (n 206) preface.

[210] C H Monro (ed), *The Digest of Justinian* vol 1 (CUP 1904).

[211] C H Monro (ed), *The Digest of Justinian* vol 2 (William Warwick Buckland ed, CUP 1909).

[212] Mackintosh (n 177) [v].

[213] Monro (ed), *Digest IX.2* (n 206) memorandum. He described Alfred Pernice's *Zur Lehre von den Sachbeschädigungen nach römischem Rechte* (Böhlau 1867) as 'the most original' and that of Joseph Willems of Brussels, *La loi aquilienne: théorie du dommage en choses en droit romain* (C Peeters 1896), as the most recent. To give an indication of size, Pernice's study contained 247 pages of text (excluding minor preliminary matter), Grueber's 279 (excluding the introduction of 35 pages) and Willems' 112 of main text.

[214] Henry John Roby, *An Introduction to the Study of Justinian's Digest Containing an Account of its Composition and of the Jurists Used or Referred to Therein, Together with a Full Commentary on One Title (de usufructu)* (CUP 1884).

elaborate. It gave a very detailed account of the Digest, with the first part amounting to 279 pages, including prefatory matter; the edition of the title *de usufructu* (D.7.1) was twenty-five pages in length, but the annotations covered 222 pages. He did not provide a translation of the text. The work was intended to aid students progressing to the Digest in the way students were helped in editions of classical texts. As well as the very elaborate and detailed introduction to the Digest, the notes to the title were, as he put it, 'legal, philological, and antiquarian', and much longer and more numerous than would 'properly accompany an edition of the Digest or of a large part of it'. Roby considered his work to be innovatory; he acknowledged no debts except to Mommsen and Savigny.[215] Two years later Roby's enormous work was made available by the Press in two separate parts: the *Introduction* and the edition of D.7.1 with its notes.[216] Each had a new preface, but the contents were otherwise unchanged. Roby had once taught at St John's College, Cambridge, and had later very briefly been Professor of Jurisprudence at University College, London. He was evidently a learned man with an excellent knowledge of the classics, whom Bryce had once apparently considered recommending for his own chair.[217] In 1887 the University of Edinburgh conferred on Roby the degree of LLD *honoris causa tantum*, the laureation address noting that his study of the Digest was 'the most valuable and learned work of the kind in the English language' and that it had been 'favourably received both in Great Britain and on the Continent', and had been translated into French.[218] Despite these accolades, his volume did not succeed in making D.7.1 the standard text with which to introduce British students to the Digest, if that had indeed been his intention.

It is quite possible that Grueber's and Roby's works were simply too elaborate for regular student use. In Edinburgh, Cambridge, and Oxford, in their differing ways, study of a title of the Digest was just one part of a student's tasks. Grueber's and Roby's books (especially the latter) were more suitable as reference works than as practical student textbooks. Muirhead, in reviewing Grueber's book, had pointed to this very problem. He commented that 'Mr. Roby has published his title *De Usufructu*, which he has furnished, from the abundance of his stores, with a wealth of notes that to many students is apt to

---

[215] ibid [vi]–vii.

[216] Henry John Roby, *An Introduction to the Study of Justinian's Digest Containing an Account of its Composition and of the Jurists Used or Referred to Therein* (CUP 1886); Henry John Roby (ed), *De usufructu: Iustiniani digestorum Lib. VII Tit. I … With a Legal and Philological Commentary* (CUP 1886).

[217] Christopher Stray, 'Roby, Henry John (1830–1915)', *Oxford Dictionary of National Biography* (OUP 2004; online edn Jan 2008) <www.oxforddnb.com/view/article/35807> accessed 17 Sept 2017.

[218] 'University of Edinburgh Graduation Ceremonial' *The Scotsman* (Edinburgh, 2 August 1887) 3. In fact, it had been translated into Italian.

prove an *embarras de richesses'*.[219] Also, teachers might want to vary the titles they prescribed, as Muirhead and Goudy had done in Edinburgh, and as was regular practice in Cambridge. This meant other works might be desirable.

In this respect, Monro had hit on a much better formula for student use. It is no surprise that Cambridge University Press reissued some of his titles as late as the 1930s. Monro's texts did not discourage through their bulk. They were not overburdened with annotations and contextual information. Monro's texts facilitated the engagement with a teacher, not with a text-book, that Muirhead considered best assisted students. The teacher had the freedom to develop the class in whatever way was most suited. There was no constraint or control from the laboured opinions of an editor. The touch was light and well judged.

Without engaging in a detailed discussion, it is obvious that some titles were much better suited for this type of teaching than others. If, for Muirhead, D.9.2 was too limited in the number of jurists extracted, it nonetheless was 'of much human as well as legal interest'.[220] It is under-standable that it was a favourite, particularly as the modern law of delictual and tortious liability developed in the twentieth century, as reflected in, for example, *Donoghue v Stevenson*.[221] But there were other popular titles. In 1922 the recently appointed Regius Professor at Oxford, Francis de Zulueta, published a translation with commentary of D.41.1 and 41.2.[222] As well as appearing in Holland and Shadwell's *Select Titles*, these had already been translated by Walker, while Monro had translated and edited D.41.1 alone. These titles had featured regularly in classes in Edinburgh, Cambridge and Oxford. Given their topics – *de acquirendo rerum dominio* and *de adquirenda vel amittenda possessione* – this was hardly surprising. De Zulueta explained that '[i]f a teacher of Roman law desires the Digest to be read, it is his business to make it readable by men who have been through the Institutes'. He stated that if 'Monro's edition of D.41,1 and Walker's of 41,1 and 2 were not out of print' he would not have undertaken the work. He stressed that the commentary was 'intended to meet an educational need, not as a work of research'.[223] De Zulueta's edition was reprinted in 1950, omitting the original preface.[224] The *condictiones* remained a popular topic, and in 1937 D T Oliver of Cambridge published a new edition with translation and notes of D.12.1 and 4–7 and D.13.1–3, exactly what Walker had once translated and published, while Monro's incomplete translation of the Digest also

---

[219]   Muirhead (n 4) 380.

[220]   ibid 380.

[221]   1932 SC (HL) 31.

[222]   Francis de Zulueta (ed), *Digest 41,1. & 2: Translation and Commentary* (Clarendon Press 1922).

[223]   ibid [5]–[6].

[224]   Francis de Zulueta (ed), *Digest 41,1. & 2* (Clarendon Press 1950).

dealt with them.[225] Yet another popular title was evidently *de furtis*. H F Jolowicz published an edition and translation with an introduction in 1940. He explained that scholarship had moved on from the time of Monro's edition.[226] There may be more to discover about this type of work. From de Zulueta, for example, we know that there had been a short-lived Oxford Digest Society that had stimulated his work on the texts.[227]

Thus, by the Second World War, several printed texts, designed for students, involving translation of a Digest title were circulating in Great Britain. These works had arisen from specific university contexts, be they Edinburgh, Cambridge, or Oxford, but they created a reservoir of titles edited with a translation that any university could use. For example, Mackintosh's translation of D.18.1 and 19.1 was recommended for one of the papers in Roman law in the Honour School of Jurisprudence in Oxford in the 1930s;[228] Jolowicz's translation of *de furtis* was prescribed in Edinburgh in 1946.[229] Availability of texts will necessarily have had a determining effect on the choice of title to teach. As the choice diminished, the same titles would be favoured again and again.

De Zulueta's, Oliver's, and Jolowicz's volumes give the impression that these editions of their respective titles reflect a greater overt engagement with contemporary studies of Roman law and also with its Continental scholarship than those of Monro, though he was a careful and learned man. All three acknowledge the assistance of Buckland, thereby pointing to the new power in the land.[230] If not of the dimensions of Grueber's volume, it is worth noting that Jolowicz's edition is somewhat larger and more elaborate than those produced by Monro. The brief note devoted to it in the *Cambridge Law Journal* alluded to the time since Monro's edition, and remarked that 'a new commentary embodying references to the contributions of, among others, Professor Schulz, Levy and de Visscher on the Continent and of Professor Buckland in England has long been overdue'.[231]

It is a subtle judgment, but these later editions of titles of the Digest, particularly that of Jolowicz, seem to have been developing into fuller, more scholarly works of greater scope than the editions of Monro, without being of the dimensions and scope of Grueber's and Roby's volumes. This is not surprising. As the study of Roman law developed in Britain in the 1920s and

---

[225] David T Oliver (ed), *Digest XII.1 and 4–7 and XIII.1–3 de condictionibus* (CUP 1937) [v].

[226] Herbert F Jolowicz (ed), *Digest XLVII.2 de furtis, Edited with Introduction, Translation and Notes* (CUP 1940) [vii]–viii.

[227] De Zulueta (ed), *Digest 41,1. & 2* (n 222) [vi]; de Zulueta (ed), *Digest 41,1. & 2* (n 224) [v].

[228] Robert Warden Lee, 'Comparative Law and Comparative Lawyers' (1936) JSPTL 1, 7.

[229] *The Edinburgh University Calendar 1946–47* (James Thin 1946) 289.

[230] De Zulueta (ed), *Digest 41,1. & 2* (n 222) [6]; Oliver, *Digest XII.1 and 4–7 and XIII.1–3* (n 225) [v]; Jolowicz (ed), *Digest XLVII.2* (n 226) viii.

[231] D T O [D T Oliver], 'Book Review' (1941) 7 CLJ 439, 439.

1930s under the influence, most notably, of Buckland and Jolowicz, a British secondary literature developed in legal periodicals.[232] From the mid-1930s the lively contributions of David Daube also stimulated scholarly work.[233] Not only would such volumes have to engage with it, but teachers also could reasonably expect students to reflect on the new scholarship, enriching their understanding of the texts.

In 1931 the noted French scholar Paul Collinet, in reviewing de Zulueta's 1922 edition of D.41.1 and 2, pointed out that, in such a work, 'the exegetical method, currently a little too neglected, reclaimed its proper place'.[234] A year later, in reviewing James B Thayer's edition of D.9.2 and D.24.1, Ernst Levy roundly condemned this type of exegetical exercise as demonstrating the excessive (*übermächtig*) reliance on a traditional method in the 'Anglo-Saxon countries'. He expressed the view that a 'Continental legal historian' would have set out a historical account and then a systematic account to expose the essentials of the issue. Had he been tempted to produce an exegetical account from the sources, he would have approached them according to their palingenesis; he would have looked at the Digest's structure only from the perspective of its compilation or of the law's development.[235] Levy's critique is one arising from late-nineteenth-century German scholarship, privileging the 'truer' or 'better' law of the earlier (or 'classical') period. When de Zulueta decided to publish *The Roman Law of Sale: Introduction and Select Texts* in 1944, he felt it necessary to point out that Levy had not really understood that these were texts to instruct students, not the products of 'traditionalism in method'; he explained that 'English Universities do not greatly value the study of Roman law unaccompanied by at least some first-hand acquaintance with the texts', which meant that if the student was to progress beyond the *Institutes* 'texts must be made accessible'.[236]

One can, however, perhaps identify a measure of influence on de Zulueta's approach arising out of Levy's critique. The former may not have set out his Digest texts according to their palingenesis, but he did include antejustinianic texts, literary as well as legal. He did not simply include the most important

---

[232] To give a few scattered examples: William Warwick Buckland, 'L'intérêt dans l'*actio furti*' (1917) 40 RHDFE 5; Herbert F Jolowicz, 'The Original Scope of the Lex Aquilia and the Question of Damages' (1922) 38 LQR 220; William Warwick Buckland, 'Digest XLVII.2 (*de furtis*) and the Methods of the Compilers' (1930) 10 TvR 117; Herbert F Jolowicz, 'The Origin of *Laesio Enormis*' (1937) 49 Jur Rev 50; William Warwick Buckland, '*Contrectatio*' (1941) 57 LQR 467

[233] For example, David Daube, 'On the Third Chapter of the Lex Aquilia' (1936) 52 LQR 523; David Daube, '*Furtum Proprium* and *Furtum Improprium*' (1937) 6 CLJ 217; David Daube, '*Nocere* and *Noxa*' (1939) 7 CLJ 23.

[234] Paul Collinet, 'Book Review' (1931) 10 RHDFE 138, 139.

[235] E[rnst] Levy, 'Book Review' (1932) 52 ZSS (RA) 533, 533–34.

[236] Francis de Zulueta, *The Roman Law of Sale: Introduction and Select Texts* (Clarendon Press 1945) [iii].

titles on sale, as had done Mackintosh; he also included extracts from the Digest with the relevant edictal material, and extracts from other titles that had a bearing on the topic, as well as printing the Sale of Goods Act, the Factors Act and extracts from the French *Code civil*. He prefaced his edition of all this primary material with a relatively lengthy introduction that had a theoretical and historical account of sale, before going on to deal in some detail with its formation, effects, rescission, variation and pacts. Does one see here as a reaction an attempt (if English in approach) at Levy's historical and systematic account?

Four years later came F H Lawson's *Negligence in the Civil Law*. Lawson stated it had 'been compiled with the same intention as Professor de Zulueta's *Roman Law of Sale*';[237] and the works are indeed very similar. This said, Lawson included, as well as D.9.2: extracts from other Roman legal texts; extracts from foreign codes (in which he included some German *Pandektenrecht* as well as extracts from the *BGB*); German and French 'Jurisprudence' and 'Doctrine'; and some Canadian statutes. The extensive introduction covered analytical and historical issues, and made references to modern law. It is important to note that Lawson's aim was to produce a text to develop the study of comparative law; he overtly distinguished what he had done from the work of other scholars such as Thayer, Monro, Grueber and so on.[238] He was consciously producing a work on the 'civil' law, not on the 'Roman', to allow students to explore the differences between the civil and common laws. He stated, however, that, because it had 'been represented' to him 'that it is still the practice of English universities to set for study the whole of a title of the Digest', he had included the whole of D.9.2, not just the parts dealing with negligence.[239]

As far as I am aware, after 1950 there were no new editions in Great Britain of any individual titles of the Digest with translations and notes, aimed at student use. In the 1950s there were lithographic reproductions of de Zulueta's *Roman Law of Sale*, of which the author produced only one edition. There was also only one edition of Lawson's *Negligence in the Civil Law*, but, as early as 1955, it was lithographically reproduced from the corrected sheets. It was reproduced again in the same way in 1962 and 1968. This meant that well into the 1970s it was a book that remained available for student purchase. By this time, the non-Roman source material had started to age;[240] one wonders if Lawson's subsidiary aim – providing a Digest title for instruction – had inevitably become the main use of the work.

---

[237] Frederick Henry Lawson, *Negligence in the Civil Law* (Clarendon Press 1950) [v].

[238] ibid vii.

[239] ibid [v].

[240] No doubt the reason for producing the two-volume Frederick Henry Lawson and Basil S Markesinis, *Tortious Liability for Unintentional Harm in the Common Law and the Civil Law* (CUP 1982). The omission of the Latin text of D.9.2 diminished its utility and perhaps longevity.

David Daube wrote in 1939 that, before the year 1908, when Buckland published *The Roman Law of Slavery*, '[t]here existed in England ... no Roman legal studies in the modern sense'. Daube went on to comment that Buckland 'has ... founded a school: a school of Roman law in which, as is obvious to one coming from the Continent, the best methods of English legal thinking are put to use'.[241] It is certainly a defensible view. And Alan Rodger repeated it in 2004.[242] But it leaves one wondering what inspired and influenced Buckland. This chapter provides some of the evidence. It is notable that Daube talked of 'best methods of English legal thinking' (one could here substitute 'British' for 'English'). In 1892 Grueber stated that the study of Roman law revived in Britain 'some forty years ago';[243] this was just as the universities started to be reformed and to reform themselves and their curriculum, the period with which this study began. Study of titles of the Digest (such as D.9.2) developed out of this reform. Is it too much to suggest that, when Daube wrote of the 'methods' of 'English' legal thinking, he had in mind this type of work as opposed to the analytical method originating with the Pandectists that was championed by Levy? What was important for the students was an engagement with the texts, rather than study of a smooth, analytical survey produced by a teacher, especially one that presupposed there was a pure law that can be reached as representing an ideal. Indeed, Grueber would have agreed with Daube.[244] It is easy to understand the popularity of studying D.9.2 and the *lex Aquilia* more generally.

---

[241] Daube (1939) (n 233) 23–24.
[242] Alan Rodger, 'David Daube (1909–1999)' in Jack Beatson and Reinhard Zimmermann (eds), *Jurists Uprooted: German-Speaking Émigré Lawyers in Twentieth-Century Britain* (OUP 2004) 233, 236–37.
[243] Grueber (n 81) xxxiii.
[244] ibid xxxiv–xxxv.

Chapter 2

William Warwick Buckland on the Lex Aquilia

David Ibbetson

1. INTRODUCTION

MS 31 in the Squire Law Library at Cambridge is a collection of miscellaneous material associated with Professor William Buckland, divided into five boxes. Among the more interesting pieces here is what appears to be a typescript of a complete set of lectures on the *lex Aquilia*, a typescript of 78 pages running to over 30,000 words.[1] Since anything new by Buckland is interesting, and the *lex Aquilia* was and remains a major topic of interest for Roman law teaching in England, the opportunity is taken to reproduce this typescript and make it available to scholars.[2]

That the text represents lectures, rather than the draft of an article or book, seems clear. It contains occasional very obviously didactic remarks addressed to an audience, such as 'When you come to translate this' referring to an apparent corruption in the Latin of D.9.2.45.4, where the use of the second person would have been wholly inappropriate in an academic work. The text is littered with expressions of opinion without supporting justifications: 'I think' or 'I suppose' could hardly have been used so frequently in an academic text, still less the occasional 'I do not know'. A number of topics are dismissed as being too unimportant or too difficult for discussion. Explicit references to secondary literature are almost exclusively to the standard works on the *lex Aquilia*; overwhelmingly they are to the two works which students would be expected to have access to, the translation of Digest 9.2 by Charles Henry Monro and the commentary on the *lex Aquilia* by Erwin Grueber, again with an English translation of Digest 9.2.[3] The only author frequently referred to beyond this is Alfred Pernice, presumably to his standard German monograph on the subject referred

---

[1] Squire Law Library, Buckland Collection, box 4.
[2] See Appendix to this chapter.
[3] Charles Henry Monro (ed), *Digest IX.2: Lex Aquilia* (CUP 1921, 1928); Erwin Grueber (ed), *The Roman Law of Damage to Property, Being a Commentary on the Title of the Digest Ad Legem Aquiliam (IX. 2), with an Introduction to the Study of the Corpus Iuris Civilis* (Clarendon Press 1886).

to repeatedly by Grueber and Monro.[4] There are occasional references to Theodor Mommsen without further elucidation; most of these, probably, were to his standard edition of the Digest, though Buckland would have been familiar with his other works. Beyond this, so far as the modern literature is concerned, there are just occasional references to the Textbook, that is, Buckland's *Text-book of Roman Law*, and passing reference to unnamed scholars. Clearly, it seems, students were not expected to engage with this modern literature.

The lectures appear to be complete, beginning with the origins of the *lex* and containing all that one would expect to see in a set of lectures on the subject. The only curiosity is that the typescript is paginated from 18 to 95. What would have constituted the first seventeen pages is wholly unclear, since page 18 undoubtedly represents the beginning of the material on the *lex*. The Aquilian lectures followed more general lectures on the law of obligations, so it may well be that pages 1–17 were on this earlier part of the course. We cannot rule out the possibility that there is a lost page or pages after page 95, since the end is perhaps rather abrupt, but if there is missing material it is impossible to guess what it might have contained.

That Buckland was the author of the lectures is overwhelmingly likely, even leaving aside the presence of the text in a collection of Buckland materials. He is known to have lectured on the *lex Aquilia* in 1927 and 1928;[5] handwritten insertions and interlineations look to be in his hand; the quality of the argumentation, with an encyclopaedic knowledge of texts elsewhere in the Digest, points to a Roman lawyer of very considerable learning as their author; and that the Textbook is referred to without naming the author points again towards Buckland himself.

The text may have been composed in two tranches. The bottom third of page 72 is blank, after the end of the section on *iniuria*; page 73 then begins the discussion of causation. Nowhere else does this happen, new topics beginning without any clear page break. That said, several times we find that a section ends at the bottom of one page and the next section begins at the head of the next one, so it may not have been unusual for him to begin a new section at the top of a page.

Occasionally there are typed interlineations, presumably the consequence of thinking taking place during the composition of the typed text. In addition, there are manuscript deletions, interlineations and additions which must show that the text was worked on subsequently. We cannot tell when these changes were made, except that they were obviously produced after the

---

[4] Alfred Pernice, *Zur Lehre von den Sachbeschädigungen nach römischem Rechte* (Böhlau 1867); and (perhaps also) *Marcus Antistius Labeo: das romische Privatrecht im ersten Jahrhunderte der Kaiserzeit* (3 vols, Buchhandlung des Waisenhauses 1873–92).

[5] (1926–27) 57 *Cambridge University Reporter* 117; (1927–28) 58 *Cambridge University Reporter* 65.

text was typed. It is a reasonable supposition that the basic typescript was produced before the lectures were delivered in 1927, though it need not have been: it is not impossible that the 1927 lectures were delivered from notes or a handwritten text, with the typescript dating from the following year. A few handwritten references to literature published in 1929 and into the 1930s (the earliest such reference is to a paper by Kunkel)[6] appearing at the head of the first page point to its having been completed before then; no account seems to have been taken of them in the text, and at the very least we should have expected the text to have shown some trace of David Daube's 'On the Third Chapter of the *Lex Aquilia*',[7] written under Buckland's supervision, had the text been altered through the mid-1930s. But these references to literature published in the 1930s do show that the text was not simply put away in a drawer and forgotten about after the lectures were delivered: the latest references are to two articles in the *Studi Albertoni*, published in 1935, and to Daube's article which appeared in 1936.

The lectures formed the second part of a course on the law of obligations in Part I of the law tripos, that is, a course aimed at students in their second year, the first part of which was studied primarily by reference to the *Institutes*. They were given three times a week over the eight weeks of the Lent term. This would have allowed for little more than three pages of the typescript per lecture, allowing plenty of time for the audience to turn to and read any text cited (assuming that they had a copy in front of them), or for the lecturer to recite the words of the texts. They would either have been delivered at dictation speed, with each clause or sentence repeated, or there would have been a good deal of time available to extemporise on the text as we have it. The first of these is the more likely: the style of the lectures, with its use of the second person, suggests it was designed to be delivered as it stood.

2. CONTENTS OF THE LECTURES

Buckland's lectures, of course, speak for themselves, but some features of them are worth drawing attention to, in terms of both their content and their style.

The origins of the lex[8]

Buckland shows a marked unwillingness to get involved in any discussion of the date or original interpretation of the *lex*. It might even be suggested that he was not interested in it. Chapter 3, as we have it in D.9.2.27.5, is

---

[6] Wolfgang Kunkel, 'Exegetische Studien zur Aquilischen Haftung' (1929) 49 ZSS (RA) 158.
[7] (1936) 52 LQR 253.
[8] Lectures, 18–20.

misquoted,[9] omitting the word *iniuria* and hence risking giving the impression that the killing of Chapter 1 had to have been without right (assuming that this was the original force of *iniuria*) but that there was no such requirement for Chapter 3; Chapter 1 is also misquoted, reading '*quanti in id anno*' rather than '*in eo anno*'.[10] He refers to the association between the enactment of the *lex Aquilia* and the *lex Hortensia*, which gave binding force to plebiscites, an association which had been made since the time of the glossators and had been found already in the Paraphrase of Theophilus, though he dates it as 247 BCE rather than 287.[11] He makes reference, somewhat elliptically, to an even older speculation about the enactment of the *lex* which linked it to Aquilius Gallus, a contemporary of Cicero, but saying only that it could not have been penned by him since Chapter 2 must have predated the introduction of the *actio mandati* and this must have been a good deal older than the first century BCE. Overall, the lack of discussion is very marked. We might suspect that it would have been rather different had Buckland been writing after the appearance of Daube's article on Chapter 3 of the *lex*, since that – more than anything that had appeared previously – made a very strong argument that the original scope of the *lex* might have been different from classical law.

The nature of the action[12]

Buckland reveals a similar lack of interest, bordering on impatience, in the name of the action, whether it is an *actio damni iniuria(e)* or *actio damni iniuria dati*. 'It does not matter,' he ends his short paragraph.[13] Whether the action is penal, by contrast, and what it means to say that it is, receives a rather fuller treatment. It would be all too easy to say that it is penal because the plaintiff can receive more than compensation, either because of the doubling of damages if the defendant denied liability or because of the recoverability of the highest value of the slave or animal in the previous year in Chapter 1, not simply the value at the time of the killing. But Buckland points out that the *actio doli*, a purely compensatory action, was undoubtedly penal, and unlike the *actio furti* it could not be brought cumulatively with a proprietary *vindicatio*. Similarly, the discussion of passive intransmissibility goes further than saying that the defendant's heir was not liable except to the extent that he was enriched by the killing or damaging. There is an example of how such

---

[9] ibid 19.

[10] ibid 19.

[11] ibid 18.

[12] ibid 20–22.

[13] Buckland had himself published a short note on this: '*Actio Damni Iniuriae*' (1927) 6 RHDFE 120. The reference to Mommsen is to his *Strafrecht* 826, a note on which is found in Buckland Collection, box 4.

an enrichment might have occurred, and a discussion of what the remedy against the heir would have been.

The plaintiff[14]

The *lex* was explicit that the action lay at the suit of the *erus*, the *dominus*. In truth this was not a difficult rule, though Buckland warned that it was not as simple as it looked. Where the thing had changed hands before the action was brought, he pointed out, with reference to texts elsewhere in the Digest, that it might have the consequence that the person who had suffered the loss might have no claim, and might not be able to require the person who had been owner at the time of the wrong to assign a claim to him. The one situation which was genuinely problematic was where a slave which was part of an inheritance was killed before the heir had entered; clearly for the heir to have an action there needed to be some sort of fiction, most obviously that the *hereditas* was the owner of the slave. The most difficult text, D.9.2.23.1, where a slave who had been freed and made heir in a will, is dealt with here, though its real issue is what, if any, damages could be recovered by the substitute.

In some situations, there would have been a decretal action against the wrongdoer at the suit of a non-owner. Sometimes, as in the case of a pledgee, the texts are complex as a result of transitions of forms of security from *fiducia* to *pignus* and from *pignus* to *hypotheca*, and the textual complexities are properly considered. Other cases, such as that of the usufructuary, are superficially simple but the texts bear traces of an early classical suggestion that a direct action might have lain; Buckland does not fight shy of facing up to this problem, where many a lecturer might simply gloss over it without comment. More awkward is his discussion of the two terms for decretal actions, the *actio utilis* and the *actio in factum*. There seems to be an assumption that the two were different, at least in classical law, though a straightforward reading of the texts more naturally suggests that even in classical law the terms were more or less interchangeable. That said, Buckland does make the important point that not all decretal actions would have the same consequence, some adopting the procedural rules of the *lex Aquilia* (such as the one-year rule for the assessment of damages under Chapter 1, or the rule of *lis crescens*), others being purely gap-filling. This is not fully worked out, either in the lectures or in the texts themselves, but it provides an important insight into the working of these actions.

---

[14] Lectures, 22–35.

The defendant[15]

It is easy to begin, as Buckland does, by saying that the person liable is the wrongdoer. But there are a number of special cases, and Buckland goes through them in detail. These include cases where liability attaches to one person to the exclusion of the person committing the act, as for example where someone with a right to command orders a subordinate to do something; cases where a master was noxally liable for his slave's wrongdoing, where different rules might have applied to the *lex Aquilia* than to other situations; cases where special rules applied, as where a commonly owned slave damaged the property of one co-owner; and miscellaneous cases, such as the free man acting as a slave. The whole treatment is very careful, and Buckland's encyclopaedic knowledge of the texts of the Digest shines through.

The active verbs of the lex[16]

The core of the *lex* is found in the notion of *occidere* (Chapter 1) and *urere frangere rumpere/corrumpere* (Chapter 3). Buckland's treatment of these, and the related issue of the scope of the praetorian actions extending liability, is to modern eyes perhaps the least satisfactory part of the lectures.

So far as the first chapter is concerned, the lectures suppose that the true test for liability under the direct action was whether the death was done by the body to the body, *corpore corpori*. This is clearly so in the *Institutes* of Gaius and Justinian, but it is not at all clear in the Digest, whose analysis consists of an extended discussion of the issue by Ulpian. Here the texts seem to be treating the question as one of statutory interpretation – is this an example of *occisio?* – rather than as one answered by the application of an abstract causal test. While it may well be that the classical juristic approach to the interpretation of *occisio* came down to asking whether the death had been brought about by direct means, to take this as the starting point for analysis (as Buckland explicitly does in a handwritten insertion)[17] risks ignoring the complexity of Ulpian's discussion. It is hardly credible that Ulpian would just have piled on more and more examples of what counted as a direct killing without stating the abstract test if he was in fact doing no more than applying this test. A more sensitive reading of his discussion points to his trying to unpick the idea of *occisio* by asking whether the killing needs to be deliberate, whether it need involve force and whether it need involve directness.

---

15   ibid 35–40.

16   ibid 40–47.

17   Buckland's pencilled note on the reverse of page 42: 'The point is not that it is not *occisio*, but that it is not an act *corpore corpori*.'

The lectures' treatment of the third chapter is yet more distorted by the unquestioning application of the directness test. This is undoubtedly present in Gaius' and Justinian's *Institutes*, but in so far as it is in the Digest at all (which it probably is) it is very well concealed. Ulpian can hardly be read as applying the abstract *corpore corpori* test without stating it, but instead providing some twenty examples (apparently not all consistent with each other) and leaving the hearers to find their own way to the solution. Looked at through unblinkered eyes, uninfluenced by Gaius, Ulpian is discussing the boundaries of *corruptio*, the interpretation of *ruptio* attributable to the lawyers of the Republic and clearly accepted by the classical jurists, and moving onwards from there.

Scarcely less problematic is the way in which the praetorian actions are dealt with in the lectures. The terminology of *actiones utiles* and *actiones in factum* is unstable in the Digest and Code, and the most economical explanation of this is that the phrases are being used more or less interchangeably, or at least non-technically, by the classical jurists. It may of course be that the terminological slippage was the result of the activity of the compilers, as Buckland hints, for it is generally accepted that there was no technical difference between them in Justinian's law; but it is not easy to believe in any wholesale compilatorial alteration which was not brought about by a need to update the texts to bring them into line with the law as it stood in Justinian's time.

The need for an act[18]

There is not much that can be said about the requirement of a positive act for Aquilian liability. The basic principle is clear; and the marginal cases, such as the doctor neglecting aftercare or the slave tasked with guarding a fire falling asleep, are transparently problematic. The Romans' difficulty in establishing a boundary between act and omission mirrors that of English lawyers. Other issues related to the act, such as the question of what counts as a single composite act and what two separate acts, uncontroversially allow of a simple description of the law.

Damnum[19]

The lectures continue by stating the need for *damnum* (loss). This is clearly the case with Chapter 3, since it was an explicit requirement of the *lex* itself, and it is unsurprisingly evidenced in the texts. It is, however, not at all clear that it was a requirement of Chapter 1, except of course to the trivial extent that the killing of a slave or animal was almost inevitably a loss to the owner.

---

[18] Lectures, 48–50.
[19] ibid 51–53.

Here, really, the question of loss went to the issue of damages, not of liability; and in the last part of this section Buckland gets very close to saying so, rather contradicting the strong statement at the start of the section saying that there had to be *damnum*. The explanation is not difficult to discern. For Buckland, Chapters 1 and 3 constitute a unity differentiated only by the type of damage; this may have been the case for Gaius' and Justinian's *Institutes*, but it was not so for the *lex* itself or for the classical jurists whose work is preserved in the Digest.

Culpa *and* iniuria[20]

The longest section of the lectures is that on *culpa* and *iniuria* (wrongfulness). Probably every lecturer finds this a topic which is difficult to address, and Buckland was no exception. The basic point is very clear. The *lex* itself required that the killing or damage have been done *iniuria*, explained by Ulpian in D.9.2.5.1 as meaning *non iure*, without right; in Gaius' *Institutes* this was explained as meaning *dolo* or *culpa*, deliberately or blameworthily, an explanation also found in the Digest. The relevant texts in D.9.2 evidence both approaches, and the lecturer's problem is to combine them. For Buckland the primary tool for the analysis was *iniuria*, the identification of situations in which an injurious act was permissible or the actor had a defence to an action. A modern lecturer might choose to stress *culpa*.

Although the focus of the lectures is on the defendant's wrongdoing, or lack of it, Buckland begins with *culpa*. This he translates as negligence, equating it to the failure to live up to the standard of care of a *bonus paterfamilias*, the predominant sense of *culpa* in the law of contract. This immediately causes problems with Ulpian's statement that *culpa levissima* is sufficient to ground Aquilian liability (D.9.2.44.pr). This is seen as 'any' failure to act as a *bonus paterfamilias*, but the difference between 'any' failure and 'a' failure is illusory, so that Ulpian's text is effectively emptied of meaning. Moreover, it is difficult to explain other texts in the Digest that classify something as *culpa* without obviously connoting any idea of the *bonus paterfamilias*. It is better to drop any idea of a determinate standard of care, in favour of a much looser notion of blameworthiness, and Buckland continues by saying that no exact definition is possible and the word is used 'in a wide sense', something approaching imputability. This means that the loose idea of *culpa* under the *lex Aquilia* is different from that found in contracts, where there was greater precision, and that there was consequently a possibility that where damage was caused in the performance of a contract the contractual rule would come into conflict with the Aquilian. This is hardly touched on in D.9.2, but Buckland uses his deep knowledge of the Digest to use texts from elsewhere

---

[20]   ibid 54–72.

to argue tentatively that in any concrete case the contractual standard was carried across into the law of delict.

The emphasis on *iniuria* pulls Buckland into listing situations in which the actor would have a defence: self-defence, 'certain intense provocations', consent or *volenti non fit iniuria*, accident, performance of an official duty, protection of rights, necessity. We might note the significant absence from this list of contributory negligence, which Buckland deals with under the heading of causation. The list provides a useful explanatory framework, though it probably imposes rather too rigid a structure on the Roman law. Moreover, it does not resolve the tension between analysis in terms of *culpa* and analysis in terms of *iniuria*, and it leaves a small residue of texts requiring further analysis.

We cannot criticise Buckland's approach, since it is the job of the lecturer here to attempt to make sense of the rather unruly Roman material. But one important observation needs to be made. The lectures' treatment is very much that of a contemporary English lawyer, shaping the law of torts – we might better say the action of trespass – through the defences that were available. The lectures were being written before the House of Lords' decision in *Donoghue v Stevenson* began to give concrete form to the tort of negligence, when there was real controversy over whether a tort of negligence existed at all. The English lawyer today, accustomed to framing his or her discussion of the law of torts in terms of the tort of negligence, puts far less weight on defences and a far sharper focus on whether the defendant was to blame; and lecturing on the *lex Aquilia* he or she will almost unthinkingly approach the subject through the lens of *culpa* rather than *iniuria*.

Causation[21]

To say that the defendant must have caused the injury is perhaps obvious, but the few texts dealing with it are highly problematic. Curiously, Buckland seems to have included it here almost as an afterthought, for he begins the part of the lectures dealing with the general conditions of liability by saying that there are three – there must have been an act, there must have been *damnum*, there must have been wrongfulness or blame – and only amends this by way of interlineation to say that there are four, adding that the defendant's wrongful act must have caused the loss. It seems unavoidable to include this to hold the whole subject together, however few texts there are.

Buckland's treatment of the texts is sure-footed. The possible contradiction between texts is resolved by careful reading of the Latin, though it is noteworthy that he does not expressly warn his audience of the misleadingly inaccurate translation of one text (D.9.2.51.pr) in Monro's edition of D.9.2.

---

[21] ibid 73–77.

One gets the impression that this was a subject that had to be dealt with, but which was being dealt with without great enthusiasm and got through as quickly as possible. Buckland may have been reflecting a dominant English lack of concern with causation at the time: perusal of the index of the then-current edition of the standard textbook on the law of torts by Sir John Salmond shows no entry for causation or cause, and the treatment of the subject in *Pollock on Torts* is little less exiguous.

The English textbooks deal with contributory negligence in terms of causation – it was only in 1945 that it became a partial defence – and it is here that Buckland deals with it too. This might most easily have been considered in terms of imputability, with *culpa* being used to determine whether the death or damage should be attributed to one cause or the other; such is the natural reading of the beginning of the barber text, D.9.2.11.pr. Buckland prefers to deal with it in the English way, as a causal defence, which does not fit easily with the Roman material. He is reduced therefore to going through a series of texts illustrating the principle, though never stating it explicitly, giving very little room for analysis.

The claim[22]

Buckland does not waste time on the formula as such, but focuses on the rule that the liability was doubled against one who denied liability, *lis crescens*. He is non-committal as to the cause of this rule, rightly so as it was included in the *lex* and any attempt to penetrate the mindset of the legislators of the third century BCE must inevitably be very speculative. That he deals with its origins at all is, no doubt, the result of that having been the subject of a discussion in Monro's book. More important is the effect of the confession of liability, and this is discussed with considerable care; the modern lecturer can read the discussion with profit.

In passing, it is said that *lis crescens* applies also to the *actio utilis* and the *actio in factum*, ignoring the point made earlier in the lectures that *actiones utiles* and *actiones in factum* might take different forms and have different functions. His authority for this is C.3.35.5, a late-third-century text which does indeed suggest this but which could perhaps be introducing a new rule and not just stating an old one. One has the impression that Buckland thought of Roman law between the first century BCE and the fourth century CE as a single entity, though accepting that there was scope for some juristic disagreement on particular points.

---

[22] ibid 78–80.

The assessment of damages[23]

The principal problems of the assessment of damages arise under the first chapter, which specified that the successful plaintiff should receive the highest value of the slave or animal in the previous year. There was disagreement over whether the year was counted back from the date of the death or from the date of the blow that led to the death, Celsus holding the former and Julian the latter, Buckland (probably) rightly saying that it was Julian's view that prevailed. Buckland explains that it was the economic value of the slave or animal that was relevant, not its sentimental value to the owner, though he draws attention to the apparent incoherence of this rule. There is not a great deal to be said about either of these rules. More problematic was the recoverability of consequential losses, normally divided into *lucrum cessans* and *damnum emergens*, though the terminology is not Roman. The principal texts here are fairly complex, and they are dealt with carefully; a modern view might see some of them somewhat differently, but Buckland's analysis reads well within the framework of the Roman law scholarship of his time. They raise the question, still alive today, of whether the plaintiff recovers the highest value of the slave (or animal) or his interest in its not being killed. The obvious answer is that they show that he recovers his interest, but Buckland takes this further and considers the situation where the owner's interest is less than the market value, and in the limit case zero. The analysis is first-rate, leading to the conclusion that it is only additions that affect the damages, not reductions in value, and that too much weight has been placed by scholars on the language of *interesse*.

Buckland's analysis is less satisfying on the inter-relationship between the one-year rule and the consequential damage rule; we might say that he largely ignores it. He is perhaps assuming that the consequential losses are recoverable if and only if they have actually been suffered, which would be sensible but which may not be consistent with Ulpian's statement (D.9.2.23.6) that everything which would have made the slave more valuable in the previous year would be brought into account. The Roman jurists themselves may not have resolved these problems.

There is almost no discussion of the assessment of damages under the third chapter, presumably because the *lex* itself referred to the recovery of the loss that had been suffered, *quanti ea res erit*, so that consequential damage was straightforwardly recoverable, and in any event the problematic situations discussed under Chapter 1 would hardly arise except in the case of death. One of the few texts in the Digest more or less clearly hinging on the point, D.9.2.29.3, is easily dealt with by assuming that the principles of *lucrum cessans* applicable to Chapter 1 applied equally to Chapter 3; and the

---

[23]　ibid 80–91.

other group of texts on Chapter 3 damages, relating to the defacing of documents and described by Buckland as 'obscure', raise real difficulties as to the assessment of the value of the loss but no theoretical difficulties worth exploring.

Concurrence of actions[24]

The final section of the lectures deals with the overlap between the Aquilian action and other actions. The matter is technical, and probably not of great interest to the majority of the audience, and we perhaps sense that it is being squeezed in at the end of a lecture course. Whatever the reason, the impression is given that it is all very rushed.

3. THE LECTURES AND THEIR AUDIENCE

'As a Tripos lecturer he was more noted for the matter than for the manner. His lectures were as full of meat as an egg, not a word was wasted ...'.[25] Kurt Lipstein, who attended Buckland's lectures in the 1930s when he was a research student, described them as having been 'excellent but beyond the reach of the undergraduate audience for their subtlety'.[26] The modern reader of the lectures will probably not be surprised at this judgment. If they had stood alone, it is hard to see that students could have done anything more than take down as much as possible of what was said and then study their notes in their own time.

Of course, the lectures did not stand alone. First of all, they were accompanied by Buckland's 'syllabus', or 'handout' as we would probably call it today. This was in essence the map of the lectures. Buckland himself was probably under no illusions about the utility of this as anything more than a map. He prefaced his lectures on the *condictiones*, given some ten years later than those on the *lex Aquilia*,[27] with a warning: 'If anyone thinks he is going to learn much from my syllabus he is mistaken.'[28] Both the syllabus, and the warning, are remarkably similar to what would be associated with the modern lecturer who chooses to use PowerPoint. Some scraps of a syllabus on the *lex Aquilia*, in all probability Buckland's, survive with a student's

---

[24] ibid 92–95.
[25] Arnold McNair and Patrick Duff, 'William Warwick Buckland, 1859–1946' (1947) 33 Proceedings of the British Academy 283, 285.
[26] Kurt Lipstein, 'Cambridge 1933–2002' in Jack Beatson and Reinhard Zimmermann (eds), *Jurists Uprooted: German-Speaking Émigré Lawyers in Twentieth-Century Britain* (OUP 2004) 761, 762.
[27] Interestingly, in the same term as these lectures were given in the law tripos (Michaelmas 1937), Buckland was giving a separate course of lectures on quasi-contract in the LLB: (1937–38) 68 *Cambridge University Reporter*, 89, 91.
[28] Squire Law Library, T Ellis Lewis Collection, box 5.

notes.[29] For the most part it seems to have consisted of headings and sub-headings linking to texts, though there is a brief summary of Pernice's analysis of the development of *culpa*. Hence, under the heading of justifications available to a defendant:

(1) Magisterial rights, 29 §7
(2) Self-defence
    i. General rule in 4 pr. and 45 §4
    ii. Robber lying in wait, 4 pr.
    iii. Thief, 4 §1
    iv. Man attacking with drawn sword, 5 pr.
    v. Slave taken in adultery, 30 pr.
    vi. Defence of property, 52 §1
    vii. Damage to third parties, 45 §4
(3) Urgent necessity
    i. Ship drive into fishing nets, 29 §3
    ii. Pulling down house to stop a fire, 49 §1
    But see 43, 24, 7, 4. and 47, 9, 3, 7.
(4) In the exercise of a private right
    i. Slave killed with permission of master, 7 §4
    ii. Moderate castigation of servant, 5 §3
    iii. Destruction of water-pipe carried through your house *nullo jure*, 29 §1
    iv. Driving off another's cattle, 39 pr., 39 §1.
    v. Setting traps where one has *jus ponendi*, 29 pr.

Useful so far as it goes, but any student simply using this as the basis of his or her understanding of the subject would, as Lipstein says, have inevitably missed all the subtlety of Buckland's textual analysis. The notes which the student responsible for the survival of this fragment took on the syllabus reveal the huge degree of simplification of what the lecturer had said.

Secondly, students would be expected to have access to the texts of Digest 9.2. The essential textbook of the course, as announced in the *University Reporter*, was Monro's edition of this, with notes,[30] and the marginalia sometimes found in copies of this book suggest that at least some students, probably all, would have had this with them in the lectures and would have glossed it with additional notes. Pencilled on the verso of many leaves in the latter parts of the lecture were page references corresponding to the pages in Monro's edition containing the texts which were being discussed, and it may well be that in the lectures he gave the page in Monro to be turned to in order to speed things up. None the less, not even a copy of Monro would help with the analysis of texts outside D.9.2; for these the student would have to go to the Digest itself, presumably after the lecture, so that any detail

---

[29] Squire Law Library, T Ellis Lewis Collection, box 2.
[30] (1926–27) 57 *Cambridge University Reporter* 1301.

in Buckland's treatment which depended on a reading of the text would in all probability have been lost.

Lectures were supplemented by supervisions provided by colleges. We have a four-volume set of notes in typescript, marked 'For Mr Wheatcroft's pupils only' and enjoining their return to Mr Wheatcroft, covering the substance of the first-year course in Roman law,[31] as well as a briefer set of typed notes on the *lex Aquilia* breaking off in the middle of the discussion of *culpa*.[32] The latter was perhaps copied by a student – a reference to Altrenus rather than Alfenus is an odd one for a teacher to make – but contains information which was not derived from Buckland's lectures, or Monro's or Grueber's commentaries, for instance that Brutus (referred to in D.9.2.27.22) wrote the work referred to in 134 BCE. The same date is given in the student note discussed above,[33] and it is a reasonable assumption that both are attributable to the same source.

The note discussed earlier gives further information about the supervision system of the period. It consists of a set of forty-one questions over eight pages, some being straightforward questions about the *lex*, some being passages for translation and comment, and some being problems. It may be incomplete, but the division questions – texts – problems, numbered consecutively, suggests that there is no substantial loss. The text is accompanied by copious notes in a spidery hand in the margins and on separate sheets, as well as by parts of Buckland's syllabus (as seen above) which are also annotated.

The printed questions typically give references to Grueber, to notes or appendices in Monro and to the main texts in D.9.2 relevant to answering the question. There is only very occasional reference to other literature: to one page in James Muirhead's long review of Grueber in the *Law Quarterly Review*, and to Edwin Clark's *History of Roman Private Law*.[34] The questions themselves are clearly designed to allow students to reproduce what they had heard or read, though no doubt a first-rate student would have had the opportunity to bring his or her critical faculties to bear. The annotations here reveal a student diligently but unimaginatively giving the 'correct' answers. We may illustrate the type of questions and answers:

> To what extent is a master or employer liable under the *Lex Aquilia* for the acts of his slaves or servants?

---

[31] Squire Law Library, MS 41. Dr W H Wheatcroft was a law 'coach' who was supervising the studies of students in five colleges at the time of his death in 1929: Obituary (1928–29) 50 Cambridge Review 369. Although a member of Downing College, he held no college fellowship; and although holding no university position he gave lectures and examined for the Law Faculty.

[32] Squire Law Library, T Ellis Lewis Collection, box 2.

[33] Above, 58.

[34] (1886) 2 LQR 379, 385; Edwin Clark, *History of Roman Private Law* (CUP 1906) (to identify jurists).

> Trace the development of the notion of *culpa* as an element of liability under the *lex Aquilia*.

The first of these is answered by stating barely the division between *culpa in eligendo* and noxal liability for a slave's *culpa*, the second by referring to the view of Pernice as given in Buckland's syllabus. The problem questions appear similarly straightforward to modern eyes. For example:

> The crew of a merchant vessel which had anchored in the Tiber, found on weighing the anchor next morning that it was entangled in a rope. In order to free the ship and its anchor they cut through the rope, which turned out to be the mooring of a fishing-boat, which, in consequence, drifted out to sea and was lost together with all the gear on board. What remedy (if any) had the owner of the fishing-boat? (29.3 & 5)

The examination questions were equally unchallenging, though students would have had to have committed to memory a certain amount of detail. For example:[35]

> Consider with illustrative cases from the Digest the proposition that for liability under the *lex Aquilia* there must have been an act.
> Illustrate from Digest 9.2 the proposition that the act done must, to create liability, be the cause of the *damnum*.
> A is in charge of his own cattle on the high road. Being called away for a moment, he asks his friend Seius, who is standing by, to look after them. Seius undertakes to do but in fact gives no attention to them. They stampede and run down and injure a slave of Maevius, one of the cattle also being damaged. What liabilities have arisen?

The analytical subtlety of Buckland's lectures might have been difficult for any but the best students to understand; but the examination neither required nor expected that they should have done so.

4. THE APPROACH OF THE LECTURES

Buckland's approach to the *lex Aquilia* is very different from the approach taken by a lecturer in England today, or at least by me and those whose lectures I attended and from whom I learned.

Most obviously, his mastery of the Roman law texts comes through unmistakeably. These are not lectures on Digest 9.2 but on the *lex Aquilia*, and there are of course references to the *lex* elsewhere in the Digest and Code as well as texts that have a bearing on it. Such an approach makes demands not only on the lecturers, demands which Buckland was pre-eminently able to cope with, but also on the audience. These are lectures apparently aimed

---

[35] *Cambridge University Examination Papers*, 1928 442–43.

at an audience with a better grounding in Roman law than could be expected in a lecture audience today; and, naturally, it could be assumed that they could read and understand Latin. Sometimes he leaves points unelaborated which tax even the expert today: for example when he says that the action on the *lex* was penal notwithstanding that it covered some of the ground of the *vindicatio*. The lectures reflect a particular culture of Roman law scholarship, typified by the books of Monro and Grueber, works which have largely (and wrongly) been forgotten.

This style of Roman law scholarship is very much at odds with what we might find today. To begin with, there is now almost certainly a far greater concentration on the book of the Digest being studied, with far less borrowing from other books of the Digest and the Code. Lawson's *Negligence in the Civil Law*, if we can think of this as the textbook for a course today, contains a text and translation of D.9.2, but relatively few texts in the *Corpus Iuris* outside this. This, it has to be admitted, makes fewer demands on both lecturer and listener in terms of their knowledge of the textual corpus of Roman law, not to mention of the whole field of private law. Intellectually, though, the modern approach allows for a more palingenetic analysis, reading texts in their context rather than treating them as fragments of knowledge which could be understood whatever the context. Peter Birks (whose lectures on the *lex Aquilia* I attended around 1990), for example, would hand out photocopies of Ulpian, 18 *ad Edictum* and use that as the basis of a large part of his lectures; it was Ulpian's meaning that we were trying to understand, not 'the' Roman law. And in a less pedagogic context, Alan Rodger's papers on the assessment of damages under Chapter 1 of the *lex* are intimately dependent on their palingenesis and not simply on their presence in the Digest. The same could be said of my own lectures' treatment of *occisio* under Chapter 1 and *corruptio* under Chapter 3: the texts cannot be seen just as a set of examples to be listed, but rather as forming an argument where what is not stated explicitly is as important as what is.

Peter Birks explained this change of attitude in terms of the 'project' of Otto Lenel, the restoration – so far as it could be restored – of the classical law by the reordering of the texts of the Digest in their original contexts.[36] The central figure in introducing Lenel's critical analysis of the texts into England was David Daube, who had been a student of Lenel's in Freiburg before coming to Cambridge. Lenel's work was opposed to the then-popular interpolationism, which had given scholars too free a rein to rewrite classical texts in the light of their own prejudices. This approach had never caught on in England, and Buckland himself published an important article making the

---

[36] P Birks, 'Roman Law in Twentieth-Century Britain' in Jack Beatson and Reinhard Zimmermann (eds), *Jurists Uprooted: German-Speaking Émigré Lawyers in Twentieth-Century Britain* (OUP 2004) 249, 253–54.

case against it.[37] But, building on the approach of the legal humanists of the sixteenth century and after, interpolationism had done something to rescue Roman law scholarship from the slavish acceptance of the texts as they had come down from the time of Justinian. English scholarship was still substantially stuck in this world of Roman law positivism, and even Buckland worked within this tradition in his lectures.

There is a second aspect, too, well brought out in the opening words of Grueber's preface to his work on the *lex Aquilia* published in 1886:

> The Board of the Faculty of Law in the University of Oxford, being convinced that a more thorough knowledge of Roman law would be the best means of advancing a scientific understanding and culture of English law, has recently encouraged candidates in the Final Honour School of Jurisprudence to exhibit a knowledge of some portion of the Digest ...[38]

We cannot penetrate too deeply into what was meant by 'scientific' here, but we should probably see it as having two dimensions: first, Roman (private) law was an integrated whole rather than split into discrete topics; and secondly it had a scholarly depth and was capable of generating principled answers to new questions. Hence, Buckland's predecessor as professor, E C Clark, had explained the role of Roman law in the reformed Cambridge law tripos of 1887 in terms of the 'scientific classification' of Justinian's *Institutes*, as well as explaining that candidates for the Ordinary degree (as opposed to the Honours degree) should not have to take papers in Roman law but could limit themselves to 'the more moderate requirement of English law'.[39] As English law and English legal education became more scientific in the 1930s,[40] so the role of the advanced study of Roman law shifted, freeing it up to become a more purely textual subject.

5. CONCLUSION

We may now be more willing to accept a multi-faceted approach to Roman law than Buckland would have been. Reading his lectures, one has a sense that he saw Roman law as a unity, the texts in the Digest an elaboration of what could be read in Gaius' *Institutes* rather than a different genre of literature entirely. We might be inclined to accept that the later classical jurists, for example, disagreed profoundly with each other's approaches or modes of analysis, in a way that I suspect Buckland would not have been. Finally,

---

[37] 'Interpolations in the Digest' (1924) 23 Yale Law Journal 345.
[38] Grueber (n 3) vii.
[39] Edwin Clark, *Cambridge Legal Studies* (CUP 1888) 15, 26.
[40] See, for example, the pioneering taxonomic study of Percy Winfield, *The Province of the Law of Tort* (CUP 1931); more generally, Frederick Henry Lawson, *The Oxford Law School, 1850–1965* (Clarendon Press 1968), 142–45.

and a reflection of our own scholarly culture, we are perhaps more willing than Buckland to historicise the law; certainly we would spend longer on the origins of the *lex* than he would, and we would be dissatisfied with his rather stark contrast between Gaius' classical law and Justinian's law, with little hint of anything in between.

Appendix to Chapter 2

NOTES TO THE READER

This transcript is of the typescript of the lectures given by Buckland in Cambridge in the late 1920s. As is the case today, the *lex Aquilia* would have been touched on in the first year; these lectures would have been given in the second or third year

I have corrected obvious errors of typing (they are very common) and added punctuation where needed, but not attempted to correct errors of fact (e.g. the dating of the *lex Hortensia* to 247 BCE in the first few lines, or the misquotation of the words of the lex); we can assume those would have been corrected orally when the lectures were given. Nor have I translated the Latin.

The text looks to have been updated several times, perhaps over several years, but the substance was largely unchanged by these corrections. I have indicated interlinear additions by \.../; words typed but deleted have been struck out (e.g. ~~Aquilis~~). Numbers in square brackets are the numbers of the pages in the initial typescript.

Reference is frequently made to:

Erwin Grueber, *The Roman Law of Damage to Property with a Commentary on the Title of the Digest Ad Legem Aquiliam (IX. 2) With an Introduction to the Study of the Corpus Iuris Civilis* (Clarendon Press 1886)

Charles Henry Monro, *Digest IX.2: Lex Aquilia* (Cambridge University Press 1921, 1928).

Alfred Pernice, *Zur Lehre von den Sachbeschädigungen nach Römischem Rechte* (Böhlau 1867); and (perhaps) *Labeo* (3 vols, Buchhandlung des Waisenhauses 1873–1895).

Students would have been expected to use the first two of these; the surviving supervision handouts refer to them continually.

Abbreviations appearing in the text are standard: h.t. (hoc titulo – D.9.2); G. = Gai.Inst.; D. = Digesta; P. = Pauli Sententiae; Coll. = Collatio legum; Ulp. =ΩRegulae Ulpiani.

For the sake of consistency, all Latin terms have been italicised. No italicisation or underscoring exists in the original manuscript.

BUCKLAND ON THE *LEX AQUILIA*

\[top margin] Rotondi[1]; Killing slaves by night Solazzi St Albertoni 1[2]; Berger St Albertoni 1[3] also; Daube[4]; Article of Kunkel ZSS 1929[5]; Thayer's book[6]/

History of the *Lex Aquilia*. We are told that it was a plebiscite introduced by Aquilius, Tribune of the plebs. \9.2.1.1/. That is all we are told of its date, and there is much doubt about this. It is early, since one of its provisions deals with the fraudulent *adstipulator* in a way which would not have been necessary if there had been an *actio mandati* and mandate is the earliest of the consensual contracts. Two very late authorities associate it with a secession of the plebs and a dispute between the orders respectively, and thus it is com-monly dated about BC 247 when the *l. Hortensia* made plebiscites binding. But the history of that rule is so uncertain that any conclusion cannot be trusted. Note that it is certainly much older than Gallus Aquilius, of the *actio doli* and the *stipulatio Aquiliana*, and has nothing to do with him. We are also told that it '*derogavit*' from all laws then existing on damage to prop-erty whether in the XII Tables or elsewhere. \D.9.2.1.pr./ '*Derogare*' means to repeal partially as opposed to '*abrogare*' which is to repeal altogether. This is a very puzzling statement. It is extremely unlikely that any early statute expressly repealed even partially anything in the Tables. Moreover, there were a number of provisions dealing with injury to property older than the *l. Aquilia* and clearly still in force with no indication of even any partial repeal. There are for instance the action for wrongfully felling trees \9.4.11/, that for turning cattle to feed on another's land \D.19.5.14.3/, and for setting buildings and the like on fire \D.47.9.9/, all still in force in later law. But there must have been some provision for damage to property more general than this before the *lex Aquilia*, and there are slight indications. Thus Festus tells us that '*rupitias*' in the XII Tables means '*damnum dederit*' and elsewhere that '*sarcito*' means make good the damage. This implies some sort of provision though '*rupitias*' is obviously in some way corrupt. It could not be a verb in the third person perfect indicative. But some have invented an action '*de rupitiis*' and Grueber talks of an action '*de servo vel quadrupede occiso*', but all this is the merest guess. We can also infer from our text that there were other

---

[1] Presumably Giovanni Rotondi, 'Della *lex Aquilia* all'Art 1151 Cod. Civ' (1916) 14 Riv Dir Comm 942.

[2] Siro Solazzi, 'Dispute Romanistiche' Studi in in Pietro Ciapessoni (ed), *Studi in Memoria di Alberto Albertoni* vol 1 (CEDAM 1935) 33.

[3] Adolf Berger, 'Dig. IX.2.4 § 1 und das "*Endoploratio*" der Zwölftafeln', ibid (n 2) 1.372.

[4] Probably David Daube, 'On the Third Chapter of the *Lex Aquilia*' (1936) 52 LQR 253, though perhaps a reference to Daube's unpublished research.

[5] Wolfgang Kunkel, 'Exegetische Studien zur Aquilischen Haftung' (1929) 49 ZSS (RA) 158.

[6] James B Thayer (ed), *Lex Aquilia (Digest IX.2 Ad Legem Aquiliam): Text, Translation and Commentary* (Harvard University Press 1929).

laws not in the XII and it may be that *derogare* is used to mean that those and the hypothetical action in the XII were repealed. But to say that all the laws were partially repealed is [19] a queer way of expressing the fact if it be a fact, that some of the laws were altogether repealed. Probably there was no question of express repeal of anything in the XII Tables, but that in the field which it covered it practically superseded earlier legislation. It is indeed said that what it means is that the XII Tables as a whole were partially repealed by it, but the actual words of our text would be a most misleading way of saying this.

The *lex Aquilia* contained, besides provisions which do not directly concern us (Textbook p.589) two enactments which are our immediate concern, and before we discuss them, we had better state them as we have them in the Digest. Chapter 1 runs (D.9.2.2.pr) '*ut qui servum servamve alienum alienamve quadrupedem vel pecudem iniuria occiderit, quanti in id anno plurimi fuit tantum aes dare domino damnas esto*' with a further provision that the damages are in *duplum contra infitiantem*, which may be not in chapter one but later on. Indeed, it must since it applies also to a later provision (D.9.2.25.1) which is corrupt but plainly applies the distinction between the *actio confessoria* and the other to a case of *vulneratio*.

The second chapter as to fraudulent *adstipulatores* (Gai 3.215,216 – his talk about the *actio mandati* only shows that he did not know it was older). In 9.2.27.4 we are told that this second chapter has gone out of use. This remark is supposed to have been interpolated by Justinian, but there is no reason for this: it was probably obsolete in Ulpian's time.

The third chapter is recorded (h.t.27.5) as follows: '*ceterarum rerum praeter hominem et pecudem occisos si quis alteri damnum faxit, quod usserit fregerit ruperit quanti ea res erit in diebus triginta proximis tantum aes dari domino damnas esto.*'

It is clear that these words are not quite unaltered. '*Ut qui*' cannot be the beginning of a *lex*: it is easily corrected to '*si quis*'. In other respects, cap [20] 1 is probably correct, subject to one point. ~~The word 'ut' was certainly not part of the lex.~~ *dominus herus/* But it is different with ch.III. The words '*ceterarum rerum*' connecting it with ch.I cannot have been those of the *lex* when we remember that there was an intervening Ch.II dealing with an entirely different matter (G.3.215, 216). And the words '*praeter hominem et pecudem occisos*' do not look at all like part of a *lex*: they are too explanatory. It has been suggested that the *lex* originally dealt only with destruction, not with damage but the case is not strong. And, in any case, it dealt with damage as early as we know anything about the law, so that the point is not very important. It is probable that it began at '*si quis*' and that it was not '*erit*' which is wrong but '*fuit*' or '*fuerit*' as Gaius has it (G.3.218). The odd fact that it says 'the value within 30 days before' and not 'highest' is noted by Gaius (3.218) and Ulpian (h.t.29.8) who speak of it as agreed that it must be read as if '*plurimi*' appeared there, though it is clear from Gaius that, till Sabinus, there had been those who maintained that the absence of this word entitled the *iudex* to fix on any value it had had within that time. The other point to be noticed as to the wording is that the *lex* did not say '*dominus*' but '*herus*' but that is not very important except as indicating what was clear anyway, that the law is ancient (h.t. 11.6).

We pass now to the consideration of the character and principles of the action. The proper name of it seems to be '*actio damni iniuria dati*' though '*actio damni iniuria*' is more common in the older texts, the *dati* being dropped and '*iniuria*' of course in the ablative. Indeed, Mommsen holds this the proper technical name. But the odd name '*actio damni iniuriae*' is still more common (e.g. G.3.210, D h.t. 27.21, 29.4, 41 etc). Whence comes this clear form? According to Mommsen it comes from an erroneous form '*damnum iniuriae*' which [21] is in fact found in two texts (D.47.2.31, P.2.31.23). According to Monro it comes from *damnum iniuria*, the dropping of the *dati* having led them to think of the *iniuria* as not in the ablative but in apposition to the *damnum*. I do not think it can be shown which is right. It is not important.

The action is penal. It is true that it includes compensation and, unlike the *actio furti*, excludes any *vindicatio*. Often indeed it would include no more than compensation. This is not unique. The *actio doli* was only for compensation but it was penal. It is not always easy to say what the characteristic is which makes an action penal; it seems to be if its aim is repression rather than mere financial adjustment. Thus in our case there might be more than restitution and a man condemned in the *actio doli* became *famosus*. Anyway it was a penal action as to the whole of the damages with all the ordinary results. Thus it was available to the *heres* but not against him unless it had already reached the stage of *litis contestatio*. Inst 4.12.1; h.t.23.8 where the words '*ceterisque successoribus*' are a typical insertion by the compilers. Our text and others add the further exception 'except to the amount to which the *heres* has profited.' This might of course happen, e.g. where the killer got a *hereditas* which the slave killed was prevented from claiming. There are two questions about this matter. How old is the rule? It is clearly as old as Diocletian (Herm. Wis. 2.1)[7] and it is generally thought that it was a gradual growth only general in penal actions in post-classical times. The other question is: what was the remedy against the *heres*? For Justinian, it is clearly the delictal action itself. But it is likely that till very late it was a *condictio sine causa*. Another result of penal character is that if several were concerned each was liable to the full penalty and the fact that one had been sued or had paid up did not in any way release the others (h.t. [22] 11.2, 11.4, 51.1). Also it was noxal (D.9.4.2, h.t. 27.1 etc) having however as we shall shortly see some peculiarities from this point of view. One point not a peculiarity can be taken here. If several of a man's

[7] *Epitome Codicis Hermogeniani Wisigothica* 2.1, in S Riccobono and others (eds), *Fontes Iuris Romani Antejustiniani* (hereinafter *FIRA*) vol 1 (G Barbèra 1941–43) 665.

slaves commit a delict he is in principle liable to pay the damages in respect of each or surrender them all. But h.t. 32 (Gaius) tells us that the praetor's edict (he speaks of 'proconsul' but that is only because he is commenting on the provincial edict) provides that in case of *furtum* the master is free from liability if he pays what would be due if one man had done it, though if he surrenders he must surrender all, and by interpretation this was extended to *damnum*. But this did not apply to all delicts, not e.g. to *iniuria* (D.2.1.9) and this text excludes it for *damnum* (D.2.1.9); but it is commonly said that this is an erroneous gloss and our 32 gives the real rule. In later law the compensatory character of the action is prominent and Justinian calls it mixed (a word he is very fond of) as being both compensatory and for a penalty (Inst 4.6.19) in language which suggests that it was penal only as to excess over compensation. But this is misleading and is probably said only to account for the right to recover profit from the *heres*. It was still noxal for the whole, and each of several participants was liable still for the whole.

The next question is: who has the action? H.t. 11.6 tells us that it is *herus* i.e. *dominus*, and in h.t. 13 Ulpian thinks it necessary to tell us that he has it in respect of a fugitive. But the rule that *herus* has it is not so simple as it looks. We are not told whether a bonitary owner was *dominus* for this purpose, but it is pretty sure that he was not. But he was not remediless. We learn from Gaius that a peregrine has not the action because statutes did not apply to peregrines except expressly, but that he has an *actio utilis* with a fiction of *civitas* (G.4.37). No doubt the bonitary owner had an *actio utilis* with a fiction of usucapion possession as in the Publician. But a more [23] difficult question arose where the *res* changed hands after the damage. In h.t 11.7 the simple rule is laid down that the buyer entitled to redhibit, being owner, has the action but, if he does redhibit, must hand over what he has received. \See D.21.1.21; 23.1; 24/ But suppose he hands over before bringing the Aquilian, what is the position? Logically it would seem he ought to have it as he would if the thing ceased to exist, but the damages would have to be handed over and would be included in the security the buyer had to give for all receipts. But in fact the text dealing with these securities contemplates only actions already begun (D.21.1.21.2) ~~so that he could no doubt be met by an exceptio doli~~. But has the vendor now the action? He was not owner when the wrong was done. Our 11.7 shows that the buyer on redhibiting ought to hand over the right of action, but suppose he has not done so as the facts were not discovered till after the redhibition. Probably the security would be made wide enough to cover this case: the buyer should then be compellable to sue and hand over. \Sale, dam. before delivery, transfer, *commoda*, acc D.19.1.13.12/ Another type of case is where there was no owner at the moment of the wrong, e.g. it was a *res hereditaria* and *heres* had not yet entered. This is discussed in 13.2 in which Ulpian quotes Celsus as saying that the purpose of the statute is that damages shall be made good to the owner, to which Ulpian adds, or is made to add, and therefore the *hereditas* is to be considered as the owner. This is rather a *non sequitur* and may be due to the compilers. The rule is discussed also in 43 where a different reason altogether is given, i.e. that the *lex* did not mean the *dominus* at the time of the wrong. But the rules we considered in the case of sale show that this is exactly what it did mean. The argument is supported by three considerations. First it is said that if it were not so the *heres* would have no *actio* for what was done before the death. But this is not true: his \right/ turns on the fact that he steps into the rights of the deceased. Then it is said that if it were not so a captive returning with *postliminium* could not sue for interim damages. But that is not true either: for we know that if he returns with *postliminium* he is regarded as having been owner all the time. Then it is said that any other [24] rule would be very hard on posthumous children, which is of course true but not to the point. Many harsh rules are law. The truth is that the rule is one of convenience, an early instance of the tendency on the one hand to think of the hereditas as having rights, and on the other to make the entry of the *heres* retrospective in effect. Further questions arise if there is a legacy of the slave. In 13.3 the case is of a *servus legatus* who was killed after entry. We are told that the legatee has the action. Clearly, for the slave vested in him on *aditio*, subject to his right to repudiate, on which it would vest retrospectively in the heres, who, as Julian says, would then have the action. See also 36.pr. But our text limits the legatee's right by the words 'provided he did not accept the legacy after the death'. This ought to be immaterial if it has already vested in him, as it had in Justinian's law. It expresses the Proculian view that it vested only on acceptance. Mommsen suggests '*vel*' for '*non*', i.e. even if he accepted after the death, which makes sense but is only a guess. The Basilica gives the text as it stands. The next text (14) discusses the case where the *heres* kills the *servus legatus*. As Monro say he is an *extraneus* as to this thing and thus legatee has the action. But the language is odd. It says that the action is '*danda*', which is appropriate to a praetorian extension – the normal word for an action lying at civil law is '*competere*', but it is possible that the text discussed a more complicated case. In 15.pr the slave is killed before the *aditio*, and thus before he belongs to the legatee. If the *heres* so kills him, the legatee has an *actio ex testamento* (D.4.3.7.5), if another the *heres* has the action as part of the *hereditas*. The text tells us that he keeps it, but if the slave had been wounded but not killed, though it is still true that the legatee was not yet owner, he must transfer the action to the legatee. The first result is strange. The probable explanation is that of Grueber, that the rule dates from a time when legatee *per vindicationem* has no personal action and if [25] there was nothing to vindicate he could not recover mere accessory rights, but if the slave still existed he could vindicate and would then have a right to the transfer of actions. But it is out of place in Justinian's law when every legatee had a personal action. \~~Thus if the heres himself kills the slave before *aditio*, legatee has an *actio ex testamento*. D.4.3.7.5~~/

The case in h.t. 34 is of the same type but a little more complex. A slave is left to two and S.S. is considering whether to accept or not. It is all clearly after *aditio*. T brings a *vindicatio* for his share. Then somebody kills the slave. Then S repudiates. T can bring the Aquilian for the whole damages as if it had been left to him alone, and 35 adds the reason that the accrual to him is retrospective. This is all plain but one wonders why it was said that T had already put in his claim for the legacy. It does not seem to matter for Justinian's law, but again it may be a survival of the Proculian view that it was not the legatee's till some act of acceptance. The author, Marcellus, had a leaning to Proculian doctrine.

The case of common ownership is discussed in several texts. The primary simple rule is that if a third party kills or damages, the owners have the Aquilian action for their proportion, which may not be equal. H.t.19 and 20. It is curious \unless in this text/ that the title does not directly discuss the case where the thing is done by one of the common owners, but it does where it is done by a slave of one of them, with rather odd results which we shall have to consider later, but the language of 27.1 shows that the common owner who damaged would be liable, for he \was/ if he was privy to the slave's doing it. It is indeed usual to treat 19 and 20 as concerned with *damnum* by one of the common owners and it may be so. Anyway the rule is clear. But there was also the remedy of *communi dividundo* (10.3.8.2).

Another group of texts deals with the case in which a slave who is killed or wounded is instituted *heres* to his owner. In h.t.23.1 Ulpian quotes Julian as laying it down that if a slave who had been freed and instituted was killed before the testator the person who actually gets the inheritance cannot claim the value of the *hereditas* under the Aquilian action for killing the slave. [26] This, as Monro says, seems obvious, for nobody ever lost the *hereditas*. But Julian adds that he will have the action for the value of the slave. This also, one would say, seems pretty obvious. He certainly would have had it if the slave had not been instituted and freed, and owing to his death this *institutio* and manumission never took effect. And, as Monro says, *non constat* that it ever would have, as the testator might have revoked it at any minute. However, Ulpian disagrees in words which are rather obscure '*ego puto nec pretii fieri aestimationem, quia si heres esset, et liber esset*', 'for if he had been *heres* he would also have been free', i.e. there was no loss to the estate as if he had not been killed he would have been free. But this ignores the point made by Monro and also the fact that it is not a question of loss to the estate, but to the owner into whose shoes the *heres* steps. It cannot be doubted that testator had the action. However most modern editors accept this reasoning though the scholiasts of the Basilica find difficulty in it and treat the case as one in which the slave survived the testator, which is certainly not the case.

This case is discussed in two other texts h.t. 15.1 \in f and 16/ and 36.1. Here a slave who is freed and instituted is mortally wounded but survives the testator and it is laid down by Ulpian \and Marcian/ and Marcellus, who cites Sabinus, that the *heres* of the freedman has no Aquilian action for the killing. For this Sabinus in 36.1 gives the sufficient reason that the slave's *heres* cannot inherit an action which the man himself could not have had. And this is the same reason in effect as Marcian gives in 16 'because the facts have reached a state in which the action could not have arisen'. 36.1 raises a further hypothesis. Suppose the slave had been only part *heres*. The other *heres* has the action and not merely for wounding but for the killing, for though he died a free man, the killing is thought of as done at the time of the actual blow. But the question arises and is not decided by the text: has he the whole action or only in proportion to his share [27] in the *hereditas*. Opinion is divided. Grueber gives him only his share, on the grounds that obligations are divided among the *heredes* by the XII Tables. This is the view of the glossators and some later commentators. Pernice gives him a claim for the whole, following the scholiasts in the Basilica and Cujas. Pernice's argument is practically given by Monro, with the addition that there is no hint in the text that it is only given for a part. It is rather doubtful, but that seems to be the right solution. On the facts the right cannot be divided. It seems to do justice, for if thus one *heres* gets more than his share, this can be adjusted in *familiae erciscundae*, while the other solution lets off the wrongdoer from part of his liability.

A further question arises. Suppose the slave did not die at all, was not '*mortifere vulneratus*'. Has he, when he becomes *heres*, an action for the wounding? There seems no reason why he should not, as he is *heres* and the action is one which the testator had. If he was freed but not instituted, he would not have it. In any case it could there be only an *actio utilis* as he is not universal successor and it must be '*suo nomine*' (h.t.13.pr). But in fact he has not even that, for when the damage was done he was another's property: a man has no action for damage done to property before he bought it. But that does not say that the *heres* himself or another would not have it. There seems no reason against it in principle, but the decision of Ulpian \23.1/, already cited and wondered at would apply here too (h.t. 23.1) for there is no loss to the estate, as the man would be free anyhow.

We shall have later to consider cases in which the *dominus* has not an action, where the *interesse* theory comes in.

Only the *dominus* has the direct Aquilian action because of the words of the *lex*, but the praetor intervened and gave either an *actio utilis* or one *in factum*. The formula of the former is not known, but probably contained a fiction '*si dominus esset*'. Let us consider the principal cases.

[28] Usufructuary and usuary. H.t.11.10, h.t.12. These texts show that they had an *actio utilis* even against the owner. They suggest questions as to the amount recoverable, for later discussion, but also raise one or two points to be dealt with now. It is clear from 11.10 (see also D.7.1.17.3) that there was a dispute, settled on the view that the *utilis actio* lay. It is clear also that the dispute was not whether any action lay, but that some jurists, Julian among them, were inclined to give the direct action. Other texts giving the action

without saying that it is *utilis* (D.4.3.7.4; 43.24.13.pr) have little significance: the word may have been dropped, as it meant little in Justinian's day. But as he was certainly not *dominus*, how came it that some gave him the direct action? According to Pernice and Grueber, the view was that as he had all the advantages of ownership he might be treated as owner as against third parties. This is unsatisfactory: he had not all the advantages of owner: he certainly was not *dominus rei*. Another possible explanation is that usufruct not being a servitude in classical law but an independent *ius*, he might be thought of as *dominus* of that *ius*, as he is sometimes called (42.5.8; cf 39.2.13.1) and given the action on that account. But the doctrine which prevailed gave him only the *actio utilis*. Then comes the question: did he exclude the *dominus*? It seems to be generally said that he did, with the corollary that he held the damages only in usufruct or quasi-usufruct. \[bottom of page] So Grueber in his L.Aq. But in Archiv für Civil pr 75 300 he adopts the view accepted above/ For neither of these opinions can I find any express warrant. It seems more probable that he recovered in the proportion which his usufruct bore to the whole value, the owner having an action for the rest. They were familiar with valuation of usufruct (e.g. D.35.2.1.9) Their method of calculating it is briefly described by Monro p.18 and more fully and and critically by Roby, de usufructu[8], pp.188 sqq.

H.t. 12 says that he has his action against the owner. The only point of interest is that he recovers '*pro portione usufructus*' an odd expression of which the most obvious interpretation is that he recovers in the *ratio* which his usufruct has to the whole value. Most people hold that it cannot mean this: indeed, as they usually hold that he recovers the whole value against outsiders they are bound to hold the same here. So they say that the allusion is to the [29] case of joint usufruct: he recovers in proportion to his share in the usufruct. This is suggested by glosses in the Basilica, but is not hinted at in the texts or the medieval gloss. I think the former view right, though the latter is argued for, not very convincingly, by Grueber pp.42 sq though he seems to have changed his mind on p.245 and taken the other view. The last words of 12 bring out the 'highest value' point. I recover the value which the usufruct would have had if the *res* had continued in the best condition which it had at any time in the previous year, whether my usufruct had begun or not.

Bona fide possessor. H.t. 11.8 says that he has not the Aquilian action but one *in factum*, and 17 tells us that he has this action even against the owner. In D.5.3.55 we hear that if he is sued by the owner he must hand over what he has recovered in the Aquilian from anyone. All this is not so straightforward as it looks.

His action is *in factum*, not *utilis*. Why? The Publician fictio '*si anno pos-*

---

[8]   Henry John Roby (ed), *De Usufructu: Iustiniani Digestorum Lib. VII tit. 1* (CUP 1886).

sedisset' seems so applicable that there must be some reason. In fact, no one but the owner or one who is substantially owner has the *actio utilis*. We saw that point in the case of usufruct. A wounded *liber homo* has it (13.pr) but he would have the direct but for the fact that one cannot exactly be *dominus* of one's limbs. The holder of an *aquaeductus* has it (h.t. 27.32) but he is *dominus* of the *caementa*, though for the moment his right is merged in the ownership of the soil. We shall see later that a pledgee has in principle only the *actio in factum*, though in his case there is a good deal of confusion and alteration of the texts.

There are two points which may be mentioned here and must be borne in mind whenever these distinctions are in question. When we speak of an *actio in factum* we are generally thinking of formulation – an action formulated *in factum*. But it is sometimes seen in another sense to mean an action given on the special facts of the case, and here nothing is said about the way in which the action is formulated. So at least it is commonly held, so that what is called an *actio in factum* may be *utilis*. Under Justinian it does not matter [30] which action it is, for they all seem to be governed by the same rules. So it is likely enough that this *actio in factum* in classical law had really nothing to do with the *l aquilia*, but was only a praetorian for simple compensation in cases where a remedy was called for and the law gave none. This is strengthened by the text last discussed, which certainly dealt originally with an *actio in factum*. It is hard to reconcile this with D.5.3.55 which contemplates the bona fide possessor as recovering the *duplum* and having to hand it over to the *dominus*. But a bona fide possessor is one who thinks he is owner. He will actually bring the direct action, so that this text may very well refer to an action brought when all parties thought he was owner. That raises the question if one sued as *dominus* could the defendant prove in defence that he was not *dominus*. Pernice apparently thinks not, but it seems to me clear that he could. There was no '*dare oportere*' unless he was *dominus*. Pernice talks of an inadmissible *exceptio de iure tertii* (p.191) but there is no need of any *exceptio* at all. We must ask ourselves then in what circumstances the bona fide possessor would bring the *actio in factum*. It must when he has ceased to be a bona fide possessor, the damage having been done while he still was, otherwise he could I suppose acquire nothing. He might be still usucapting but he might not: the *res* might have a *vitium* which barred this but this would not prevent his being a bona fide possessor. \As against an outsider he appears to recover the ordinary damages though as we have seen he may have to hand them over to the *dominus* D.5.3.55/ ~~The unit of damages we shall consider later: here it is enough to point out that~~ If he is suing the *dominus* all he can recover \I suppose/ is what he could keep against the *dominus* vindicating, primarily his expenses on useful improvements for which he had a right of retention. \But there is no text/ If the damage amounted to destruction and it was a *res mancipi* bought or a thing bought with a *stipulatio duplae* \from non owner/ he could recover twice the price he had paid, for since he had not been evicted and now cannot be he has lost the action on the *stipulatio* [31] or *actio auctoritatis* as the case may be. If he had not given anything for it there was no such claim, nor if he had bought with a simple warranty against eviction, *stipulatio habere licere*, for he can recover on this if the title proves defective even though the *res* has ceased to exist.

The pledge creditor. This is, as in the case of *furtum*, a very puzzling case. In h.t. 30.1 the case is considered of destruction by a third party. It tells us that the debtor has the action, as of course he has, for he is owner, and goes on in a very obscure manner to consider the question whether creditor has an *actio utilis*, since he may have an *interesse*. The debtor may be insolvent, or the personal action for the debt may be barred by lapse of time. All this may be genuine, but it decides nothing. Then comes an incoherent passage which has long been suspected as having been due to Justinian. It says that it is unfair for the wrongdoer to be liable to both debtor and creditor. Then comes a clause which says 'unless indeed you say that the debtor does not suffer, since what the creditor recovers will be imputable to the debt and he can recover any excess since the creditor may not make profit out of the *res*.' Here it is to be noticed that the comment begins with the question whether it is not unfair to the person liable to the Aquilian and goes on as if the question has been of unfairness to the debtor. Then it goes on 'or perhaps you might give the debtor, ab initio, an action for the excess of the damages over the debt.' Then it sums up: 'And therefore in those cases in which an action is given to the creditor because the debtor is insolvent or his action time barred he will have the action to the amount of the debt to be accounted for to the debtor, and the debtor will have the Aquilian action for the excess of the claim over the debt.' This summary differs in one fundamental way from what is said before. Above it is suggested that he has the action because he may have an *interesse*. The summary gives him the action only if he actually has this [32] interest. What conclusion can be drawn from this confused stuff? It is generally agreed that the conclusion represents Justinian's law, but has all been altered. But where does the corruption begin. Some say at '*sed hoc iniquum*', some at '*vel ab initio*' – I think at '*nisi si quis*' though even the beginning does not look quite right. No conclusion can be drawn for classical law. In Justinian's law he has the action within the limits stated, whether direct, *utilis* or *in factum* does not appear. It does not matter much in his time. It has indeed recently been maintained that the pledgee has no such action at all in classical law, even *in factum*, where a third party damaged it. The ground is that he did not need it, as he could claim cession of actions by the action *pigneraticia contraria*. But that seems to me uncertain.

Where the owner does the damage, h.t. 17 gives the pledgee an *actio in factum*. But D.20.1.27 gives him where the thing is damaged an *actio 'quasi damni iniuriae ad quantum interest'*, and no such action but an *actio ad exhibendum* if the thing is destroyed. Note these seem to give only compensation and the former at least is in its present form due to Justinian. In the case where *ad exhibendum* is given it must have been hypothec, for no one was liable to this action unless he had physical possession. In the other it may be *pignus*. It is clear that the text has been altered. What it originally said we do not know. But one who has the civil *actio ad exhibendum* might conceivably have as alternative the *actio in factum*, which might be more profitable. The text does not expressly exclude him. If he had it for mere damage, as I suppose he had, it is not easy to say why he should not have it for destruction. But here too we do not know the classical law.

There is difficulty in all these pledge cases owing to the fact that in classical law pledge was superseding *fiducia*, and there is uncertainty: there [33] was some uncertainty among the lawyers themselves as to how far rules were carried over from one institution to the other. The debtor in *fiducia* would not have the Aquilian and the creditor would. That is perhaps why Paul expresses the fact that in *pignus* the debtor it.

Holders of other rights *in rem*. It is generally held that these had an *actio utilis*, but I do not know on what authority this reposes. It is probable that *emphyteuta* had it, but that is post-classical. It is probable that holder of a superficies had an *actio in factum* \causa cognita 43.18.1.pr/. As to ordinary servitudes there is no authority, which is strong evidence that they had no such action. In h.t. 27.32 we are told that the man with a right of aquaeduct has an *actio utilis* if the *caementa*, the materials for his waterway, which he put there are damaged, but this is not because he had a servitude but because he has a latent ownership in the materials, and it is not *directa* only because this ownership is latent. No conclusion can be drawn for other servitudes, except such as leave a latent ownership in materials, e.g. if I have servitude to navigate your lake and I erect a landing stage. This would seem to be Pernice's view – at least he does not I think anywhere suggest that a servitude as such gave any sort of Aquilian acton. It does not seem to be necessary for interference with a servitude was dealt with by interdicts. However, Grueber lays it down in general terms that a servitude gave the *utilis actio*, but in general textbooks, though it is commonly said that the holder of a right *in rem* has it, I do not usually find a direct statement that a servitude as such gives it.

Holders of rights *in personam*. In general, they have not the action in any form. Thus it is denied to *commodatarius* in h.t. 11.9 which tells us it is for the *dominus* to sue. In h.t. 54 it is shown that it belongs to the promissor not the promisee in a *stipulatio*. A vendee has no action before delivery (D.18.1.13.12) (for seller on Grueber, 250 \middle/, read buyer). In 18.6.13 where a vendee has it the [34] ownership seems to have passed. But there are two cases which raise difficulty. In h.t. 41 Ulpian agrees with Marcellus that \where a will is tampered with/ the testator has no action on the ground that there is no *damnum*, which seems debateable. But he quotes Marcellus as also holding that \heres and/ legatee have no right. He demurs on the ground that the will is the evidence of their right. This must be after the death of testator. But he does not go so far as to say they have the action: he merely puts a sort of question mark to Marcellus. ~~Of course~~ the *heres* ~~would~~ \might if it was done after the death/ have it as owner, but the legatees have no sort of right in the document. But if he has not entered the *heres* is not yet owner and in D.4.3.35 we are told that in that case he \and legatees/ have an *actio doli.* ~~It would seem that legatees ought to have simply this or iniurarum~~ \There might be *iniuriarum*/ according to circumstances, if it was done intentionally. How if it was done by sheer negligence? He might possibly have had an *actio in factum*, but not in relation to the Aquilian, but as Paul says (h.t. 33.1) '*in damnis quae lege aquilia non tenentur, in factum datur actio.*' There were even in classical law hosts of cases in which an *actio in factum* is given where equity calls for a remedy and there is no *dolus.*

The other text is h.t. 27.14. Ulpian quotes Celsus as saying that if you sow deleterious weeds in your neighbour's cornfield to the damage of his crop, the owner, or if the land is let, the *colonus* can bring the interdict *unde vi aut clam* or an *actio in factum*, but if the *colonus* brings the latter he must give security that the *dominus* will not take further action. It then continues 'for it is one thing to corrupt or change a thing so that the *l. aquilia* applies and another, without changing it to add something which is hard to separate.' On this text there are several things to be said.

i Notwithstanding the concluding words of the text the *actio in factum* mentioned is that connected with the *lex Aquilia*, as appears from h.t. 20 which says that such dealings are *quasi corruptio.*

[35] ii Even taken as it stands the text does not give the *colonus* as such an *actio in factum* for *damnum iniuria datum* to the thing hired, as is sometimes said. It is only the crop which is damaged and gives him the right. And while the wrong was done before the crop was his, the *damnum* can hardly be said to occur till the crops are his. It is the fact that the act was done before which differentiates him from the lodger, who has the action *directa* but not in respect of the building but only in respect of his furniture (h.t. 27.8).

iii There is no reason to doubt the classicality of the rule, though there are all sorts of opinions on this, into which we need not go. It has however been altered in some way. Thus the *cautio* by the *conductor* is out of place. If no damage was done except to the crop the *dominus* has suffered no damage and could have no claim. If damage is done to the field, as may be, for seeds lie latent, there is no reason why he should be barred by the action of *colonus.* Again the clause '*sed et in factum agendum, et si colonus eam exercuit*' is very ungrammatical: *eam* requires *actio* not *agendum.* \[at foot of page] ~~In h.t. 13.pr Ulp thinks it necessary to tell us that an owner had the action on account of a runaway. This seems obvious: he is still dominus./~~

The next question to consider is against whom the action lies. Of course the plain ordinary rule is that it lies against the wrongdoer, but there are some cases which are specially mentioned by reason of peculiarities and these we must discuss.

i In h.t. 37.pr we are told by Javolenus that if the act is done by A's hand but by the command of B, A is not liable if he was bound to obey B, but B is, and we see the same rule in more general terms in D.50.17.167[9]. *Is damnum dat cui iubet dare, eius vero nullla culpa est qui parere necesse est.* \~~See also 9.2.44.1.~~/ If A was not bound to obey then both A and B will be liable. This is clearly laid down, e.g. in 47.10.11.3, though not in so many words in connexion with this delict. The question then arises: what is this *ius imperandi* – who has it? No one has a right to order [36] another person to do a wrong. The allusion is to persons whose lawful orders you are bound to obey, and whose order therefore excuses you, partly because of their inevitable ascendancy over you and partly though the ordering to do what actually is a wrong it may not be obviously so. A slave's master tells him to kill a pig. He does so. It turns out to be another man's pig. The slave is excused, but the master will presumably be liable, or may be, for negligence. Monro gives a list of persons with the *ius imperandi*. It is not of course exhaustive: one might for instance add the *paterfamilias*. Even if the slave sees that it is a wrong he may still be excused, but there is a limit. The rule is laid down in D.50.17.157.pr the slave is excused by the order of the master or one who is in the practical position of master, such as tutor or curator (and I suppose we may add fructuary or bona fide possessor), provided the act done has not the *atrocitas* of a *facinus* or *scelus*. It does not tell us where to draw the line. In D.9.4.2 we are told that a slave was excused by his master's order, as to the *l Aquilia*, while apparently theft was on the other side of the line. The same *lex* tells us further that incitement was not necessary: the owner of the slave was liable if he knew and did not prohibit when he could, though this of course in no way excused the slave. ~~The same rule is laid down in 9.2.44.1.~~ \h.t. 41.1/ \[at foot of page] An obvious case of *ius imperandi* is that of public officials. But this does not say that they will not be liable. In h.t. 29.7 we are told that municipal magistrates may be liable *ex Aquilia* and in D.18.6.14 there is an Aquilian action against an aedile who destroyed property in excess of his duty./

    ii Common owners. We have already seen that common owners were liable to each other, but the case must be mentioned where the damage is done ~~by the slave of one of the common owners or the wrong is done~~ by a common slave to the property of one of his owners. H.t. 27.1 \tells us/ ~~dealing with the latter case we are told~~ that if the master knew he will be directly liable to his co-owner of the slave, but that if he did not there was no noxal action, the reason assigned being the rather absurd one that otherwise the slave might by doing more damage than half of him was worth secure that he should be transferred to the other owner. Julian in D.9.4.41 gives a reason based on principle. Any common owner was liable [37] *in solidum* on delicts of the common slave, and there was a rule that that no one could be noxally

[9] Really D.50.17.169.

liable and entitled in respect of the same slave. The same rule is brought out in D.11.3.14.2 and 47.10.17.9 etc. Of course the matter can be adjusted *in communi dividundo*, and there will be a right of *'pro noxae deditione'* in such a case. 47.2.82.pr note that there is a corruption in the text: it should be *'ut mihi'* \i.e. 27.1/: perhaps Mommsen is correct in suggesting [*'utri'*] as in the rendering in the Basilica.

iii If the pledgee damages the thing we are told (h.t. 18) by Paul that the owner has the aquilian and also the *actio pigneratitia 'sed alterutra debebit esse contentus actor.'* Paul gives the same decision in the same words in 19.2.43 where a *conductor* injures the slave hired. Both *ex locato* and aquilian lie *'sed alterutra contentus actor esse debet,'* but here adds the further explanation *'idque officio iudicis continetur apud quem ex locato agatur.'* Gaius lays down the same principle in general terms in other words in 13.8.18.1 and in 47.7.9 where again we have *'contentus esse debet.'* \[at foot of page] Monro (p.23) cites a number of texts which show exceptions, some treating the actions as merely alternative, some showing Aquilian for any possible excess, some as here suggesting that both actions lie but one must be remitted in some way./ What does this mean? This raises one of the most thorny topics in Roman law, that of the *consumptio litis*. I shall not go into it but deal with it very dogmatically. It does not refer to *litis consumptio* by *litis contestatio*: it certainly is not *eadem res*. It refers to what is called judicial consumption. The *iudex* in a number of cases where justice required it might refuse to give judgment without either surrender of the other action or security against bringing or some similar precaution. But there is a difficulty. There might be more recoverable under the *lex* than under the contract. There are a number of texts e.g. D.13.6.7.1; D.44.7.34.2 which say that the aquilian can still be brought for any excess over the mere compensation recovered in the other action. No doubt this must be read in here for Justinian's law but it is doubtful if it is classical. To the later classics the compensation aspect of the Aquilian was more prominent than the penal.

[38] iv In h.t. 38 Javolenus tells us that if a slave bona fide possessed is damaged by a slave of the bona fide possessor there is an Aquilian action, of course noxal. *'Omnimodo'* seems to mean 'whether the holder was *sciens* or not' and the text is dealing only with the noxal action. The fact that the case chosen is that of *damnum* by a slave of the holder, i.e. the former holder, for the tenses show that he is no longer in possession so that there is no question of a *vindicatio*, suggests the notion that a bona fide possessor could not be liable for his own act, for how can a man be guilty of *dolus* or *culpa* in regard to a thing which he supposes to be his own? But we are told elsewhere that he can be sued under the *lex Aquilia*, and since harm done could be claimed for in a *vindicatio* both were available and \if/ one was brought the other must be released as in the last case, with no doubt under Justinian the same restriction as to any excess \5.3.5.5/.

v We have already seen that the *dominus* himself may be liable for damage to property in the hands of pledgee, fructuary, bona fide possessor h.t. \11.8/, 12, 17.

vi In h.t. 56 Paul tells us that if a wife has damaged her husband's property she is liable '*pro tenore legis Aquiliae*'. And in 27.30 Ulpian tells us that if a man lends his wife pearls to use and she makes holes in them to put them on a necklace, she is liable *ex aquilia*, whether still married to him or divorced. In 24.1.37 Julian says that a woman is liable for damage to things given her by her husband (such a gift was not valid) '*maxime si post divortium id commiserit*'. It is not quite clear that this last text is any authority for bringing the action for what was done during the marriage – '*maxime*' often seems to mean 'at any rate if'. But the text of Ulpian is clear. It seems to conflict with the rule in C.5.21.2 which excludes any penal or infaming action between the parties to a marriage. But this is said in connexion with a theft and Gaius in D.25.2.2 states the rule as excluding any '*turpis*' actio, and in view of the prominence of the compensatory element in it, the rule in classical law was as [39] stated by Ulpian. Why '*pro tenore*'? It seems to refer to the actual words of the *lex* as being wide enough to cover this case.

vii In h.t. 3̶1̶ \13.1/ Ulpian quotes Julian as saying that a free man, *bona fide serviens* to me is liable to me *ex aquilia*. Obviously. The point is that though like a slave he is not one, the rule of no action between slave and master does not apply. Elsewhere we are told of an *actio in factum* for harm done by him (40.12.12.6). It is confined to *dolus* and refers primarily to other than physical harm. It says that under the *lex* he is liable for *culpa* but 41.1.54.2 says that even here he is not liable for such slight negligence as other people are. It looks like a hasty addition by the compilers.

viii Though noxal liability is only slightly touched in our title, it must be noted that that under the *lex* it had some peculiarities. Just as only the *dominus* can be sued noxally (h.t. 11.6, 27.3) not a bona fide possessor as in *furtum*, and an owner is liable for a *fugitivus*, though not in *furtum* for lack of *potestas*, which here means legal and physical power to produce (ibid; I.4.11; 9.4.21.3; 47.2.17.3). The point is that owing it seems to the wording of the *lex* (we have not this part) only *dominus* is liable and he is liable whether he has potestas or not.

ix Personal capacity (h.t. 5.3) Since the harm must be *iniuria*, wrongful, no one is liable who is not capable of forming judgments. Thus a *furiosus* is not liable. He presumably would be if it were in a lucid interval, though we are told this only of crimes (U.1.13.14). It is also doubtless true of other *mente capti* e.g. idiots, who, of course, have no lucid intervals. But obviously diffi-cult questions arise of which we hear nothing. Our text put on the same level infants who are conclusively presumed incapable. An *infans*, for Justinian, is one under 7; earlier it meant literally one who could not yet speak. As to *impubes* the law is, as our text shows, more complex. Labeo applies the rule of [40] *furtum* making him liable if he is *doli capax*: in this case *doli* or *culpae capax*. This is of course a question of fact to be determined in each case. The same rule is laid down in 47.2.23 both for theft and *damnum*. Naturally they get more *capaces* as they approach puberty and thus it is said that if they are *prope pubertatem* they are liable. Grueber states this as a separate rule: such persons are capable of *dolus* etc. D.44.4.4.26.

We pass now to the general scope of the statute. It is not a comprehensive statute dealing with liability for damage. It deals only with a definite class of objects and it was only gradually that it acquired the comprehensiveness we find in the texts. Its first *caput* deals with the killing, *occisio*, of another man's slave or quadruped of the kinds which feed in herds, *pecus* (h.t. 2.pr \In 4.3.pr/). Just what these are is discussed in the rest of the text. Sheep, goats, oxen, horses, asses and mules, and even swine, though there was some hesitation about this, but not wild animals such as bears, lions and panthers, even though held in confinement. I suppose the same would be true of a private pack of wolves, though these feed in herds. ~~Nor is anything said of dogs.~~ \ Dogs also are not *pecudes* (h.t. 29.6)./ There was some difficulty about elephants and camels as these though for private purposes and so owned are by nature wild: the texts say that these are of mixed nature and therefore ought to come under the first *caput*. This solution is commonly put down to Justinian, partly because it is illogical, the same reason would equally well account for their exclusion, and also because the compilers were notoriously fond of the word '*mixtus*' and of mixed categories. The classics probably excluded them, just as they excluded them from *res mancipi*, though they were used for work, on the ground that they were essentially wild (G.2.16; Ulp.19.1).

There must be *occisio*. What is *occisio*? Primarily it is not simply 'killing' but killing in a particular way, as opposed to ~~the more general word~~ *necare* (Festus s.v. *occisio*). Apparently on etymological grounds \h.t. 51.pr a *caedendo vel caede*/ it meant cutting down with [41] a sword or club, or at any rate by direct impact by the killer. This is the basis of h.t. 7.1, which mentions strangling or kicking or butting or with sword or stick, while '*necare*' means killing in some other way. In practice the construction was a little wider. In h.t. 7.2 where a man too heavily laden threw off his load and it fell on and killed a slave, this was *occisio*. In h.t. 7.7, G.3.219, Inst 4.3.16, it is *occisio* to throw a man over a bridge so that he is drowned or to kill a child by dashing his head against a stone. Actually to administer poison so that it causes death is *occisio* (h.t. 9.pr) or to apply a noxious ointment (Inst 4.3.7; h.t. 9.1). So too to kill by throwing a javelin (h.t. 9.4). To urge a dog on to a man was enough according to Labeo, but this was not accepted except where the wrongdoer was holding the dog (h.t. 11.5). In h.t. 31 cutting a tree so that it falls on a man and kills him is *occisio* (Inst 4.3.5). It is of course not essential that he dies at once: it is occisio if he ultimately dies of it with no other cause, h.t. 21.1, 51, 52\.pr/; Inst 4.3.6). Technically put it must be *corpore corpori* (G.3.219, Inst 4.3.16). Where the killing was not so direct it might be called '*necare*' e.g. h.t. 9.2, 49. It is not *occisio*: it is rather '*causam mortis praestare*' (h.t. 7.8, 9.pr, 11.1, 49\.pr/, 51.pr) This was not within the *lex* or its juristic extensions. But in many such cases the praetor provided a remedy; such are shutting up slaves or cattle so that they die of starvation (G.3.219; Inst 4.3.16; h.t. 29.7; C.3.35.5); driving so hard that the horse is destroyed (G and Inst citt); frightening sheep so that they go over a precipice (ibid); inducing a man with no justification to climb a tree or go down a well and he is killed (ibid); pushing another so that he falls on and kills a man (h.t. 7.3); giving poison but not directly administering it (h.t. 7.6, 9.pr); putting a sword into a lunatic's hands and he kills (h.t. 7.6); frightening a horse so that it throws and kills its rider (h.t. 9.3); sending a man to an ambush where another kills him (ibid); holding a man while another kills him (h.t. 11.1); setting a dog on a man without holding it (h.t. 11.5); furiously driving so that the cart is upset and kills someone (19.2.13); destroying my bees by smoke (h.t. 49.pr). Note that if you strike a man and he dies of the blow this is *occisio*, though it was a blow not [42] at all likely to kill, but owing to his state he did in fact die. You were in *culpa* and he dies of your act (h.t. 7.5).

There are various things to be said of these cases.

i These cases are mentioned in connexion with *occisio*, but they apply equally to cases under the third chapter. Indeed, the case of bees is under the third chapter, since bees are not *pecus* and it is hard to see why we are told that this is not *occisio*. Similarly, some of the illustrations to come under cap. III would apply equally here. \[on reverse of previous leaf] The point is not that it is not *occisio*, but that it is not an act *corpore corpori*./

ii Two of the cases look at first sight rather strong: holding a man while another kills him and sending him to an ambush where he is to be killed. But they are quite logical. It is indifferent, as we shall see, whether it is *dolo* or *culpa*.

iii Though not covered by the *lex*, the praetor gave an action. When we have to ask what action this was we get a puzzling story from the texts. In the four cases given by Gaius and the Institutes it is a *utilis* Aquilian action. Only two of these appear in our title. In one of these, shutting up to starve, (h.t. 29.7) an *actio in factum* is given, and in the code, in the same case, an *actio utilis* (C.3.55.5). In the other case, sheep caused to go over a precipice (h.t. 53), it is described as an *actio in factum ad exemplum legis aquiliae*, a hybrid name. In all the many other cases in our title it is an *actio in factum*: we hear nothing of an *actio utilis* for this kind of case. In the case of furious driving, from another title (19.2.13.pr) it is *utilis*. What inference is to be drawn from this confused story? This is a matter on which '*quot homines, tot sententiae*'. My own opinion is that in classical law the *actio utilis* was the remedy where there was a real killing but it was not direct enough to be an *occisio*, though it is quite possible that the \jurists/ gave also an *actio in factum* where my act caused the death but I could hardly be said to have killed at all, e.g. where I have let your horse loose and he falls down a shaft. It is not possible to set limits in such cases. In Justinian's time the distinctions are immaterial

(D.3.5.46.1; Monro App. 4) and in this title, though not all over the *Corpus Iuris*, they have commonly substituted the *actio in factum* for the *utilis* of the original. It no longer means '*in factum concepta*'. It is just one setting out the facts and it made no real difference which it was.

[43] The only other word to be considered in this connexion is the word '*alienum*' (h.t. 2.pr) As this is in the *lex* it is impossible for a man to be directly liable for what he does to his own slave, and that is why pledgee, fructuary etc have only the praetorian action in one form or another. Also it implies that the thing must be the subject of property. Thus a free man could not have the direct action for damage to his person. This belongs to *caput* 3 but we may note that he had an *actio utilis*. But there was none if he was killed, at least if it was a *paterfamilias*, since the *heres* could not inherit an action which the deceased could never have had. It is nowhere expressly said that there is no action in this case, but it is an obvious inference from the language of many texts e.g. 9.1.3 from which it is also to be inferred that it was the same if he was a *filiusfamilias*, though one might have expected the *paterfamilias* to have an action. \I note the special edict in Inst 4.5.1 – res dej. et effusae/

Before passing to the conditions of liability, damage and *iniuria* which are the same for both *capita*, we will consider the wording and scope of cap. 3, which we have already stated and criticised as to its authenticity.

It tells us \9.2.27.5/ that the action lies for any *damnum*, other than killing slave or *pecus* by *occisio*, by *urere frangere* or *rumpere*, burning breaking or *rumpere* which is difficult to translate. Monro makes it 'breaks up', Grueber 'break'. Pernice seems to avoid translating it. In a german translation of the Digest it appears as *verdorben* which seems to mean 'spoil'. A french translation makes it '*briser*' which again means to spoil. But in fact it does not much matter, for we are told that the unanimous interpretation of the jurists was that rumpere meant '*corrumpere*' i.e. any kind of actual damage to the thing (9.2.27.13) \The words *urere frangere* being, as is not unusual, covered by the more general word: h.t. 27.16./ The damages are estimated in a different way, this we shall take later, but some verbal difficulties have already been considered.

Here too to bring the statute into play there must have been damage actually by the body to the body, *corpore corpori*, and we will look at the illustrations of [44] this point. It must be done by the body. One result of this is that those cases which we see giving an *actio utilis* under *caput* 1 will not come directly under *caput* 3 as the language of 3 might suggest, precisely because it was not done *corpore*. But *vulnerare* in circumstances which would be *occisio* if he died comes under ch. 3 as in h.t. 27.17 where wounding with stick or whip or fist or weapon either breaking the skin or causing a bump is enough. The title from 27.5 onwards gives a great number of illustrations of cases for the application of caput 3. They show how wide the notion of *corrumpere* was, but are not so far very interesting though several will call for discussion from other points of view. They do not necessarily involve destruction, though destruction of things like bees and dogs and captive wild beasts, which do not come under *pecus*, is covered by it (h.t. 27.12; 29.6; 49.pr). Of the first of these texts we have the original in the *collatio* and it shows that the jurists of the first century some of them doubted whether this was the case with bees, since they could not be said to be tame. Celsus held that it did and this clearly prevailed. Among the illustrations given are: setting a house or its contents or other property on fire (h.t. 27.7, 8, 11, \C3.35.2/, Coll 12.7); spoiling wine or turning it to vinegar (h.t. 27.15); \throwing my grapes about so that they are spoilt: h.t. 27.26/; cutting or soiling clothes (h.t. 27.18); striking an *ancilla* or animal, causing miscarriage (h.t. 27.22; h.t. 32.pr); overloading a beast to its damage (h.t. 27.23); scuttling a ship (h.t. 27.24); breaking something lent you or entrusted to you to work on (h.t. 27.29, 30, 35); breaking open my doors or pulling down my house \or wall/ (h.t. 27.31; C.3.35.2; h.t. 50; \45.5/); letting a thing fall off a wagon to the damage of a passer (h.t. 27.33); making pitfalls or traps into which something falls and is damaged (h.t. 28; h.t. 29.pr); cutting away a man's balcony wrongfully overhanging your land (h.t. 29.1); causing damage to a ship or its cables or nets by careless navigation (h.t. 29.2, \3/, 4); ~~cutting a ship's mooring cable (h.t. 29.3)~~; erasing valuable securities (h.t. 40-42); assault doing damage (h.t. 52.1); careless management of a wagon, doing damage (h.t. 52.2); careless riding in company, doing damage (h.t. 57); picking a man's fruit before it is fit, otherwise than for theft (h.t. 27.25); \defacing a picture or a book D 47.2.31; burning or cutting down my wood: C3.35.1)/; [45] injuring trespassing cattle by too violent ejectment (h.t. 39.1).

These are fairly straightforward, but there are others which I put at the end because they need discussion in connexion with the cases in which praetorian actions are allowed. The direct action is expressly given where wine is spilt: we are told that it is '*corruptio*' (h.t. 27.15) and so it seems is h.t. 27.21 where money is dropped out of my hand into the sea, and we are told that the Aquilian lies and also an *actio in factum*, and apparently also in 27.20 where grain and sand are mixed, *quasi de corrupto*. There are others in which it is said that an Aquilian action lies, which would prima facie mean the direct, but may mean only some form of Aquilian action, e.g. throwing my grain into the river (h.t. 27.19); handing over animals for test without notice that they are dangerous (h.t. 52.3); frightening an animal so that it does damage, or letting out a slave incompetent for the work (h.t. 27.34). Of course it is only if there is *dolus* or *culpa*, but with that requirement we are not concerned for the moment. Let us now pass to the cases in which a praetorian action is given. Starting a fire and going to sleep so that it spreads to a neighbour (h.t. 27.9; Coll 12.7.7); carelessly looking after a fire with the same result (ib.). It is a *utilis actio*, having a furnace against a party wall causing damage (h.t. 27.10; Coll 12.7.8). Here it is an *actio in factum*; damaging my aquaeduct (27.32, *actio utilis*, but this would have been direct if I had been *dominus*); employed to put a protective covering on a cask, holing it so that the wine is spilt (h.t. 27 35, an *actio in factum*); consuming another's wine (h.t. 30.2) *actio utilis*; driving animals into a narrow space so that they go over a precipice (h.t. 53) *actio in factum ad exemplum legis Aquiliae*. Gaius (3.202) gives an *actio utilis*. Sowing weeds so that the crop is spoilt (h.t. 27.14) *actio utilis*; loosing a bound slave so that he escapes and is lost (Inst 4.3.16; D.4.3.7.7) really under cap. I *actio in factum*. Pushing B so that C is damaged. B is not liable *actio in factum* against the pusher (h.t. 7.8); Throwing things into the sea (D.19.5.14.2) *actio in factum*.

These cases raise two questions. On what principle are we to determine when the direct and when a praetorian is to be given? On what principle is the *actio utilis* given in some cases and the *actio in factum* in others? [46] There is a familiar scheme in the Institutes (4.3.16) which settles the whole thing more or less. If it is by the body to the body, *corpore corpori*, the direct action lies. If it is not by the body but is to the body, *corpori non corpore*, an *actio utilis* lies. If it is neither *corpore* nor *corpori*, an *actio in factum*. But this is open to several objections. It does not deal with the case where it is *corpore non corpori*, but I think they mean an *actio in factum* in that case. It does not quite agree with Gaius (3.219). He gives a direct action if it is *corpore corpori* and an *actio utilis* is if is to the body but not by the body, *corpori non corpore*. He says nothing about an *actio in factum* in any case. That seems to mean that for him the *actio in factum* which certainly lay in some cases (Coll 12.7.5, 8) has nothing to do with the *l. Aquilia*, but was one for compensation where no actual harm was done to the *res*, but loss followed, e.g. if a stable door is unlocked and a horse is lost. But in later classical law it has come to be connected with the *l. Aquilia*, for the Collatio 12.7.8 speaks of an *actio in factum exemplo legis Aquiliae* and it was then no doubt as it was in Justinian's time subject to similar rules as to damages etc. A third difficulty is that it does not agree with the Digest, and the texts in the Digest do not seem to agree altogether. In some of the cases no reconciliation is needed, for though the text speaks of the Aquilian action the writer is not concerned with the question which of them. But some do raise a difficulty. In h.t. 27.15 we are told expressly that the direct action lies where wine is spilt, but where a hole was carelessly knocked in a cask and the wine was spilt it is a praetorian action (h.t. 27.35) and where the wine is carelessly drunk an *actio utilis* (h.t. 30.2). I do not know how to reconcile these decisions. For knocking money out of your hand into the sea, Sabinus gives clearly a direct action, observing that in some cases an *actio in factum* will also lie (h.t. 27.21). But in 19.5.14.2 Pomponius denies that the direct action will lie but gives an *actio in factum*. As this is in his 'ad Sabinum' it is likely that he is correcting Sabinus. In h.t. 27.18 if grain is thrown into the sea, a direct action lies, but this is normal for the grain is spoilt; it is *corpori* and *corpore*. Cutting a mooring rope so that the ship is wrecked gives only an *actio in factum* (h.t. 29.5). Yet it is [47] much the same thing. I suppose it is like holding a man while another kills him. You facilitate the harm but do not actually do it. In h.t. 27.20 mixing grain with sand seems to give the direct action '*quasi corruperit*' as in h.t. 27.18 where it is obviously direct '*quasi ruperit*'. In h.t. 27.14, which is also a case of deleterious mixture which is difficult to separate it is an *actio in factum*, which seems the right remedy. Perhaps two things can be said on the whole matter. The earlier jurists Sabinus (h.t. 27.21) and Mela (h.t. 27.34) give the direct action more freely than the later ones. It is possible that this sort of thing gave rise to disputes and the praetor introduced the *actio utilis* on someone's advice precisely to settle these questions. The other point is that the line between direct and indirect could never have been easy to draw and we must remember that it mattered nothing in Justinian's time and very little in Ulpian's time which action it was.

It is no easier to determine when an *actio utilis* lay and when an *actio in factum*. We need not repeat the illustrations. It is all the more confusing because we get once or twice the expression '*actio in factum ad exemplum legis Aquiliae*' (h.t. 53, Coll 12.7.5 and 6 taken together). But that expression suggests the *actio utilis*, as in h.t. 12 '*danda est mihi ad exemplum legis Aquiliae actio*'. It does not seem possible to get a clear principle. The history may be that in earlier classical law there was a *utilis actio* if actual damage were done to the thing, *corpori*, but indirectly, not *corpore*, but that if the thing was not damaged at all but merely rendered unavailable, then however direct it was, the *lex* had nothing to do with the matter, but in many cases an *actio in factum* was given in suitable cases merely for compensation. Before the end of the classical age (the Collatio suggests this) this action was associated with the *lex* as to e.g. mode of assessment of damages and that thereafter, and especially under the law of Justinian, there is no great care in distinguishing the fields of the two actions.

[48] We have now to consider the elements of liability. They may be stated under ~~three~~ \four/ heads. There must be an Act. There must be *Damnum*. The thing must be done *iniuria*, without legal justification. \The wrongdoing must be the cause of the damage./

Act. The delict is the breach of a *ius in rem* and *iura in rem* never impose positive duties. It follows that if I am liable for damaging your property it must be for doing something, not for merely abstaining \D.7.1.13.2/. There was no legal obligation for instance on a passer by to pull a sheep out of a stream in which it was drowning, though any decent man would. But the rule is not always easy to apply. In the vast majority of the cases in the texts the act is obvious, but it is not always so. H.t. 8 gives the limitations which we must notice. In h.t.pr a surgeon operates properly but does not attend to the patient afterwards and he dies. Here all that he actually did was properly done. But his act imposed on him an obligation to avoid possible evil consequences. There was the necessary act. This is I suppose what Grueber means by his odd statement, that the operation was affected by *culpa*. It can be contrasted with h.t. 8.1. A muleteer for lack of skill cannot hold in his mules and they do damage. Or he is unable for lack of strength. Or the same thing occurs in the case of a horseman. Here the wrong is in the original act: he had no business to undertake a dangerous thing which he was not qualified to do. In h.t. 27.9 we have a much discussed text. We have the same text in a different form in Coll. 12.7.7. The case in the Digest is this. The slave of a *colonus* lights a fire in a furnace and goes to sleep and the fire being unguarded burns down the house. Neratius says that if his master, the *colonus*, told him to do it, knowing he was likely to neglect he is liable under the contract and the end of the text shows that there was a *actio utilis a lege Aquilia* and we are told that it is no defence that he only did a natural thing in going to sleep. He ought to have taken precautions: it is the same case as in h.t. 8.pr. Then we get a more complex hypothesis. One slave lit the fire and did all that [49] he ought to. Another, appointed to watch it neglected it with resulting damage. The difficulty is that the first did nothing wrong; the second did nothing at all. The conclusion is that there is the action – *utilis* of course as it was not corpore. Where is the act? Monro in his long note admits that he cannot find it and is inclined to doubt the existence of the rule. I might add that while some of his criticism seems captious, e.g. the fact that they are slaves and could not be liable at all, since it is not said the action is brought against the slaves, he does in his statement of Grueber's argument bring out its weak points. There are two answers to the difficulty offered by Grueber, neither satisfactory. We are told that he has taken a responsibility which imposes the duty and this undertaking is an act. But a usufructuary by accepting the usufruct undertakes responsibilities as to maintenance but if he neglects them he is not liable *ex Aquilia* (D.7.1.13.2). Again we are told that he has acted, he '*neglegenter custodiit*'. He began his guard. This is an answer so far as the facts of this case go, but the real question is: suppose his master ordered him on guard and he took no notice. It is moreover to be noted that in the Collatio the case is put on a level with that of the doctor who neglected after treatment. This fact coupled with the argument in the text which puts the fact that he has done nothing as a poser seems to make it clear \that this is the real question/. There is also the fact that liability under the *lex* is constantly associated with '*culpa*' (e.g. h.t. 5.1 and 2; Gai 3.211) \ In 47.10.1.pr *damnum culpa datum* appears as the description of the wrong/ and the original meaning of *culpa* is carelessness in act, not in omission, the proper name of which is *neglegentia*. It is difficult to see the act here. Clearly the case was doubtful \There is clearly something more than a mere omission and/ they somehow linked up the act of one slave with the carelessness of the other. Or it may be that just as they made a master liable for what was done under his *iussus*, they saw a sufficient act in the master's order. One would like to know how they would have dealt with the case where it was a friend who had been simply asked to look after the [50] fire and did not. Or he had a mandate or was hired to do it. Some recent writers hold that this is post-classical: classical law refused the action, but it is difficult to think this of a rule laid down here and in the Collatio 12.7.7. In h.t. 27.10 building the oven and having fires in it is the act. We need not now consider the *cautio damni infecti* for threatened damage. It does not seem to matter whether it was a party wall or all the neighbour's. Grueber thinks that had it been all the neighbour's no action would lie. An absurd result, and in the text he cites (39.2.7.2) there was no act.

Note though it does not at the moment concern us that on the next text (27.11) Monro and Grueber have long but not very helpful notes. If *colonus* was not careless in choosing slaves he is liable only noxally, and we know that in later law he could be sued *ex locato* on their acts and release himself by *pro noxae deditione*. Probably in the earlier classical law he could not have been sued on the contract at all. The words from '*sed haec*' to the end are probably Justinian but though absurdly expressed they state an old rule. *Colonus* is personally liable for *culpa in eligendo*. Of course it is not for having such slaves that he is liable. It is for putting them on to this work when he knew they were not competent. '*Cur*' is odd – we should have expected '*quod*', but it has been shown that easterns did so use a '*cur*' and Ulpian came it seems from Syria. But the best evidence that the words are an addition is the fact that we have also this text in the Collatio (12.7.8) and there the words do not occur.

It is hardly necessary to say that for distinct damages to the same thing distinct actions lie, just as if I steal a slave and then kill him. I am liable to both *furti* and *damni iniuria* (h.t. 27.pr). So if I wound and afterwards kill him I am liable to two actions (h.t. 32.1) though a series of blows in the same assault are one act for this purpose. An odd result of the fact that killing and wounding are under distinct provisions is that if I wound a man and pay damages and he then dies, a new action is not barred by the first. In strictness damages would be cumulative, but in fact, as this would be unfair, as it was a single act it was held that an *exceptio doli* would make the plaintiff recover no more than if he had sued for killing in the first instance, i.e. the threat of it would cause him to put in a *taxatio* (h.t. 46, 47).

[51] ~~We have now to consider the other~~ requirements of liability, ~~damnum and iniuria.~~

Damnum. The rule is that there must be a *damnum* to the plaintiff in respect of property. The *lex* does not express it exactly as damage to property but as here: '*si quis alteri damnum faxit, quod usserit*' etc, and it is these latter words that express the limitation to actual physical harm to the thing. \[foot of page] Thus in h.t. 41.pr in f. where a man tells other people of the contents of private documents entrusted to him, he may do monetary harm, but there is no Aquilian action. There may be an *actio iniuriarum*./

It is not necessary to give illustrations of ordinary cases of *damnum*: those we have just stated are enough. But there are some special cases to be considered. Since it must be in respect of property and a freeman's members are not property there is no direct action for damaging them. But as we have seen a man has an *actio utilis* for damage to a member (h.t. 13.pr) and a *paterfamilias* has for similar damage to his *filiusfamilias*. The text which tells of this does not say that it is *utilis* (h.t. 5.3-7.pr) but it must be. See also h.t. 7.4. It did not lie for killing a freeman, though we may remember that the praetorian action for *res dejectae* did (Inst 4.5.1) but for a fixed penalty. Here there is no *actio in factum* even. It is also noticeable that the *actio de pauperie* lay where a *filius* was damaged (D.9.1.3) and nothing is said about its being *utilis*. This action is given by the XII Tables and is usually said to be civil. It is possible that the pauperies is described as *damnum facere* (D.9.1.1.3) since nothing is said about *res*, the direct action lay. It is also not impossible, as older editors have thought, that for some reason not known to us the action was *in factum*. The fact that the *damnum* must be to the owner led to difficulties we have already considered where the damage was done to a *res hereditaria* (h.t. 13.2). In h.t. 23.7 we have the case of a slave child under one year killed. It is a little difficult to see any value at all in such a slave but presumably it had some for the action lies and we are elsewhere told that if a slave who had no value at all ('*nullo pretio*') is made worse than he was there is no Aquilian though there may be *iniuriarum* (h.t. 27.17). The mode of estimation of this *damnum* we shall have to consider later. [52] But something may be said here as to whether there is damage or not. In the first place it does not matter that the damage was temporary: the fact that the injured slave has completely recovered is no defence. '*lege aquilia agi potes et sanato vulnerato servo*' (h.t. 45.1). It must be a *damnum* estimable in money. Thus in D.9.3.7 in connexion with a cognate action we are told that if a freeman is disfigured merely no action lies, for this cannot be valued. Our own courts find no difficulty. Moreover the context shows that this does not cover such disfigurement as creates an economic loss, e.g. disqualifying him from his profession. Monro p.20 does not bring out this point. Similarly in h.t. 33.pr we are told that it must be economic loss '*non affectiones aestimandas*'. If your slave who is your natural son is killed you can recover only damages based on his market value, not on the fact that if he had belonged to someone else you would have been ready to give a lot of money for him. As Monro says, you must add 'in the same circumstances'. It is worth noting that h.t. 1 must not be read as meaning that these sentimental damages could be recovered by an *actio in factum*. It is a new proposition, referring to the same kind of *damnum*, but one not within the *lex*. And if one performs unlawfully an operation on the slave which increases his value, there is no Aquilian – there is no loss, though as the text says there may be an *actio iniuriarum*, or one under the edict of the aediles or for fourfold (h.t. 27.28). These other remedies are puzzling. There is no other mention of this edict, but it is supposed to have been a provision in the aediles' edict on sale of slaves. The alternative fourfold action is quite unknown and hardly intelligible. Fourfold of what? Presumably the value of the slave. As Grueber points out, the Basilica omit the word '*aut*' making the fourfold not an alternative but the remedy under the edict, which may be correct.

In h.t. 27.17 we have a text which is clear enough as it stands but which also exists in Coll. 2.4 in a very different form, i.e. with a very different rule. Our [53] text says that if the slave is not reduced in value but expense has been incurred these are recoverable – a simple illustration that the damage is not the less *damnum* because the slave has been cured, for of course if he had been offered for sale before treatment he would have brought less. But the Collatio omits the words '*Aquilia enim eas ruptiones quae damna dant persequitur*' making its '*ergo*' follow the statement that there is no \Aquilian/ action if a slave of no value is wounded, and goes on to say that if he is not less valuable but expense has been incurred in curing '*in haec nec mihi videri damni Aquilia lege agi posse*'. This is the exact opposite, and the question arises: is it the classical law? We will not discuss it – it is I think a blunder of some scribe, for it is sheer nonsense. \[marker for insertion, but nothing inserted]/

For completeness two cases must be mentioned which have already been discussed. There is the case of the promisee killing an undelivered slave \(h.t. 54)/ when the promissor is already *in mora*, so that the risk is on him. Can he be said to suffer any *damnum* since he was already liable for the value of the slave and the promisee's act has released him. I think the answer is that he formally has the action, just as he certainly would if a third person had killed him, but justice requires either an *exceptio* or *denegatio actionis*. This accounts for the language '*non recte experiri*'. In Justinian's time these distinctions however meant little. There is also the case of the buyer who is going to redhibit (h.t. 11.7). The buyer has the action though it can hardly be on account of any *damnum* to himself, as he is bound to hand over what he recovers if he does redhibit.

The case in D.4.3.18.5 has already been sufficiently discussed. \promisee, 3rd p. de dolo/

[54] We pass now to the most important of the requirements: the act must have been done *iniuria*, contrary to law, imputably \h.t. 3, *oportet esse iniuria factum*/ \[at foot of page] which excludes liability if it is done by one incapable of *iniuria*, e.g. a lunatic or *infans* or beast or by the accidental fall of a tile (h.t. 5.2). Of course fall of a tile might create liability./ As it is often expressed it must have been done *culpa*, where *culpa* is used in a wide sense. The title contains a large number of texts illustrating this matter which we shall have to work through. But there are some general principles which can be dealt with first.

The first point is that it does not matter, as far as this action goes, whether it was wilful or merely negligent so long as it was unlawful. The damages were the same. But obviously there might be other liabilities which might be affected by this point. Thus in h.t. 5.1 after saying that it need not be contumelious, as *iniuria* must, but it suffices that it be *iniuria*, contrary to law, that is to say '*culpa*', which is no doubt a gloss, it adds that there might also be an *actio iniuriarum* with different and independent damages but that the Aquilian action lies where damage was done with no intention to harm.

So in h.t. 23.9 it is said that if the slave is killed *dolo* there may be criminal proceedings under the *lex Cornelia de sicariis* and the judgment in one does not prejudice the other. And 5.pr \self-defence/ gives a case of the same kind. The absence of any distinction between wilful and negligent damage merely reflects the fact that the law is very ancient. The damage is more prominent than the conception of guilt. If you do damage you must pay for it unless there is something which excuses you.

Not only was *culpa* in the ordinary sense on a level with *dolus*: it might be the slightest negligence. '*In lege Aquilia et levissima culpa venit*' (h.t. 44.pr), any failure to attain the standard of a *bonus paterfamilias*. And this raises a difficult question. It is clear that the existence of a contractual or quasi-contractual relation between the parties did not exclude the Aquilian: we have seen many cases and that there is often a choice of actions but the plaintiff must choose. He must renounce the second action or give security not to bring it (see e.g. h.t. 18; 27.11 etc). This raises no difficulty where, as in most cases, the contract or quasi-contract calls for the same degree of care. But it may happen that it [55] does not. Thus in deposit the liability is only for *dolus*. If a depositee carelessly damages the *res* he is not liable under the contract. Is he liable *ex Aquilia* or does his contract protect him? The question is not directly answered in the texts and has been much discussed. The dominant view is that the existence of the contract makes no difference in this respect, that e.g. a depositee who negligently damages the *res* though not liable *ex deposito* is liable under the *lex Aquilia*. The other view is not without strong supporters, e.g. Pernice. The texts give no direct answer and as Monro says the fact that they do not say in stating the liability that it might be modified if there was a contract is evidence that it did not make any difference. \ and the fact that it is a *ius in rem* that cannot be affected by an ob. is urged./ But the *argumentum a silentio* is not very strong. Monro indeed observes that the arguments both ways are very weak. Apart from texts the strongest arguments against the dominant view is that it goes a long way towards making nonsense of the rule in deposit, for in most cases of negligent harm it will be some physical damage which gives an Aquilian and again the argument a *silentio*, i.e. the fact that none of the texts which tell us that the depositee etc are liable only for *dolus* (or *culpa lata*) say that nevertheless there may be a liability *ex Aquilia* though this limitation is stated in other connexions. Thus in 40.12.12.6, 13 we are told of an *actio in factum* against one who is claiming his liberty and who had been a *bona fide serviens* who did damage *dolo malo*. The text says that this covers only *dolus* but adds that there is a liability *ex Aquilia* if it was only *culpa*. There is of course here no question of any contract or the like limiting responsibility. So in D.47.4.1.2 the same point is made. There is not much force in the argument that as it is a *ius in rem* this cannot be affected by an *obligatio*. That is not true. If I have expressly agreed that you shall be in no way liable for damaging the thing I cannot sue, yet the damage is breach of *ius in rem* and the agreement is only obligation. In fact the argument begs the whole question as we shall see when we come to the texts. Of these there are several to consider.

[56] In h.t. 5.3 after laying it down that the Aquilian lies for wounding or killing an apprentice \slave/ it continues with a case. A cobbler's apprentice \a freeman/ did a job badly, his master hit him on the nape of the neck with a last and destroyed one eye. Julian is quoted as saying that there is no *iniuriarum*, as it was not done to insult, but by way of admonishment he doubts whether there is \or is not/ any *actio ex locato*, the master having a right to *levis castigatio*. Then Ulpian adds that he has no doubt the Aquilian lies. At first sight this looks in favour of the dominant view: there is the Aquilian though it may be doubtful whether there is *ex locato*. But we must look more closely. In the first place it is Julian who doubts on one point and Ulpian who is certain on another: non constat that Ulpian shares the doubt. Further Julian's words may mean and probably do mean that he doubts whether there is not an *actio ex locato* since the master has a right only to light castigation. This is confirmed by D.19.2.13.4 where Ulpian again quotes from Julian the same case. And there Julian says 'there is an action *ex locato* since though the master has a right of *levis castigatio* he has not here observed this limit.' It is also clear that in that text the allusion to the Aquilian is an addition by the compilers and this may be, it is so held by some, the case in our text. Add further that if the actio ex locato is excluded because the master has not exceeded his right of *levis castigatio* this must necessarily have excluded the Aquilian also, since there could be no *culpa* at all. The text is no support to the dominant view.

Another text more or less in point is h.t. 11.pr. A barber was shaving a slave in a place where people were playing ball. One of the players hitting the ball somewhat violently hit the barber's hand with the result that the razor cut the slave's throat. On these facts, says the text, whoever was guilty of *culpa* was liable *ex Aquilia*. This is Mela's view and it seems obvious and not very helpful. However, Proculus says the *culpa* is in the barber and Ulpian agrees that if he did it where the game was usually played or people constantly passed he is to [57] blame. But he adds: if the man voluntarily put himself in the hands of the barber in a dangerous place he has only himself to blame. It is possible to consider this – most people do – as a case of contributory negligence which, as we shall see later, may bar the claim. But it can be looked at in another way. It may be said that the customer agreed to take the risks, and this pact in the contract of hiring bars the claim *ex Aquilia* also. If that is so the same would be true of the case of the implied term in deposit. The same point arises in h.t. 27.29. A craftsman employed to decorate a bowl by piercings breaks it. He is obviously liable *ex Aquilia* unless as the text says it was not due to want of skill but to a defect in the bowl itself. It then adds, and this is what concerns us, that therefore it is the practice of such workmen to agree that they shall not do it at their own risks and this frees them both under *ex locato* and the Aquilian. Now what they contract out of is liability for negligence, i.e. the point is not to be raised whether he might not by greater care have avoided breaking it: he does not want to contract out of what he is not liable for, defects in the *res*. \[at foot of page] In 19.2.13.5 it is noted that he is not liable if it is from defects in the thing but it is added that of course he can later take this risk on himself if he likes (unless?)/ Here too an agreement under the contract is a defence on the *Aquilia*, and it is not obvious why the same should not be true of the implied term in deposit. Nor it is simply an implied term since it can be contracted out of D.16.3.1.6: *Si convenit ut in deposito et culpa praestatur, rata est conventio.* In h.t. 27.23 we are told that if a man overloads a mule so that it is injured he is liable *ex Aquilia*. This is obvious but it is to be compared with D.19.2.30.2. Mules were let to be loaded with a certain weight. The hirer put heavier loads on them and they were injured. Both *ex locato* and Aquilian are available, within of course the restrictions already mentioned. Now what would happen if they were not loaded above the agreed amount and that a careful muledriver would have known that this was too much and they were in fact damaged? Pernice who takes the view that I am supporting says that it follows *e contrario* from the text that in that case there would be neither action. I am not quite sure that it does, but if it does, then [58] again we have the terms of the contract excluding an Aquilian liability which would otherwise exist. But even so it is not strong for it can be answered that '*volenti non fit iniuria*'. If I do only what you authorise me to do exactly you cannot have any remedy against me. Altogether it seems to me that the weight of evidence is in favour of the view that a depositee was not liable for slight negligence *ex Aquilia*. But it is only fair to say that I think most people take the other view.

   We have seen that the liability depends on *iniuria* or *culpa* in a wide sense. What is this *culpa*. The Romans do not define it: they rarely generalise. They do not begin from a general idea. They do not say *culpa* is so and so there-fore this that and the other are *culpa*. They take concrete cases and say that this that and the other is *culpa* and we have to find out the general concep-tion if we can. And it may very well be that no exact definition is possible. The general character of it is conduct involving dealing with another man's property in a way which is unauthorised and therefore prima facie unlawful, without grounds of excuse recognised by law. Thus if I hand you a thing to look at and you break it this is unlawful, for I did not authorise you to deal carelessly with my property. Since all voluntary conduct is either inadvertent or intentional, wilful or careless, all cases can be brought under the rubrics of *dolus* or *culpa* in the ordinary sense, but the terminology of the texts wants some care. We are told that it is *culpa* to undertake to drive a team not having the necessary strength and we get the catchword '*infirmitas culpae adnumeratur*' (h.t. 8.1). Obviously the expression is loose: it is not *culpa* to be weak, but it is *culpa* to do things affecting the property of others without giving due weight to the fact that you are too weak for the job. This loose-ness of expression has led to the suggestion that the phrase is interpolated, but there seems no reason for this. In like manner it is *culpa* to undertake skilled work without having the necessary skill, and we are told in the same way that '*imperitia culpae adnumeratur*' (D.19.2.8.5; 50.17.132) which is [59] taken from the same place as the remark that '*infirmitas culpae adnumeratur*': to which expression the same objection can be \made/ and has been made. It is clear that in both these expressions '*culpa*' is used in the wide sense of imputability, as if a man undertakes skilled work knowing that he has not the skill, this is in fact *dolus* rather than *culpa* in the technical sense.

We may now go on to consider the excuses which may operate in defence though the act is prima facie done '*iniuria*'. The principal are the following.

i Self-defence. The texts in our title are 4, 5.pr and 45.4, and their rule is pretty clear. The principle is clearly laid down in h.t. 4.pr, '*adversus periculum naturalis ratio permittit se defendere*' and in h.t. 45.4 '*vim enim vi defendere omnes leges omniaque iura permittunt*'. In the first case it is against a *latro*, in the other against assault. The same rule is laid down in D.43.16.1.27. But there are limitations on this right. The circumstances must be such that it seemed, and would seem to a careful man, necessary. Thus (h.t. 45.4) notes that even though you killed him when he was attacking you, still that is no reply to an action if you did it not really in defence but out of anger to get a bit of your own back. (When you come to translate this note the corruption: '*damni culpam*' means nothing; Mommsen's suggestion '*damni quiddam*' is usually accepted.) The case of robbery illustrates these principles. The XII Tables laid it down that it was permissible to kill a nocturnal thief provided you shouted (h.t. 4.1). We need not consider the reason for the require-ment of '*clamor*' and also a thief by day if he was armed. This says nothing about its being necessary in self-defence, but the original of our 5.1 is in the Collatio (7.3.2) and states the rule of the XII Tables and expresses a doubt of Pomponius whether it be still in force and adds as our text has, following it, if when he could have arrested him he preferred to kill him, he will be liable. Our text takes this over but for the citation to the XII Tables it sub-stitutes for the rule of the XII Tables the case of killing '*metu mortis*', i.e. in self-defence. Two points however [60] must be made here. The text says 'if he could have arrested him', which makes the killing allowable not only in defence, but in order to secure his capture. But this does not seem to be true, for in D.48.8.9 it is said that the killing is excusable only if he could not be spared without danger to yourself. Clearly in other cases you have no right to kill him after he has started to run away (h.t. 7.4). Another point is that this defence is good only as against the wrongdoer himself. In h.t. 45.4 the case is put of one who intending to throw a stone at his assailant hits somebody else he is liable. Monro supposes that he mistook him but I think the text means that he made a bad shot.

ii Certain intense provocations. As we have just seen it was not in general permitted to kill or wound merely in revenge. The only case mentioned in the title is that of a *servus alienus* caught in adultery (h.t. 30.pr). This is put in very general terms, but in fact the right was subject to severe limits as to persons and circumstances into which we need not go. The matter is also discussed under the *Cornelia* concerning murder but it does not appear that the protection extended to any but sexual cases.

iii Consent, '*volenti non fit iniuria*'. So far as this is exact consent to what is done it is obvious, but the practical case is that of consent to something of which what is done is a probable consequence. In some cases it is difficult and perhaps unnecessary to distinguish this from what is called contributory negligence. We may take as a typical case of exact consent that of a man who hires mules for an agreed load and though he does not exceed that load it is too much and the mules are injured: there is no action either on the contract or under the lex (arg. 19.2.30.2). In h.t. 7.4 it is said that if two free men fight in a wrestling contest or in the public *certamina*, and one hurts the other. There is no action because it is not done for *iniuria* but for glory and manliness. But this does not apply to slave because these don't '*certare*'. I do not think much of this [61] reasoning. The rule certainly does not apply only to these public contests, for if slaves do not take part in them the point could not arise. It applies actually to any private form of contest which may very well lead to damage to a party & the parties know it. It rests on consent and it did not apply to slaves because they could not consent to anything to the damage of their masters. This appears from the end words which say that the rule did apply to slaves if they engaged in contests of this kind, not in a public contest, with their owner's consent. To all these cases it may be said that there is no *culpa* at all.

iv Accident. Here too there is no *culpa* and some of the cases we have been discussing might equally come under this head. A few other illustrations may be taken. In h.t. 7.3 A is knocked by B against C and injures him. There is no liability in A, whether there is in B or not. So far as A is concerned there is no *culpa*. In 7.2 if a man carrying a load not unduly heavy and not carelessly, slips and hurts a man, there is no liability for there is no *culpa*. In h.t. 45.3 two men are leaping over a fire. They collide and fall and one is burnt. The text says that there is no action unless it is known which upset the other, which looks absurd but is of course true. What I think it would come to in practice is that there would be no action unless it were shown that one intentionally collided with the other. For I should have said that leaping over the fire in company with others, whether at the feast of Palilia, founder's day or any other occasion, was an occasion on which you must have known and your master too that collisions were extremely likely. In h.t. 52.4 they were playing at ball. The player was running for the ball and another pushed him over and his leg was broken. Here too we are told that this was *casus* rather than *culpa* – it is in fact 'the rub of the green'. And the last text \57/ illustrates the same point. A number are riding together. Without any negligence, one horse bumps against another and upsets its rider and its legs are broken. Here too there is no action: it is *casus*.

[62] v Performance of \official/ duty. This illustrated in h.t. 29.7. It tells us that municipal magistrates if they do *damnum iniuria* may be liable *ex Aquilia*, for instance if having seized cattle under a judgment they refuse to allow them to be fed so that they die. There is an *actio in factum*. Or if they damage them whether the seizure had been in order or was mistaken. But if one resists lawful seizure there is no liability for violence to make him submit. The text goes on to make the obvious statement that if a slave lawfully seized hangs himself the official is not liable. Note that this does not deal with the higher magistracy, who have *imperium*. They could not be sued during their office. Grueber thinks that the word *violentius* here means 'in excess of duty' but I do not think it does: it means what Monro says, 'proceeds to forcible measures'. If it did mean what Grueber supposes it would imply a rule that such an officer acting in good faith was not liable even where he exceeded his powers, but I do not think that there is any such rule, though corresponding rules do exist in many systems \cf 18.6.13.14/.

vi Protection of rights. This is dealt with in a text which has been much discussed, h.t. 29.1. The facts are that A has built out over his wall a roof which hangs over B's land. B cuts it away. Proculus says that there is an Aquilian action. The proper course was to bring an action denying the servitude. But where a man who had no servitude made a waterway through my house, Severus rescripted that I had a perfect right to do away with it, and the text adds in words which must be those of Ulpian who is quoting him, that the distinction is perfectly sound, since in the first case (hic) he built something out of his own building; in the other he did something on another man's land. Grueber's translation 'was protecting himself' is curious: it really means 'was roofing'. The reason given wants some expansion. Pernice says that the point is that the waterway is in his legal possession, the roof is not; but that seems hardly enough. As Grueber puts it, the waterway is part of his land: it is his since it is part of his [63] land. It would be absurd if I by digging a trench on your land could compel you to bring an action before filling it up. H.t. 39 deals with cattle trespassing on my land. It says that if a mare in foal is grazing on my land (I do not think it need mean has been turned out to graze on my land as Monro says) and slips her foal while she is being driven out there will be an Aquilian action if he struck the mare or drove her violently \consulto/ but not if he ejects her with the care which the circumstances clearly require. The word 'consulto' makes a difficulty and its meaning is not clear. Pernice and Grueber explain it on the view that he had no right to hit her at all, but he had a right to drive her out even it would seem violentius but that if he did it 'consulto' i.e. with a view to damaging her, he would be liable, just as you have as we saw a right to resist force by force, but if you do not do it merely in resistance but to get a bit of your own back that is an *iniuria* (h.t. 45.4). But it does not seem quite satisfactory. Suppose he knew her condition and chased her violently off not of malice but out of sheer carelessness. Would he be liable? Not on this reasoning, but I think he would. I think *consulto* if it means anything means knowing her condition, and this would be indifferent if he struck her. But it is rather doubtful. In h.t. 39.1 we have a general rule. In driving cattle you must do it as you would your own. You have your action if they have done any harm. You may not lock them up. You should drive them out without violence or tell their owner to come and take them away. There was no action for a mere trespass on your land.

vii Necessity. This topic presents some difficulty. It is illustrated by several texts, which leave certain questions open. In h.t. 29.3 we are told on the authority of Labeo that if my vessel is driven by the force of the wind on to the anchor cables of another and the sailors cut away these cables, this being the [64] only way in which the ship can be extricated, there is no action. This no doubt assumes that the ship's crew were in no way to blame for getting their ship into that position. This appears from the following words which say that the same is true if the ship is so driven in among fishermen's nets, and it is added that if this resulted from their negligence an Aquilian action would lie. Note too that sect. 3 says 'if there was no other way of saving themselves', not 'if they reasonably thought there was no other way'. What would be the law if, the moment the cables were cut the wind changed and the ship drew clear? In any case, if there was *culpa*, bad navigation, no question arises as to liability: the person who gave the order would be liable to the direct action. H.t. 49.1 begins with a statement of principle on the point which is unfortunately corrupt. It seems to say that *damnum* gives the action only where there is *iniuria*, and that there usually is *iniuria* except where the act is done '*magna vi cogente*', in conditions of urgent peril. But that does not help us much. It then states and discusses a case. A man whose house is in danger of fire pulls down his neighbour's to check the fire. Ulpian quotes Celsus filius as holding that there is no action on the *lex*, for he did it inspired by reasonable fear that the fire would reach him and thus, whether the fire gets so far or is put out before, there is no action. In 47.9.3.7 Ulpian again discusses the case. Here the fire seems to be actually in the neighbour's house which he pulls down. After rejecting an opinion of Labeo on a point which does not concern us he quotes Celsus as saying, as before, that no Aquilian action will lie, as there was no other way of protecting himself. This reason is not quite the same. In our case it was reasonable fear that his house would be burnt: here it seems to be assumed that the house would inevitably have been burnt down. In 43.24.7.4 Ulpian again discusses the case. Here he begins by saying that Celsus doubts but there is reason to think there is corruption, that it should be Gallus Aquilius, Celsus not being quoted. But he quotes Servius as saying that if a magistrate did it no action lies, but that if a private person did, the danger is no defence unless the fire actually did reach the house which was pulled down. The reason given is that there is no *iniuria* and no *damnum* since the house would have been burnt in any case. [65] This is a bad reason, so far as the *damnum* point is concerned, inconsistent with what we get in our title in another connexion. We are told (h.t. 51) that if A mortally wounds C, i.e. so that he is sure to die, and B then kills him, B is liable for the killing. The question is: are these texts in accord or in conflict? Something turns on the meaning of '*sive pervenit*' in our text. '*Pervenit*' where? Monro and Grueber think it means the house of the defendant. But that seems impossible: the pulling down of the intervening house prevented that. To my mind it must mean the house that was pulled down, and in that case there is a conflict. Our text makes reasonable fear that your house would burn down a defence; the other makes it one only if the fire reaches the house pulled down, which does of course show that your fear was reasonable. As Pernice says, the real question is how much proof is needed that the fear was reasonable. The view of Servius requiring demonstration that the house would have been burnt is a rigid view of an early jurisprudence; that of our text which requires you only to show in whatever way you can that your fear was reasonable is the view of classical and later law.

But three points suggest themselves. Monro says that in 43.24.7.4 Servius contradicts himself. I do not see this: what he says is the fact that it was done to check a fire is a defence if a magistrate did it, but not if a private owner did it; he must also show that the fire did actually reach the house that was pulled down. Also there must be limits to the right. I cannot burn down your house because otherwise my hens will die of the cold even if I have no other way of protecting them. The damage avoided must bear some quantitative relation to that done. I suppose it must not be greater than that avoided, but our text seems to imply that it may be as great. But if my house is a hut and yours a palace I cannot think I had a right to pull it down to save mine. But we have no more information. Also, while most systems free from criminal liability on such facts they commonly require compensation. There is just a hint of this in 43.24.7.4 where corrupt words seem to mean that if there was reasonable ground of fear but the fire did not get so far damages would be only *in simplum*, i.e. all penal aspect of the Aquilian action is cut out.

There is one other point of principle to be mentioned. The act must be done [66] *iniuria*, either negligently or wilfully, but even where it is wilful there need be no intent to injure me. To use a maxim of our law '*Malitia agreditur personam*'. Thus in h.t. 27.8 where a man intends to burn down my house but burns down a neighbour's too he is liable to him, and though he had no desire to injure lodgers he is liable to them for their furniture destroyed. And in h.t. 45.2 where I kill a man whom I suppose to be free, killing of whom would involve no civil liability, but in fact he is your slave, you have the Aquilian action.

We can now proceed to discuss those texts, not yet fully analysed, in which the question of *iniuria* is considered.

H.t. 11.pr. The barber case. Already considered, but notice that the ball hits the barber's hand so that it is *impulsus*. It is not the act of the barber at all. Suppose you hold the barber to blame for shaving in such a place, he is liable, but ought it not to be an *actio utilis*: did he not rather *causam mortis praestare*?

The contributory negligence point we shall take later. Monro thinks that if it was in a place where people constantly pass, which the text gives as a case of negligence in the barber, it is not so because such an accident is not so likely there, but that seems to be not the point of view. What the text means is that by choosing such a spot he renders himself likely to meet with not precisely this mishap, but to have his hand joggled at a critical moment.

H.t. 27.34. A hires a slave to drive mules. The man ties the mule's rope to his thumb. The mule breaks away, tears off the man's thumb and rushes to destruction. If he was let as a qualified muleteer there is an actio ex ~~locato~~ \conducto/ for breach of warranty, the loss of the mule coming into account. The point is that by acting in that silly manner he had no control over the mule. The damage may seem a little remote, but some sort of damage is probable and any specified form would be unlikely. Ulpian adds that on the same fact an Aquilian action lies, but it would I suppose be *utilis* or *in factum*. But if the mule broke away because some boy struck or frightened it, its owner and the owner of the slave have Aquilian actions against the frightener. That is plain enough, subject to a question of [67] contributory negligence, which will be taken later. But it all leaves certain questions open. If he had been simply hired as a slave, not as a mule driver, there would be no action on the contract: would there be an Aquilian? I think so – a noxal action. Grueber, following the gloss, thinks it noxal in the first case, but to me that is very doubtful. He argues from h.t. 27.11. But that is different. In that text there is no suggestion of any carelessness in the master, or breach of warranty: it makes the master liable on the contract for his slave's act which would be a breach if he himself had done it, with a right of '*pro noxae deditione*'. There is no hint in our text that if sued ex locato the owner could have got off in this way. Another question is: does the intervention of the frightener prevent the owner from being liable? That is the kind of point we shall have to consider in dealing later with the principle that the act must be the cause of the *damnum*.

H.t. 29.2 ~~and 3~~. The first case is at first sight simple. Your ship comes into collision with my dinghy. If it is through the fault of the *nautae* they are liable *ex aquilia* and it does not matter whether the harm was done by steering into the dinghy or by taking in your steering oar so that the ship was out of control (my rendering of the obscure words) or by hand. In all these cases there is a direct action, *corpore*. But the text adds that if it was due to the breaking of a rope (*casus*) or to no one's being on board, there is no action against the *dominus*. There are two difficulties. To have a ship at large in traffic with no one on board is carelessness. You can make it clear by striking out the '*aut*' when it is the case of a ship breaking from her moorings. But this is not justified as the *aut* is confirmed by the Basilica. The other point is that while the beginning says there is an aquilian action against the sailors if they are careless the last part says there is an action against the *dominus* in certain events. This 'lame contrast', as Monro calls it and it certainly is, can be explained in a way which also explains the last point. There was an *actio in factum* against the owner of the ship for *damnum iniuria* by those he employed on board, and this says that on such facts this action does not lie (Textbook p.593) since there was no *damnum in*[68]*iuria* by anyone on board the ship. There is nothing in the text to exclude liability on the part of any person who turned the ship loose in this dangerous way. The text has no doubt been abridged. Note that '*tu*' at the beginning has become '*dominus*' at the end.

The case in 3 we have already considered under the head of necessity.

H.t. 29.4 is pretty obvious. If one ship runs into another there is an aquilian action against the steersman or *ducator*, probably captain. ~~will lie ex Aquilia~~ But if there was no negligence but it was caused by the force of a gale, no action will lie against the *dominus*. Obviously no aquilian lies against him: it is not *culpa* to own a ship. There is the same 'lame contrast' and it is to be explained in the same way. The edictal *actio in factum* does not lie against the *dominus* unless there was negligence on board. Then the text decides another point. Suppose there was negligence and the Aquilian is brought; can the edictal *actio in factum* also be brought. No: the Aquilian suffices. This language means that it is not formally barred, for it is not *eadem causa* exactly but that if they bring the other they will either be met by an *exceptio doli* or nonsuited *officio iudicis* or perhaps in the first action be compelled to give security against bringing the other. That this *actio in factum* against the *dominus* is the explanation of the 'lame contrast' is suggested by the fact that in the Basilica these texts are not discussed under the Aquilian but under a heading concerned with the liability of the ship itself. I suppose it may be the origin of our admiralty real actions.

H.t. 30.3. A man sets fire to straw or thorns on his land: it spreads and does damage to crops on other land. The question is whether this was due to his stupidity or negligence. If, for instance, he did it on a windy day, this is *culpa* and he is liable to an *actio utilis* or *in factum* – he provided the cause of the harm. But if he acted with due care, but a sudden gust of wind carried the fire over there is no *culpa* and no liability. Of course, doing all that was necessary includes watching it, to see that it does not spread. The same [69] case is discussed in Coll. 12.7.5.6. It is a different text and it makes it clear that the remedy is an *actio in factum* or *utilis*. But it shows that the matter had been discussed, and it distinguishes this case from that in h.t. 27.8 where the direct action lies for setting fire to my house and so burning my neighbour's too, on the ground that in the present case '*non principaliter hic exussit sed dum aliud agit, sic ignis processit*' (Grueber's reference should be to Coll. 12.7.3, not 12.7.2). The reasoning is a little obscure for it seems to make the distinction turn on whether it was *dolus* or negligence, which does not seem to be material. The truth is that once they began to extend the statute there was no very definite line to take and hence differences of opinion and not very consistent solutions. In Justinian's time it did not matter.

H.t. 31. A man is cutting branches from a tree or handling things on a scaffold. Something drops and kills a passing slave. Mucius Scaevola is quoted by Ulpian in a rather involved sentence as saying that if it is a public way or even a private place where there is a way and people may be expected to pass, it is *culpa* to let a thing drop without giving a warning or only giving a warning when it is too late to avoid the danger. But if it is in a private place where there is no reason to expect any person to be then it is not necessarily *culpa* even if no warning at all is given. But even there if he sees someone coming not to give warning is *dolus* and therefore *culpa* in the wide sense and he is liable. This is straightforward: it is a trite illustration commonly given in our books on Homicide. If one is inclined to carp one may say that it would not necessarily be *dolus* even here. For suppose he thought wrongly that the passer saw what was happening. It could then be no more than negligence. Or suppose in fact that he was right and the passer did see, but took no precautions: there would not then be even any *culpa*. \The same point is made in h.t. 28 – traps are set where they have no business to be. This is *culpa* and if a passer is damaged he has an action unless he is notified or knows of the danger and can provide against it./

[70] H.t. 52.1. A shopkeeper puts a lamp on a stone in the street outside his house. A passer walks off with it, the shopkeeper runs after him, catches him, demands the lamp and holds him to prevent his running away. The man hits at him with a whip *in quo dolor erat*, which seems to mean was of the sort that would hurt badly, in order to make him let go. Then a fight arose in which the shopkeeper knocked out one of the man's eyes. Someone consulted Alfenus – it is an early case – in the republic, whether this was not free from liability as the injured man had first struck him with the whip. Notice that up to that point the shopkeeper had been quite within his rights. The answer was that since the other man had begun the fighting he had no claim unless the shopkeeper wilfully put out his eye. But if he had begun the violence, e.g. by assaulting the man who had the lantern, then he would have been guilty of culpa and so been liable. He would have been quite entitled to hold the man for he was a thief running away with his lantern. I do not know whether it was technically night, but at any rate the thief '*telo se defendit*' and one can't help wondering whether in Alfenus' time this point would not have been raised. There does not seem to be any doubt that it was theft. Note as one result that while a man has a right to commit assault in self-defence, provocation of other kinds is not a justification.

H.t. 52.2. This, as Monro says, is a long but simple case. Two loaded wagons were being drawn by mules up the slope at the side of the Capitoline hill. The front one got tilted over. Just what that means is not quite clear, but I suppose it to be that the load had slipped back a bit so that the rear went down and the shafts went up, so that the mules could get no foothold. The drivers tried to put matters right by holding up the rear. But nevertheless or perhaps because of this the wagon began to go back. The drivers of the rear

~~wagon~~ \then/ got out from between. The wagons collided and the back one was driven on to a slave boy behind and [71] crushed him. His owner asks against whom he can claim. The long response begins with the remark that the law depends on the facts and goes on to consider divers hypotheses consistent with the facts as stated. Let us take them in order.

If the drivers got out of the way unnecessarily, when they could have held up the front wagon and the mules could not hold it, no action lies against the owner of the mules but the Aquilian lies against the men, or, I suppose, noxally against their owner if they are slaves. The reason assigned is that it is much the same to let go a thing you are holding so that it does harm as if you failed to hold a young donkey in your charge or threw something.

If the mules because they were frightened at something drew back and the drivers ran out in terror of being crushed there is no action as to the men, but there is one against the owner of the mules. The text of this part is corrupt.

If neither men nor mules were in any way to blame, not being able to hold up the wagon, there is no action in respect of either of them.

In any case there is no action against the owner of the mules of the rear wagon for they were forced back.

Lawyers of this age received no fee and this opinion is worth it. It is an elementary lecture on the principles of the *lex*. In truth the facts are not so stated as to allow of a valuable opinion. There is something to be said in each hypothesis.

In the first as elsewhere it seems to be assumed that nobody else could possibly be liable. But it looks as if the load was too heavy for the hill and also as if the load had been badly stored, and both these would make somebody liable.

As to the second hypothesis the action must be the *actio de pauperie*. But why should this lie. It depends on how they were frightened. If it was a case of vicious shying then *de pauperie*, but if a third person frightened them he would assuredly [72] be liable (h.t. 9.3; 27.34).

The third hypothesis is badly stated: it makes the point that neither mules nor man could hold it, but the point is whether both could.

Note also that the men are not excused if they ran out when they and the mules together could have held it up, but only if the mules began to go backward. Yet that is rather a fine calculation to require them to make when the thing is slipping back on them. I should have thought that a reasonable fear that they could not hold it would be enough. It is an early case and refinements of this type may be later.

H.t. 57. I lent you a horse. You went out riding with friends. One of them rode his horse against yours. You were thrown and the horse's thighs were broken. The case is simple. There is no action on contract or for *damnum* against you, but if there was carelessness on the part of the man who rode into you there is an Aquilian action against him. It then says that there is no action against the owner of the colliding horse. I should have thought there might be *de pauperie* if the horse had the trick, which some have, of suddenly boring against its neighbour. The only other thing to say is that the case of the man who broke his horse's thighs by falling off is a good companion to that of the man who had his eye knocked out by a blow at the back of his neck.

That ends all I have to say about *iniuria* as an element in the liability.

[73] The next point is that the wrongdoing must be the cause of the *damnum*. The principle is simple and logical. If you intend to do a certain harm and before your act has produced its result some other cause intervenes and either prevents the harm or does it independently, you have not done it and are therefore not liable. This is simply illustrated by h.t. 15.1. A slave is mortally wounded but before he dies of the wound he is lost in a shipwreck or the fall of the house. (We shall deal later with the '*alio ictu*'). You are not liable for killing him but only for wounding, though on the facts this would not usually make much difference. But the fact that he was sold or freed before he died would not make any difference: it is none the less true that you killed him. Julian's language is curious but it brings out a point which we shall have to consider later. If he does actually die of your wound you are regarded as having killed him at the time of the wounding. Julian says that the shipwreck has not allowed it to appear whether you did kill him. This makes it a question of evidence. Nothing but actual death would prove that the wound was mortal. But it seems more rational to say that the drowning killed him and you did not. But there is a point here to which we shall shortly recur. Conversely if you wound a man not mortally, but there is neglect for which you are not responsible so that he dies you have not killed him. This text (h.t. 30.4) can be usefully compared with h.t. 52.pr. There the fact that he dies of the wound and there was no negligence is proof that the wound was mortal – *res ipsa loquitur*. So in h.t. 27.34 though the slave who tied the rope to his thumb was careless, yet the third person who '*turbavit*' the mule caused the damage.

Difficult questions arise where there are two or more woundings by different people. We can start with the proposition that if a man gives two wounds on different occasions he is liable to two actions, though not of course if in a single assault he inflicts more than one wound (h.t. 32.1). And where several people let fall a heavy thing which none of them could have moved alone they are still equally liable under the *lex* (h.t. 11.4). That leads us to a type of [74] case which is not quite the same but is dealt with in the same way. A number of people attack a man and he dies of their assault. In h.t. 51.1 Julian discussing primarily successive attacks lays down rules applicable to this case. All are liable for killing. He says you must either say all are or none is and that whatever may be said logically for this last solution, the contrary rule is established, in the public interest, on the authority of the '*veteres*', the republican jurists, lest wrongful acts go unpunished. He says that it is like the case of several men carrying off a thing none of them individually could have moved. Ulpian in h.t. 11.2 quotes and approves this opinion, adding that if it is clear which wound killed the man, that one is liable for the killing, the others only for wounding. He adds also, what we know from other sources, that what one pays does not release the others as it is a *poena*. Passing to the actual case of successive assaults it must be said that there is much controversy. It is commonly held that there is conflict in the texts, but not all think this and I think the view that there is not is right. The rule of the texts as I understand them is as follows.

If it is clear which killed him that one is liable for killing, the others (we assume only two assaults) are liable only for wounding. But if it is uncertain all are liable for killing. H.t. 11.2 and 51.1.

If A mortally wounds him and B afterwards does something which would certainly kill him and does kill him, B has killed him, not A. This is laid down by a wealth of authorities, Celsus, Marcellus, Julian and Ulpian, h.t. 11.3, 15.1. The second man's killing is as if he had died in an earthquake – that caused his death, not A. h.t. 15.1.

If A's wound was mortal and B's certainly shortened his life, though it is not certain that it would have killed apart from B's both are liable for the killing. Thus the rule saving A applies only where the wound by B would certainly kill. The mere fact that it shortened his life does not protect A, nor of course the fact that it may have done so. If B had cut the victim's finger, that might have shortened his life, but it is no protection to A any more than a spell of cold weather, which might have the same effect.

[75] The alleged conflict is between h.t. 11.3 and 15.1 on one side and h.t. 51.pr on the other. It is enough to say that this view assumes that the words 'he died *ex alio vulnere*' and '*alius postea exanimaverit*' which are those of h.t. 11.3 and show that the second wound was a mortal one in itself mean the same as 'he died *ab alio ictus*' not '*ictu*' which is the language of h.t. 51.pr. They do not mean the same. The second wording means that he died sooner for the second blow, but there is nothing in it to suggest that this would have killed without the other. There is no break of causation. The text has however a peculiarity which has suggested that it is altered. It says '*lege Aquilia teneri*', but that is not the question. Both are liable in any case under one head or the other. The question is whether A or B or both are liable under cap. 1 *de occiso*.

A further question arises under this head of causation. What if there were other causes operating of which you were not aware but without which your act would not have done the harm? There is no systematic discussion of this but it seems that this had in general no effect if there was a wrongful act. If you struck a blow which would have done no harm but for the fact that the victim was in a bad state of health, this is no defence. H.t. 7.5. If you wounded a man already mortally wounded and caused his earlier death you were liable for killing (h.t. 51.pr). That raises the question how far contributory negligence is a defence. It might be inferred from h.t. 31 that it is no defence where the act was done '*dolo*'~~from h.t. 31~~, but it is difficult to reconcile that with the notion of cause, however reasonable it is in itself. In h.t. 52.pr a slave is wounded but dies owing to negligent treatment by the *dominus*. The wounder has not killed. But it is not suggested that the original wounder was merely negligent. It does seem to have been a defence in case of culpa but the texts are not satisfactory. The rule is called by continental writers '*culpa* compensation' which is an inconvenient expression, as it suggests reduction of liability by set off rather than exclusion of it altogether. It has however some justification in the texts, though not in this connexion. We are told that one guilty of *dolus* cannot object to *dolus* in the same transaction. It is compensated (D. 18.1.57.3; D.4.3.36). It is found in connexion with negligence. Thus we are told that where *socii* have both been guilty of negligence [76] '*ipso iure compensatione negligentiae facta*' \(16.2.10.pr)/ but the context makes it clear that this is set off in the ordinary sense: it is no authority for its use in the case where the negligence either has no effect at all or completely excludes liability. As Monro says, the expression is a bad one.

　　We can preface our discussion of the few actual texts by saying that we must not think of contributory negligence as a case in which the act would not have produced its effect but for some extraneous circumstance like the dying of a slave from a slight blow because he was very weak, but rather as analogous to the case of successive mortal wounds by two men and the man dies of the second, that is it is a case in which the act is prevented from being the cause of the harm by reason of an intervening cause. This is in fact somewhat paradoxically expressed in D.50.17.203, cited by Pernice. 'Where a man suffers *damnum* by his own *culpa* he is not regarded as having suffered *damnum*.' In D.13.6.23 we are told that if I lend you a horse to ride to a certain place, and, with no carelessness on your part the journey is too much for the horse, you are not liable: the *culpa* is mine. I ought not to have lent the horse for a job too heavy for him. This is not contributory negligence, for it is said that there is no *culpa* on the part of the borrower. The barber's case, the slave whose throat was cut may also, as the later part of the text (h.t. 11.pr), shows be thought of as a case of contributory negligence. The barber was careless in setting up his chair there. You are negligent in letting him shave you there. The text does not decide the point. Proculus thought it seems that the *culpa* was in the barber: I suppose he would have said that the customer called on the barber's knowledge as to whether it was safe or not. Or you can look at it in another way. He has tacitly agreed to be shaven there, in which case no *culpa* need be thought of on either side. If I agree to let you carry me over a tight rope and without carelessness on your [77] part \I fall/, there is no question of *culpa*. But this creates a fresh difficulty in our case. Would a slave's contract involving serious danger to him bind his master in any way, even *de peculio*? See 17.1.54.pr. We will not pursue this.

　　In h.t. 28.pr traps were set where they ought not to be, and were dangerous to the public. This is *culpa*. But a passer by had due warning and yet walked carelessly into the trap. There was no liability. This is contributory negligence, such as breaks the chain of causation.

In h.t. 30.4 a slave is wounded in a way which would not be fatal. The master neglects the injury and the man dies. This is contributory negligence in a sense, but as the wound was not mortal it was really an independent cause of death. It would be more in point if the wound had been mortal. Of course he is liable for the wounding.

H.t 31 is the familiar case of the man letting branches fall from the tree. We have already said enough about this, but one point may be made. We are told that if it was on private ground where no-one was to be expected the man is liable only for *dolus*. Suppose the woodman saw him coming and deliberately dropped the limb on him, but in fact the passer saw that the limb was just about to fall and nevertheless went on and it fell on him. Is there any liability? I cannot find a good answer.

In h.t. 52.3 some oxen were sold and delivered on approval. During trial a slave of the buyer was gored by one of them. If the sale was complete of course no action: it was his ox who gored his slave. This would not exclude liability under the contract if the vendor knew they were vicious and concealed the fact. \under the ed. edict/ If the purchase was not yet complete, so that they were the vendor's, we are told that there is no liability if it was through the man's negligence but that there was if it was through the vice of the ox. Suppose both were true: the man was careless, the ox was vicious. The plain interpretation of the text is that in that case there would be no liability: it is a case of contributory negligence. Note also that the whole liability assumes that the vendor knew or ought to have known that the beast was vicious.

[78] We pass now to the claim. We need not spend time over the formulation of the action in classical law. It was, the direct action, presumably in ius as it enforced a claim given by the civil law, and there is the fact pointed out by Lenel, that it must have been since otherwise a fiction would not have been necessary to extend it to peregrines as Gaius says there was (G.4.37). Nor shall we discuss the burden of proof which except in one point which will soon arise incidentally has no special peculiarities in this case.

The first point that the action is *duplex contra infitiantem*. Denial creates double liability (h.t. \2.1/ 23.10; \C.3.35.4;/ G.3.218; 4.171 etc.) This character it shares with many other actions and it is a debated question what the origin is. It is not that it is penal, for many penal actions have not this character and some have it which are not regarded as penal e.g. the *actio ex testamento* for a legacy of a *certum per damnationem*, a rule modified by Justinian. The prevalent view, due to Huschke, but modified in detail by later writers, is that it is due to the words *damnas esto* in the Statute. Wherever this occurred in an early statute or other document it gave a right to *manus iniectio* and that when *manus iniectio* disappeared all those cases had a rule of double liability *contra infitiantem*, the liability of the *vindex* in *manus iniectio* having been for double. There is evidence that this last point is true, but there is a good deal of conjecture about the whole thing. See Monro's Appendix 2. The chief difficulty is that we are told that the *lex* expressly provided that it should be *duplex contra infitiantem* (h.t. 2.1). If the remedy was by *manus iniectio* this must have been provided by the *lex* and the other provision would have been unnecessary. But we will not spend time on it.

Two questions are of more direct importance. The first is: what must he admit to avoid double liability, the fact of killing or the liability? Is it for instance possible for him to escape the double liability by saying, 'I killed him, but it [79] was in self-defence?' The answer is no. A rubric in the Collatio says that the confession is *'iniuria occidisse'* (Coll. 12.7) and h.t. 25.2 and 26 tell us that in the *actio confessoria* i.e. not *contra infitiantem*, the *iudex* has no issue in the case to try, but only to settle the damages if these are in dispute. But the second question raises a difficulty. That is the effect of a false confession. In h.t. 23.11 Ulpian quotes Julian as saying that even if the defendant has admitted, it is still open to him to prove that the man had not been killed at all. All that the confession does is to relieve the plaintiff of the need of proving that the defendant was the person liable. But there will be no liability if the man has not been killed at all. Paul in the next text (h.t. 24) says that the need for this rule is made clear if we think of a case of wounding, for how can the amount of damage done by the wound be estimated if there is no wound? And in h.t. 25.pr Ulpian says that if in fact the slave is dead but was not occisus by any one, the confession is not binding. But our texts show that the burden of proving that the man is not *'occisus'* is shifted to the defendant. \It seems that his attempt to do this is not *infitiatio*./ What is the principle of all this? Our title helps us no further, but there are other texts dealing with the matter. In D.11.1.14.1 it is said that confessions are valid only if what is confessed is possible in nature and law. In 11.1.13.pr it is said that the confession is of no account if there was in fact no liability at all in anyone. In D.42.2.4 it is said that a confession that you killed is binding if the man was in fact killed by someone. It all therefore turns on a curious notion of possibility. But this kind of impossibility is really a confusion. It is in a sense impossible that I could have killed him if he has not been killed, but it is equally impossible if he was killed by someone else, and yet I might not prove this. It is not really impossible at all, for though he has not been killed he [80] might have been. Monro's discussion in App.III puts this very clearly. The practical rule emerging is as he says that by *confessio* I could take over a liability, but could not create one which did not exist. It ought to follow that if he had been killed by someone but in circumstances not creating liability this is a defence after confession, for there is no liability. The wrong is *'iniuria occidisse'* and he is not *'iniuria occisus'*. But there is no authority.

In h.t. 25.1 we learn that a procurator, a tutor, a curator or *'quivis alius'* can confess on behalf of another and that an *actio utilis confessoria* will lie against him. There is something wrong in the text. Either *'aut'* before *absentem* must come out or *'aut pupillum aut adultum'* must be added to make sense. The latter seems the most probable though Grueber prefers the former on the ground that this gives only three persons while four cases are mentioned. But *'absentem'* serves for both *'procurator'* and *'quivis alius'* who is a *procurator voluntarius*. *'Eos'* means the procurator etc. The action is *utilis* as it is not against the actual person liable. It is a Rutilian formula with procurator's name in the *condemnatio*. *Actio iudicati* would be against the principal, except in the case of the *'quivis alius'*: here it would not be unless his act was authorised or ratified.

Does this double liability on denial arise in the *actio utilis* and *in factum?* The title shows no difference and the matter seems to be settled by C.3.55.5 where the action is *in duplum contra infitiantem* where cattle are shut up and starve, which is sometimes said to give the *utilis* (G.3.219) and sometimes *in factum* (h.t. 9.2). And whatever may have been the earlier classical law there was no substantial difference in effect.

We now pass on to the estimation of damages under cap. I. The rule is that the plaintiff can claim the highest value the thing has had within the previous year (h.t. 2.pr) i.e. 365 days (h.t. 51.2) where the injury and the death are not simultaneous the killing is held to have been done at the time of the act. This is the Sabinian view expressed by Julian and accepted, though the Proculian Celsus had held otherwise (h.t. 21.1). At the time of the *lex* the *'quanti in eo anno plurimi fuit'* was just what we should call the market value of the thing in itself, \[at foot of page, without insertion marker] More useful matter in Von Tuhr Baseler Fschr für Jhering[10]/ [81] as the Institutes tell us (4.3.10) the jurists extended this by interpretation and included in the value for the purposes of the *lex 'non solum perempti corporis aestimationem, sed eo amplius quidquid preterea perempto eo corpore damni vobis allatum fuerit'*. This is expressed in h.t. 21.2 in other words *'quanti interfuit non esse occisum et hoc iure utimur ut eius quod interest fiat aestimatio'*. It is worth noting that this is not quite the same thing. The words in the Institutes contemplate additions to the value and additions only: the other form expressing the *'interesse'* rule might take into account circumstances which made your interest in the man less than his corporal value. How far it did so: how far the later compensation aspect of the action easily produced this effect we shall consider later. We can complete our summary of the general principle by saying that these extraneous considerations are commonly classed under the heads which are very familiar, *lucrum cessans* and *damnum emergens*, of which it is as well to say that though they are convenient catchwords they have no Roman authority. Not much illustration is given or is needed of the 'value' in the limited sense without these accretions. In h.t. 33.pr we are warned that we have to

---

[10] Andreas von Tuhr, 'Zu Schätzung des Schadens in der *Lex Aquilia*', in *Festschrift der Juristischen Facultät Basel zum 50jährigen Doktorjubiläum von Rud v Jhering* (Reinhardt 1892).

consider commercial value not '*pretium affectionis*'. Thus if you have a slave
who is your own illegitimate son and he is killed you can recover what such
a slave would raise in the open market, not what you yourself, his father,
would have been prepared to give for him if he had belonged to someone
else. You are none the richer, says Pedius, because you have a son whom
you would buy for a lot if another had him. More important is the point
also made that if your son is my slave and he is killed I cannot recover what
I could sell him for to you, but only what he is worth in the open market. I
am not sure that that is very logical for if I did sell him to the father I should
be so much the richer. But the rule is clear. ~~In h.t. 55 we have a rather puzzling text. I have promised to A either~~ \There are several texts dealing with
the valuation '*retrorsum*' within the previous year./ [82] H.t. 23.3 is a simple
illustration. A slave of mine is killed; he was or had been valuable as an
artist. Within the previous year he had lost a thumb. I can recover what he
was worth before the accident, since '*artes cum pollice amisisset.*' H.t.23.5: a
slave who had been a faithful servant fell into bad ways. Within a year after
he had gone to the bad he was killed. I can recover what he was worth before
his '*mutatio morum*', and the next text (23.6) sums it up by saying that '*omnia
commoda*' which had made him more valuable within the previous year come
in. So in G.3.214, Inst 4.3.9, we learn that if a slave who is now *clodus* or
luscus or *mancus* (lame or one-eyed or in any way maimed) is killed within a
year of the arising of the defect I can recover as for a sound man.

As we have seen, *damnum emergens* comes in. There are many types of this.
The simplest is expenses to which we have been put: '*damnum consequimur at
amisisse dicemur quod aut consequi potuimus aut erogare cogimur*' (h.t. 33.pr in f).
In h.t. 7.pr and again in h.t.27.17 we are told that one can recover expenses
incurred in curing the wound, and I suppose the same would be equally
true if expense was reasonably incurred in trying to cure him but he died
nevertheless. I am not sure that this is expressly said anywhere, but it follows
from the fact that the master is bound not to neglect treatment, otherwise
he will lose his claim for the killing. There are many forms of this so-called
damnum emergens, most of them familiar. Where I was bound to hand over a
slave under a penalty (and I am not released by the death) the amount of the
penalty comes in (h.t. 22.pr). If one of a troupe of actors or musicians or of
a team of horses, a *quadriga*, or one of a pair of mules, is killed I recover not
merely the value of him as one thing, but the lessening of value of the others
as being no longer a complete team (h.t. 22.1; Inst 4.3.10; G.3.212). The text
gives as an illustration one of a pair of twins. I suppose this means what
are called identical twins, so that they make a well matched pair of running
footmen.

In h.t. 23.4 a slave who had committed many frauds on his master was
killed as [83] he was about to be tortured to make him disclose his accomplices. Labeo held that the damages will include my interest in finding
out the frauds committed by him (and, as Monro says, his friends), not

merely what he himself made away with. It seems to be implied that if I find out the facts by torture I shall be able to recover the money and not otherwise. But there is the difficulty which we shall get in other connexions, that unless I know the amount from other sources the damages cannot be assessed, and if I do the torture would not be necessary. This difficulty is never handled clearly. In h.t. 27.17 we have the rule already mentioned that medical expenses can be recovered, but the case is worth mentioning again, since this text also occurs in the Collatio and lays down there the rule that medical expenses cannot be recovered if in the long run the slave is none the worse, but we have already considered this. In 37.1 h.t. there is another form of *damnum emergens*. A beast has committed *pauperies* and an action on it has reached *litis contestatio*. The beast is killed by a third party. Death of the animal after *litis contestatio* does not release me as death before would, so that I shall have to pay the full damages since I cannot surrender. I can therefore recover what it was worth to me to surrender him rather than pay the damages. In h.t. 47 we have the case of a slave who is wounded and an Aquilian action is brought and then he dies. This gives me another action, for the things come under distinct chapters. But if I bring it there will be an *exceptio doli* the next text says, \limiting the claim/ to what is enough to make up what I should have recovered if I had sued for the killing in the first instance. H.t. 55 gives a complex illustration. I owe B *ex stipulatu* Stichus who is worth 10 or Pamphilus who is worth 20. So that the choice being with me, I can free myself at a cost of 10. Before there is any *mora*, the promisee kills Stichus. What can I recover? The answer is that as he killed the cheaper it is the same as if a stranger had done it. What then have I to claim? What have I lost? If there had been no killing I [84] would have handed over S and have retained P, worth 20. As it is S is dead and he I must hand over P, keeping nothing. ~~He has~~ \I have/ lost 20 and this can be claimed. Suppose P died after S was killed, still before *mora*. As things stand ~~he loses~~ \I lose/ nothing by the killing, but ~~he is~~ \I am/ entitled to recover what ~~he~~ \I/ stood to lose at the time of the killing, and if P had died before S was killed, within a year the *annus retrorsus* still entitles ~~him~~ \me/ to recover the 20. The case of killing after *mora* we shall consider shortly (h.t. 54).

We will now consider the cases of '*lucrum cessans*' so called. The most familiar are two. If a slave has been instituted *heres* but he is killed before he has accepted at his master's order, the value of the *hereditas* can be recovered (h.t. 23.pr; 51.pr; Inst 4.3.10; G.3.212). We have already considered the difficulties which arise where he is killed after being instituted with liberty by his own master \h.t. 23.1/. Again, if a man is made *heres* on the condition that he frees Stichus and Stichus is killed before this is done, he cannot now satisfy the condition and can therefore recover the value of the *hereditas* (h.t. 23.2). Note however that this will be without the value of the slave, since to get the *hereditas* he must lose the slave. It has therefore been suggested that the '*etiam*' of the text is meaningless. But that is not so since the slave may well have been worth more within a year before and there may have been other accessory advantages. All these he will still get under the value of the slave; all that he loses by freeing him is his present value. And a case might be conceived under which he would not lose the *hereditas* and therefore could not claim its value. This would be so if the slave were killed purposely by someone having an interest, in order that the condition should not be satisfied, for then the condition would be regarded as satisfied. Note further that *damnum emergens* and *lucrum cessans* must be ascertained and reasonably certain. A mere expectation of a *hereditas* is not enough. We have seen texts which seem to imply that the *hereditas* of a living person [85] was a *lucrum* for this purpose (h.t. 41). But we must assume in the case that the testator is dead, and in h.t. 23.2 it is clearly said that the testator must be dead.

Since the year is reckoned back from the wounding, that being regarded as the date of the killing, if a man is killed by two wounds by different people at different times, his value may not be the same for both; the year will go further back for the first wounder and value may have changed in the intervening days (h.t. 51.2). But suppose the wounds inflicted by the same man at different times, which date is taken? If it cannot be said which was the fatal blow, I do not know the answer. I should think the first, since the killing began then. But there is another point. Since the killing is dated from the wounding, if, after he was wounded but before he died, a testator died who had instituted him *heres*, I suppose this would not come in as the year is backward not forward. How if there were two wounds and it occurred between the two? It is possible to say that he was being killed all the time and the year would be a year plus the days between the two woundings. The texts give, so far as I know, no solution.

We must now consider cap. III from this point of view. We have already noted that the period is only 30 days and that till Sabinus since the word '*plurimi*' was not in the *lex* there were lawyers who held that the *iudex* might take any value he pleased that the thing had within the thirty days. There is not so much room in this case for *lucrum cessans*, since a wounded slave can enter on a *hereditas* or be manumitted. Before discussing the illustrative cases, there is one important point to be taken. The lex says that the defendant must pay the highest value within the previous thirty days '*quanti ea res erit, plurimi*' (h.t 27.5) '*erit*' should be '*fuit*' as it is in another text (h.t. 29.8). That suggests the impossible rule that however small the harm the whole must be paid, with the effect that one who had done any harm would be likely to destroy the res altogether: it would cost him no more. It is sometimes said [86] that he could take the thing but there is no evidence whatever for this \in this action, though there is something like it in *servi corrupti* 11.3.14.9/. In fact, though it is nowhere expressly laid down, there is little doubt that what he paid was the difference between its highest value within the previous 30 days and the value after the damage, the word '*res*' in the phrase '*quanti ea res erit*' meaning not the physical thing damaged but the *interesse*. Indeed h.t. 24 seems conclusive, for it is clear that the damages are based on the harm done by the wound not on the value of the man. H.t. 7.pr suggests the same thing but it is not so conclusive, since the freeman is not a *res* and could not be valued. It does not seem to me that h.t. 27.17, cited by Monro (p.38) proves anything, but it raises a curious question. If the slave was quite worthless but I did spend money on curing him, can I recover this? The logical answer, I suppose, is: No: it was not an expenditure called for on economic grounds at all.

In h.t. 29.3, the case of careless damage to my fishing nets, we are told that I can recover the value of my nets which are presumably destroyed, but not the value of the fish which I might have caught if I had had the nets, as *non constat* that I should have caught any. The reason does not seem to be very good, for it is easy to imagine cases in which it was quite obvious that I should. The same result however can be reached in another way. This loss of fish is no part of the value of the net: it is *lucrum cessans* and hypothetical *lucrum cessans* however probable was never allowed. It must be some specific and ascertained loss. Thus where my slave was killed it would be of no use for me to prove that an *extraneus* who has since died was going to make him *heres* if he had not been killed.

One group of texts raises difficulty as to the estimation of damages, where documents are tampered with. In h.t. 41.pr the case is put of a will the provisions of which have been wrongfully erased. Marcellus ~~doubts whether~~ \ denies that/ there is any action, for how can the damage be estimated. Ulpian comments that that is very [87] true of the testator, but not in the case of legatee or *heres*, for the will is the evidence of their right, so that they will have the action. ~~It should be direct though the end of this passage speaks of actio in factum. It is likely however that this is, as Grueber says, corrupt, and that it was really furti as in D.47.2.27.3.~~ The same doctrine, that for alteration or cancelling of documents there is an Aquilian action, is also laid down in h.t. 40 to which we shall recur, in h.t. 41.1 and 42 and 47.2.27.3 and 47.2.32.1. But in all these cases there is a difficulty. If there are other evidences of your right you suffer no *damnum*. If there is no other evidence you suffer no *damnum*. This is fully discussed in D.47.2.32.1. The answer given is not very satisfactory. You sue on the contract and lose for lack of evidence. Then further evidence turns up, but you cannot sue again on the pact. This loss you can prove by your new *actio* when you sue *ex Aquilia*. This is Paul. It compels you to bring the action on the contract first, and it makes your claim depend on further evidence turning up, which our text does not suggest. In h.t. 40 there is a rather more complex case. There is a *chirographum* of a conditional debt and there are other witnesses. But these witnesses may not be on hand when the condition is satisfied. The text says I can sue at once and shall get judgment, but it will not be put in force unless the condition happens. Here there are two difficulties. This is a conditional judgment, and judgment could not be conditional (49.4.1.5). Further it ought to require that the witnesses were not available when the condition happens, otherwise you suffer no *damnum* since you can still prove your debt. This has led to the suggestion that the solution is a hasty interpolation which I think is very probable. There is a further difficulty. In *chirographa* the plaintiff no doubt will be the owner. So too the testator so long as he lives is owner of the will, but on his death it is part of the *hereditas* and will not belong to the *heres* till he has [88] entered, and never to a legatee at all. And in D.4.3.35 it is said that where a will is so tampered with the heres has only an *actio doli* till he has entered, and it gives the legatees an *actio doli* also, which means, as Grueber says, that they have no other. As the author is Ulpian, who is also the author of our 41, there is a difficulty. Grueber thinks that our text gives the *heres* the action only after *aditio* (p.149) and, as Monro says, the fact that he is called '*heres*' and not '*heres scriptus*' suggests the same thing. But if he has entered, what *damnum* has he suffered? None except in the case where he was also *heres ab intestato* and has so entered but gets a less share than he would under the will. As to the legatee, his action could not be direct. Perhaps this is why at the end of 41.pr we are told the action is *in factum*, which it would not be for a *heres* who has entered. Grueber however suggests that '*in factum*' is corrupt and should be '*furti*' as it is in 47.2.27.3, for deletion of a will was *furtum* if it was done *lucrifaciendi gratia*. But it is all very obscure. We must not forget that under Justinian it mattered nothing what you called it.

We have several times mentioned, and it is discussed in all the books, the tendency to a gradual replacement of the crude 'value' of the *lex* by the *interesse* of the plaintiff. We have seen how this has been used to explain the introduction, which must have been very early, of *lucrum cessans* and *damnum emergens*, and it has an obvious bearing on the right of a non-owner to claim. It is an interesting question how far this worked the other way, how far, that is, the action was excluded or restricted on the ground that the owner had no real interest or an interest less than the value. Some apparent examples of this are not real examples. Thus one of common owners could recover only in proportion to his share, and though if he sues noxally he can get surrender of the whole if his share is not paid this is because surrender is not divisible (h.t. 27.2) and it does no injustice to the owner of the wrong-doer, since he is quit of any further liability. See too h.t. 19, 20 ante. [89] So too the usufructuary has the action, *utilis*, to the extent of the usufruct (h.t. 11.10 and 12) and no doubt as we have already said the unit of value in an action by the owner is the value of the *nuda proprietas*. In the case of pledgee, already discussed, a long winded text (h.t. 30.1) reaches the conclusion, not quite consistent with what is said earlier in it, that the pledgee has the action if, and only if, the personal action on the debt is time barred or the debtor is insolvent, that his claim is limited to the amount of the debt, and that if he has the action the owner's unit is the excess value over the debt. This is probably due to Justinian: we do not know the classical law.

But these are all cases where there is a rival claim to the action. The real question is: how far did this '*interesse*' principle bar the owner if in fact he did not stand to lose anything, but no one also had the action. A slave has been sold and the price paid, but he is wrongfully killed before delivery. Has the vendor the Aquilian action as he loses nothing, the risk not being on him? A man has received a legacy under a *fideicommissum* to free a slave. The slave is wrongfully killed. Has he the action: the risk is not on him. Or the *fideicommissum* was to hand him over to someone. He is released by the death here too. I think in general he has the action, but not always for his own benefit, but the texts are not quite consistent. Let us look at them. In some cases the rule is clear that the *dominus* has the action though his *interesse* is hard to see. The vendor has it for he is bound to transfer it to the vendee as part of the *commoda rei* (D.19.1.13.12). He could not transfer it unless he had it. The buyer about to redhibit has it, with the same obligation to transfer it (h.t. 11.7). He has no real *interesse*, since if the slave is dead without his fault he is released. The *heres* has it if a *servus legatus* is killed or harmed before entry. If it is mere harm he must transfer it to the legatee as before (h.t. 15.pr). If it was killing he keeps it on the technical ground that as the death occurred [90] before the legacy vested the legacy was void. If it was only wounding he must transfer it as before. All these are clear and on the face of them disregard the '*interesse*' point. But they are all cases in which it may be said that the action is allowed only to provide a remedy for the person actually concerned, who, for technical reasons, has not the action himself. But this seems the wrong way to put it. On principle, '*interesse*' is immaterial: the words of the *lex* are clear. But there are cases in which on equitable grounds the praetor or some other authority will refuse the action. The foregoing cases clearly do not call for his intervention in this way.

Some difficulty however is created by a group of texts which have to do with promises to do something. It is clear that a promissor is released from liability if the thing promised ceases to exist without his fault or *mora*. In D.4.3.18.5 the thing has been destroyed by a third party. Justice requires attention to the interests of the injured promisee and that the wrongdoer shall not go unpenalised. We should therefore expect the same solution as before: the promissor has the action but must transfer it. But that is not what we get. The text says that '*plerique putant*' (which shows that the point had been discussed) that the promisee has an *actio doli* against a wrongdoer and therefore the promissor has no Aquilian action. This applies the '*interesse*' rule but not the *interesse* principle, for the '*ideoque*' shows that the action is refused not for lack of *interesse* but to avoid a double liability. It is really an unfair decision, too favourable to the wrongdoer, for by the *actio doli* he will recover only exact compensation for his loss, whereas the liability under the *lex Aquilia* might be very much greater in view of the *annus retrorsus* and the *lucrum cessans* and *damnum emergens*. It will be observed that it is clearly a praetorian intervention. It is not said that the action does not lie, but that '*actio tibi denegabitur*', the regular phrase for such intervention. [91] In h.t. 54 the first case is of a thing promised destroyed by the promisee before delivery and before any *mora*. The promissor has the Aquilian, though he is clearly released from his promise and has no more *interesse* than in the case just discussed. The text then considers the case supposing the killing had occurred after *mora*, when as a result of *mora* the risks were on the promissor so that if it had been done by a third party he would still have had to satisfy his obligation and the '*interesse*' would be obvious. But where the promisee did it, of course, the promissor is released, but that as the promisee has done about the only thing which would release the promissor we are told that he has done the wrong rather to himself than to the promissor and therefore the promissor has not the Aquilian. Here too the language is noticeable. It is said '*non recte experietur*'. This language again suggests not the application of a principle but refusal of the action which would prima facie lie on account of the special facts of the case. The *interesse* principle is directly applied. It does not do justice. It is favourable to the wrongdoer for he loses only the present value of the man, while under the Aquilian it might have been a great deal more in view of *annus retrorsus, lucrum cessans* and *damnum emergens*. But the small number of texts in which this '*interesse*' principle is applied leave us much in the dark. I should sum up the matter by saying that too much weight has been attached to the use of the word '*interesse*' in h.t. 21.2, where the real point is additions on account of interesse not deduction. Altogether the '*interesse*' principle cannot be regarded as having been thought out or consistently applied, nor, as it seems to me, is its operation reasonable where it is applied.

[92] Concurrence of the Aquilian with other actions

i With contractual or quasicontractual actions. These are illustrated in our texts for *locatio* (h.t. 5.3, 7.8, 37.11, 27.34, where it is called *ex locato* in one place and *ex conducto* in another); and *pignus* (h.t. 18). Other titles give other examples. *Societas* (17.2.\47-/50), divisory actions (10.2.16.5; 10.3.8.2 and 10) and other actions which though in rem deal to some extent with obligations, e.g. *rei vindicatio* (6.1.13,14) and *hereditatis petitio* (5.3.36.2) and others. We have already considered these cases. As they were not *eadem res* one did not formally bar the other but a plaintiff could be compelled either by *exceptio doli* or action of the *iudex* in the first action to renounce the other. If he brought the contractual action first there are many texts which entitle him still to sue for any excess he might have recovered had he brought the Aquilian. And this seems to be the law for Justinian's time. As to concurrence of the Aquilian and *condictio furtiva* there are difficulties too great for us to tackle: D.7.1.23.

With delictal actions. The wrong may be combined with other delicts. If I commit two delicts in relation to the same thing, I am liable for both and judgment or satisfaction by one does not relieve me from the other liability. (47.1.1.pr). If I steal your slave and afterwards kill him I am liable both for *furtum* and for *damnum*. If after stealing him I flog him before killing I shall be liable also for *iniuria* (47.1.2). So if a slave freed by the will damages property before the *heres* enters and also after he is free by the entry he is liable to be sued for double damages by the *actio in factum* of D.47.4 for what he did before freedom and the Aquilian for what he did afterwards (h.t. 48). It is somewhat puzzling to find in D.47.2.28 that if one steals a document and later erases it '*nihil ad poenam adicit*'. Probably he is not speaking of the Aquilian. It is thought of as a second theft. While every fresh *contrectatio* is a fresh theft there is no action for each such handling.

There is more difficulty when we come to the common case in which the same [93] act is two delicts. The problems raised are too difficult for us to study in detail and a few words must suffice. It is clear from h.t. 5.1 and 2; 27.pr and 41.1 that the same act might give rise to the Aquilian and the *actio iniuriarum* or to the Aquilian and the *actio furti*. It is another question how far they were absolutely cumulative. It is to be noted that the *actio furti* is purely for a penalty, while the Aquilian includes compensation. And, while the Aquilian and the *actio iniuriarum* both include compensation, it is compensation for different things, the Aquilian being in respect of material loss and the *actio iniuriarum* in respect of wounded feelings (D.9.2.5.1; D.47.10 15.46). Thus the two cases of concurrence would not necessarily be treated in the same way. \I have the value of *iniuria*./ As h.t. 5.1 shows the one action was no formal bar to the other in the accepted doctrine. But there is a text which has been altered (D.44.7.34.pr) which shows that there were jurists who held that there was a formal bar and others who held that there was no formal bar, but that if the Aquilian had been brought the *iudex* would absolve in the *actio iniuriarum* on the ground that it was not *bonum et aequum* to condemn when he had already been condemned to the value of the thing, the point being that '*ex bono et aequo*' occurred in the formula for *iniuria*. They held also that if *iniuriarum* had been brought the Aquilian still lay but the *iudex* would limit the *condemnatio* to any excess. How much of this is classical it is impossible to say, but that is Justinian's law. The text contains some confusions which I have not mentioned, e.g. making the point depend on actual payment instead of *condemnatio*. Whether there were any jurists who held that they were absolutely cumulative is disputed. I think there were, but we cannot go into this.

Where the Aquilian concurs with the *actio furti* we have different considerations. Often of course the one or the other lies according to intent and [94] circumstances (h.t. 27.21; 27.26), but here there is no question of concurrence. But where both might lie there is no text anywhere, so far as I have seen, which says that the bringing of either action had any effect on the other (h.t. 41.1; D.47.2.27.3). They seem to be absolutely cumulative. This is reasonable, for the compensation element is really the most important factor in the Aquilian and is completely absent from the *actio furti*. But it is fair to say that there are great differences of opinion on these points.

Other remedies are mentioned in the title which might arise out of the

same facts. The '*damnum infectum*' of h.t. 27.10 is not a case in point, for
that proceeding lies when and only when the damage is threatened and has
not yet happened (D.39.2.2) so that there can be no Aquilian action. In h.t
27.14 where crops are damaged by sowing tares among them, we are told
that besides the *actio in factum* of *dominus* or *colonus* which we have already
considered, either can bring the interdict '*quod vi aut clam*'. Its scope is very
different. It applies only to injuries in connexion with land (D.43.24.1.4). It
is one of the interdicts open to anyone with any sort of *interesse*, e.g. a *colonus*
with only a *ius in personam* (D.9.2.27.14; 43.24.11.14 and 12). It is only for
the actual damage (D.43.24.15.12) and thus if compensation has been got in
any other way the interdict does not lie (D ib and 9.2.27.14). But it and the
Aquilian do not formally bar each other as our text shows it is a judicial bar:
judgment will not be given unless security is given against taking the other
proceeding. In later law, though perhaps not in classical law, if the interdict
was brought first the Aquilian still lay for any excess (D.47.7.11).

Another competing action was the special action for cutting down trees.
There were in fact two of these actions, one under the XII Tables, *de arboribus succisis*, [95] and one under the Edict, *arborum furtim caesarum*, which is
that mentioned in h.t. 27.26. They were both in operation in classical and
later law. The former was of no importance since the penalty was 25 asses,
which is why the praetor, as in *iniuria*, introduced a more practical action for
damages. It was not repealed by the *lex Aquilia*. The praetorian action is of
course later than the *l. Aquilia*. The fields of the two actions were not quite
the same: there was nothing about '*furtim*' in the case under the XII Tables.
The field of the praetorian action and that of the Aquilian were not quite the
same, e.g. if the trees were ripe for cutting there was no *damnum* \h.t. 27.26/.
But if they were immature the two overlapped. Here too the same rule was
laid down. There was no formal bar, but only excess could be recovered
in the second action, which would not necessarily be the Aquilian since
arborum furtim caesarum was always for double damages (D.47.7.7.7). How
the damages were assessed where there was no stealing and they were ripe for
cutting I do not know. The action under the XII and the praetorian action
are muddled in the Digest.

We have already considered the *actio in factum* against one *bona fide serviens*. There is no formal bar but no double recovery.

There might also be *servi corrupti*, but we have little information. Their
fields are not quite the same as for *servi corrupti* the damage need not be
physical; it was only for *dolus* and always *in duplum*. There was no formal
bar (11.3.3.1 and 4; 48.5.6.pr). The classical rule was probably that where
the harm was physical and done *dolo* there would be *absolutio* in the second
action, except perhaps as to any excess, but that *servi corrupti* would not bar
the Aquilian if it proved to be only *culpa*, or vice versa if it proved not to be
physical. An interpolated phrase at the end of D.48.5.6 makes them absolutely cumulative, but this is unlike the rule in other cases.

Chapter 3

'This Concern with Pattern':
F H Lawson's Negligence in the Civil Law

Paul Mitchell

I. INTRODUCTION

When Frederick Henry Lawson's *Negligence in the Civil Law* first appeared in 1950, English-speaking reviewers were quick to register that this was an important moment. Lawson had become the first Professor of Comparative Law at the University of Oxford only two years earlier, and Owen Hood Phillips, writing in the *Modern Law Review*, evidently felt that a celebration was in order. '[W]e congratulate Professor Lawson', he wrote, 'on putting this admirable tool at the disposal of teachers and students, the University of Oxford on providing him with an appropriate chair, and the Clarendon Press on furnishing an excellent production at reasonable cost'.[1] Other reviewers, while less effusive, were overwhelmingly positive in their assessments.[2]

In praising the work for its value to teachers and students, Hood Phillips was echoing Lawson's own description, in the opening sentence of the Preface, as a

> book ... compiled with the same intention as Professor de Zulueta's *Roman Law of Sale*, namely that of introducing the student, through the detailed study of the Roman law on a particular topic, 'to a general familiarity with the basic concep-tions of most continental systems, such as an educated English lawyer ought to possess'.[3]

Lawson had set about this task by providing the complete text and transla-tion of D.9.2 *ad legem Aquiliam*; texts and translations of other Roman legal texts; extensive extracts from a range of 'foreign codes' (stretching chrono-logically from 1794 to 1945, and geographically from the Soviet Union as far west as Mexico); and, finally, some Canadian statutory materials together with an article on the Saskatchewan Automobile Accident Insurance Acts. To guide students through this extraordinary range of materials, he had

---

[1] Owen Hood Phillips (1952) 15 MLR 255.
[2] Wolfgang Friedmann (1951) 9 U of Toronto LJ 142; Arthur von Mehren (1952) 66 Harvard LR 190; Ben Wortley (1951) 33 J Comp Legis & Int Law 111; Hessel Yntema (1952) 1 AJCL 294. For a notably less enthusiastic appraisal see Reginald Dias (1952) 11 CLJ 306.
[3] Frederick Henry Lawson, *Negligence in the Civil Law* (Clarendon 1950) v.

written a lengthy introduction (of nearly eighty pages), which combined systematic and historical analysis. It was, without doubt, a highly accomplished scholarly performance. But it was also, for reasons which I will now go on to explore, a peculiarly ambiguous and even enigmatic book, which was expressive of Lawson's own conflicted instincts about the importance of Roman law both generally and in his own professional identity, as well as being profoundly shaped by the historical conditions in which it was written. My aim is not to debunk, or to diminish Lawson's achievement; rather, it is to show how that achievement is more complex, and harder won, than we might previously have thought.

II.

A closer look at the reviews of *Negligence in the Civil Law* begins to alert us to the fact that the book is a more complicated work than it might first appear. For, while its reception was overwhelmingly positive, reviewers' characterisations of it were strikingly disparate. For Henri Lévy-Bruhl, both this and Zulueta's book on sale were 'essentiellement des livres de droit romain (c'est ainsi qu'il faut traduire «civil law»)'; the non-Roman materials, he explained, were included solely to allow a precise measurement of Roman law's influence on modern law to be undertaken.[4] Reginald W M Dias, similarly, assumed that Roman law was the central focus, and took Lawson to task for including too much else.[5] Wolfgang Friedmann and Ben Wortley, by contrast, praised the book as an exercise in comparative method (although Wortley particularly admired Lawson's treatment of strict liability, which Friedmann singled out for criticism).[6] Owen Hood Phillips was also impressed by the work as a piece of comparative scholarship, but, as he explained, comparison should be undertaken 'with one eye on law reform', a position which neither Friedmann nor Wortley expressly endorsed in their reviews.[7] Perhaps the most perceptive of the English language reviewers was Hessel Yntema, writing in the *American Journal of Comparative Law*. Yntema detected that the book was formally experimental: it could, in part, be seen as an updated edition of the *lex Aquilia*, 'but it is considerably more'.[8] 'The additional materials', Yntema continued, 'have effectively shifted the center of gravity of the volume from the Roman to the comparative law of negligence'.[9] The result was 'a work ... of equal interest as a model text for

---

[4]   Henri Lévy-Bruhl, *L'Année sociologique* (1940/1948–), Troisième série, T 4, 338.
[5]   Reginald Dias (1952) 11 CLJ 306, 306–07.
[6]   Wolfgang Friedmann (1951) 9 U of Toronto LJ 142; Ben Wortley (1951) 33 J Comp Legis & Int Law 111.
[7]   Hood Phillips (n 1) 255.
[8]   Hessel Yntema (1952) 1 AJCL 294.
[9]   ibid 294–95.

the student, a scholarly contribution of Roman law, and an illuminating synthesis of the corresponding modern laws'.[10]

The sense that Lawson was trying to do two things at once was at the heart of rather sterner assessments by Max Kaser and Wolfgang Kunkel. Kaser characterised Lawson's introduction by inventing the compound adjective 'historisch-dogmatische'.[11] It was not a happy hyphen: in Kaser's view, Lawson had chosen to create an internal methodological conflict, and had not convincingly resolved it. Kunkel, writing in the *Zeitschrift für ausländisches und internationales Privatrecht*, was, if anything, more unforgiving. He was particularly troubled by Lawson's habit of treating contemporary material alongside the *lex Aquilia*, commenting that: 'Manchmal ist der abrupte Übergang von der historischen Darstellung des römischen Rechts zu modernen rechtsvergleichenden Problemen etwas verblüffend. [Sometimes the abrupt transition from the historical presentation of Roman law to modern comparative law problems is rather confusing.]'[12] More damagingly:[13]

> Überhaupt entspricht der Aufbau der Einleitung vielfach nicht den Anforderungen, die wir an die Systematik einer solchen Darstellung zu stellen gewohnt sind. Dies macht das Studium des Buches für den deutschen Leser nicht gerade bequem, erklärt sich aber, wie mir scheint, z.T. aus der ganz anderen Denkweise des englischen Juristen ...
> [Above all, the structure of the introduction often fails to meet the standards which we, in the system of such an exposition, are accustomed to. This makes the study of the book not exactly comfortable for a German reader, but, it should be said, it seems to me, that it sometimes casts light on the quite different ways of thinking of the English jurist ...]

Here, then, in a rather unexpected quarter, was an acknowledgement of the distinctive English contribution to *lex Aquilia* scholarship, with a helpful tip for how to recognise it: it was distinctly below German standards.

III.

Kaser and Kunkel's critiques of Lawson's introductory essay offer a starting point for closer analysis. What, exactly, had confused and discomforted these eminent scholars of Roman law in a student book on the *lex Aquilia*? Kaser complained about the abruptness of the transition between ancient Roman and modern materials. But that, if anything, tended to simplify

---

[10] ibid 295.
[11] Max Kaser (1953) 70 ZSS (RA) 481.
[12] Wolfgang Kunkel, 'Zeitschrift für ausländisches und internationales Privatrecht' 17 Jahrg H1 (1952) 139, 141.
[13] ibid 141.

the issue. Consider the following passage, in which Lawson addresses the meaning of '*iniuria*' under the *lex Aquilia*:[14]

> We know that as late as the classical period and, so far as appearances go, in the time of Justinian an action could be brought on the lex itself only if the death or injury resulted from direct contact between the body of the wrongdoer and the thing (*corpore corpori*). Translated into the language of English law this means that the lex penalized only trespasses. Now we know that originally all trespasses were prima facie wrongful, and that it was only at a comparatively late date that the question was squarely raised whether a voluntary act giving rise to damage which was neither intended nor reasonably foreseeable could be a trespass. So rare were the cases that the point was finally settled as late as the second half of the nineteenth century in England, though earlier in America, that no action for trespass to the person will lie unless the act was wilful or negligent; but the medieval rule was one of strict liability, and down to the end of the eighteenth century the defendant could escape only if he pleaded and proved inevitable accident. Indeed, before the advent of firearms and swiftly moving vehicles most trespasses would naturally be wilful, and the most obvious defences would be that the defendant had acted in self-defence or was otherwise justified in what he did; and we may perhaps infer that originally the qualification of liability introduced by the word *iniuria* meant strictly that the defendant must not have acted *iure*, i.e. in pursuance of some right.

What is distracting here is not so much the abruptness of a transition between ancient and modern as the movement forwards and then back across different time periods. We move from Justinian to medieval England, cursorily note the development of the forms of action, then glance at later technological changes and their potential effect on legal rules, before circling back to *iniuria* again. The effect feels rather like a five-minute tour of the British Museum with an excited guide: we might catch a glimpse of items that it is worth going back to look at later, but the overall experience is bewildering. The final step, in particular, is troubling. Lawson's suggestion that '*iniuria*' carried a sense of 'without right' is etymologically plausible, and supported by juristic examples.[15] But to argue backwards, as Lawson does, and to assert – almost in passing – that carelessness is a quintessentially modern concept associated with 'firearms and swiftly moving vehicles' tends to diminish the persuasive force of his arguments. Even on its own terms the thesis is a weak one: it is hardly as if the Romans lacked weapons and vehicles that could cause accidental injury; indeed, several important juristic examples are concerned with precisely such sources of damage.[16] But it is the underlying logic of the argument that is most disconcerting: Lawson apparently did not feel

---

[14] Lawson (n 3) 14–15.
[15] Eg Inst.4.3.5; D.9.2.52.1.
[16] Eg Inst.4.3.4 (javelins); D.9.2.52.2 (carts).

that there was a problem with shuttling back and forth across the centuries and invoking nineteenth-century English decisions on the forms of action to elucidate the meaning of Latin words used two millennia earlier.

What Lawson felt justified this kind of free-ranging practice was the conviction that English lawyers and Roman jurists thought about things in the same way. In his discussion of the dividing line between the direct action on the *lex* and *actiones in factum* he even imagines a kind of intellectual camaraderie:[17]

> Where the direct action on the lex failed, the praetor gave actions in factum … and there was the same preoccupation in the minds of the classical jurists as to the boundaries between the actions as in the minds of the English common lawyers of the eighteenth century. Any Roman jurist would have enjoyed dealing with the problem raised in the *Squib Case*.[18]

'Enjoyed' strikes an important note here: these legal issues are being seen as intriguing intellectual puzzles, on which lawyers (of any era) could test their ingenuity and analytical powers. English and Roman lawyers are united in friendly rivalry, rather than divided by two millennia and unimaginably different social conditions.

At times Lawson's eagerness to identify the Roman jurists with their contemporary counterparts risked becoming programmatic, as in this discussion of abuse of rights:[19]

> To use the terminology of modern French law, did Roman law make a person liable for abus de droit? Or did it agree with English law in holding in principle that what a man has a right to do, he may do maliciously without making himself liable? Perhaps these questions are not very important so far as the Lex Aquilia was concerned, for the occasions on which a person could do physical damage to another in the exercise of a right were rare and the right was in each case strictly limited. But they were important for the *actio doli* and, presumably, for the little-known *actio generalis in factum* of Justinian's law, which, far more than actions on the lex, were the ancestors of the modern action for wrongful damage. It is therefore worth while to consider them.

'Perhaps' and 'presumably' are made to do a suspiciously large amount of work here, and it is difficult to avoid the feeling that what is really sustaining this discussion is not so much an analysis of the Roman texts as the author's deep commitment to the position that the Romans *must have been* like us, and *must therefore* have faced the same dilemmas. Here perceived similarity between Rome, England and France was being used to draw bold – it might even be said unwarranted – conclusions about Roman law. But perceived

---

[17] Lawson (n 3) 24.
[18] That is, *Scott v Shepherd* (1773) 2 W Bl 892.
[19] Lawson (n 3) 15–16.

similarity could also have the opposite effect: by exerting pressure it could restrict a jurisdiction's ostensible freedom of movement, as the following passage on the defence of contributory negligence illustrates:[20]

> In the United Kingdom the Maritime Conventions Act, 1911, substituted [the] principle [of apportionment of damage according to blameworthiness] for the old Admiralty rule which pooled the damage and divided it equally between the parties where a last clear chance could not be found; and, after spreading from Quebec to a number of other Canadian provinces and a few American States, it has at last been applied to England and Scotland by the Law Reform (Contributory Negligence) Act 1945. Whether the whole loss ought still to be thrown on one of the parties to the exclusion of the other if he can be shown to have carelessly omitted to take the last clear chance of avoiding the accident – as is still the case in Admiralty since the Act of 1911 – is a question that has been much canvassed and hardly settled as yet. Although I am inclined to think it is in accord with the policy of the new Act that the search for a last clear chance should entirely cease, I am bound to refer, not only to the statement of Esmein to the effect that French courts often neglect a slight negligence of one of the parties – which would not in itself be hostile to my thesis – but also to the case of *Camelyre C. Leduc*, which might be called the French *Davies v Mann*.[21]

What is remarkable about this passage is not so much the argument that the 'last opportunity' doctrine might still be good law, as the reasoning invoked to support it. In 1950 English courts hardly ever referred even to English textbooks,[22] so there was really no need for anxiety about an English court relying on Esmein's contribution to the *Traité pratique de droit civil français*.[23] Nor was an English court – either then or now – likely to consider itself bound by French decisions on delict. As a matter of precedent, of course, English courts were not bound to follow French decisions; and even the softer role of influence was unlikely to be enjoyed when a statute had recently reformed the area, as had happened with the 1945 legislation in England. Lawson knew this. When he says he is 'bound to refer' to the French material he cannot be identifying sources that might influence an English court, so he is clearly not engaged in attempting to predict how an English court might decide the issue in the future.[24] What, then, is he doing?

---

[20] ibid 57.

[21] *Davies v Mann* (1842) 10 M & W 546 introduced into English law the principle that, where a question of contributory negligence was raised, the party who had had the last opportunity of avoiding the occurrence of the damage was to be regarded as having caused it.

[22] Neil Duxbury, *Jurists and Judges: An Essay on Influence* (Hart 2001).

[23] Marcel Planiol and Georges Ripert, *Traité pratique de droit civil français* (Librairie générale de droit & de jurisprudence 1925–34).

[24] When the Court of Appeal, in *Jones v Livox Quarries Ltd* [1952] 2 QB 608, decided that the last opportunity doctrine was no longer relevant, there was, unsurprisingly, no mention of French law.

There is a teasing mimicry of judicial language in 'bound to refer', an ironic insistence that, whatever the mundane rules of precedent might say, a proper decision cannot be reached without considering the French case and treatise. We might perhaps say, provisionally, that Lawson wanted to find the best, in the sense of the most intellectually satisfying, answer, no matter where it might come from.

It was this pursuit of the most intellectually satisfying answer, irrespective of time and jurisdiction, that Kaser and Kunkel found so jarring. To return to Kaser's bipartite adjective, 'historisch-dogmatische', the norms of legal historical writing privileged careful chronological sequencing and painstaking attention to legal development; dogmatic writing called for a rigorously self-contained analytical treatment of a particular system. Lawson's approach was cheerfully iconoclastic of both genres. There was a gaping hole in his chronological treatment between the Basilica (ninth century CE) and the Prussian Code (eighteenth century) and, as we have seen, his historical arguments were idiosyncratic. At the same time, there was no attempt to conform to the conventions of dogmatic writing: ideas from Roman, English, French, German and other legal systems merrily jostled for position on their merits. The result was an exposition that was both *atemporal* and *atopical*: it was rooted in neither time nor place. Hessel Yntema, in a passage already quoted, had written that Lawson's inclusion of contemporary materials had moved the book's centre of gravity; but, rereading the book today, it can be difficult to avoid the feeling that Lawson had done something far more radical than that, by abolishing the centre of gravity altogether.

IV.

The immediate explanation for the unusual methodology of Lawson's book was not far to seek. As the opening sentence of the Preface acknowledged, Lawson had taken Francis de Zulueta's treatment of sale as his starting point.[25] Zulueta's rather more staid work compared the Roman and English law of sale, and had been designed for students sitting the Oxford Finals paper on the subject, which covered D.18.1 and the English law relating to sale of goods. In 1947 Lawson informed readers of the *Journal of the Society of Public Teachers of Law* that 'We have made considerable though not revolutionary changes in the Oxford Law School', which included a new paper: 'Roman Law of Delict and Quasi-Delict (with Gaius III.182–225; IV.75–79; Justinian, *Inst.* IV.1–5, 8–9; Digest IX.2; and the English Law of Negligence, etc)'.[26] The appearance of *Negligence in the Civil Law* in 1950 can,

---

[25] Lawson (n 3) v, referring to Francis de Zulueta, *The Roman Law of Sale: Introduction and Select Texts* (Clarendon Press 1945).

[26] Frederick Henry Lawson, 'Changes in the Law Courses at Oxford' (1947–1951) 1 JSPTL ns 112. Lawson here misquoted (perhaps misremembering) the examination rubric, which

therefore, be explained in terms of meeting an immediate practical student need.

But the explanation can only be partial. The Oxford Finals paper examined candidates on the English law of negligence, a subject on which Lawson barely touched. This was a pity, because his earlier comparative analysis of duty of care had been extraordinarily prescient and perceptive, and similar insights into other aspects of negligence would have been invaluable.[27] The Oxford paper was also more Romanist than Lawson's book – indeed, the Romanist emphasis in the Oxford syllabus invites us to read one aspect of the book in a new light: in the Preface Lawson apologises for having included the whole of Digest 9.2, because, as he explains, several texts in that chapter deal with matters outside negligence, such as succession. 'But it has been represented to me', he continues, 'that it is still the practice of English Universities to set for study the whole of a title of the Digest, and omission would make the book less available for that purpose'.[28] Lawson's own institution, apparently, was one of the offenders. Clearly there was not a straightforward relationship between the Oxford paper and Lawson's book; this complexity, I suggest, was expressive of Lawson's own ambivalent attitude towards Roman law itself.

V.

Professors of Comparative Law seem to have had something of a gift for revelatory opening sentences in their autobiographical writings. Otto Kahn-Freund, Lawson's immediate successor in Oxford, astounded close friends and colleagues by his statement that 'the most important single fact of my life is that I am a Jew'.[29] Lawson could not quite match that. But, given the career that he was looking back on, his opening sentence was still eye-catching: 'I always wanted to be a historian.'[30] It was an ambition he would achieve only after retiring from his Oxford chair and becoming a part-time lecturer at the University of Lancaster.[31] In the meantime, Lawson had forged himself an Oxford career to be envied: he read classics, history and law at the Queen's College and then, after a precarious period, was awarded a Research

---

referred to 'the English law of Torts', not 'the English law of Negligence'. See, further, Benjamin Spagnolo, elsewhere in this volume 000.

27 Frederick Henry Lawson, 'The Duty of Care in Negligence: A Comparative Study' (1947–48) 22 Tulane LR 111.

28 Lawson (n 3) v.

29 Mark Freedland, 'Otto Kahn-Freund (1900–79)' in Jack Beatson and Reinhard Zimmermann (eds), *Jurists Uprooted: German-Speaking Émigré Lawyers in Twentieth-Century Britain* (OUP 2004) 299, 302 (quoting from an unpublished memoir).

30 Frederick Henry Lawson, 'F.H. Lawson: A Bibliography' in Peter Wallington and Robert Merkin (eds), *Essays in Memory of Professor F H Lawson* (Butterworths 1986) 11.

31 Stanley Hussey, 'Harry Lawson at Lancaster' in Wallington and Merkin (n 30) 7.

Fellowship in Roman Law at Merton College in 1925. A Tutorial Fellowship at the same college followed and, in 1931, he was appointed All Souls Reader in Roman Law. The Chair of Comparative Law arrived in 1948, which he held for sixteen years.[32]

The centrality of Roman law, in the positions Lawson held, is striking. And that makes all the more striking Lawson's own consistent denials that he had any real expertise in the subject. Thus, describing his appointment to the Research Fellowship, he comments that 'my classical background made me an obvious candidate'.[33] Well, yes, but a background in classics was hardly a unique advantage in 1920s Oxford. His account of appointment to the Readership goes a step further: 'Although I never became a real Roman law specialist, on appointment as All Souls reader in Roman law [1931–48] I became, as it were, second in command of the subject.'[34] This makes the appointment sound like an almost comical misunderstanding: *somebody, somewhere* (in Oxford) must – at the very least – have been led to believe that Lawson was an expert Roman lawyer, we might think. Of course, there may be issues of tone and style here: by all accounts Lawson was a modest, self-deprecating man, and it would be uncharacteristic of him to boast. But there is, nevertheless, a powerful sense of a career shaped by opportunities, in which Lawson found himself occupying roles which, by their very titles, implicitly laid claim to an expertise that he would not have chosen to profess.

Lawson's ambivalence about his own Roman law expertise was particularly noticeable in his book reviews. The sheer number of reviews of Roman law books that he wrote, and which were published in an international array of leading journals, is both an ironic counterpoint to his denials of expertise, and also rather suggests that book review editors were under the same impression as the electors to the All Souls Readership. The reviews themselves are lucid and authoritative, but often also noticeably ambiguous and sometimes evasive about their author's standing. Lawson seems to have felt most confident about claiming the perspective of a professional Roman lawyer when writing for a non-lawyer readership. In his admiring assessment of Fritz Schulz's *History of Roman Legal Science* in the *English Historical Review*, for example, he hailed it as 'one of the most important books on Roman law published in this century', with the kind of sweeping confidence that implied expert familiarity with other pretenders to such an accolade.[35] He then went on to highlight that some aspects of the book would be 'of the greatest interest to the professional Roman lawyer', and proceeded to enumerate those points. He did not go quite so far as to say 'of the greatest

---

[32]   Barry Nicholas, 'Professor F H Lawson 1897–1983' in Wallington and Merkin (n 30) 3, 4–5.
[33]   Lawson (n 30) 11.
[34]   ibid 11.
[35]   Frederick Henry Lawson (1947) 62 EHR 86.

interest to the professional Roman lawyer *like me*', but that was the inescapable implication. When writing for a more legally expert readership, such as that of *Rabels Zeitschrift für ausländisches und internationales Privatrecht*, Lawson's self-positioning was very different. In a short review for that journal of Kaser's *Das römische Privatrecht*, which showed that there were no hard feelings about Kaser's earlier, less than effusive, reception of *Negligence in the Civil Law*, Lawson described Kaser's book as[36]

> the most up to date comprehensive textbook of Roman law, which is now the first reference book for all professional Romanists. Those whose main interest is in the modern law can leave on one side the encyclopaedic footnotes, with their references to controversial literature, and read only the admirably lucid text, in which the author shows his great gifts as an expositor and historian.

Is the first sentence quoted here a description of Lawson's own practice, or a report of colleagues' habits? Does Lawson place himself in the 'professional Romanists' category, or the 'main interest in the modern law' camp? The remainder of the review leaves one in some doubt. In the next paragraph 'English lawyers' are identified as the kinds of 'non-specialist' who might find the book interesting, and we might be tempted to detect here a note of self-identification. Ten lines later, however, this hypothesis buckles as Lawson characterises post-Justinianic Roman law in the West:[37]

> Everything tends to become relative, in a way that is not unfamiliar to English lawyers. There is more than a suspicion that this is not merely vulgarisation, but a conquest of Rome by the provinces. Certainly we have always known that *praescriptio longi temporis* and *pacta et stipulationes*, both institutions of doubtful tonality, were provincial in origin.

Lawson is not, of course, repudiating his identity as an English lawyer here; he is drawing on it – but he is also demonstrating an expertise and familiarity with the primary materials that give him the air of a professional. It is as if he has categorised Kaser's potential readers into professionals and non-specialists, only to occupy a third space himself.

VI.

While it is possible to explain Lawson's ambivalence about his own standing as a Roman lawyer in terms of his innate modesty, or as a manifestation of the anxieties inherent in being a generalist,[38] it can also be linked with his

---

[36] Frederick Henry Lawson, 'Rabels Zeitschrift für ausländisches und internationales Privatrecht' 27 Jahrg H 1 (1962/63) 174, 174–75.

[37] ibid 175.

[38] Lawson would have accepted this description of himself: Frederick Henry Lawson, 'Comparative Law: A Generalist's Apology' (1960–61) American Bar Association Section on

views about the merits of Roman law as a discipline. For one way in which Lawson was emphatically not a professional Romanist was in his consistent denials that Roman law should be studied in isolation, as an end in itself. There is a tantalising glimpse of his generalist, and generalising, impulses in his very first publication, a review of Leopold von Wenger's *Der heutige Stand der römischen Rechtswissenschaft*, in which he identified a distinct role in Roman law studies for English lawyers:[39]

> Surely a comparison of the English forms of action with the remedies afforded by the formulary system is worth making. It might be of the utmost value in the detection of interpolations in the Digest. There are signs that this is already being realised in Germany.

It is striking to see here, so early in his career, the conviction – repeated in *Negligence in the Civil Law*[40] – that the Roman formulary procedure and English medieval forms of action were so deeply similar that they could be fruitfully compared at this level of detail. Lawson did not identify his potential *Mitarbeiter* for such a project, and it seems to have come to nothing.

Four years later, in an important two-part article on the Basilica in the *Law Quarterly Review*, Lawson included a sketch of English Roman law studies that was noticeably more troubled:[41]

> Except to some extent in Scotland and the countries of the Roman-Dutch Law, Roman Law has little practical value. The student reads it as part of his juristic training and for purposes of comparison, and may hope by means of it to bridge the gap between our English modes of legal thought and those in vogue on the Continent of Europe and in Latin America. The advanced student of Roman Law pursues a purely academic study unless, perhaps, he hopes by his research into the details of the classical law to show that certain misguided tendencies in modern juristic development lack classical authority. In this country, at all events, we have no such hopes to add zest to our study.

The 'purely academic study' of the 'advanced student' is hardly made to sound very satisfying here, and the passage as a whole is an important early statement of one of Lawson's abiding preoccupations. He would return frequently to the theme that the study of Roman law was valuable because it provided an introduction to modern civil law;[42] in the 1950s this position became significantly more sophisticated as Lawson articulated the idea that Roman law contained a basic conceptual grammar which civil law systems

---

International and Comparative Law Bulletin 5.

[39] Frederick Henry Lawson (1927) 17 Journal of Roman Studies 245, 246.

[40] See text to n 17.

[41] Frederick Henry Lawson, 'The Basilica' (1930) 46 LQR 486 (1931) 47 LQR 536, 553.

[42] Eg Frederick Henry Lawson, 'The Teaching of Roman Law in the United Kingdom' in *L'Europa e il diritto romano. Studia in memoria di Paolo Koschaker* vol 2 (Giuffrè 1954) 271, 281.

had inherited, and which had to be mastered before those systems could be properly understood.[43] The passage also embodies another important aspect of Lawson's ideas on Roman law, although rather less obviously than the point about Roman law as an introduction to civil law, and that is to talk of the reasons for 'studying Roman law' in a way that tended to blur the distinction between teaching and research. The 'student' in the second sentence of the quotation is obviously an undergraduate; the 'advanced student', who initially sounds rather like a graduate student, is, in fact – as the end of the passage makes clear – an established academic. Indeed, if we take the 'we' of the last sentence literally, the All Souls Reader in Roman Law was an 'advanced student' too.

Many of Lawson's views about the value of Roman law were expressed in lectures to students, reviews of books aimed at a student readership or articles about teaching the subject, and that can make it especially difficult to distinguish pedagogical propositions from broader intellectual claims. For instance, Lawson's arguments about the underlying grammar of Roman law in civil law were designed to encourage students, such as the audiences of his *A Common Lawyer Looks at the Civil Law* or 'The Approach to French Law', to take up Roman law.[44] But, elsewhere, Lawson could be alert to the ideological commitments that a grammar of Roman law might entail: in a review of a book on Soviet civil law, in the *Slavonic Review*, he drew readers' attention to Russia's Roman law tradition, and was particularly struck by the way in which a Soviet code provision designed to create strict liability for damage had been reinterpreted by the courts to turn on fault. 'No doubt there are very good socialist reasons for the change', he observed, surely ironically.

> We are not to think of the Soviet Courts as being unduly favourable to defendants; for in most cases where the damage is serious the plaintiff will have been in contact with some vehicle or machine, and most vehicles and machines are the property of the Soviet Government. None the less, it may be suspected that the change in standpoint was to some extent brought about by the steady tendency of professional lawyers to bring the Law under the categories with which they are familiar, and to persist in their secular habits of thought.[45]

---

[43] Eg Frederick Henry Lawson, *A Common Lawyer Looks at the Civil Law* (University of Michigan Law School 1953) 4; Frederick Henry Lawson, 'The Approach to French Law' (1958–59) 34 Indiana LJ 531, 533.

[44] Frederick Henry Lawson, *A Common Lawyer Looks at the Civil Law* (University of Michigan Law School 1953); Frederick Henry Lawson, 'The Approach to French Law' (1958–59) 34 Indiana LJ 531.

[45] Frederick Henry Lawson, review of Vladimir Gsovski, *Soviet Civil Law: Private Rights and their Background under the Soviet Regime* (1950) 28 Slavonic and East European Review 557, 560.

VII.

A similar articulation between teaching and research can be made in relation to Lawson's views on patterns, as expressed in pedagogical and more scholarly contexts. He devoted an entire lecture at Boston University to the theme of 'Roman Law as an Organizing Instrument', going so far as to say that 'the claims of Roman law depend ... chiefly on the extraordinary services it has performed and may, yet, I hope, perform in organizing thought and action in the law'.[46] There followed an elegant celebration of the way that the Romans, as 'a people of engineers, or perhaps rather of grammarians, who were not interested in mathematics or philosophy',[47] had conceived of private law as a system of interlocking parts, as well as an overview of Roman law's importance in medieval Europe. Lawson's conclusion, however, was anxious to avoid anything other than modest pedagogical claims: 'You will see that I am not making extravagant claims for Roman law in American legal education. I am asking for the average law teacher to teach it to the average law student as a teacher in a primary school would teach elementary English grammar.'[48]

Lawson's interest in patterns and system went well beyond the pedagogical, however: it was central to his professional identity, and an impulse that visibly animated much of his best scholarship. Indeed, in an address to a breakfast meeting of the American Bar Association Convention in 1960, he came close to making such an interest the defining feature of legal scholarship: 'cultivat[ing] the bird's eye view' was, he said, the 'only' way an academic lawyer could make 'his own peculiar contribution to legal study'.[49] At its best, this kind of approach allowed Lawson to make some impressively original points: his overview of the principles of negligence liability, for instance, enabled him to point out that English law needed a duty of care concept not so much to define when claims could be brought as to define the circumstances in which negligence liability should cease.[50] Similarly, his approach to the Roman law of contract yielded some bold and compelling claims about the underlying concerns that had inspired the fourfold classification of consensual contracts.[51]

---

[46] Frederick Henry Lawson, 'Roman Law as an Organizing Instrument' (1966) 46 BULR 181, 182.

[47] ibid 190.

[48] ibid 203–04.

[49] Frederick Henry Lawson, 'Comparative Law: A Generalist's Apology' (1960–61) American Bar Association Section on International and Comparative Law Bulletin 5. See also the reference to an 'addiction to bird's eye views of comparative legal history' in Lawson's affectionate piece on Edward Jenks: 'Jenksiana' (1961) 6 JSPTL (ns) 115.

[50] Lawson (n 27).

[51] Lawson (n 44) 121–25. The less convincing aspect of the 'bird's eye view' approach can be seen in Frederick Henry Lawson, 'Some Paradoxes of Legal History' (1966–67) 15 AJCL 101, where the analysis is unsatisfyingly sketchy. The bird could fly too high to be able to see things properly.

VIII.

Quite how deeply committed Lawson was to the identification and elaboration of patterns can be seen in an extraordinarily revealing, but little known, essay he published in 1956. Entitled 'Reflections on a Thirty Years' Experience of Teaching Roman Law', this short contribution delicately blended pedagogy, scholarship and autobiography to produce the closest thing to an intellectual self-portrait that Lawson would ever write.[52] His starting point was the difficulty in sustaining students' interest in Roman law beyond their studies of the *Institutes*. Roman 'case law', Lawson observed (referring, presumably, to the Digest),[53]

> is in a sense too grown-up, too dry, for students who have got through the Institutes. It certainly cannot compete with cases in the modern law reports, whether English or South African. It is also too terse and it deals with an unfamiliar world, so that the problems have to be restated in more modern terms to become real.

The result was that 'the lawyer who has left Roman law for a more modern system usually does stay away from it unless for some reason he becomes a specialist in Roman law'.[54] Lawson, however, was not a usual lawyer – 'I have come back to Roman law via comparative law and have found many things in it which could have meant little to me at an earlier stage.'[55]

He then went on to explain 'how I came to find renewed enjoyment in the study, or rather the contemplation, of Roman law'.[56] The immediate inspiration had been Schulz's *Principles of Roman Law* and Jhering's *Geist des römischen Rechts*, in which Lawson perceived that the authors tried 'to get below the surface of Roman law to see what the Romans were really driving at'.[57] 'In truth', Lawson continued,

> Roman lawyers have usually been concerned, excessively so as I must think, to ascertain the actual rules of Roman law at different periods, and not enough with its importance in the scheme of world history and above all not enough with its real shape and pattern.[58]

This was not a point that had occurred to him only recently: 'I had almost from the start, over thirty years ago, suspected that in this shape or pattern

---

[52] Frederick Henry Lawson, 'Reflections on a Thirty Years' Experience of Teaching Roman Law' 1956 BSALR 16.
[53] ibid 16.
[54] ibid 16.
[55] ibid 16.
[56] ibid 17.
[57] ibid 17.
[58] ibid 17–18.

lay the real fascination of Roman law, though it took many years for it to become at all clear except in a few places.'

Lawson's early instincts had been affirmed, he made clear, by the salutary experience of writing on Roman law for the non-specialist readership of *Chambers Encyclopedia*:[59]

> I had to try to tell the ordinary man how and why Roman law is important and to disengage its main institutions and principles, especially if they are of permanent value, from antiquarian detail. It was largely an exercise in the art of omission; and in order to make the account run like a story I had to see what sort of a pattern Roman law could be made to exhibit ... the task fascinated me and intensified my interest in Roman law.

'Perhaps', he concluded, 'this concern with pattern has become an obsession. I have indulged in it more than once. But I think it is hard to be a lawyer and not to have it in some measure.'[60]

Having set out this stirring, if perhaps slightly defensive, scholarly credo, the essay then takes a turn which, as we have already seen, is not uncharacteristic of Lawson's writing: it focuses the ideas back on teaching, arguing that 'every attempt should be made to bring home such patterns to the student of Roman law, and I think that by such means the second, difficult stage in the study of Roman law has some chance of being bridged'.[61]

The final section of the essay addressed an alternative way of making Roman law appealing to students who were already familiar with the *Institutes*: the comparative method. 'In my experience', Lawson was happy to report, 'this way of treating Roman law has captured the imagination of many of the most intelligent students, and has made Roman law fairly real to a large number of others'.[62] Strikingly, given the title of the chair that Lawson held at the time, he made no claims for the underlying intellectual benefits of comparative law as a scholarly activity, but moved quickly to address the objection that comparative law was most appropriately undertaken with systems from the same historical period:[63]

> I think the best answer to this question is that the limited nature of the Roman sources enables one to keep the comparative study within bounds. How often is one not forced in comparative work on purely modern law to look for explanations outside pure law in the social habits or economic developments of different peoples? One can do very little of that with Roman law; one is kept down to pure law. However unsatisfactory that may be in the long run, it is good in the short run ...

---

[59] ibid 18.
[60] ibid 18.
[61] ibid 19.
[62] ibid 19.
[63] ibid 20.

As Lawson acknowledged in the final sentence of the quotation, this was not an entirely happy justification. He had, previously, emphasised that social and economic conditions often illuminated Roman legal doctrines, and had taken to task the author of an introductory book (aimed at students) who had neglected such conditions.[64] Later he would make the same point in more emphatic and general terms:[65]

> Much that passes for comparative law is little more than a placing side by side corresponding pieces of different legal systems. It comes very near to pure description. Doubtless many, if not most, comparative lawyers have started by being merely curious about foreign law; they have developed into comparative lawyers when they have come to search for the reasons underlying resemblances and differences. This leads one away from any exclusive preoccupation with the history of technical devices or bodies of supposedly self-developing doctrine into the whole social, political and economic history of nations.

In 'Reflections', however, he was taking the directly opposite approach to the use of the comparative method in teaching, and advocating a pedagogical position that risked arbitrarily closing off promising avenues of intellectual inquiry for no better reason than the convenience of the examiners. This was a rare, uncharacteristic instance of Lawson's broader intellectual commitments working against his philosophy of teaching, and it is worth pausing for a moment to ask ourselves what he felt was gained by this awkward self-contradiction. In the passage from 'Reflections' quoted above there is an insistence on *purity* and, in particular, on 'pure law' uncontaminated by socio-political or historical context; it is, surely, a return to the vision of legal rules as a series of abstract, eternal, intellectual puzzles on which all lawyers can test their wits, and which is prominent, as we have already seen, at key moments in *Negligence in the Civil Law*.[66] Lawson's position, as expressed in 'Reflections', that this kind of analysis was good only 'in the short run', invites us to read *Negligence in the Civil Law* as embodying an approach that even its own author did not believe held good 'in the long run', and that makes the question of Lawson's authorial voice in *Negligence in the Civil Law* an intriguingly complicated one. At most he was only provisionally committed to the 'pure law' view. But was he going further? Was he deliberately pushing the 'pure law' approach to its limits in order to encourage intellectually inquisitive readers to become dissatisfied with it? Was the disorientating shuttling between different eras and places a way of exhibiting – almost satirising – the method's inherent shortcomings? Was he, in short, hoping to provoke in readers exactly the kind of responses that the German critics had expressed?

---

[64] Frederick Henry Lawson, review of Herbert F Jolowicz, *Historical Introduction to the Study of Roman Law* 1933 JSPTL 40, 40–41.

[65] Lawson (n 49) 5.

[66] See text accompanying n 17.

As well as raising questions about Lawson's authorial strategies in the *Negligence* book, 'Reflections on a Thirty Years' Experience of Teaching Roman Law' is also particularly valuable for the light it casts on Lawson's sense of himself as a Roman lawyer. He certainly did not wish to be grouped with that body of scholars who were 'concerned, excessively, so I must think, to ascertain the actual rules of Roman law at different periods', but nor did he identify himself as a comparatist. He was a seeker of patterns, a status which aligned him, rather winningly when we remember that he was nearly sixty and an Oxford professor, with second- and third-year under-graduates. He also shared, or at least sympathised with, such students' taste for the law they were studying to be 'real', and it is worthwhile pausing for a moment to consider what, exactly, he understood by this cryptic adjective. One possibility, on which he published a full-length article shortly after 'Reflections', was the correspondence between legal concepts and the factual reality to which they applied,[67] but this does not seem to have been a problem peculiar to Roman law. What Lawson seems to have had in mind can best be gathered by looking at two prominent instances of unreality that he identifies: the 'unfamiliar world' of ancient Rome requires problems 'to be restated in more modern terms to become real';[68] and, 'it is very easy to detach the more antiquarian and unreal parts [of Roman law from the syllabus], such as the texts dealing with manumission and the complications of classical marriage'.[69] 'Unreal' in these examples means unfamiliar by reason of remoteness in time and historical conditions, or having no direct counterpart in current English law. Lawson seems to have had rather low expectations – perhaps the bitter fruit of thirty years' experience – about his students' imaginative range and intellectual curiosity.

Despite Lawson's upbeat account of the experience, the same note of constricting presentism resonates in his description of writing for 'the ordinary man'. When Lawson says, 'I had to try to tell the ordinary man how and why Roman law is important'[70] we surely hear the sentence continuing 'for him, today'. The 'ordinary man' is imagined from the outset as a somewhat sceptical, impatient individual, who will be receptive to a 'story' so long as there is no 'antiquarian detail'.[71] Why such a person would be both curious about Roman law and yet, at the same time, resentful of historical data is less than obvious, and it is difficult to avoid the feeling that Lawson's imagined 'ordinary man' was a kind of caricature of his Oxford students, who, as a result of

---

[67] Frederick Henry Lawson, 'The Creative Use of Legal Concepts' (1957) 32 NYULR 909.
[68] Lawson (n 52) 16.
[69] ibid 17.
[70] ibid 18.
[71] Cf Stefan Collini, 'Realists' in *Common Writing; Essays on Literary Culture and Public Debate* (OUP 2016) 123, particularly at 130: 'The insistence on the perspective of the "plain man" by writers who are, almost by definition, rarely plain themselves should always be suspect.'

the structure of their course, had no choice about studying Roman law, but could sometimes be persuaded to like it. Lawson's main strategy for bringing this about was, essentially, to focus on topics where it could appear not to matter that some sources were two thousand years older than others: everybody could seem to be thinking about the same problems. For someone who 'always wanted to be a historian', this professional commitment to an anti-historical methodology must have had its ironic moments.

IX.

Lawson's insistence that Roman law should be seen 'in the scheme of world history',[72] as part of a larger story, raises a further intriguing question about his own *Negligence in the Civil Law*: what was that book's grand narrative? Lawson's own later description of the work as a 'source book'[73] and reviewers' characterisations of it as, for instance, 'a rich mine'[74] might suggest that it was nothing more than a collection of materials. But a closer examination of the book itself invites a more sophisticated interpretation.

Lawson very clearly did not envisage (or encourage the idea) that readers would begin at the beginning and read linearly. The Introduction, he explained, was 'intended ... to furnish the student with an intelligible order in which to read the texts'.[75] True to his word, the opening page of the Introduction informs readers that 'one of the first steps for a student to take when studying a [Digest] title is to rearrange the fragments';[76] the subsequent exposition implicitly indicates the appropriate sequence. But the Preface also suggests, more tantalisingly, that this is a book with 'an argument', even though that argument is never expressly set out.[77]

The allusion to an 'argument' is made to explain the inclusion of extracts from Canadian legislation on road traffic accidents and an entire academic article on the Saskatchewan automobile accident scheme. What these provisions had in common was their rejection of a fault-based model of compensation for damage, although what they put in its place varied considerably: the Ontario legislation excluded all claims by gratuitous passengers in motor vehicles, for instance, while the Saskatchewan scheme ensured that a minimum of compensation was available to all motor vehicle accident victims irrespective of fault. Undoubtedly these statutes represented new ways of responding to personal injury and property damage, but readers

---

[72] Lawson (n 52) 18.

[73] Frederick Henry Lawson, 'The Teaching of Roman Law in the United Kingdom' in *L'Europa e il diritto romano. Studia in memoria di Paolo Koschaker* vol 2 (Giuffrè 1954) 271, 283.

[74] Arthur von Mehren, review of F H Lawson, *Negligence in the Civil Law* (1952) 66 Harvard LR 190.

[75] Frederick Henry Lawson, *Negligence in the Civil Law* (Clarendon Press, 1950) vi.

[76] ibid 1.

[77] ibid v.

looking for 'an argument', for which the Canadian materials were supporting evidence, may have been left feeling uncertain about what exactly that argument was.

There is, perhaps, a hint of Lawson's thought processes in the dustjacket text. 'This book', it is said, 'is designed as an instrument to be used in the comparative study of the Law of Torts, a subject which has everywhere remained less affected by governmental changes than almost any other branch of private law'. The Canadian statutes represented an obvious exception to that statement, being very much governmental initiatives. Later in the same text the Canadian innovations are described as 'some of the most advanced developments in the law of motor accidents', and 'advanced' here may perhaps be meant to signal approval as well as denoting that these were the most recent materials.

A couple of years later, in a review of Albert Ehrenzweig's *Negligence without Fault*, Lawson felt that he could be more outspoken.[78] Ehrenzweig's book had argued for the imposition of strict liability on business enterprises for damage caused by risks closely bound up with those enterprises' normal activities. Lawson approved: 'the thesis is an interesting one and seems to point in the right direction'; but he also proposed applying something like the Saskatchewan road traffic scheme to business enterprises as a way to reach the same result.[79] A review of another of the prolific Ehrenzweig's books endorsed the importance of insurance-based solutions in road traffic cases, although Lawson added that 'Perhaps each country will have to work out its own salvation.'[80] This, we might notice, introduces a note of relativism, an acknowledgement that different jurisdictions could legitimately arrive at different solutions to the same problem – and is the exact opposite of the 'pure law' approach.

It seems strange, at first sight, that Lawson should feel unable to say in a book what he had no difficulty in saying in book reviews, particularly when the statements in question went to the underlying narrative of the book as a whole. Lawson never explained why he had chosen to adopt such a cryptically light touch. Perhaps, this being a student text, he wanted to leave the students to work things out for themselves. But there is also a more intriguing possibility, which is that the political context in which the book was published made it embarrassing to express this argument in a book on Roman law. What Lawson would be saying, we should remember, was that the individualised focus on fault in Roman law was no longer appropriate for modern conditions, and should be replaced by collective schemes in

---

[78] Frederick Henry Lawson, review of Albert A Ehrenzweig, *Negligence without Fault* (1952) 1 ICLQ 112.

[79] ibid 113.

[80] Frederick Henry Lawson, review of Albert A Ehrenzweig, *'Full Aid' Insurance for the Traffic Victim* (1955) 4 ICLQ 585, 586.

which the priority was society's obligation to help the injured. This would have uncomfortably echoed the German National Socialists' antagonism to Roman law, as expressed in their party programme: 'We demand that Roman law, which serves a materialist world order, be replaced by German common law'.[81] The Nazis' central contention was that basic Roman legal principles such as absolute property rights, and the validity of contracts of sale despite the price not being a fair reflection of the value of the counter-performance, promoted selfishness at the expense of social welfare.[82] Leading German Roman law scholars, including Fritz Schulz and Max Kaser, had been at the forefront in arguing that Roman law, properly understood, was richly communitarian,[83] and there was a danger that Lawson's criticisms of fault would have sounded like a reiteration of the Nazi line. It would have been perfectly understandable if he had opted to avoid any possible confusion by omitting an outspoken treatment of the topic from his book.

X. CONCLUSION

Negligence in the Civil Law is little read today. Readers interested in its subject matter are more likely to consult the extensively revised version, *Tortious Liability for Unintentional Harm in the Common Law and the Civil Law*, which Lawson produced in collaboration with Basil Markesinis in 1982.[84] But it would be a great pity if it disappeared entirely, because, as I hope I have shown, it embodies a distinctive (and distinctively British) engagement with classical Roman legal texts, in which fundamental questions (and anxieties) about the aims of Roman law teaching and scholarship are never very far from the surface. As an expression of what Kunkel called the 'ganz andere Denkweise des englischen Juristen' [quite other ways of thinking of the English jurist] and of Frederick Henry Lawson's own methods and ideas in particular, it remains a rich, rewarding and occasionally surprising source.

---

[81] Michael Stolleis, 'Was There "Progress in Legal History" during the Nazi Period?' in *The Law Under the Swastika: Studies on Legal History in Nazi Germany* (Thomas Dunlap tr, University of Chicago Press 1998) 48, 49.

[82] James Q Whitman, 'Long Live the Hatred of Roman Law!' Rechtsgeschichte 2/2003, 40.

[83] Stolleis (n 81) 53–56.

[84] CUP 1982. The revisions apparently brought the work up to German standards: Werner Lorenz (1983) Juristen Zeitung 38 Jahrg. Nr. 3 (4 Feb 1983) 119: 'Dies alles ist ganz auf der Höhe der deutschen wissenschaftlichen Diskussion.' [This all reaches the level of German scientific discussion.]

Chapter 4

Students' Digest:
9.2 in Oxford in the Twentieth Century

Benjamin Spagnolo

1. INTRODUCTION

This chapter surveys teaching and learning connected with Digest 9.2 against the background of the changing place of Roman law in the Oxford curriculum over the course of the twentieth century. The chapter considers five snapshots, taken at twenty-year intervals from 1920 to 2000, chosen for consistency and convenience but also because they roughly sample the tenures of the twentieth-century Regius Professors of Civil Law in Oxford. While Henry Goudy demitted in 1919, a year before the date of the first snapshot, the picture revealed in 1920 is still broadly representative of his period (1893–1919). The year 1940 falls in the last third of Francis de Zulueta's era (1919–48); 1960 elides the relatively brief tenure of Herbert Jolowicz (1948–54) with that of David Daube (1955–70); 1980 is midway through Tony Honoré's stint (1971–88); and the final snapshot, taken in 2000, falls a little over ten years into Peter Birks's professorship (1989–2004). Each snapshot indicates where Digest 9.2 fits into the curriculum, who was teaching the subject, what books students used and what types of questions they were asked in their examinations.

2. 1920: AN ADVANCED UNDERGRADUATE PAPER

Harold Hanbury, a staunch defender of Roman law,[1] though himself later Vinerian Professor of English Law, took the Second Public Examination in the Honour School of Jurisprudence in Trinity Term 1920. While he was to be the Vinerian Scholar – the top Bachelor in Civil Law (BCL) student – in 1921, in the Final Honour School (FHS) in 1920, the examiners placed him in the second class, along with ten others. There were five in the first class, four in the third class and two in the fourth class.[2] Sixty-nine other can-

---

[1] See Harold Hanbury, 'The Place of Roman Law in the Teaching of Law To-day' (1931) JSPTL 14.

[2] See 'Nomina Candidatorum qui in Jurisprudentia honore digni sunt habiti' in *Oxford University Gazette* (1920.07.28) No 1622, 849, 849–50.

didates satisfied the examiners that year, out of a total cohort of 101,[3] the number reflecting the fact that jurisprudence was then regarded as one of the 'softer honour schools'.[4] The examiners were the still relatively new Regius Professor of Civil Law, Francis de Zulueta; Sir John Miles (Chairman of the Faculty, Merton College); and William Stallybrass (Brasenose College).[5] The exam the students sat was called the Second Public Examination but it might well have been their first examination in law. For example, Hanbury came up to Oxford on a classical scholarship,[6] so would have taken Honour Moderations in classics for his First Public Examination, rather than the Preliminary Examination in jurisprudence.[7] He would not, therefore, have sat the compulsory three-hour paper on Gaius, Books I, II.1–97 and III.88–225 that was set for the Preliminary Examination in that period.[8]

On the other hand, Roman law was one of four compulsory disciplines in which FHS candidates were examined, alongside general jurisprudence, the history of English law and international law.[9] In 1920, there were two Roman law papers in the FHS: the first on the *Institutes* of Gaius and of Justinian and the second, which could be omitted by a candidate not aiming at the first or second class, on Digest 9.2.[10] It was common from at least 1860 to set different papers 'for those who aimed at a class and for those whom aimed at a mere pass'.[11] The Board of the Faculty had agreed in 1884 that '[a] title of the Digest, to be changed from time to time, might advantageously be prescribed

---

[3] See 'Nomina Examinandorum Secunda Publica Examinatione in Schola Jurisprudentiæ' in *Oxford University Gazette* (1920.05.27) No 1616 Supplement (2) 699, 701–02; 'Schedulæ Suppletoriæ' in *Oxford University Gazette* (1920.06.23) No 1620, 806, 806.

[4] Daniel Greenstein, 'The Junior Members, 1900–1990: A Profile' in Brian Harrison (ed), *The History of the University of Oxford, Volume VIII: The Twentieth Century* (Clarendon Press 1994) 45, 57. See also Frederick Henry Lawson, *The Oxford Law School, 1850–1965* (Clarendon Press 1968) 137.

[5] See 'Nomina Candidatorum qui in Jurisprudentia honore digni sunt habiti' (n 2) 850.

[6] Robert Stevens, 'Hanbury, Harold Greville (1898–1993)' in *Oxford Dictionary of National Biography* (OUP 2004; online edn Jan 2008) <www.oxforddnb.com/view/article/52096> accessed 4 December 2017).

[7] The latter route also necessitated a candidate's taking an additional subject at Responsions (or equivalent entry examination), together with the Examination in Holy Scripture that was a compulsory element of the First Public Examination: see University of Oxford, *Oxford University Handbook* (Clarendon Press 1917) 106, Table II. The Preliminary Examination in jurisprudence did not become part of the First Public Examination until 1921: Lawson (n 4) 132.

[8] Regulations of the Board of the Faculty, 'Preliminary Examination', reg 2.2 in University of Oxford, *The Examination Statutes* (for the academical year 1917–18, Clarendon Press 1917) 94. Since the regulations normally apply prospectively, those cited, here and below, are the regulations governing the course at the time the candidate commenced studying.

[9] Statutes of the University of Oxford, Title VI s 1.C §6.4 in ibid 92–93.

[10] ibid 95.

[11] Lawson (n 4) 23.

in addition to the Institutes of Gaius and Justinian'.[12] Digest 9.2 was the title initially chosen by the Faculty to cultivate 'a more thorough knowledge of Roman law'[13] than the overview provided by the *Institutes*.[14] In line with the policy that the title should be periodically changed,[15] Digest 18.1 *de contrahenda emptione* was prescribed from 1897[16] to 1908, when Digest 9.2 was reinstated.[17] Since he obtained the second class, we know that Hanbury sat the paper on Digest 9.2 in 1920.

From published lists, we know that de Zulueta lectured on the *Institutes* for three terms in the academic year 1919–20, and took 'informal instruction' (seminars)[18] on the Edict and on problems in legal history; it was Jolowicz, the All Souls Reader in Roman Law and later de Zulueta's successor as Regius Professor, who lectured on Digest 9.2, in the Trinity Term before the exam.[19] The syllabus for the paper simply prescribed 'Digest IX, 2, *ad legem Aquiliam*';[20] for that reason, and because the Oxford tutorial system entailed both that candidates would often be examined by academics who had not taught them and that individual tutors had wide discretion as to what and how they taught any given subject,[21] the Faculty regulations of the

---

[12] University of Oxford Faculty of Law, *Minutes of the Board* (1884.02.09) 23; Oxford University Archives FA 4/6/1/1 at 18. The Committee making the recommendation comprised Thomas Erskine Holland (Chichele Professor of International Law), Erwin Grueber (Reader in Roman Law), John Moyle (New College and Jesus College) and Charles Shadwell (Lincoln College): University of Oxford Faculty of Law, *Minutes of the Board* (1883.05.12) 4; Oxford University Archives FA 4/6/1/1 at 4.

[13] Erwin Grueber (ed), *The Roman Law of Damage to Property, Being a Commentary on the Title of the Digest Ad Legem Aquiliam (IX. 2), with an Introduction to the Study of the Corpus Iuris Civilis* (Clarendon Press 1886) vii.

[14] University of Oxford Faculty of Law, *Minutes of the Board* (1884.05.10); Oxford University Archives FA 4/6/1/1 at 29, 32.

[15] Reaffirmed by the Board a decade later: University of Oxford Faculty of Law, *Minutes of the Board* (1894.12.03); Oxford University Archives FA 4/6/1/2 at 2, 2.

[16] Regulations of the Board of the Faculty, 'Final Honour Examination', reg 2.2 in University of Oxford, *The Examination Statutes* (for the academical year 1896–97, Clarendon Press 1896) 78.

[17] Regulations of the Board of the Faculty, 'Final Honour Examination', reg 2.2 in University of Oxford, *The Examination Statutes* (for the academical year 1908–09, Clarendon Press 1908) 95.

[18] Lawson (n 4) 173.

[19] 'Michaelmas Term, 1919: Schedules of Lectures authorized by Boards of Faculties and the Board of Studies for Music' in *Oxford University Gazette* (1919.10.09) No 1591 (Supplement (2)) 29, 33; 'Hilary Term, 1920: Schedules of Lectures authorized by Boards of Faculties and the Board of Studies for Music' in *Oxford University Gazette* (1920.01.15) No 1601 (Supplement) 307, 309; 'Trinity Term, 1920: Schedules of Lectures authorized by Boards of Faculties and the Board of Studies for Music' in *Oxford University Gazette* (1920.04.23) No 1611 (Supplement (3)) 545, 547.

[20] Regulations of the Board of the Faculty, 'Final Honour Examination', reg 2.2 in University of Oxford, *Examination Statutes 1908–1909* (n 17) 95.

[21] Lawson (n 4) 170–71; Barry Nicholas, 'Jurisprudence' in Michael Brock and Mark Curthoys

period customarily prescribed a list of books, rather than topics,[22] in which 'the subject may be studied'.[23] The examiners could, therefore, expect all candidates to be familiar with these works. Nine books (in English, German and French) were suggested for the paper on the *Institutes*;[24] only Erwin Grueber's commentary on the *lex Aquilia*[25] was prescribed for the paper on Digest 9.2.[26] As Grueber explains in his Preface, the work was designed with the FHS course in mind, and conceived 'as a text-book for students who only know the elements of Roman law, as they are explained in lectures on the Institutes'.[27] It forms part of a contemporary flourishing of Digest titular literature,[28] commentary on the Roman texts being, according to Grueber,

(eds), *The History of the University of Oxford, Volume VII: Nineteenth-Century Oxford* (Clarendon Press 2000) 385, 387.

22　Lawson (n 4) 22.

23　In some subjects, the Board of the Faculty formally distinguished between 'books recommended to be read and books suggested for reference': University of Oxford Faculty of Law, *Minutes of the Board* (1884.02.09) (n 12) 20.

24　Justinian, *The Institutes of Justinian* (John Moyle ed, 5th edn, Clarendon Press 1913); Gaius, *The Institutes of Gaius and Rules of Ulpian* (James Muirhead ed, T&T Clark 1880); Gaius, *Gai Institutiones, or, Institutes of Roman Law by Gaius* (Edward Poste ed, 4th rev edn, Clarendon Press 1906); James Muirhead, *Historical Introduction to the Private Law of Rome* (Henry Goudy and Alexander Grant eds, 3rd edn, A&C Black 1916); Édouard Cuq, *Les institutions juridiques des Romains* (2nd edn, Librairie Plon 1904); Georg Friedrich Puchta and Paulus Krueger, *Cursus der Institutionen* (10th edn, Breitkopf und Härtel 1893); Rudolph Sohm, *The Institutes of Roman Law* (James Ledlie tr, 3rd edn, Clarendon Press 1907); Paul Girard, *Textes de droit romain* (4th edn, Rousseau & Cie 1913); Paul Girard, *Manuel élémentaire de droit romain* (6th edn, Rousseau & Cie 1918).

25　Grueber (n 13).

26　Regulations of the Board of the Faculty, 'Final Honour Examination' (n 17) 95.

27　Grueber (n 13) vii.

28　Other examples of Digest titular literature down to 1930 include: Balthazard-Marie Emerigon, *An Essay on Maritime Loans, from the French of M. Balthazard Marie Emerigon; with notes: to which is Added an Appendix, Containing the Titles de Exercitoria Actione, de Lege Rhodia de Jactu, and de Nautico Fœnore, Translated from the Digests and Code of Justinian, and the Title Des Contrats à la Grosse Aventure ou à Retour de Voyage, from the Marine Ordinance of Louis XIV* (J E Hall ed, Philip H Nicklin & Co 1811); Thomas Holland and Charles Shadwell (eds), *Select Titles from the Digest of Justinian* (Clarendon Press 1881); Bryan Walker (ed), *Selected Titles from the Digest: Part 1: Mandati vel Contra: Digest XVII. I* (CUP 1879); Bryan Walker (ed), *Selected Titles from the Digest: de Adquirendo Rerum Dominio and de Adquirenda vel Amittenda Possessione: Digest XLI.I and II* (CUP 1880); Bryan Walker (ed), *Selected Titles from the Digest: de Condictionibus: Digest XII.I and IV–VII and Digest XIII.I–III* (CUP 1881); Bryan Walker (ed), *Selected Titles from the Digest: de Servitutibus: Digest VIII* (Deighton, Bell, & Co 1881); Bryan Walker (ed), *Selected Titles from the Digest: Digest IX* (Deighton, Bell, & Co 1883); Bryan Walker (ed), *Selected Titles from the Digest: Digest XVII.2: Pro socio, and X.3, communi dividundo* (Deighton, Bell, & Co 1883); Henry Roby, *An Introduction to the Study of Justinian's Digest: Containing an Account of its Composition and of the Jurists Used or Referred to therein, together with a Full Commentary on One Title (de Usufructu)* (CUP 1884); James Kelleher, *Possession in the Civil Law: Abridged from the Treatise of von Savigny to which is added the Text of the Title on Possession from the Digest, with Notes* (Thacker 1888); Charles Henry Monro (ed), *Digest XIX.2: Locati Conducti* (CUP 1891); Charles Henry Monro (ed), *Digest XLI.1: de* 'the peculiar method in which topics of Roman law are dealt with in this country'[29] and, in at least one instance, 'the selection of titles being determined by the Oxford law curriculum'.[30] Grueber's work consists of translation, commentary, 'systematic exposition' and a summary 'intended ... to give a short and precise survey of the whole topic, and the connection of its single parts with one another [... and ...] also to enable the reader to find quickly each particular point he wants to be informed on'.[31] It is still useful – and still used – by students, 130 years after its publication.

The 1920 FHS examination paper confirms that students were not expected to stray far from direct application of the Digest texts or from themes picked out in Grueber's commentary. The paper consists of five questions, all of which, it seems, had to be attempted in the two hours available.[32] The first question calls for a short essay on the original text and early literal interpretation of Chapter 1.[33] A reasonable answer, to be composed in twenty-four minutes, might correspond more or less to Grueber's remarks under the heading 'The fundamental provisions of the lex Aquilia',[34] which proposes amendments to the text, and in his commentary on D.9.2.7.1, which, in point of fact, describes the early interpretation of *occidere* as 'strictly literal'.[35] The second question requires students to translate and comment on D.9.2.4.1 and D.9.2.52.1, passages plainly linked by the thief

---

Adquirendo Rerum Dominio (CUP 1900); Charles Henry Monro (ed), *Digest* XVII.2: *Pro socio* (CUP 1902); Charles Henry Monro (ed), *Digest* IX.2: *Lex Aquilia* (CUP 1928); Thomas C Jackson (ed), *Justinian's Digest (Book 20): with an English Translation and an Essay on the Law of Mortgage in the Roman Law* (Sweet & Maxwell 1908); Graham Trapnell (ed), *The Institutes of Gaius (Extracts): The Digest: Title* XLV. I: *De Verborum Obligationibus* (Swan Sonnenschein & Co 1908); Francis de Zulueta (ed), *Digest 41, 1 & 2: Translation and Commentary* (Clarendon Press 1922); Samuel Leathley (ed), *The Roman Family; and de Ritu Nuptiarum, Title* XXIII *(2) from the Digest of Justinian* (Blackwell 1922); James B Thayer (ed), *Lex Aquilia (Digest IX.2 Ad Legem Aquiliam): Text, Translation and Commentary* (Harvard University Press 1929); James Thayer (ed), *On Gifts between Husband and Wife: Digest* XXIV.1, *De Donationibus inter Virum et Uxorem: Text and Commentary* (Harvard University Press 1929). It has been suggested that the selection of titles for advanced study may have become 'fairly conventional': Frederick Henry Lawson, 'Reflections on a Thirty Years' Experience of Teaching Roman Law' (1956) BSALR 16, 16.

29 Grueber (n 13) vii.
30 De Zulueta (n 28) 5. On a related note, de Zulueta also expresses his thanks to an 'Oxford Digest Society': ibid 6. Sadly, it appears from the reprint edition that this gathering was 'short-lived': Francis de Zulueta (ed), *Digest 41, 1 & 2* (reprint of 1922 edn with Latin text of Mommsen and Krüger, Clarendon Press 1950) Preface. Little else is known of the Society: Lawson (n 4) 174.
31 Grueber (n 13) ix.
32 On this style of paper, where all questions must be attempted, but in respect of a slightly earlier period, see Lawson (n 4) 23.
33 University of Oxford, *Honour School of Jurisprudence (Final Examination): Trinity Term, 1920* (Oxford University Examination Papers, No 1961, 1920).
34 Grueber (n 13) 196–99.
35 ibid 19.

and legitimate self-defence, and expressly related to one another in Grueber's commentary.[36]

The third question offers four short scenarios, in English, in which advice is sought, while the fourth question extracts five short cases directly from Digest 9.2 (albeit without attribution), and asks for analysis on the points raised about damages. On the assumption that the student will delve no further than the rules discerned in the Digest and commented upon in Grueber, it is entirely feasible for him to address each of these cases in the five minutes or so available. The final question calls for a reasoned response about the liability of a *bona fide* possessor to the *dominus* and of the *liber homo bona fide serviens* to the possessor; again, both topics are specifically treated by Grueber.[37]

In the first two decades of the twentieth century, Digest 9.2 was studied in an advanced paper for the most promising undergraduates. It was a self-contained subject, closely focused on learning the text and perhaps, in practice, on learning Grueber's commentary. While it might be said, as Lawson remarked of questions in the 1850s, that the examination 'called for nothing but intelligent reading and a reasonably good memory',[38] the paper on Digest 9.2 nonetheless required students to reason casuistically and to engage, in detail, with sources of law, fault, loss and damage, causation and title to sue and be sued.

3. 1940: A SPECIAL POSTGRADUATE PAPER

Immediately after the FHS, Hanbury took the BCL. Like that of the FHS, the contemporary syllabus for the BCL required examinations in jurisprudence, Roman law, English law and international law.[39] The Roman law component comprised two papers: one addressing the principles of Roman private law as set out in the *Institutes* of Justinian (thus complementing the contemporary focus on Gaius in the FHS) and the other addressing a special subject.[40] In Hanbury's year, 1921, the choice of special subjects was between ownership and possession (Digest 41.1–2) and the theory of contract (Digest 45.1).[41] Jolowicz lectured on the first and de Zulueta on the second,[42] though it is to be supposed that neither otherwise had much

---

[36] ibid 9.

[37] ibid 242–43 and 47, 226.

[38] Lawson (n 4) 23.

[39] Statutes of the University of Oxford, Title VI s VI §2.1, University of Oxford, *The Examination Statutes* (for the academical year 1921–22, Clarendon Press 1921) 232.

[40] Regulations of the Board of the Faculty, regs II.1–2 in ibid 237.

[41] Regulations of the Board of the Faculty, reg II.2 in ibid.

[42] 'Hilary Term, 1920: Schedules of Lectures' (n 19) 309; 'Trinity Term, 1920: Schedules of Lectures' (n 19) 547.

contact with students.[43] It may be that these subjects were thought to have been particularly relevant to the English lawyer; in this period, passing the FHS or the BCL exempted a candidate from the Roman law paper in the bar exam and from two of the five years' articled clerkship required for practice as a solicitor.[44] Ownership and possession, in particular, was offered as a special subject in the BCL from at least 1893, and was compulsory from 1923 to 1966, after which it remained an option until 1974.[45] Property had always been emphasised in Oxford's Roman law curriculum, mirroring, as Lawson observes, the Law School's late-nineteenth-century focus on real property and succession in English law.[46] He further notes, more generally, that the Digest titles addressed in the advanced papers 'were always on subjects which were concurrently studied in English law'.[47] Other options that were available at various times as special subjects in the BCL included the contract *emptio venditio* and the contracts *locatio conductio* and *mandatum*;[48] ownership and possession in Roman-Dutch law and the theory of contract in Roman-Dutch law;[49] the contracts *locatio conductio* and *societas*;[50] the law of theft;[51] and the law of *condictiones*.[52] Digest 9.2 featured as a discrete special subject from 1933 to 1940,[53] by which time Hanbury, having been a Fellow of Lincoln since 1921, was one of four members of the Faculty absent on national service, together with William Hart (Wadham College),

---

[43] Lawson (n 4) 166.

[44] University of Oxford, *Oxford University Handbook* (n 7) 152–53.

[45] See Regulations of the Board of the Faculty, reg II.2 in University of Oxford, *The Examination Statutes* (for the academical year 1893–94, Clarendon Press 1893) 142 and University of Oxford, *Examination Statutes 1921–22* (n 39) 237; Regulations of the Board of the Faculty, 'Examination for the Degree of Bachelor of Civil Law', reg (B)2 in University of Oxford, *The Examination Statutes* (for the academical year 1966–67, Clarendon Press 1966) 444; Regulations of the Board of the Faculty, 'Degree of Bachelor of Civil Law', Examination, regs 1, 3(B)4 in University of Oxford, *Examination Decrees and Regulations for the Academic Year 1973–1974* (Clarendon Press 1973) 528–29.

[46] Lawson (n 4) 24.

[47] Lawson (n 28) 19.

[48] Regulations of the Board of the Faculty, reg II.2 in University of Oxford, *Examination Statutes 1893–94* (n 45) 142.

[49] Regulations of the Board of the Faculty, reg II.2 in University of Oxford, *The Examination Statutes* (for the academical year 1910–11, Clarendon Press 1910) 201.

[50] Regulations of the Board of the Faculty, reg II.3 in University of Oxford, *The Examination Statutes* (for the academical year 1922–23, Clarendon Press 1922) 229.

[51] Regulations of the Board of the Faculty in University of Oxford, *The Examination Statutes* (for the academical year 1928–29, Clarendon Press 1928) 245; University of Oxford, *The Examination Statutes* (for the academical year 1940–41, Clarendon Press 1940) 299.

[52] Regulations of the Board of the Faculty in University of Oxford, *The Examination Statutes* (for the academical year 1951–52, Clarendon Press 1951) 349; University of Oxford, *Examination Statutes 1966–67* (n 45) 443–46.

[53] Regulations of the Board of the Faculty in University of Oxford, *The Examination Statutes* (for the academical year 1932–33, Clarendon Press 1932) 263; University of Oxford, *Examination Statutes 1940–41* (n 51) 299.

Richard Holdsworth (University College) and John Morris (All Souls Lecturer in Private International Law; Magdalen College).[54]

With the Second World War underway, only nine candidates are recorded for the BCL exam in Trinity Term 1940;[55] two were placed in each of the first and second classes and one in the third class.[56] The students had apparently been offered 'informal instruction' in the *lex Aquilia* in Michaelmas Term 1939 by Harry Lawson, then Fellow of Merton and All Souls Reader in Roman Law.[57] No books were prescribed by regulation for them to study. Their examiners for the BCL were Robert Lee (Rhodes Professor of Roman-Dutch Law), Sir William Holdsworth (Vinerian Professor of English Law), Arthur Goodhart (Corpus Professor of Jurisprudence) and Geoffrey Cheshire (All Souls Reader in English Law; Exeter College).[58]

The paper indicates that six questions were to be answered, implying that there were three hours available (though this is not made explicit).[59] Candidates were obliged to attempt one or both of question 1, requiring translation (and only translation) of the run of texts from D.9.2.33.pr to D.9.2.36.pr on the assessment of damages, or question 2, requiring translation and comment on the largely unrelated texts D.9.2.25.2 (assessment of damages where defendant admits liability), D.9.2.27.32 (*actio utilis* for destruction of aqueduct), D.9.2.48 (damage inflicted by a slave manumitted by will, both before and after *aditio*) and part of D.9.2.55 (before delivery, *stipulator* kills one of two slaves promised in the alternative). As with the FHS paper of twenty years earlier, competent answers to these questions might be made in the thirty minutes available on the basis of nothing more than Grueber's, Monro's or Thayer's commentaries.[60] The same may be said of question 7, calling for analysis of six short cases taken directly from Digest 9.2 (again without attribution), question 9, offering five short scenarios in English for examination, and perhaps also question 6, asking about the remedies available in the case of damage cause by three different animals and by a slave.

The essay questions, too, suggest that students were not expected to stray far from Grueber. Question 3, on the law prior to the *lex Aquilia*, is addressed directly by his section on 'The relation of the lex Aquilia to the former law

[54] University of Oxford Faculty of Law, *Withdrawal of Members of the Faculty for National Service* (1940); Oxford University Archives FA 4/6/2/4 at 135, 135.

[55] 'Names of Candidates in the Examination for the Degree of Bachelor of Civil Law in Trinity Term, 1940' in *Oxford University Gazette* (1940.05.16) No 2293, 669.

[56] 'Names of Candidates who in Trinity Term, 1940, were adjudged worthy of Honours' in *Oxford University Gazette* (1940.07.18) No 2300, 804.

[57] 'Michaelmas Term, 1939: Schedules of Lectures' in *Oxford University Gazette* (1939.06.23) No 2257 (Supplement) 825, 828.

[58] 'Trinity Term, 1940: Names of Candidates' (n 56).

[59] See University of Oxford, *Examination in the Faculty of Law for the Degree of BCL: Trinity Term, 1940* (Oxford University Examination Papers No 3892, 1940).

[60] Monro (n 28) on the LA; Thayer (n 28) on the LA; Grueber (n 13).

as to damage to property'.[61] Question 4, about general exceptions to liability, is systematically treated in his section on 'The requirement of iniuria'.[62] Question 5 calls for discussion of a quotation from Grueber about acts and omissions, by reference to texts: precisely the kind of analysis that he undertakes himself under the heading 'The nature of the act, which entails liability under the Aquilian law'.[63] Finally, question 8 is a variation on the theme of the original provisions of the *lex* and the structure of its chapters, which, as noted in relation to the FHS question on the same theme, is addressed in Grueber's section, 'The fundamental provisions of the lex Aquilia'.[64]

Although the BCL is a postgraduate degree, there is a striking re-use of the same questions (or minor variations on them), not just among BCL papers between 1933 and 1940 but also between papers in the BCL course on Digest 9.2 and the FHS course. Of the 1940 BCL paper, questions 1,[65] 2(a),[66] 2(b),[67] 2(c),[68] 2(d),[69] 3,[70] 4,[71] 5,[72] 6,[73] 7(c),[74] 7(e),[75] 7(f),[76] 8,[77]

---

[61] Grueber (n 13) 185–96.

[62] ibid 214–22.

[63] ibid 208–14.

[64] ibid 196–99.

[65] University of Oxford, *Second Public Examination: Honour School of Jurisprudence: Trinity Term, 1895* (Oxford University Examination Papers No 860, 1895) question 5(a); University of Oxford, *Examination in the Faculty of Law for the Degree of BCL: Trinity Term, 1936* (Oxford University Examination Papers No 3658, 1936) question 2(c) (in part).

[66] University of Oxford, *Examination in the Faculty of Law for the Degree of BCL: Trinity Term, 1934* (Oxford University Examination Papers No 3540, 1934) question 2(c).

[67] University of Oxford, *Second Public Examination: Honour School of Jurisprudence (Final Examination): Trinity Term, 1921* (Oxford University Examination Papers No 2022, 1921) question 2(c); University of Oxford, *Examination in the Faculty of Law for the Degree of BCL: Trinity Term, 1933* (Oxford University Examination Papers No 3481, 1933) question 6(c).

[68] University of Oxford, *Second Public Examination: Honour School of Jurisprudence (Final Examination): Trinity Term, 1911* (Oxford University Examination Papers No 1548, 1911) question 4(b); University of Oxford, *FHS Paper 1921* (n 67) question 2(d); University of Oxford, *BCL Paper 1936* (n 65) question 2(f).

[69] University of Oxford, *FHS Paper 1911* (n 68) question 4(c); University of Oxford, *Second Public Examination: Honour School of Jurisprudence (Final Examination): Trinity Term, 1919* (Oxford University Examination Papers No 1903, 1919) question 6(c) (in part); University of Oxford, *BCL Paper 1933* (n 67) question 2.

[70] University of Oxford, *Second Public Examination: Honour School of Jurisprudence: Trinity Term, 1896* (Oxford University Examination Papers No 904, 1896) question 1; University of Oxford, *Second Public Examination: Honour School of Jurisprudence (Final Examination): Trinity Term, 1912* (Oxford University Examination Papers No 1598, 1912) question 2; University of Oxford, *Second Public Examination: Honour School of Jurisprudence (Final Examination): Trinity Term, 1915* (Oxford University Examination Papers No 1759, 1915) question 1(a); University of Oxford, *Second Public Examination: Honour School of Jurisprudence (Final Examination): Trinity Term, 1918* (Oxford University Examination Papers No 1868, 1918) question 5(a).

[71] University of Oxford, *Second Public Examination: Honour School of Jurisprudence (Final Examination): Trinity Term, 1917* (Oxford University Examination Papers No 1841, 1917) question 5.

9(b)[78] and 9(d)[79] had all appeared in some form before. Even excluding the comment and short problem questions, where some repetition might reasonably be expected, close equivalents of the essay questions in the 1940 paper can be found in nine previous FHS papers and two previous BCL papers.

The detailed study of Roman law expected of the 1940 postgraduate BCL student tracked the areas of English law upon which the contemporary curriculum focused. The paper on Digest 9.2 was concentrated, like its 1920 undergraduate equivalent, on close textual analysis and casuistic application, in order to developed a refined, if practical, understanding of the legal rules and their operation. While the study of other areas of the law had, by this time, 'perforce become critical',[80] the style of examinations in Roman law seems unreformed. Nonetheless, the essays, commentary and short problem questions tested students' appreciation of the historical evolution of the law and its sources, and required them to engage with particular instances of the general concepts of fault and exceptions, acts and omissions, loss and injury, assessment of damages, title to sue and causation.

4. 1960: AN UNDEMANDING UNDERGRADUATE PAPER

In 1960, Hanbury, now Vinerian Professor of Law, was made an honorary Queen's Counsel;[81] he would shortly serve as Acting Dean of Law at the new University of Ife (now Obafemi Awolowo University) in Nigeria.[82] It

---

[72] University of Oxford, *FHS Paper 1896* (n 70) question 5; University of Oxford, *FHS Paper 1912* (n 70) question 3; University of Oxford, *FHS Paper 1918* (n 70) question 2; University of Oxford, *BCL Paper 1936* (n 65) question 7(a).

[73] University of Oxford, *FHS Paper 1912* (n 70) questions 4(c)–(e) (in part).

[74] University of Oxford, *BCL Paper 1936* (n 65) question 2(a).

[75] University of Oxford, *FHS Paper 1895* (n 65) question 3; University of Oxford, *BCL Paper 1934* (n 66) question 3(a); University of Oxford, *Examination in the Faculty of Law for the Degree of BCL: Trinity Term, 1937* (Oxford University Examination Papers No 3717, 1937) question 6(b).

[76] University of Oxford, *Second Public Examination: Honour School of Jurisprudence: Trinity Term, 1894* (Oxford University Examination Papers No 831, 1894) question 5(d); University of Oxford, *Second Public Examination: Honour School of Jurisprudence: Trinity Term, 1910* (Oxford University Examination Papers No 1499, 1910) question 3(c); University of Oxford, *FHS Paper 1921* (n 67) question 2(a); University of Oxford, *BCL Paper 1936* (n 65) question 2(d); University of Oxford, *BCL Paper 1937* (n 75) question 6(c).

[77] University of Oxford, *Examination in the Faculty of Law for the Degree of BCL: Trinity Term, 1938* (Oxford University Examination Papers No 3778, 1938) question 4.

[78] University of Oxford, *FHS Paper 1919* (n 69) question 5(d); University of Oxford, *FHS Paper 1920* (n 33) question 3(b).

[79] University of Oxford, *Examination in the Faculty of Law for the Degree of BCL: Trinity Term, 1935* (Oxford University Examination Papers No 3600, 1935) question 6(a).

[80] Lawson (n 4) 143.

[81] Stevens (n 6) 3.

[82] Lawson (n 4) 168.

was still possible to proceed to the FHS in Jurisprudence having taken some
other subject for the First Public Examination[83] but a student who did take
Law Moderations (as the Preliminary Examination had been called since
1932)[84] would have been obliged to sit a paper in Roman law.[85] At this time,
the Moderations paper covered sources, property and the general outline of
the law of persons, succession and delict, studied in connection with relevant
passages of Justinian's *Institutes*.[86] As a result of reforms to the FHS syllabus
in 1934,[87] 1950[88] and 1953,[89] candidates for the Second Public Examination
were now examined in:

(1) general jurisprudence;
(2) a branch of Roman law;
(3) law of land or Roman-Dutch law;
(4) contract;
(5) torts;
(6) three of the following:
    (a) a second branch of Roman law,
    (b) constitutional law,
    (c) the history of English law,
    (d) international law.[90]

So far as Roman law was concerned, the pattern from 1950 until 1997 was
to offer two papers in the FHS: Roman Law I covered contracts and quasi-
contracts as set out in Gaius's and Justinian's *Institutes*, together with the
law of sale, with reference to Digest XVIII.1; Roman Law II covered the
following:

(a) The Roman Law of Delict and Quasi-Delict, studied historically in connexion with the following texts: Gaius, III. 182–225; IV. 75–9; Justinian,
Inst. IV. 1–5; 8–9.

---

[83] ibid 162.
[84] See Statutes of the University of Oxford, Title VI s 1.B §8.1 in University of Oxford, *The Examination Statutes* (for the academical year 1931–32, Clarendon Press 1931) 35.
[85] Statutes of the University of Oxford, Title VI s 1.B §7.1 in University of Oxford, *The Examination Statutes* (for the academical year 1957–58, Clarendon Press 1957) 55.
[86] Regulations of the Board of the Faculty, 'Law Moderations', reg 1 in ibid 56.
[87] See Regulations of the Board of the Faculty in University of Oxford, *The Examination Statutes* (for the academical year 1934–35, Clarendon Press 1934) 120–23.
[88] See Statutes of the University of Oxford, Title VI s I.C §7 in University of Oxford, *The Examination Statutes* (for the academical year 1950–51, Clarendon Press 1950) 129 and Regulations of the Board of the Faculty in ibid 129–30.
[89] See Statutes of the University of Oxford, Title VI s 1.C §7 in University of Oxford, *The Examination Statutes* (for the academical year 1953–54, Clarendon Press 1953) 128 and Regulations of the Board of the Faculty in ibid 128–33.
[90] See Statutes of the University of Oxford, Title VI s I.C §7.1 in University of Oxford, *Examination Statutes 1957–58* (n 85) 127.

(b) The Roman Law of Damage to Property, studied in connexion with Digest IX.2. Candidates will be expected to compare the Roman Law with the corresponding portions of the English Law of Torts.

Candidates for either paper I or paper II will be required to show a sufficient knowledge of the principles of Roman Law.[91]

Grueber's and Monro's *lex Aquilia* continued to be prescribed as core reading for Roman Law II.[92] More generalist works were also prescribed, in relation to both Roman law papers.[93]

There were 255 candidates in the FHS in 1960; seventeen firsts, ninety-eight seconds, eighty-four thirds, thirty fourths, one aegrotat, one passed overstanding for Honours[94] and twenty-four fails (of whom eleven were awarded a pass degree).[95] Around 178 candidates (69 per cent of the cohort) took Roman Law II as one of their option papers.[96] The examiners commented upon this in their report:

> The continued popularity of this paper, despite the poor results last year, is presumably accounted for by the fact that the syllabus is narrow and choice of topics for questions very restricted.[97]

The paper was considered less exacting than options in legal history or public international law and a lighter load may have been attractive to stu-

---

[91] Regulations of the Board of the Faculty, reg 2 in ibid 128.

[92] ibid.

[93] ibid 128–29. Under 'texts' were prescribed: Frederick Henry Lawson, *Negligence in the Civil Law* (Clarendon Press 1950). Justinian, *The Institutes of Justinian* (n 24); Francis de Zulueta, *The Institutes of Gaius* vol 2 (Clarendon Press 1953); Francis de Zulueta, *The Roman Law of Sale: Introduction and Select Texts* (Clarendon Press 1945). Under 'general' were prescribed: William Warwick Buckland, *A Text-Book of Roman Law from Augustus to Justinian* (2nd edn, CUP 1932); William Warwick Buckland, *A Manual of Roman Private Law* (2nd edn, CUP 1939); William Warwick Buckland, *The Main Institutions of Roman Private Law* (CUP 1931); André Giffard, *Précis de droit romain* (4th edn, Librairie Dalloz 1951); Paul Girard and Félix Senn, *Textes de droit romain* (6th edn, Rousseau & Cie 1937); Salvatore Riccobono and others, *Fontes iuris Romani Antejustiniani* (2nd, amended, edn, G Barbèra 1940–43); Paul Girard and Félix Senn, *Manuel élémentaire de droit romain* (8th edn, Rousseau & Cie 1929); Herbert F Jolowicz, *Historical Introduction to Roman Law* (2nd, corrected, edn, CUP 1954); Robert Warden Lee, *Elements of Roman Law: with a Translation of the Institutes of Justinian* (4th edn, Sweet & Maxwell 1956); Raymond Monier, *Manuel élémentaire de droit romain* (6th edn, Domat Montchrestien 1947); Fritz Schulz, *Principles of Roman Law* (M Wolff tr, Clarendon Press 1936); Fritz Schulz, *Classical Roman Law* (Clarendon Press 1951).

[94] That is, the candidate was ineligible for an Honours degree because he had exceeded the number of terms permitted after matriculation.

[95] University of Oxford Faculty of Law, *Report of the Examiners for the Final Honour School of Jurisprudence 1960* (1960.10.17) L(6)36; Oxford University Archives FA 4/6/2/8, 1.

[96] University of Oxford Faculty of Law, *Final Honour School of Jurisprudence 1960: Optional Papers* (1960.03.18) L(60)13; Oxford University Archives FA 4/6/2/8, 1.

[97] University of Oxford Faculty of Law, *FHS Examiners' Report 1960* (n 95) 3.

dents whose syllabus in jurisprudence, contract, torts and constitutional law now encompassed a greater body of material (and was now the subject of reading lists) than it had at the start of the twentieth century.[98] The most significant difference between the Roman Law II paper and its predecessor is, of course, that the syllabus covered delict and quasi-delict at the level of the *Institutes*, as well as *damnum iniuria* treated in depth by reference to Digest 9.2. Accordingly, in the examination of 1960,[99] only seven of the twelve passages for translation and comment are taken from Digest 9.2; of the essays, questions 6 and 7 directly concern the *lex Aquilia*, while answers to questions 5 and 8 ought to refer to it at least in part; of the short problem scenarios, *damnum iniuria* is central to questions 9(b) and 10(c), and is also implicated in question 10(a). Seven of the ten questions are, in style, familiar from the papers stretching back into the nineteenth century. One type of question calls for translation and comment or historical commentary on short excerpts in the original Latin (with many of the excerpts repeated from past papers). A second type calls for advice or discussion of very short scenarios that pick up, more or less directly, fact-patterns addressed in the Digest. The rubric for the 1960 paper offers candidates the choice to answer four or five questions, meaning that they would have had twelve to fifteen minutes to devote to each of the three parts in this style of question, if the duration of the paper (not indicated in the original) were three hours, or eight to ten minutes, if it were two hours. The essay questions, too, invoke familiar themes and, it is submitted, are neither more nor less open than essay questions in earlier FHS or BCL papers. Question 6, for example, asking, 'To what extent were self-defence, necessity, and mistake defences to an Aquilian action?' can be put alongside similar past questions that candidates might have answered on the basis of Grueber's section on 'The requirement of iniuria', where categories of lawful excuse are systematically treated.[100] Given the similarity in the style of questions and the time available to answer them, as well as the near-identity of the materials prescribed, it seems unlikely that what was expected of students taking the delict paper differed significantly from what was expected of candidates in the Digest 9.2 papers twenty, forty or even sixty-five years earlier. Even so, Lawson suggests that 'in some quarters a more exacting view of Romanistic study began to prevail over a limited but conscientious study of the original texts'.[101]

One aspect of the syllabus regulations might be thought to entail a more exacting approach: the expectation, specifically noted in the syllabus, that students compare the Roman law with corresponding portions of the

---

[98] Lawson (n 4) 152–53.

[99] University of Oxford, *Second Public Examination: Honour School of Jurisprudence: Roman Law II* (Examination Paper No 5265, 1960).

[100] Grueber (n 13) 214–22.

[101] Lawson (n 4) 164.

English law of torts. The motivation behind this instruction is both clear and pedagogically sound, at least where the material is taught and examined in an appropriate fashion. This does not, however, appear to have been the case, even allowing for the prescription of Lawson's *Negligence in the Civil Law* as a core text. All of the essay questions in the 1960 paper, for example, expressly and exclusively direct attention to Roman law, leaving little scope for, or benefit in, referring to equivalent English law principles. The examiners expressed their views on the issue in their report:

> One difficulty in setting and marking this paper arises from the rubric in the Examination Statutes which requires the candidate to compare the Roman Law of Damage to Property (i.e. in this context <u>damnum iniuria datum</u>) with the corresponding portions of the English law of torts. Most candidates say nothing about English law. Probably they take the view, for which there is much to be said, that <u>damnum iniuria datum</u> is the wrongful infliction of patrimonial loss and that in English law, with the possible exception of the action <u>per quod servitium amisit</u>, there is no tort which is conceived in this way. At the moment, candidates are not in practice penalised for omitting comparison with English law. On the other hand, if comparisons are to be required, the analogies between <u>furtum</u> and English criminal law, and between liability for damage done by animals in the two systems are closer and more interesting than any which can be made between <u>damnum iniuria datum</u> and the English law of torts. Again, if there is anything to which Chapter 1 of the lex Aquilia 'corresponds', it is, surely, the English law of homicide, rather than any part of the law of torts. At the moment, candidates who act on the principle that every word in the rubric must have a meaning are faced with the difficulty of deciding, e.g. whether the Roman plaintiff's slave 'corresponds' in English law to his servant, his chattel, or (when contributory negligence is discussed) to the plaintiff himself. We feel that, at the moment, when faced with these puzzles, the candidate has no solid ground to walk on.[102]

The examiners went on to recommend that the offending part of the regulation be removed or, alternatively, that the relevant part of the English law of torts or criminal law be specified.[103] A Committee was duly convened to review the rubric, comprising David Daube (Regius Professor of Civil Law), Harry Lawson (Professor of Comparative Law), Tony Honoré (Rhodes Reader in Roman-Dutch Law; Queen's College) and Barry Nicholas (All Souls Reader in Roman Law; Brasenose College). The Committee plainly did not share the puzzlement of the examiners (of whom Tony Honoré had been one)[104] as to the available 'correspondence' and as to the possibility of

---

[102] University of Oxford Faculty of Law, *FHS Examiners' Report 1960* (n 95) 3.
[103] ibid 3.
[104] The Examiners were Jack Butterworth (New College), Rupert Cross (Magdalen College; later Vinerian Professor of English Law), Tony Honoré (Rhodes Reader in Roman-Dutch Law, Queen's College; later Regius Professor of Civil Law), David Yardley (St Edmund Hall)

useful comparison between Roman and English law. Their unanimous rec-ommendation was a broader amendment to the rubric: expecting students 'to compare the Roman law with the relevant portions of the English Law of Torts and English Criminal Law'.[105] The Board referred the recommenda-tion to the Faculty.[106] The proposed rubric was defeated by eleven votes to eight; a proposal to delete the words 'and English Criminal Law' was tied with eight votes in favour and eight against; instead, it was agreed that 'the Committee should consider the rubric again with special reference to the desirability of ... specifying particular torts and crimes for comparison'.[107] The Committee's second report considered that it was not 'practical to specify the portions of the Law of Torts with which comparison would be required, since only certain aspects of any given tort would be relevant in a Roman context. (Trespass, conversion and nuisance, for example, fall from the Roman point of view partly into Delict, partly into Property.)'[108] In relation to criminal law, the Committee considered specifying homicide and 'Larceny, False Pretences, Embezzlement and Fraudulent Conversion' but thought that the latter, in particular, 'would impose on the candidate an undue burden in the shape of a complicated branch of English law which is at present included in Law Moderations and not in the Final School'.[109] The Committee's ultimate recommendation, that the rubric (continue merely to) require candidates 'to compare the Roman Law with the relevant portions of the English Law of Torts',[110] was accepted by the Board[111] and the rubric retained this form until 2013.[112]

The study of Digest 9.2 in 1960 was in transition: the delict paper in which it featured was regarded as easier than many and, while it appears that the older style of learning, based on commentaries and close analysis of the texts

and Anthony Rogerson (Trinity College): 'Class and Pass Lists for Trinity Term 1960' in *Oxford University Gazette* (1960.08.19) No 3053 (Supplement) 1565, 1574.

[105] University of Oxford Faculty of Law, *Report of the Committee on the Revision of the Rubric for Roman Law II in the Honour School of Jurisprudence* (1960.12.16) L(61)7; Oxford University Archives FA 4/6/2/8, 1.

[106] University of Oxford Faculty of Law, *Minutes of the Board* (1961.01.28) L(61)vi, vi; Oxford University Archives FA 4/6/1/5 at 66, 66 (item 4).

[107] University of Oxford Faculty of Law, *Minutes of the Faculty Meeting* (1961.02.27) L(61)26; Oxford University Archives FA 4/6/2/8, 2 (item B). See also University of Oxford Faculty of Law, *Minutes of the Board* (1961.04.03) L(61)xiii, xiv; Oxford University Archives FA 4/6/1/5 at 72, 73 (item 12).

[108] University of Oxford Faculty of Law, *Second Report of the Committee on the Revision of the Rubric for Roman Law II in the Honour School of Jurisprudence* (1961.05.30) L(61)44; Oxford University Archives FA 4/6/2/8, 1.

[109] ibid.

[110] ibid.

[111] University of Oxford Faculty of Law, *Minutes of the Board* (1961.06.10) L(61)xxv, xxv; Oxford University Archives FA 4/6/1/5 at 82, 82 (item 11).

[112] University of Oxford Faculty of Law, *Student Handbook (Undergraduate Students) 2012–2013* (2012) 75.

of Digest 9.2, still prevailed in practice, comparison with English law was formally required and debates in the Faculty reveal that this was understood to be a desirable objective. A wider range of source materials was prescribed, though largely limited to textbooks and commentaries. A potentially broader reach can be discerned in some examination questions, though others continued to focus on careful casuistic explanation and application of legal rules and principles. Nonetheless, the subject matter of the examination required students to convey an understanding of archaisms and the historical evolution of the law, the interplay between fault and exceptions, classic problems of causation and the relationship between remedies and substantive law.

5. 1980: AN ADVANCED COMPARATIVE PAPER

Hanbury was long retired by 1980 and, following the death of his wife, he moved to live in South Africa.[113] Although the 'Roman Law of Delict' was reinstituted as an optional BCL paper from 1975, none of the thirty-one students took this option in 1980,[114] so it is convenient, for now, to continue to follow the FHS paper in Roman Law II (Delict). Aside from those who passed the First Public Examination in another subject (which was still possible), candidates in the FHS would, at the prior stage of Law Moderations, have been examined in Roman law, criminal law and constitutional law.[115] The Roman law component at Moderations now encompassed sources, property, the formulary system and delict, in both Gaius's and Justinian's *Institutes*, together with the general outline of the law of persons.[116] For the FHS itself, in addition to four compulsory papers in jurisprudence, contract, tort and land, candidates were required to sit four optional papers from a choice of fourteen, including Roman Law I and Roman Law II. While the prescribed texts for the contracts and sale course (Roman Law I) had been amended slightly in 1969,[117] the syllabus for Roman Law II was, apart from insignificant linguistic changes, identical to that set out above. After 1969, no books were prescribed by regulation; there is, unfortunately, also a gap in the Bodleian Library's holdings of lecture lists for the early 1980s. It is therefore difficult to trace the process by which tutorials in Roman Law II (as distinct from tutorials for Roman law in Moderations) increasingly came to be the preserve of specialists, the generalist college tutor who could teach

---

[113] Stevens (n 6) 3.

[114] University of Oxford Faculty of Law, *Bachelor of Civil Law 1980: Examiners' Report* (1980) L(80)54; Oxford University Archives FA 4/6/2/14, 1.

[115] Statutes of the University of Oxford, Title VI s I.B §13.1 in University of Oxford, *Examination Decrees and Regulations 1977* (for the academical year 1977–78, Clarendon Press 1977) 61.

[116] Regulations of the Board of the Faculty, 'Law Moderations', reg 1 in ibid 61–62.

[117] See Regulations of the Board of the Faculty, reg 6 in University of Oxford, *Examination Decrees* (for the academical year 1969–70, Clarendon Press 1969) 142.

across the FHS having already been in decline from the middle of the centu-ry.[118] As noted below, the demands of the paper were by now more exacting: because it no longer comprised mere close study of the texts, it became both more difficult for a generalist to teach and also less of a 'soft' option for stu-dents. Evidencing the decline in popularity, the *Examiners' Report* for 1980 indicates that eighteen candidates offered Roman Law II: 7 per cent of an overall cohort of 252. Of that overall cohort, twenty-seven candidates were awarded firsts, 201 seconds, nineteen thirds, two passes and three fails.[119] Of the Roman Law II candidates, the examiners said:

> Though there were no outstanding scripts, the general standard was good and none of the candidates was really weak. The text questions were better answered than the essays, and the problems tended to be the weakest part of the papers.[120]

The rubric for the 1980 FHS examination paper required candidates to answer four questions from ten, including at least two of the four comment questions available; five of the ten passages for comment are taken from Digest 9.2. While some of the excerpts are, not unexpectedly, familiar from previous papers, in contrast to earlier practice, the instruction is not 'trans-late and comment' but '[c]omment, without translating';[121] this change had taken effect in 1973 and is one of several features arguably indicating a more intense focus on substance and analysis than in previous decades. Another feature is the express direction, not merely in the rubric but also in the text of particular questions, to compare Roman and English law, as in questions 5 to 7:

> 5. Gaius and Justinian say that, whereas contractual obligations are of different sorts, all delictual obligations are of the same type. Why do they take this view of delictual obligations? Could the same be said of the English law of torts?
> 6. In what circumstances, apart from contractual obligation, do Roman and English law require persons to take action in order to prevent harm to others?
> 7. What is the difference between the noxal and personal liability of an owner for the act of his slave? Is there a parallel distinction in English law as regards the employer's liability for the act of his employee?[122]

Question 8, about damages under Chapter 1 of the *lex*, does not invite similar comparison but it is the only one of the four essay questions not to do so. The comparative dimension of teaching Roman law is, accordingly,

---

[118] Lawson (n 4) 173.

[119] University of Oxford Faculty of Law, *Final Honour School of Jurisprudence 1980: Examiners' Report* (1980) L(80)53; Oxford University Archives FA 4/6/2/14, 2.

[120] ibid 9.

[121] University of Oxford, *Honour School of Jurisprudence: Roman Law II (Delict)* (Examination Paper 2L5, 1980) questions 1–4.

[122] ibid.

more fully expressed in this paper than in its predecessors. It is submitted that the style and scope of the essay questions, as well as the time available to complete them – given that only four answers are required in three hours – call for answers of a more sophisticated kind than had been sought even twenty years earlier. This is not only a function of their comparative dimension but also a product of more open questioning: inviting analysis, not merely description, and argument, not merely recitation of knowledge. Plainly, the paper is not entirely open to interpretation: the comment questions and the two two-scenario short problem questions (out of which three scenarios arguably involve *damnum iniuria*) all demand specific knowledge of the texts and application to the facts.

Despite the lack of formal change to the syllabus, the study of Digest 9.2, in the context of the paper on delict and quasi-delict, changed appreciably between 1960 and 1980: no longer could it be regarded as an easy option for students. The newer style of examination questions called not for mere comment and competent application but conceptual and evaluative analysis of, for example, primary and secondary liability; the roles of intention and fault; and the theory of damages. Moreover, the significant potential for insight to be gained by comparing the Roman and English law was now fully realised and rigorously tested in the examination.

6. 2000: AN ADVANCED ROMANIST PAPER

Hanbury died in March 1993, at nearly ninety-five years old, so we examine Digest 9.2 at the end of the twentieth century without him. Although it was still technically possible to proceed to the FHS having taken a subject other than law for the First Preliminary Examination, this was exceptional by 2000 and, accordingly, candidates had generally taken Law Moderations, with papers in criminal law and constitutional law and one of either Roman law or 'Introduction to Law'.[123] Of the cohort of 259, 149 candidates took the Roman law paper and 109 Introduction to Law.[124] The content of the Moderations course had again shifted slightly: students now studied sources, property, contract and delict, in both Gaius's and Justinian's *Institutes*.[125] The FHS itself now offered two BA programmes, identical save that Course 2 involved spending a year taking courses at a partner European university.[126] Jurisprudence, contract and tort were at this time compulsory papers, as

---

[123] Decree, para 1 and Regulations of the Board of the Faculty, 'Law Moderations', regs 1–2 in University of Oxford, *Examination Decrees and Regulations 1997* (for the academical year 1997–98, OUP 1997) 64–65.

[124] University of Oxford Faculty of Law, *Law Moderations – Hilary Term 2000: Moderators' Report* (2000.05.25) L(00)67, Appendix A; Oxford University Archives FA 4/6/2/27A, 1.

[125] See Regulations of the Board of the Faculty, reg 1 in University of Oxford, *Examination Decrees 1997–98* (n 123) 65.

[126] Decree, para 3 in ibid 241–42.

was one of either land law or administrative law (land law having once been alternative to Roman-Dutch law and then a compulsory paper; the choice between land law and administrative law was offered between 1998 and 2006).[127] Candidates were required to take four additional optional papers from a choice of nineteen 'Standard Subjects', together with a ninth paper chosen from a list of four 'Special Subjects'.[128] One of the Standard Subjects was Roman Law (Delict): this was straightforwardly Roman Law II, the paper having been rebranded in 1998, when the contract-focused Roman Law I was dropped.

The formal structure of the BCL degree remained unchanged through most of the twentieth century, until a short-lived experiment with a Preliminary Examination for students other than graduates of the FHS, from 1960[129] to 1970,[130] and the equally short-lived experiment with offering both a one-year and a two-year BCL, from 1991[131] to 2000,[132] after which only the one-year variant survived. When the Preliminary Examination for the BCL was first introduced, a paper on the *Institutes* of Justinian was compulsory, and the paper on ownership and possession was one of four compulsory papers that candidates sat for their Final Examination, together with papers in two special subjects.[133] In 1967, however, candidates for the Preliminary Examination were given the choice between a paper on the general principles of Roman law and a paper on the general principles of the common law, and the Roman law of ownership and possession became a special subject, that is to say, an optional subject rather than a compulsory one.[134] Roman law thus ceased to be a mandatory element in the degree of Bachelor of Civil Law. The Digest 9.2 paper having last been offered in the BCL in 1940, an optional paper encompassing the *lex Aquilia* was not offered again at postgraduate

---

[127] Regulations of the Board of the Faculty in ibid 242–43.

[128] ibid.

[129] See Regulations of the Board of the Faculty, 'Degree of Bachelor of Civil Law' in University of Oxford, *The Examination Statutes* (for the academical year 1960–61, Clarendon Press 1960) 366–67.

[130] See Regulations of the Board of the Faculty, 'Degree of Bachelor of Civil Law' in University of Oxford, *Examination Decrees* (for the academical year 1970–71, Clarendon Press 1970) 534–35.

[131] Regulations of the Board of the Faculty, 'Degree of Bachelor of Civil Law', reg 1 in University of Oxford, *Examination Decrees and Regulations 1991* (for the academical year 1991–92, OUP 1991) 698–99.

[132] Decree, §2 in University of Oxford, *Examination Decrees and Regulations 1999* (for the academical year 1999–2000, OUP 1999) 905–06 and Regulations of the Board of the Faculty in ibid 908–10.

[133] Regulations of the Board of the Faculty, 'Degree of Bachelor of Civil Law' in University of Oxford, *Examination Statutes 1960–61* (n 129) 366–67.

[134] Regulations of the Board of the Faculty, 'Degree of Bachelor of Civil Law' in University of Oxford, *Examination Statutes 1966–67* (n 45) 443–46.

level until 1974.[135] That paper, entitled the Roman Law of Delict and Damage to Property, had the same syllabus as the undergraduate Roman Law II paper, and was not available to any student who had taken Roman Law II in the FHS.[136] When the Faculty began to offer the MJur degree in 1992, principally for the benefit of students whose legal training was not in a common-law jurisdiction,[137] candidates were permitted to choose from certain papers in the BCL, including the Roman Law of Delict and Damage to Property, and also from certain papers in the FHS, including Roman Law (Delict). Though, as noted, the syllabus for these two delict courses was the same, different examination papers were set.[138]

Since the syllabus for the delict course was identical wherever offered, and since the cohorts were now usually relatively small, be they drawn from the FHS, the BCL or the MJur, it was natural that the teaching should be combined. The lecture lists record that Peter Birks led seminars for two hours in each week of Hilary Term and for two weeks of Trinity Term 2000, combining the cohorts from the FHS and the BCL.[139] In that year, three candidates took the undergraduate course in Roman Law (Delict), one of whom achieved 'considerable sophistication in the analysis of the texts' and, with it, a first-class mark.[140] Although a BCL paper was set, the relevant *Examiners' Report* does not indicate how many students took the paper; it does not appear that any MJur candidates sat either form of the delict paper.

The FHS and BCL exam papers follow the same format: four questions calling for comment, without translation, on a series of passages in the original Latin, five essay questions and a short problem question. Of the passages for comment, seven of eleven in the FHS paper and eight of twelve in the BCL paper concern *damnum iniuria*. There are, predictably enough, familiar passages amongst them: D.9.2.13.pr, for example, has been a perennial favourite of the examiners. Three of the essay questions in each paper invoke *damnum iniuria*, exclusively or in part, and both papers' problem questions involve damage to property. One interesting feature is that the style of question expressly calling for comparison between Roman law and English law is

---

[135] Regulations of the Board of the Faculty, 'Degree of Bachelor of Civil Law', reg 3(B)5 in University of Oxford, *Examination Decrees and Regulations 1978* (for the academical year 1978–79, Clarendon Press 1978) 556.

[136] ibid.

[137] See, generally, Decree, §§1–4 in University of Oxford, *Examination Decrees and Regulations 1992* (for the academical year 1992–93, OUP 1992) 753–56.

[138] The duplication was eventually suppressed in 2003: see Special Regulations, 'Degrees of Bachelor of Civil Law and Magister Juris', Schedule A in University of Oxford, *Examination Regulations 2003* (for the academical year 2003–04, OUP 2003) 892–93.

[139] University of Oxford Faculty of Law, *Lecture List for Hilary Term 2000* (2000) 3, 5; University of Oxford Faculty of Law, *Lecture List for Trinity Term 2000* (2000) 2, 4.

[140] University of Oxford Faculty of Law, *FHS Jurisprudence 2000: Examiners Report* (2000); Oxford University Archives FA 4/6/2/27B, 2, 6, 25.

entirely absent from both papers – though the syllabus for each course still indicates that candidates will be required to make this comparison.[141] This may be a function of changing preferences of the setters of the papers but it might also be conjectured that the scope and detail of the secondary materials to which students were now directed furnished them with the means to discuss the Roman law in greater depth than before, permitting a shift of emphasis and interest. For example, whereas a student answering question 1 of the 1920 FHS paper on the original text and early interpretation of Chapter 1 of the *lex Aquilia* was formally prescribed only Grueber's commentary, the section on 'The Lex as Enacted' in Birks's reading list directed students of the 2000 FHS course to no fewer than nineteen sources, ranging across three languages and eight decades.[142] Moreover, the evolution from questions calling for predominantly descriptive rather than predominantly analytical answers, which was evident in the 1980 FHS paper, now appears essentially complete: nowhere in Grueber could candidates find a ready-made answer to the 2000 BCL question 'Was Aquilian *culpa* just a matter for the tribunal of fact?' Of course, the Regius Professor had contributed much of the new literature himself; accordingly, we see his interest in, say,

---

[141] Regulations of the Board of the Faculty, 'Honour School of Jurisprudence', reg 5.2 in University of Oxford, *Examination Decrees 1992–93* (n 137) 204 and Regulations of the Board of the Faculty, 'Degree of Bachelor of Civil Law', reg 5 in ibid 758.

[142] A copy of this list was kindly provided to the author by Professor Helen Scott. The works prescribed were: Frederick Henry Lawson and Basil S Markesinis, *Tortious Liability for Unintentional Harm in the Common Law and the Civil Law* vol 1 (CUP 1982); Reinhard Zimmermann, *The Law of Obligations: Roman Foundations of the Civilian Tradition* (OUP 1996); Hans Ankum, '*Quanti ea res erit in diebus XXX proximis* dans le troisième chapitre de la *lex Aquilia* : un fantasme florentin' in Étienne Dravasa (ed), *Religion, société et politique: Mélanges en hommage à Jacques Ellul* (Presses Universitaires de France 1983) 171; Guillaume Cardascia, 'La Portée primitive de la Loi Aquilia' in Alan Watson (ed), *Daube Noster: Essays in Legal History for David Daube* (Scottish Academic Press 1974) 53; John Kelly, 'Further Reflections on the "Lex Aquilia"' in Luigi Aru (ed), *Studi in Onore di Edoardo Volterra* vol 1 (Giuffrè 1971) 235; Fritz Pringsheim, 'The Origin of the «Lex Aquilia»' in *Droits de l'Antiquité et sociologie juridique: Mélanges Henri Lévy-Bruhl* (Sirey 1959) 233; A Bernard, 'A propos d'un article récent sur le chapitre 3 de la loi Aquilie : Contenu. Nature de la réparation' (1937) 16 RHDFE 450; Peter Birks, 'Wrongful Loss by Co-Promisees' (1994) 22 Index 181; John Crook, '*Lex Aquilia*' (1984) 62 Athenaeum 67; David Daube, 'On the Third Chapter of the *Lex Aquilia*' (1936) 52 LQR 253; William Gordon, 'Dating the *Lex Aquilia*' (1976) Acta Juridica 315; Tony Honoré, 'Linguistic and Social Context of the *Lex Aquilia*' (1972) 7 IJ 138; J A Iliffe, 'Thirty Days Hath *Lex Aquilia*' (1958) 5 RIDA 493; Herbert F Jolowicz, 'The Original Scope of the *Lex Aquilia* and the Question of Damages' (1922) 38 LQR 220; John Kelly, 'The Meaning of the *Lex Aquilia*' (1964) 80 LQR 73; Otto Lenel, 'H.F. Jolowicz, The Original Scope of the *Lex Aquilia* and the Question of Damages (The Law Quarterly Review XXXVIII, 220 f.) (Review)' (1922) 43 ZSS (RA) 575; Henri Lévy-Bruhl, 'Le deuxième chapitre de la loi Aquilia' (1958) 5 RIDA 507; Geoffrey MacCormack, 'On the Third Chapter of the *Lex Aquilia*' (1970) 5 IJ 164; Constantin St. Tomulescu, 'Les trois chapitres de la *lex Aquilia*' (1970) 21 IURA 191.

Ulpian's treatment of the *lex Aquilia*[143] feature in contemporary examination questions.[144]

In 2000, Digest 9.2 was studied by undergraduates and by postgraduates of both civilian and common-law training, as part of an advanced paper that was much more Romanist in scope and intent than its comparativist 1980 equivalent. The dominant approach of the start of the century took Digest 9.2 as a self-contained source for study; at the end of the century, close study of the classical and Justinianic texts was enriched by exploration of a wide literature, incorporating elements of legal history, private law theory and comparative law. Accordingly, students were required both to develop a sophisticated understanding of the legal rules and principles and also to confront the difficulties of historically layered texts and divergent juristic views in a deeply critical and evaluative fashion.

7. CONCLUSION

Twentieth-century teaching and learning in Oxford vividly illustrates the 'very British pursuit' of studying the *lex Aquilia*. Digest 9.2 was a subject of focused study in compulsory or optional papers at undergraduate or graduate level in all but twenty-nine years of the century. While it ceded its place as the topic for the 'advanced' paper in Roman law to other titles of the Digest in those twenty-nine years, it has been offered every year from 1950 to the time of writing. The nature and scope of teaching and learning of Digest 9.2 did not, however, remain static over the century. At the start of Hanbury's career, Digest 9.2 was a subject of in-depth study in an undergraduate degree in which Roman law was compulsory at all stages. Nonetheless, both the undergraduate FHS paper of 1920 and the postgraduate BCL paper of 1940 reveal a narrow syllabus and a narrow style of questioning: a close but not deeply critical understanding of the texts, probably cribbed from Grueber's commentary on the *lex Aquilia*. For that reason, what had begun life as an advanced paper for those aiming at a class had, by 1960, become something of a 'soft' option. From the middle of the century, however, Digest 9.2 was taught more contextually, as the Digest-focused component of a course that examined delict and quasi-delict more broadly. It was also taught more

[143] Peter Birks, 'Ulpian 18 *ad Edictum*: Introducing *Damnum Iniuria*' in Robert Feenstra and others (eds), *Collatio Iuris Romani* vol 1 (Gieben 1995) 17.

[144] University of Oxford, *Honour School of Jurisprudence: Roman Law II (Delict)* (Examination Paper DJUR106, 1994) question 9; University of Oxford, *Honour School of Jurisprudence: Roman Law II (Delict)* (Examination Paper DJUR0606, 1995) question 8; University of Oxford, *Examination for the Degree of BCL: The Roman Law of Delict and Damage to Property* (Examination Paper 4764, 1996) question 9; University of Oxford, *Examination for the Degree of BCL: The Roman Law of Delict and Damage to Property* (Examination Paper EBCL4764, 1999) question 6; University of Oxford, *Examination for the Degree of BCL: Roman Law (Delict)* (Examination Paper EBCL4791, 2003) question 10.

comparatively, with increasing attention to direct comparison between the Roman and English law in the fields covered by the *lex*. Notwithstanding a relevantly identical syllabus, the last part of the twentieth century saw Digest 9.2, and Roman law generally, treated in an appreciably more scientific fashion, with wider reference to secondary literature and a concerted effort to ask more open and analytically demanding examination questions: it was a 'soft' option no longer.

Notwithstanding changes in audience, method and intensity, the value in studying Digest 9.2 has remained constant, perhaps explaining its persistence and longevity in the syllabus. Lawson said, of teaching Roman law generally, that it affords valuable 'breadth and universality';[145] that it is 'educational', even where it is not directly 'useful'.[146] Studying Digest 9.2 certainly assists in training lawyers to be capable of thinking analytically, conceptually and independently – unbound by the constraints of a single, national legal system. However, Digest 9.2 is arguably 'useful' as well. Just as Lawson describes the Roman jurists as 'concerned above all to provide the ordinary man with a simple but sufficient armoury of legal tools which will enable him to do his business',[147] it might be said that Digest 9.2 offers students a toolkit for studying law – and, as Grueber reminds us, a conveniently self-contained one.[148] It exposes students to different kinds of law-making, in *lex*, *interpretatio* and praetorian decree. It illustrates the interaction between procedure and substance, in the *lex* and the *actiones utiles* and *in factum*. It reveals evolution and increasing sophistication of law over time, in the expanding range of claimants and defendants, the evaluation of injury and loss and in the search for principle in *culpa*. In the sentiment of James Bryce reported by Lawson,[149] it offers a link between theoretical jurisprudence and positive law, through its engagement with concepts of intention, fault, causation, compensation and punishment. In terms of method, it absorbs students in casuistic and analogical reasoning of a kind familiar to the common law. Given the long-acknowledged parallels between the Roman and modern law of wrongs,[150] Digest 9.2 offers substantive parallels,[151] as well as tools honed by comparative method. By coming to grips with Digest 9.2, students are exposed to fundamental concepts and alternative solutions. By directing their minds explicitly to the comparisons, they develop a better understanding of their

---

[145] Lawson (n 4) 156.

[146] ibid 176.

[147] Lawson (n 28) 21.

[148] Grueber (n 13) vii.

[149] Lawson (n 4) 30.

[150] Francis de Zulueta, *The Study of Roman Law To-day* (Clarendon Press 1920) 9.

[151] Just as Julian and Ulpian are cited in *Fairchild v Glenhaven Funeral Services Ltd* [2002] UKHL 22; [2003] 1 AC 32 (HL(E)) 113–15 [58]–[60] (Lord Rodger of Earlsferry), so, too, are the facts of *Fairchild* conjured in University of Oxford, *Honour School of Jurisprudence: Roman Law (Delict)* (Examination Paper DJUR0605, 2003) question 10.

own law: unpicking rules and exposing background assumptions, developing critical standards and new methods of analysis, and better appreciating the close relationships between law and society, law and culture, and law and language. As Hanbury put it, 'a grounding in the Roman law ... enormously clarifies the mind of the beginner in its English counterpart';[152] it does so perhaps nowhere so clearly as in Digest 9.2.

Teaching and learning connected with Digest 9.2 in Oxford over the course of the twentieth century was marked by both continuity and change. Further changes were still to come: the injunction to compare *damnum iniuria* to the English law of torts would be downgraded[153] and the set texts would be prescribed in English translation (from 2010), a change that would have horrified Hanbury, who thought that, in 'abandon[ing] Latin as our medium for the study of Roman Law, we may be doing nothing less than resigning hope of gaining treasure that still lies buried in the storehouses of the Corpus Juris'.[154] Lawson was more sanguine; in his contemplation, Roman law would be 'strong enough to stand fairly close study in a good translation',[155] and so it has proved so far. These changes, however, belong to another century, and the story of Digest 9.2 in Oxford after the turn of the millennium is still being composed.

---

[152] Hanbury (n 1) 21.
[153] From 2014, a stated learning outcome for the Final Honour School was the 'capacity to reflect on [the classical jurists' ideas and methods'] influence on English common law'; the course promised to 'discuss fundamentals of the law of delicts/torts, aided by the comparison with English cases': University of Oxford Faculty of Law, *Student Handbook (Undergraduate Students) 2014–2015* (2014) 45.
[154] Hanbury (n 1) 23.
[155] Lawson (n 28) 20.

Part II

Case Studies

Chapter 5

Revisiting D.9.2.23.1

Joe Sampson[1]

1. INTRODUCTION

The preoccupation with the *lex Aquilia* that has characterised much of anglo-phone Roman law scholarship in recent decades might leave the bemused onlooker wondering what there could possibly be left to say. If the centuries of rigorous exegesis at the hands of dedicated Romanists, who doubtless had greater sensitivity for the nuances of the Latin texts than any lawyer working on Roman sources today, have failed to exhaust the Digest's mysteries, perhaps they are destined to rest unsolved. But this would downplay the importance of methodology and its development in Roman law scholarship. Although the same texts have been subjected to countless scrutineering interpretations, the way in which a given mind approaches a source can have a profound effect on the outcome of each analysis. For much of modernity the focus of Romanist scholarship has been on the identification of the 'truth' of the text, on the assumption that the Byzantine compilers of the sixth century through obfuscation or manipulation warped the message of classical law, in a sense mirroring the humanist endeavours of fifteenth- and sixteenth-century jurists.[2] Though intellectually impressive, there is an inherent risk in such a method of twisting the source material to suit one's own argument. It is only in recent years that the approach of Romanist scholarship has snapped back to something reminiscent of the *mos italicus* of medieval Europe.[3] Though we do not approach the sources of the *Corpus Iuris Civilis* with the same quasi-religious respect of those jurists, we are more willing than our immediate predecessors to take the texts at face value. On the supposition of textual authenticity, unless confronted with undeniable anachronism or linguistic implausibility, can we make sense of the source

---

[1] Most of the ideas in this chapter have their roots in Civil Law II supervisions held in Cambridge between 2013 and 2017. My thanks are owed to my co-supervisor, David Ibbetson, and years of enthusiastic and engaging students who constantly cast fresh light on the topic.

[2] David Johnston, 'Justinian's *Digest*: The Interpretation of Interpolation' (1989) 9 OJLS 149.

[3] On whose methods see generally James Gordley, *The Jurists: A Critical History* (OUP 2013) ch 2; Peter Stein, *Roman Law in European History* (CUP 1999) 45–49.

material? A return to this methodology, of explaining rather than editing, has encouraged a new generation of Roman lawyers to approach the sources with fresh eyes, and to dream up novel solutions to old problems.

To illustrate the impact of this shift in methodology, this chapter will consider an old chestnut: damages under Chapter 1 of the *lex Aquilia*, and in particular the differing views of Julian and Ulpian in D.9.2.23.1. The starting point for most past analyses of this troublesome text has been the inadequacy of the Latin, and the assumption that elements of it are inter-polated.[4] This chapter will take a different tack: assuming that everything that survives in the text is authentic (though not necessarily complete as a description of the scenario), is it possible to make sense of the approaches to damages taken by Julian and Ulpian? A variety of solutions will be explored, ranging from those that leave the text unaltered to those that introduce the minimum of additional detail. It will be argued that through the addition of one particular fact, namely the insertion of a condition on the inheritance, it is possible to develop a solution to the text that makes sense of everything that *is* contained therein, without the need to resort of accusations of interpolation. Ultimately, however, the best we can aspire to is coherence and the identification of possible understandings of the issue behind the text. The 'truth' of the text, if such a thing exists, is likely forever beyond our grasp.

2. THE OVERALL PATTERN OF DEVELOPMENT

In order to understand the significance of D.9.2.23.1, it is first necessary to understand the way in which damages under Chapter 1 of the *lex Aquilia* were calculated, and how the answer to this question evolved over the course of Roman legal history. The text of Chapter 1 is provided by Gaius in D.9.2.2.pr: 'Lege Aquilia capite primo cavetur: "Ut qui servum servamve alienum alienamve quadrupedem vel pecudem iniuria occiderit, quanti id in eo anno plurimi fuit, tantum aes dare domino damnas esto".'[5]

The seven words that have spawned centuries of controversy – '*quanti id in eo anno plurimi fuit*' – set out the measure of damages. Superficially straightforward, the successful claimant was entitled to 'the most the thing was [worth] in the last year'. This retrospective period of valuation likely attests to the early context of the *lex Aquilia*, where the types of property

---

[4]   Eg Max Kaser, *Quanti ea res est* (Beck 1935) 180; James B Thayer (ed), *Lex Aquilia (Digest IX.2 Ad Legem Aquiliam): Text, Translation and Commentary* (Harvard University Press 1929) 79; Frederick Henry Lawson, *Negligence in the Civil Law* (Clarendon Press 1950) 96.

[5]   D.9.2.2.pr: 'It is provided in the first chapter of the *lex Aquilia*: "that whoever should wrong-fully kill a male or female slave belonging to another or a four-footed grazing animal, so much as it was worth at its highest in that year, let him be condemned to the owner in so much bronze".'

protected by Chapter 1 (namely slaves and *pecudes*, or four-footed grazing animals) might have fluctuated in value significantly from season to season.[6] Were you to kill my ox in the depths of winter, you might incur a relatively trivial level of liability. With no fieldwork to be done, the ox would be just another mouth to feed. At such a time, the cost of replacing the ox would be relatively low, certainly when compared with the cost of replacing him come harvest season. By allowing a full year within which to identify the highest value the killed property had held, Chapter 1 ensured that no claimant would ever go undercompensated, erring instead on the side of overcompensation.

Chapter 1's measure of damages was ostensibly objective, at least in origin. It is common in the literature to speak of the original remedy as offering the *pretium*, or price.[7] This was the value of the slave in the marketplace, the price any owner could hope to obtain for his sale, blind to any additional value he might hold to his present owner alone. As much is made clear in the view of Sextus Pedius, a jurist of the late first century CE, as reported by Paul:

> ... *Sextus quoque Pedius ait pretia rerum non ex affectione nec utilitate singulorum, sed communiter fungi: itaque eum, qui filium naturalem possidet, non eo locupletiorem esse, quod eum plurimo, si alius possideret, redempturus fuit, nec illum, qui filium alienum possideat, tantum habere, quanti eum patri vendere posset ...*[8]

By contrast, Chapter 3 of the *lex Aquilia* calculated damages according to the claimant's *damnum*, or loss: '... *quanti ea res erit in diebus triginta proximis, tantum aes domino dare damnas esto*'.[9] The difference in approach between the two chapters' remedies is striking, and since at least the time of Gaius there has been a desire to reconcile the two. Gaius himself, at least in his *Institutes*, analysed Chapter 3 in line with Chapter 1, offering the highest value the damaged property had held in the previous thirty days.[10] Although Gaius

---

6 Guillaume Cardascia, 'La portée primitive de la Loi Aquilia' in Alan Watson (ed), *Daube Noster: Essays in Legal History for David Daube* (Scottish Academic Press 1974) 53; David Daube, 'On the Third Chapter of the *Lex Aquilia*' (1936) 52 LQR 253, 259.

7 Eg Giuseppe Valditara, *Dall'aestimatio rei all'id quod interest: evoluzione del criterio di stima del danno aquiliano* (Gianni Iuculano Editore 1995) ch 1. The language is also used in the texts to refer to the bare market value of the killed thing, e.g. D.9.2.23.1, D.9.2.23.3, D.9.2.23.5, D.9.2.27.17, D.9.2.33.pr, D.9.2.36.1, D.9.2.55.

8 D.9.2.33.pr: '... And Sextus Pedius says that the values of things are to be taken not by the feelings of individuals or the use to them, but as their common worth; and hence the person who possesses his natural son is none the richer because he would redeem him for a very large amount if another possessed him, nor has the person who possesses the son of another the amount for which he could sell him to his father ...'.

9 D.9.2.27.5: '... whatever that matter will be worth in the nearest thirty days, let him be condemned to pay so much bronze to the owner'. The thirty-day period referred to in the text is barely attested to in the Digest, and appears to have fallen out of use by classical law.

10 Gai.Inst.3.218.

claims to be offering the view of Sabinus, there is scant evidence for this view finding a wider application.[11] The logical impracticalities of a value-based approach to damages under Chapter 3 were made abundantly clear by Daube.[12] Indeed, when the leading Romanists of his day failed to see the wisdom of his interpretation of *damnum* as loss,[13] he went to significant lengths to point out the absurdity of adhering to Gaius' account of damages, joking that the reason for Romans having such cumbersomely long names was the inevitable necessity of noxally surrendering a child from family to family each time they kicked a ball through a window or scratched a wall, lest their hapless father be forced to pay the highest value of the house in the last thirty days: 'Children, unless totally disabled, were never more than transient members of a family'.[14]

The evidence of the Digest supports Daube's reading of *damnum* as loss rather than value. Perhaps the clearest text is D.9.2.27.28, in which the castration of a child is said not to entail a claim on Chapter 3 for want of *damnum* – the wrongful act in fact makes the boy more valuable.[15] And since Daube's seminal work on *damnum*, there have been no significant challenges to his interpretation of damages under Chapter 3. Instead the issue has returned to the question of the degree of harmonisation of the two chapters' remedies. If Chapter 3 did not realign its remedy to mirror Chapter 1, might Chapter 1 perhaps have been made to mirror Chapter 3?

Answering this question has proved fiendishly difficult, largely because the textual evidence seems to point in different directions. Perhaps the most comprehensive analysis of the evolution of Chapter 1's remedy sees a gradual shift towards a *damnum*-based analysis, articulated in terms of a shift from *pretium* to *interesse*.[16] This connotes the movement from price to interest, or from objective value to subjective interest. The starting point of this development is the identification of the word 'value' inserted into the English translation of the damages clause with '*pretium*'.[17] However, it is not inconceivable that the minds behind the *lex Aquilia* were already thinking of Chapter 1 in terms of subjective value from its inception. After all, a

---

[11] Paul appears to attach significance to a thirty-day period in D.44.7.34.2, but references in D.9.2 are virtually non-existent.

[12] David Daube, 'On the Use of the Term *Damnum*' in *Studi in onore di Siro Solazzi* (Jovene 1948).

[13] Eg Fritz Schulz, *Classical Roman Law* (Clarendon Press 1951) 590.

[14] David Daube, *Roman Law: Linguistic, Social and Philosophical Aspects* (EUP 1969) 67–68.

[15] D.9.2.27.28: *Et si puerum quis castraverit et pretiosiorem fecerit, Vivianus scribit cessare Aquiliam, sed iniuriarum erit agendum aut ex edicto aedilium aut in quadruplum* ('And if someone castrates a boy and makes him more valuable, Vivianus writes that the Aquilian will not lie, but an *actio iniuriarum* will have to be brought, or an action on the edict of the aediles or for fourfold').

[16] Valditara (n 7).

[17] See above, 165.

cornerstone of Daube's thesis is that *damnum* was always a term for subjective loss.[18] On the assumption that Chapter 3 was enacted at the same time as Chapter 1, the draftsman of the *lex Aquilia* was comfortable articulating damages in subjective terms. Nevertheless, as has already been seen, Sextus Pedius appears to be describing Chapter 1 in terms that are indicative of a *pretium*, or objective, analysis.[19]

The endpoint of this development is a claim for the owner's *interesse*, analysed as in Chapter 3 according to the loss suffered as a result of the wrongful death. To be analysed in a manner truly harmonious with Chapter 3, the one-year period would have to disappear. If this position was reached in classical law, it must have been very late in the day. Although there are several texts that might represent an *interesse* analysis in combination with the original one-year rule, only one text seems truly indicative of an *interesse* analysis under Chapter 1:

> *Legis Aquiliae debitori competit actio, cum reus stipulandi ante moram promissum animal vulneravit: idem est et si occiderit animal. Quod si post moram promissoris qui stipulatus fuerat occidit, debitor quidem liberatur, lege autem Aquilia hoc casu non recte experietur: nam creditor ipse sibi potius quam alii iniuriam fecisse videtur.*[20]

The scenario Papinian has in mind requires some unpacking. It begins with a straightforward *stipulatio*. Aulus asks Brutus whether Brutus will promise to deliver to him a horse,[21] and Brutus duly offers the promise. The first permutation of the facts has Aulus kill the horse before Brutus has delivered it, and before Brutus is in *mora*. Clearly Brutus has an action under Chapter 1 for the killing. But what if Aulus kills the horse when Brutus *is* in *mora*? Ordinarily *mora* has the effect of shifting the risk to the party who is wrongfully delaying the fulfilment of his obligation.[22] And so logically the loss ought to be borne by Brutus. But Papinian would deny both parties an action under Chapter 1. For Aulus, this seems only reasonable – it would be perverse were he to recover for the horse which he himself killed, simply

---

[18] Daube (n 6) 102–08.

[19] D.9.2.33.pr.

[20] D.9.2.54: 'An action on the *lex Aquilia* is available to a debtor where the stipulator wounds the promised animal before he is in *mora*; the same applies if he kills the animal. But if the stipulator kills it when the promisor is in *mora*, the debtor is released but in this case he will not rightly have an action on the *lex Aquilia*, for the creditor rather than any other person appears to have done the wrong to himself'.

[21] It is assumed that Papinian has made it a case about killing in order to bring into focus the calculation of damages under Chapter 1. This assumption seems sound given the distinction drawn between wounding and killing in the first sentence. Nevertheless, the animal isn't identified. It is conceivable that the animal killed is not a *pecus* and this is straightforwardly a Chapter 3 text, although that would render the point behind the text somewhat obvious.

[22] William Warwick Buckland, *A Text-Book of Roman Law from Augustus to Justinian* (Peter Stein ed, 3rd revised edn, CUP 1963) 550.

because Brutus was in *mora*.[23] As Papinian says, Aulus appears to have done the wrong to himself. But why does Brutus not have an action? After all, the horse was still his property – should he not receive the highest value it had in the previous year? Reasons are not provided, but the implication seems clear: Brutus has not suffered any loss. Were Papinian thinking of damages in the terms dictated by the text of Chapter 1, there would be no good reason for denying Brutus an action. He is the owner of a killed *pecus*, and so is entitled to the highest value it had in the last twelve months. By denying an action, Papinian appears to be rejecting this measure of damages and instead analysing the facts in a manner harmonious with Chapter 3's focus on *damnum*.

A text of Papinian on the *actio doli* suggests that Papinian was not an outlier in his approach to Chapter 1 of the *lex Aquilia*.[24] In the text, the facts of which closely mirror D.9.2.54 (though it is simply an *animal* that is killed, and not expressly a *pecus*), Neratius and Julian are reported as saying that an *actio doli* ought to lie. Implicitly, this means that there cannot be liability on Chapter 1 of the *lex Aquilia*, as an *actio doli* could only be brought where no other action was available.[25] On the assumption that the killed *animal* was a *pecus* and that the proper form of redress would be a claim under Chapter 1 rather than Chapter 3 of the *lex Aquilia*, it would appear that both Julian and Neratius are analysing damages according to the loss suffered by the claimant rather than in terms of value.[26] Paul gives a similar opinion in a parallel case involving a killed slave, which undeniably would lead to liability under Chapter 1.[27] Thus it would appear there is a significant pool of evidence for an *interesse*-style analysis being applied to Chapter 1 certainly in late classical law, and perhaps significantly earlier.

By late classical law damages under Chapter 1 of the *lex Aquilia* were being analysed by some jurists in terms consonant with damages under Chapter 3. Significantly more controversial is the universality of this *interesse* analysis in the early third century. Of central importance is the position of Ulpian, a contemporary of Paul and Papinian. This focus would appear inevitable given the sheer preponderance of texts by Ulpian in the Digest title on the *lex Aquilia*. But the interest he inspires is only furthered by the sheer difficulty of identifying a consistent position behind the manifold scenarios he discusses.

The starting point is Ulpian's generic statement of the function of the damages clause in Chapter 1, which he expressly links to the calculation of

---

[23] A point of controversy was whether loss caused by the fault of the party not in *mora* still fell on the head of the party in *mora*.

[24] D.4.3.19.

[25] D.4.3.34; D.4.3.5.

[26] Of course, if the claim *is* brought under Chapter 3 this would be perfectly orthodox and would render the text somewhat pointless.

[27] D.4.3.18.5.

the claimant's *damnum*.[28] But when he begins applying this rule to concrete examples, it becomes clear that the one-year rule is still alive and well. Of particular importance is the string of texts in D.9.2.23, which deal with the various facets of a slave that can be taken into account when calculating damages. The perennial favourite of examiners in Roman law comes in D.9.2.23.3, where a skilled painter loses his thumb at some point in the last year. It is of no consequence that the slave actually killed was not a skilled painter, so long as he held such value in the last twelve months: '... *posse eum Aquilia agere pretioque eo aestimandum, quanti fuit priusquam artem cum pollice amisisset*'.[29] So too where the slave fell into bad habits in the year before his death.[30]

Ulpian's position is concisely summarised in D.9.2.23.6: '*In summa omnia commoda, quae intra annum, quo interfectus est, pretiosiorem servum facerent, haec accedere ad aestimationem eius dicendum est*'.[31] It has been suggested that this last text is a post-classical or Byzantine gloss, designed to explain the preceding texts in a unitary fashion.[32] Consequently, it might be misrepresenting Ulpian's views, and perhaps even obscuring a pure *interesse* pattern of analysis with an anachronistic appeal to the one-year period. In particular, the allegedly pseudo-Ulpian's use of the phrase '*in summa*' has been found objectionable.[33] These concerns are unfounded. Texts from across the Digest can be marshalled as evidence of Ulpian's tendency to use that phrase in precisely the same fashion, namely to tie together a handful of examples on particularly thorny issues.[34] Unless one were to doubt the legitimacy of each of these texts, there seems little cause to suspect D.9.2.23.6 of subterfuge. Moreover, it has been convincingly argued by Rodger that one of the other thorny texts in D.9.2.23 must be about the operation of the one-year rule.[35] It seems difficult to ignore the likelihood that the one-year rule was an important part of Ulpian's understanding of damages under Chapter 1.

---

[28] D.9.2.21.pr: *Ait lex: 'Quanti is homo in eo anno plurimi fuisset'. Quae clausula aestimationem habet damni, quod datum est* ('The lex says: "the highest that slave was worth in that year". This clause contains the evaluation of the loss which had been caused').

[29] D.9.2.23.3: '... he can bring an Aquilian action for his price to be valued at what it was before he lost his skill with his thumb'.

[30] D.9.2.23.5.

[31] D.9.2.23.6: 'In sum, it has to be said that all those things which would make the slave more valuable within the year of his being killed are added to the valuation'.

[32] Gerhard von Beseler, 'Romanistische Studien: Zur Sachbewertung nach dem Aquilischen Recht' (1930) 50 ZSS (RA) 25; Valditara (n 7) 216–17, Kaser (n 4) 177.

[33] Valditara (n 7) 217.

[34] D.13.4.4.1; D.21.1.4.4; D.39.3.1.15; D.44.5.1.6. For jurists other than Ulpian using the phrase in a similar way, see D.39.3.2.pr (Paul); D.40.12.23.1 (Paul); D.43.24.16.2 (Paul); D.46.2.34.2 (Gaius); D.49.14.17 (Modestinus).

[35] Alan Rodger, 'Labeo and the Fraudulent Slave' in A D E Lewis and D J Ibbetson (eds), *The Roman Law Tradition* (CUP 1994).

3. D.9.2.23.1 AND ITS SIGNIFICANCE

Central to recreating Ulpian's view, and the broader question of the evolution of damages under Chapter 1 of the *lex Aquilia*, is D.9.2.23.1:

> *Iulianus ait, si servus liber et heres esse iussus occisus fuerit, neque substitutum neque legitimum actione legis Aquiliae hereditatis aestimationem consecuturum, quae servo competere non potuit: quae sententia vera est. Pretii igitur solummodo fieri aestimationem, quia hoc interesse solum substituti videretur: ego autem puto nec pretii fieri aestimationem, quia, si heres esset, et liber esset.*[36]

The text reports a dispute between Ulpian and Julian as to the quantum of damages recoverable in a claim under Chapter 1 of the *lex Aquilia*. The facts are slightly unusual, and the conclusion that they are incomplete seems difficult to avoid. A testator has directed that his slave be free and heir. The slave is killed – whether before or after the testator dies is unclear – and it is the substitute heir or the *heres legitimus* (heir on intestacy) who is bringing the claim. What is this claimant entitled to recover? Firstly, can the claimant, who after all only has this inheritance by virtue of the slave's death, treat the inheritance itself as an aspect of the slave's value, effectively receiving it a second time through delictual recovery? On this point, Julian and Ulpian concur: the inheritance cannot be recovered through an *actio legis Aquiliae*. Julian restricts recovery only to the slave's price, what anyone would hope to get in the marketplace for the hapless heir. But Ulpian would not allow even that minimal recovery. Denying as he is the most objective element of the slave's value – the price tag imposed in the market – it seems that Ulpian would allow the claimant a valueless claim, or more probably would deny an action altogether.

It is clear from the preceding text that an inheritance is *capable* of being recoverable under Chapter 1 of the *lex Aquilia*, and that both Ulpian and Julian considered it as such. In 9.2.23.pr, Ulpian relies on a statement of Neratius to that effect.[37] Julian gives a similar opinion in 9.2.51.2.[38] The key difference between those texts and D.9.2.23.1 is that the inheritance has already been received here, whereas it is lost for good in D.9.2.23.pr, D.9.2.23.2 and D.9.2.51.2. Thus while we might say that an inheritance could be recovered through the tangential recovery of consequential loss, it could

---

[36] D.9.2.23.1: 'Julian says, if a slave is killed who has been directed to be free and to be heir, neither the substitute nor the *heres legitimus* will recover by the *actio legis Aquiliae* the value of the inheritance which could not come to the slave; this opinion is true. And [he says that] only the price [of the slave] should be valued, because this alone seems to be the interest of the substitute. However, I think that we should not value the price either, because if he were heir he would also be free'.

[37] D.9.2.23.pr: '*Inde Neratius scribit, si servus heres institutus occisus sit, etiam hereditatis aestimationem venire*'.

[38] D.9.2.51.2.

not be recovered as an aspect of the slave's value where already received.[39] The far more difficult task is explaining how the two jurists disagree about whether there can be any recovery of the slave's value at all.

4. AN AMBIGUOUS CHRONOLOGY

At the outset of his article on this problematic text, Rodger identifies its central riddle: who dies first, the slave or the testator?[40] There are, he argues, drawing upon centuries of tradition, two presumptions that anyone seeking to understand this text must choose between. Either the slave died before the testator, or we are missing factual detail.[41] Though he ultimately opts for the former chronology, on the grounds that it does not require mutilating the text or introducing additional elements to make an argument work, he argues that it is inconsequential which reading is adopted:

> The matter is not crucial, since either supposition is sufficient to deal with the point of title to sue. On the first hypothesis, the substitute or heir on intestacy will sue as heir to the testator who owned the slave when he was killed. On the second assumption [that the facts are missing a condition preventing the slave from inheriting immediately], the slave was still a slave when killed, though a slave of the inheritance. The substitute or heir on intestacy can sue upon entry.[42]

Rodger's thesis flows from this initial decision to have the slave die before the testator. This is a decision that matters. As will be argued in due course, the solutions that have been offered to this text thus far do not adequately explain every aspect of it. In particular, Ulpian's final sentiments prove a difficult fit for any attempt at solving this text. For this reason, Beseler simply cut out the clause entirely in his reconstruction of D.9.2.23.1, while others have labelled it an interpolation.[43] Here it will be argued that the only way to understand Ulpian's final comment is to see D.9.2.23.1 as falling into a series of texts on the interest of an owner in a *statuliber* – a slave who had been promised his freedom under a condition in a will – which occupied a curious middle ground between property and liberty.[44] But for this solution

---

[39] Corroborated by the sorts of characteristics explored as aspects of the slave's value in D.9.2.23: talents or skills (D.9.2.23.3), knowledge (D.9.2.23.4) and characteristics or behaviours (D.9.2.23.5). These are all aspects internal to the killed slave, unlike a legal artifice such as an inheritance that is attached to his person.

[40] Alan Rodger, 'Damages for the Loss of an Inheritance' in Alan Watson (ed), *Daube Noster: Essays in Legal History for David Daube* (Scottish Academic Press 1974) 289, 289–90.

[41] Typically taken to be an omitted condition – see the reconstruction of the first sentence of D.9.2.23.1 by Beseler (n 32) 27: '*Iulianus ait, si servus sub condicione liber et heres iusssus occisus fuerit …*'.

[42] ibid 290.

[43] Beseler (n 32) 27; e.g. Kaser (n 4) 180.

[44] This is a solution that Rodger explores, but in relation to D.9.2.23.2 rather than D.9.2.23.1: Rodger (n 40) 295–96.

to be viable, the insertion of a condition into the text is inevitable, or else the slave could not have been a *statuliber*.

However, it should be noted that the straightforward binary choice – that we must either insert a condition or else get out the scissors and begin editing the text – presented by Rodger and earlier generations of Roman lawyers might be overly simplistic. Once the door is opened to the insertion of missing detail, there are a great many possibilities that might explain how it is the slave died after the testator despite being an *heres necessarius*. Firstly, the scenario under discussion could have been complicated by a formal defect preventing the inheritance from vesting immediately. This could be as simple as there being an as-yet unmet condition on the inheritance, as in D.9.2.23.2 and suggested by Beseler.[45] Indeed, it will be argued that given Ulpian's reasons for denying the claimant the value of the killed slave, this is by far the most likely omitted detail. But it is equally conceivable that the vesting of the inheritance could have been delayed by the process of opening the will. Rights under an inheritance were not allowed to vest until the will was formally opened.[46] For a will to be validly opened, the praetor had to procure the appearance of all its witnesses, who in turn had to acknowledge their seals.[47] Provided a majority of witnesses turned up, the will could be opened and read in their presence.[48] Were the slave to be killed within this window, of course he could not become heir, and so any claim would have to be brought by the substitute or heir in intestacy. And even once the will had been validly opened, the slave would still have to enter into the *hereditas* to be free and heir, providing a further window for his death that would make sense of the facts of D.9.2.23.1.

A further possibility is raised by the ambiguity in the death of the testator. Under the *senatusconsultum Silanianum* where an owner of slaves was killed, the will would not be opened (and so the estate would not vest) until the slaves had been tortured to discover the truth of the matter.[49] This rule is couched in the language of vengeance, with the inheritance being suspended until vengeance had been doled out. The unfortunate household slaves were the targets of this bloodlust, in addition to the actual wrongdoers. It was intended to punish slaves for not protecting their master, regardless of whether they were complicit in the crime. Thus Ulpian says that slaves ought not to be tortured where the master was killed by poison rather than violent means, as there is very little that could be expected of a slave in defending against such threats.[50]

---

[45]   Beseler (n 32) 27.
[46]   Buckland (n 22) 312–19.
[47]   D.29.3.4: 'Cum ab initio aperiendae sint tabulae, praetoris id officium est, ut cogat signatores convenire et sigilla sua recognoscere'.
[48]   D.29.3.6: 'Sed si maior pars signatorum fuerit inventa, poterit ipsis intervenientibus resignari testamentum et recitari'.
[49]   Buckland (n 22) 312 n 8; D.29.5.

Where the master had been killed, the will could not be opened until the slaves had been tortured. This rule is stated clearly by Ulpian:

> *Quod ad causam testamenti pertinens relictum erit ab eo qui occisus esse dicetur, id ne quis sciens dolo malo aperiendum recitandum describendumque curet, edicto cavetur, priusquam de ea familia quaestio ex senatus consulto habita suppliciumque de noxiis sumptum fuerit.*[51]

Moreover, Ulpian also specifically states that this provision applies to necessary heirs, such as the slave in D.9.2.23.1.[52]

When dealing with putative omissions of factual detail the only limit on an argument is imagination. Perhaps the best that can be aspired to is coherence. And it will be argued that the only way to make sense of all that survives in D.9.2.23.1, without recourse to cutting out clauses or identifying interpolations, is to read into the text an unmet condition. It is only through such a condition that the slave can be rendered a *statuliber*, and it is only through treating him as a *statuliber* that Ulpian's basis for denying the claimant the slave's value makes sense. But before turning to this line of argument, it is first necessary to assess the adequacy of the range of solutions offered by the existing literature.

5. SOLUTION ONE: FROM SUBJECTIVITY TO OBJECTIVITY

Rodger's path through D.9.2.23.1 is to see the text as representing 'a fundamental shift in attitude towards the assessment of damages'.[53] Julian represents the old orthodoxy, an objective approach to damages that simply asks what the highest price was that the slave commanded in the last year. That this particular claimant, the substitute or necessary heir, could never have owned the slave is apparently irrelevant: 'Julian does not see any need to enquire about the particular plaintiff whose identity cannot affect the objective valuation of the loss which has occurred'.[54] Ulpian represents a move towards subjectivity, writing 'in an age when the concept of *interesse* is better understood'.[55] Straightforwardly, there is no world in which this particular

---

[50] D.29.5.1.18: '*Quod si quis puta veneno vel etiam quo alio quod clam necare soleat interemptus sit, ad hoc senatus consultum vindicta mortis eius non pertinebit: hoc idcirco, quia totiens puniendi sunt servi, quia auxilium domino non tulerunt, quotiens potuerunt ei adversus vim opem ferre et non tulerunt: ceterum quid potuerunt facere adversus eos, qui veneno vel quo alio more insidiantur?*'

[51] D.29.5.3.18: 'It is provided in the edict that no one shall, knowingly and with fraudulent intent, see to the opening, reading out, and copying of what has been left by way of testamentary disposition by someone who is said to have been killed, before questioning of that household under the *senatusconsultum* has taken place, and the guilty parties have been executed'.

[52] D.29.5.5.pr.

[53] Rodger (n 40) 291.

[54] ibid 292.

[55] ibid 292.

claimant, whether the substitute heir or the heir on intestacy, could have owned this particular slave. The only way in which the inheritance could ever have reached the claimant's hands, and bring with it the cause of action, was if the slave first died. The damages clause is reread to award 'the highest value *to the claimant* in the last year'.[56] This is not, however, the same as a pure *interesse* reading akin to that offered by Papinian in D.9.2.54. Elsewhere Rodger argues that Ulpian was still adhering to the one-year rule.[57] Rather, Ulpian represents a step beyond the objectivity of Julian on the path towards a pure *interesse* analysis of damages under Chapter 1 of the *lex Aquilia*. As already noted, adopting this view renders insignificant the question of whether it was the slave or the testator who died first, as in either case the claimant is bringing an action in his own name. Nevertheless, he thinks it more likely that the slave died before the testator.

6. SOLUTION TWO: DIFFERING CONCEPTIONS OF ACTIVE TRANSMISSIBILITY

Rodger's solution presupposes that the claimant is bringing the action in his own name. This is not obviously the case. An alternative solution, advanced by Valditara, relates to how different jurists understood restrictions on the transmissibility of delictual actions.[58] In its essentials, his argument is that Julian belonged to a class of jurists that held that an heir's inherited delictual action was to be conceptualised as an action brought by the heir on behalf of the deceased – rather than an action in the heir's own name, for his own loss. Support for this position is drawn from 9.2.36.1:

> *Si dominus servum, quem Titius mortifere vulneraverat, liberum et heredem esse iusserit eique postea Maevius exstiterit heres, non habebit Maevius cum Titio legis Aquiliae actionem, scilicet secundum Sabini opinionem, qui putabat ad heredem actionem non transmitti, quae defuncto competere non potuit: nam sane absurdum accidet, ut heres pretium quasi occisi consequatur eius, cuius heres exstitit. Quod si ex parte eum dominus heredem cum libertate esse iusserit, coheres eius mortuo eo aget lege Aquilia.*[59]

It is the view of Sabinus provided in the middle of the text that is shared by Julian. Returning to D.9.2.23.1, Julian's position now seems understand-

---

[56] ibid 292.

[57] Rodger (n 35).

[58] Valditara (n 7) 69–70.

[59] D.9.2.36.1: 'If an owner orders that a slave, whom Titius has mortally wounded, be free and his heir, and afterwards Maevius becomes heir to him, Maevius will not have an *actio legis Aquiliae* against Titius; that is, according to the opinion of Sabinus, who thought that an action could not be transmitted to the heir which could not have been available to the deceased. For it would clearly be absurd that the heir should recover the value of the dead person whose heir he is. But if the owner orders that he should be part-heir and free, his co-heir can sue on the *lex Aquilia* on his death'.

able. The substitute heir, or the heir in intestacy, is bringing the action on behalf of the deceased testator. Damages are to be calculated according to the highest value the slave had in the last year. The question of whether Julian is understanding value to mean the objective market price, or the value of the slave to this particular owner, becomes immaterial as they are likely identical. The institution of the slave as heir had no value to the testator – he already owned the estate, and didn't stand to gain in the least from the slave being heir. That particular fact had no bearing on the slave's value to the testator, and so it is equally irrelevant to the substitute or heir in intestacy bringing the action on the testator's behalf.

This understanding of active transmissibility is borne out in other contexts. For example, Valditara points to D.11.3.8 on the *actio servi corrupti*: '*Sed et heres eius, cuius servus corruptus est, habet hanc actionem, non solum si manserit in hereditate servus, sed et si exierit, forte legatus*'.[60] In this text, an heir is allowed an action for the spoiling of a slave who no longer belongs to the estate, having been bequeathed to a third party upon the testator's death. It is of no consequence to Paul that the slave is not the property of the heir, because he *was* the property of the testator. Rodger addresses this line of argument about transmissibility, but gives it short shrift: '[Kaser] does not cite any authority for this assertion that the value of the claim as opposed to the claim itself transmits to the substitute. Nor does there seem to be any'.[61] Both Rodger and Kaser seem equally convinced of the obviousness of their diametrically opposed positions. In this, they unwittingly reflect an attitude millennia old. Cicero, exhibiting the bulldoggish tendencies of a lawyer in his cups that is often on display to this day, describes the following drunken interaction with a friend:

> *Illuseras heri inter scyphos, quod dixeram controversiam esse, possetne heres, quod futurum antea factum esset, furti recte agere. Itaque, etsi domum bene potus seroque redieram, tamen id caput, ubi haec controversia est, notavi et descriptum tibi misi, ut scires id, quod tu neminem sensisse dicebas, Sex. Aelium, M'. Manilium, M. Brutum sensisse: ego tamen Scaevolae et Testae assentior.*[62]

Cicero's drinking companion is on the side of Kaser. Surely it is obviously that the *heres*, who is after all stepping into the shoes of the deceased, brings

---

[60] D.11.3.8: 'The heir of a man whose slave has been made worse can also have this action, not only if the slave has remained in the inheritance but also if he has left it, perhaps as a legacy'.

[61] Rodger (n 40) 292.

[62] Cic. *Fam.*, VII, 22: 'You jeered at me yesterday amidst our cups, for having said that it was a disputed point whether an heir could lawfully prosecute on an embezzlement which had been committed before he became the owner. Accordingly, though I returned home full of wine and late in the evening, I marked the section in which that question is treated and caused it to be copied out and sent to you. I wanted to convince you that the doctrine which you said was held by no one was maintained by Sextus Aelius, Manius Manilius, Marcus Brutus. Nevertheless, I concur with Scaevola and Testa'.

an action as his representative? But despite the apparent obviousness of this conclusion, the point was disputed in Cicero's day, and the disagreement conceivably continued into classical law.

Valditara's solution has the advantage of explaining the text as it is, without the need to introduce any additional detail. It does not, however, directly address the reasoning provided by Ulpian in the text's final clause: '*quia, si heres esset, et liber esset*'.[63] This statement, which appears to turn on the status of the slave, does not neatly map onto any argument about transmissibility. It also stretches credulity to suggest that Ulpian fell so markedly out of sync with other leading jurists of the day on a matter as fundamental to the operation of procedure as the transmissibility of actions. While the text of Cicero clearly shows that the issue was contentious in the last days of the Republic, there is little in the way of textual evidence to suggest the controversy survived into high classical law.

7. SOLUTION THREE: DIFFERING PERCEPTIONS OF THE RELEVANT OWNER AT TIME OF DEATH

It is possible that Valditara is right in identifying the transmission of actions to heirs as being the issue at the heart of the text, but that he focuses on the wrong point of detail. Though possible, it seems unlikely that Ulpian would fall so markedly out of line on as fundamental a point of law as in whose name an heir brings an action. The view attributed to Julian, and seen in the writings of Sabinus and Paul, is the same one identified by Kaser as so orthodox that it didn't require explanation, much to Rodger's puzzlement and Cicero's consternation.[64] But can we make sense of D.9.2.23.1 on the assumption that Julian and Ulpian shared an understanding of the way in which actions were transmitted to heirs, i.e. that the substitute heir or necessary heir brings an action on behalf of whoever the owner was at the moment the slave was killed rather than in their own name?

Logically this seems to lead to an impasse. If Julian and Ulpian both agree that the claimant is suing in the name of his predecessor, how can they disagree on whether the claim entails recovery of the slave's value? The only plausible explanation is that they disagree on who the relevant predecessor is. Julian argues that the slave had a value to the relevant owner, Ulpian argues that it was valueless. Julian's position seems the more obviously correct line to follow if we assume the claim is being brought on behalf of the testator, to whom the slave clearly had value. But it is not necessarily the case that the action is brought on behalf of the testator. Between the death of the testator and someone entering onto the estate, the slave is not free. He is the property of the *hereditas*, which Ulpian somewhat elliptically says

---

[63] D.9.2.23.1.
[64] Kaser (n 4) 180; Rodger (n 40) 292.

elsewhere is 'deemed to be owner'.[65] But this is a peculiar brand of ownership stemming from a peculiar conception of legal personality.[66] It can only
be seen as tokenistic or symbolic – although the *hereditas* (more properly, the
hereditas iacens) owns the slave, it has no powers over the slave, for the simple
fact that there is no human actor who can actually exercise those powers.
Instead it is said to *'personam defuncti sustinet'* until the heir enters onto the
estate.[67] So far as this 'owner' is concerned, the slave is property, but he is
not an asset, and his value cannot be realised. Translated into Latin, he is a
not a *bona* but a simple *res*.[68] The *hereditas* is, as an incorporeal form of property itself, incapable of transferring, selling or otherwise converting the slave
to its benefit. The only reason the Romans would resort to thinking of the
hereditas as owner of the slave is to avoid the alternative – branding the slave
a *res nullius*, and so rendering it capable of being acquired by a third party.
Having the *hereditas* own the slave during the lapse in human ownership of
the estate evades this problem, and ensures continuity in the ownership of
the slave. It just results in an awkward lacuna in which the slave is property
without being, in economic terms, an asset.

While in this penumbral state the slave is killed, and the right to bring
the *actio legis Aquiliae* vests in the *hereditas*, which is of course incapable of
realising it through litigation. Whatever defect was stalling entry onto the
inheritance is remedied, and so the substitute or heir in intestacy inherits
and enters onto the estate. And Ulpian asks what value the slave had to the
relevant owner at the time of the killing, namely the *hereditas*. This involves
drawing a fairly subtle distinction between having ownership of the slave,
and being able to realise the slave's value. Although the *hereditas* owned the
slave, that ownership was valueless due to the basic incapacities of the *hereditas* in a commercial sense. All of the avenues by which an owner can realise
the value of his property were closed off to the *hereditas*. It couldn't sell
the slave, or use him as security for a loan, or even put him to work. It was
restricted to bare ownership. By contrast, the *hereditas* can suffer loss – it can
be caused to have less than it ought to have – and so claims brought under
Chapter 3 on behalf of the *hereditas* could still result in damages.[69] But for
Chapter 1, the language of which refers to value rather than loss, the claim
is essentially worthless to the *hereditas* as the relevant owner at the time of
death.

This reading of the text casts doubt on the supposed evolution that

---

[65] D.9.2.13.2: '*Si servus hereditarius occidatur, quaeritur, quis Aquilia agat, cum dominus nullus sit
huius servi. Et ait Celsus legem domino damna salva esse voluisse: dominus ergo hereditas habebitur.
Quare adita hereditate heres poterit experiri*'. Note the caginess of Ulpian's use of *habebitur*. See
also D.28.5.31.1, D.43.24.13.5, D.47.4.1.1.

[66] Patrick Duff, *Personality in Roman Private Law* (CUP 1938) ch 7.

[67] D.41.1.33.2.

[68] D.1.8.1.pr: '*... nam res hereditariae, antequam aliquis heres existat, nullius in bonis sunt*'.

[69] D.9.2.43.

occurred in the century between Julian and Ulpian. If the two jurists are seen as disagreeing about on whose behalf the action is brought, it becomes possible to see both jurists as applying a subjective analysis. Julian is asking 'what is the highest value the slave had *to the testator* in the last year?' while Ulpian asks 'what is the highest value the slave had *to the hereditas* in the last year?'[70] Its principal problem is the likelihood of Julian and Ulpian disagreeing about the identity of the relevant owner. If the text is to be interpreted as concerning active transmissibility, this is a problem that needs to be surmounted. Two solutions can be tentatively offered, though neither is satisfactory. The first goes to the conceptualisation of the *hereditas* as a *dominus*. This was clearly a controversial issue throughout classical law. The jurists were uncomfortable with applying the language of *dominus* to the *hereditas iacens*. On this, Duff argues that

> the personification [of the *hereditas iacens*] is not worked out or consistent. The texts which definitely call the *hereditas* '*dominus*' do so as a slovenly afterthought, and it seems that even the compilers did not really regard the *hereditas iacens* as a Person.[71]

We have textual authority for Ulpian treating a *hereditas* as something equivalent to a *dominus*, but lack the same for Julian.[72] It is entirely possible that they disagreed. The point might further be compounded by the actual language of the *lex Aquilia*, which refers to the *erus* rather than the *dominus* of the killed property.[73] These two terms are treated as functionally equivalent, by Ulpian no less than by more modern scholars.[74] However, even if at least some classical jurists were content that an incorporeal entity like the *hereditas* could be a *dominus*, it is not so obvious that it could be an *erus*.[75] Relocating the point of disagreement from something as procedurally fundamental as the transmissibility of actions to the interpretation of an archaic term renders the differing approaches of the two jurists far more plausible. But it is a necessarily speculative argument.

The second relates to an identifiable trend in Julian's thinking in other doctrinally problematic areas of the *lex Aquilia*. To a greater degree than Ulpian, Julian is willing to interpret the law in a manner favourable to the claimant. The clearest example of this is D.9.2.51.pr–2, in which Julian argues that the year within which the highest value is to be identified should be counted back from the moment the mortal wound is struck, rather than

---

[70] And it should be remembered that Papinian reports Julian as offering a subjective approach to damages under Chapter 1 in D.4.3.19. See above, 168.

[71] Duff (n 66) 166–67.

[72] D.9.2.13.2.

[73] D.9.2.11.6: '*Legis autem Aquiliae actio ero competit, hoc est domino*'.

[74] D.9.2.11.6. Gaius also sees the two as equivalent: Gai.Inst.3.154a.

[75] Admittedly this is unclear due to the sheer paucity of Roman sources from which the meaning of *erus* might be derived.

from the moment of death. Making sense of this text has spawned an impressively creative literature.[76] However, the reason Julian himself gives seems the most plausible:

> ... *nec mirum, cum uterque eorum ex diversa causa et diversis temporibus occidisse hominem intellegatur. Quod si quis absurde a nobis haec constitui putaverit, cogitet longe absurdius constitui neutrum lege Aquilia teneri aut alterum potius, cum neque impunita maleficia esse oporteat nec facile constitui possit, uter potius lege teneatur* ...[77]

This is straightforwardly an argument from policy.[78] He interprets the scenario in the way that will give the claimant his best shot at fully realising the value of his claim, or conversely to maximise the penalty imposed on the defendant for the wrong he has committed. He counts back from the moment a mortal wound is struck rather than the time of death to give the claimant a full year within which to identify the slave's highest value, circumventing the scenario where a slave lingers at death's door for weeks or months. He attributes the claim in D.9.2.23.1 to the testator rather than the *hereditas* for the same reason – to take the line later adopted by Ulpian is to allow the nefarious killer to evade liability, a possibility described by Julian in D.9.2.51.2 as '*absurde*'.[79]

8. SOLUTION FOUR: *STATULIBER*

There are a variety of ways in which the active transmissibility interpretation of D.9.2.23.1 can be made to work, but none is entirely satisfactory. They entail either suppositions about the conceptualisation of a quasi-person for which there is incredibly little textual evidence or arguments from policy. Though the latter is more persuasive than the former, seeing Julian as driven by policy has left Roman law scholars unconvinced when explaining his views on the meaning of *occidere*, and so is unlikely to fare batter in this context. Moreover, all of the solutions explored thus far ought to inspire dissatisfaction for their failure to explain the final clause in the text: '*quia, si heres esset, et liber esset*'.[80] This purports to be Ulpian's reason for denying the substitute

---

[76] Eg Helen Scott, 'Killing and Causing Death' (2013) 129 LQR 101; Adriaan Johan Boudewijn Sirks, 'The Slave who was Slain Twice: Causality and the *Lex Aquilia*' (2011) 79 TvR 313.

[77] D.9.2.51.2: '... Nor is this surprising, since each is understood to have killed the slave in a different way and at a different time. And if anyone should think that what has here been laid down by us is absurd, he should reflect that it would be far more absurd to lay down that neither should be liable on the *lex Aquilia*, or one rather than the other; for on the one hand wrongs should not go unpunished, and on the other is it is not easy to lay down which should rather be liable on the *lex* ...'.

[78] Danilo Dalla, '*Giuliano e il longum intervallum in tema di applicazione dell'Aquilia*' (1974) 187 Archivio giuridico F Serafini 145.

[79] D.9.2.51.2: 'absurd'.

[80] D.9.2.23.1: '... because if he were heir, he would also be free'. On the curious position of the

heir an action, and it does not accord with an *interesse* approach to damages. Rather we get the somewhat elliptical statement that the price is not to be taken into account because 'if he were heir he would also be free'. There appears to be something about the status of the slave that is causing Ulpian pause. Admittedly the clause does have the quality of a marginal gloss that snuck into the text at some point, and so might be thought to represent not Ulpian's reasoning but that of some earnest student or scholar in centuries past.[81] But this temptation ought to be resisted, at least for the time being: taking the text as it is preserved, is there any way to make sense of Ulpian's curious caveat? On its face, it is difficult to see the point at which Ulpian is driving. Of course, had the slave actually been the heir he would have been free. But the only reason the inheritance – and so the action – has reached the hands of the substitute or necessary heir is because the slave was not free and heir. Slavery is archetypally a binary notion: one is either free or a slave. The unfortunate heir might have been on the path to freedom, but he was nevertheless a slave at the moment of his death. But it seems that Ulpian sees significance in the promise of freedom. The looming release from servitude, albeit when subject to a condition, gave the slave a status that was somewhere between freedom and slavery: he was a *statuliber*, a slave to whom freedom had been promised under a will, subject to the satisfaction of a condition.[82] The significance of this curious status can be seen primarily in the law of property, where questions arose as to whether the state of conditional freedom passed with the slave when, for example, he was sold or usucapted.[83] In most respects the slave remained the property of the heir until the condition on his freedom was met.[84]

A significant exception to this general proposition was the manner in which the slave's value was calculated in an action brought by the heir. It would appear that the slave retained his value to the heir so long as the condition placed on his freedom went unmet. But as soon as that condition was met, even if after the death of the slave, the slave was retrospectively deemed to have lost any value to the heir. Though not expressly stated in D.9.2.23.1, the idea can be seen across a number of actions. In relation to the *lex Falcidia*, Papinian is uncharacteristically straightforward:

> *Si servus sub condicione libertate data vita decessit, si quidem impleta condicio quandoque fuerit, heredi non videbitur perisse: quod si defecerit, in contrarium ratio trahit, sed quanti statuliber moriens fuisse videbitur.*[85]

---

statuliber generally, see William Warwick Buckland, *The Roman Law of Slavery* (CUP 1970) 286–91.

[81] Indeed, this appears to be Rodger's conclusion on the clause: '… it is just a false – and presumably compilatorial – explanation of the classical decision which Ulpian may not have deigned to expound'. Rodger (n 40) 292.

[82] D.40.7.1.pr.

[83] D.40.7.2.pr.

[84] Buckland (n 80) 286.

[85] D.35.2.11.1: 'If a slave is granted his freedom under a condition and dies, and if the condition

The ambiguous state of the slave gives rise to an ambiguous approach to damages. We cannot allow the slave's occupation of a halfway point between servitude and freedom to obfuscate the calculation of damages – it is necessary to definitively classify him one way or the other. And so Papinian claims that the identification of the slave as either free or property turns on whether the condition placed on his freedom has been met, whensoever (*quandoque*) that might happen. Translated into the context of the *lex Aquilia*, if the condition that prevented the slave from becoming free and heir is satisfied before the substitute heir can bring an action for his death, the slave is deemed to have no value to the heir.

The same idea can be seen in relation to the *condictio furtiva*:

> *Si servus furtivus sub condicione legatus fuerit, pendente ea heres condictionem habebit et, si lite contestata condicio exstiterit, absolutio sequi debebit, perinde ac si idem servus sub condicione liber esse iussus fuisset et lite contestata condicio exstitisset: nam nec petitoris iam interest hominem recipere et res sine dolo malo furis eius esse desiit. Quod si pendente condicione iudicaretur, iudex aestimare debebit, quanti emptorem invenerit.*[86]

Here Julian argues that the ability of the heir to bring the *condictio furtiva* turns entirely on whether or not the condition has been met, even after *litis contestatio*. Where the condition is met, the heir ceases to have any interest in the slave. This logic is provided by Ulpian in relation to the *actio furti*:

> *Si statuliber subreptus sit vel res sub condicione legata, deinde, antequam adeatur, extiterit condicio, furti iam agi non potest, quia desiit interesse heredis: pendente autem condicione tanti aestimandus est, quanti emptorem potest invenire.*[87]

Across these various contexts it is possible to see a clear principle. Where an action requires an assessment of the value of a *statuliber* to an heir, the focus has to be on whether the condition attached to his freedom has been met. Where it hasn't been met, the *statuliber* remains a slave in the eyes of the law, and so the heir is entitled to his value calculated as for any other slave. But

---

is satisfied thereafter, the heir will not be seen to have lost by his death. But if the condition remains unsatisfied, the contrary reasoning applies, though he will be seen as having died as a *statuliber*'.

[86] D.13.1.14.pr: 'If there is a conditional legacy of a stolen slave, so long as the condition goes unsatisfied the heir has the *condictio*. If the condition is satisfied after *litis contestatio*, absolution has to follow, just as where a slave is freed under a condition that is met after *litis contestatio*. This is because the claimant no longer has any interest in recovering the slave, who has left his property without any fraud on the part of the thief. But if judgment is given while the condition remains unsatisfied, the judge ought to evaluate damages according to how much a buyer could be found for'.

[87] D.47.2.52.29: 'If a *statuliber* or some property subject to a condition in a legacy is stolen, and then, before entry onto the inheritance, the condition is satisfied, the *actio furti* cannot lie because the heir no longer has an interest. But so long as the condition remains unsatisfied, the judge ought to award damages based on the amount for which a purchaser could be found'.

where the condition has been met, even after the death of the *statuliber*, the grant of freedom operates retrospectively to deny the heir has any interest in the slave, negating even causes of action that accrued before the condition was satisfied.

Returning to D.9.2.23.1, it is possible to see Ulpian as providing a style of reasoning consistent with this principle. It does require the insertion of a condition that is satisfied following the death of the slave into the facts behind the text. But it is only through such an insertion that sense can be made of the final clause of Ulpian's reasoning. While it is not implausible that, in accordance with much that has been written on this text in the past, the text illustrates a stepping stone in the evolution from objective to subjective damages under Chapter 1 of the *lex Aquilia*, such explanations do not square with Ulpian's own explanation for his denial of damages.

9. CONCLUSION

Definitively answering the mysteries of D.9.2.23.1 is likely an unattainable goal. But modern Roman law scholarship does not seek such conclusivity. The goal is not to uncover the truth of Roman law, or the truth of the texts, but to approach the source material as a puzzle awaiting a solution. Four such solutions have been offered in relation to a single problem in this chapter, each of which can be made to sound eminently plausible. The purpose of this chapter is not to present any one of them as 'the answer' to the riddle of D.9.2.23.1, but to show how significantly methodology can shape the approach of scholarship, especially in an area with as narrow as evidential basis as Roman law. The fourth solution has been arrived at only through a belief in the need to make sense of Ulpian's final comments about the status of the slave. If the impulses of earlier generations to jettison that clause as a postclassical gloss or Byzantine interpolation had been followed, such an answer would have likely not been reached, as there was no reason to strive towards it. Today's willingness to take the *Corpus Iuris Civilis* at face value, and the sometimes Sisyphean task this entails of making sense of the texts as they stand rather than in an edited form, means there are plenty of puzzles left to be solved for the dedicated Roman lawyer.

Chapter 6

Reflections on the Quantification of Damnum

Alberto Lorusso

1. INTRODUCTION[1]

The *lex Aquilia* is a plebiscite traditionally dated to 286 (or 287) BCE.[2] It consists of three *capita*. The first deals with the unlawful killing of a slave[3] or a *pecus*[4] belonging to someone else. The second chapter is concerned with the contract of *adstipulatio* and imposes 'liability on a secondary creditor who wrongfully released the debtor as against the principal creditor'.[5] The third chapter focuses on wrongful damage to property generally by means of burning, breaking or breaking apart.

The wording of the first chapter is preserved in D.9.2.2.pr, a fragment of the second-century jurist Gaius's commentary on the provincial edict: '*Lege Aquilia capite primo cavetur: "Ut qui servum servamve alienum alienamve quadrupedem vel pecudem iniuria occiderit, quanti id in eo anno plurimi fuit, tantum*

---

[1] The following chapter is based on Alberto Lorusso, *Riflessioni sulla stima del danno nel terzo capo della lex Aquilia* (Università degli Studi di Modena e Reggio Emilia, 2011) with all its limits.

[2] The traditional dating is based mainly on the information reported in Theophilus' *Paraphrasis* (Theoph. 4.3.15). For a recent account of the controversies surrounding the dating, see Alessandra Bignardi, who proposes the end of the third to the beginning of the second century as the most probable period for the approval of the *lex Aquilia*: A Bignardi, 'Teoph. Par. 4. 3. 15: ancora sulla data della *lex Aquilia*' in *Annali Ferrara. Scienze Giuridiche, nuove serie*, 3 (Università di Ferrara 1989) 1. She bases her theory on the fact that it is difficult to reconcile the content of the text of the *lex Aquilia* with the tensions between the patricians and plebeians in the period indicated by Theophilus. For an opposing view, see for example Maria Floriana Cursi, who uses arguments derived from Serrao (Feliciano Serrao, *La 'jurisdictio' del pretore peregrine* (Giuffrè 1954) 41): Maria Floriana Cursi, *Iniuria cum damno. Antigiuridicità e colpevolezza nella storia del danno Aquiliano* (Giuffrè 2002) 155. The uncertainty over dating has its roots in the relationship of the Romans with statutes as a source of law: see Mario Bretone, *Storia del diritto romano* (Laterza 1987) 182 as well as Fritz Schulz, *Prinzipien des römischen Rechts* (Duncker & Humblot 1934) 5.

[3] Bretone underlines that the *lex* does not make this aspect explicit: see Bretone (n 2) 203.

[4] Slaves and beasts of draught or burden are treated as equivalents, as Gaius indicates in D.9.2.2.2. The *pecudes* are beasts used for agricultural exploitation, beasts of burden, or generally employed in economical activities, as is demonstrated by the list that Gaius provides.

[5] Paul du Plessis, *Borkowski's Textbook on Roman Law* (OUP 2010) 320.

aes dare domino damnas esto"'.[6] The wording of the second chapter is less clear. In D.9.2.27.4 Ulpian reveals *'Huius legis secundum quidem capitulum in desuetudinem abiit'*, while the compilers of Justinian's *Institutes* settle the matter in eight words (Inst. 4.3.12): *'Caput secundum legis Aquiliae in usu non est'*. Gaius, in his *Institutiones*, comes closest to the actual wording of Chapter 2. In Gai.Inst. 3.215, we read: *'Capite secundo aduersus adstipulatorem, qui pecuniam in fraudem stipulatoris acceptam fecerit, quanti ea res est, tanti actio constituitur'*. Finally, the content of the third chapter is reported in D.9.2.27.5 where Ulpian reports: *'Tertio autem capite ait eadem lex Aquilia: "Ceterarum rerum praeter hominem et pecudem occisos si quis alteri damnum faxit, quod usserit fregerit ruperit iniuria, quanti ea res erit in diebus triginta proximis, tantum aes domino dare damnas esto"'*.[7]

This contribution will focus on the first and third chapters, since the second chapter had already fallen into desuetude by the start of the classical period. In keeping with the general theme of this volume, I will approach the sources without any preconceptions, an approach typical of Anglo-Saxon academia, with a view to offering a critique of Continental scholarship on the question of the quantification of *damnum*.

Traditionally,[8] according to Continental scholarship, the third chapter of the *lex Aquilia* provided that, irrespective of the extent of the damage caused to the object, the wrongdoer was obliged to pay the highest value of the object in the previous thirty days to its owner (hereafter referred to as 'the traditional view/interpretation'). The gist of this view is that although the concept of *damnum* was gradually enlarged through juristic interpretation to include consequential loss, the quantification always included the highest value of the object in the previous thirty days. When this traditional view is compared to the calculation of *damnum* in Chapter 1 (the highest value of the slave or *pecus* in the year preceding its destruction), it would seem that the main difference between the two chapters was the differing time periods

---

[6]   On the various reconstructions of the text of the law, see Paul van Warmelo, 'A propos de la loi Aquilia' (1980) 27 RIDA 334; Robert Warden Lee, *The Elements of Roman Law* (Sweet & Maxwell 1952) 386; Francesco de Robertis, *Damnum iniuria datum* (Laterza 2000) 55; Erwin Grueber (ed), *The Roman Law of Damage to Property, Being a Commentary on the Title of the Digest Ad Legem Aquiliam (IX. 2), with an Introduction to the Study of the Corpus Iuris Civilis* (Clarendon Press 1886) 4.

[7]   With reference to the wording, see van Warmelo (n 6) 337; Andrew Borkowski, *Textbook on Roman Law* (OUP 1997) 329; Alessandro Corbino, *Il danno qualificato e la lex Aquilia* (CEDAM 2008) 42; John Crook, 'Lex Aquilia' 1984 (72) Athenaeum 73; Michael Crawford (ed), *Roman Statutes* (Institute of Classical Studies 1996) 723; Grueber (n 6) 196; Hans Ankum, *'Quanti ea res erit in diebus XXX proximis* dans le troisième chapitre de la *lex Aquilia* : un fantasme florentin' in Étienne Dravasa (ed), *Religion, société et politique: Mélanges en hommage à Jacques Ellul* (Presses Universitaires de France 1983) 171; Gustav Heimbach, *Basilicorum libri V* (Mercati 1850) 290; de Robertis (n 6) 55.

[8]   For a recent survey of the literature, see Giuseppe Valditara, *Damnum iniuria datum* (Giappichelli 2005) 9 n 54.

(thirty days vs one year). Bernard, comparing the texts of Chapters 1 and 3, as they appear in D.9.2.2.pr[9] and D.9.2.27.5, observed that:

> pour arriver à l'interprétation courante du chapitre 3, il faut: *a*) suppléer le mot *plurimi* qui n'est pas dans le contexte, car condamner à *la valeur* dans les 30 jours passés ne signifie rien; *b*) traduire *erit*, temps de futur, par un temps du passé: *fuerit*, *fuit* ou *fuisset*, alors que la version *erit* n'est pas douteuse; *c*) enfin, admettre que *ea res* signifie la *chose endommagée*, comme dans le chapitre 1 ...[10]

while Zimmermann underlined that the two chapters have four differences: if the first chapter has a term of one year, the third has one of thirty days. 'Secondly, this period is not retrospective but prospective: it is the 30 days *after* the infliction of the wound that matter, not the month preceding this event'. Then, in the third chapter, the word '*plurimi*' that appears in Chapter 1 does not appear 'and fourthly (and perhaps most surprisingly): the principle of the real value seems to determine assessment of the compensation here too', therefore, regardless of the fact that a slave was killed or 'merely bumped into or scratched', his *dominus* would have had the right to claim the entire value: 'Damage worth three pence, slave worth 300 pounds: the wrongdoer had to pay 300 pounds'.[11] The remainder of this contribution will be devoted to providing arguments against this traditional interpretation of Chapter 3.

2. ARGUMENTS AGAINST THE TRADITIONAL INTERPRETATION

The first argument concerns the centrality of *damnum*. A comparison of Chapters 1 and 3 shows that *damnum*[12] was the central common element, since it was impossible to obtain a *condemnatio* (in other words a judgment) under the action, unless it could be demonstrated that the wrongful act had caused a diminution of the patrimony of the owner of the *res*.[13] The first chapter focused on the unlawful destruction of living objects, both slave and animal belonging to a specific group. The second chapter dealt with the destruction of a non-physical object, namely the credit that had been

---

[9] Gaius, 7 *ad edictum provinciale*: *Ait lex: 'Quanti is homo in eo anno plurimi fuisset'. Quae clausula aestimationem habet damni, quod datum est.*

[10] A Bernard, 'A propos d'un article récent sur le chapitre 3 de la loi Aquilie: Contenu. Nature de la réparation' (1937) 16 RHDFE 450.

[11] Reinhard Zimmermann, *The Law of Obligations. Roman Foundations of the Civilian Tradition* (Juta 1990) 962.

[12] For reasons of space, I will not discuss the meaning of *damnum*; I refer the reader to my dissertation.

[13] Lawson underlines a text by Ulpian reported in in D.47.10.7.1. Here, Ulpian clarifies that the first chapter of the *lex Aquilia* is based on the economic loss that occurred as a result of the killing of a slave or a *pecus*: Frederick Henry Lawson, *Negligence in the Civil Law* (OUP 1950) 74.

terminated by the release of the debtor.[14] In both cases, the *dominus* or the *creditor* suffered loss corresponding to the value of the *res corporalis* or *incorporalis* in question. The third chapter, on the other hand, provided for an action even though the object had not been destroyed.[15] It is only in the third chapter that the word *damnum* occurs, while the first and second chapters describe a result, but the common element that unifies the three chapters of the *lex Aquilia* is clearly the existence of a *damnum*.[16]

The reason why the word *damnum* appears only in Chapter 3 is because in the first two chapters the wrongful act is already described sufficiently, while in the third, the conduct of the wrongdoer rather than the result is described.[17] As Lawson observed: '*damnum* came to be thought of as the gist of all actions on the *lex*'[18] and the chapter, whether the first or the third, only mattered in relation to the *quantum* of the *damnum*. This is confirmed by various Roman legal sources. In D.9.2.1.pr, Ulpian, referring to the *lex Aquilia* in general, described it as the *lex* that *derogavit* all others dealing with damage: '*Lex Aquilia omnibus legibus, quae ante se de damno iniuria locutae sunt, derogavit, sive duodecim tabulis, sive alia quae fuit: quas leges nunc referre non est necesse*'.[19] This also explains the full name of this plebiscite, the *lex Aquilia de damno*.[20]

---

[14] For a range of opinions on this matter, see Édouard Cuq, *Les institutions juridiques des Romains* (2nd edn, Librairie Plon 1904) 206; van Warmelo (n 6) 337; Carlo Augusto Cannata, 'Il terzo capo della "*lex Aquilia*"' (1995–96) 37–38 BIDR 118. Giuseppe Grosso, 'La distinzione fra «*res corporales*» e «*res incorporales*» e il secondo capo della «*lex Aquilia*»' in Antonio Guarino and Luigi Labruna (eds), *Synteleia Vincenzo Arangio Ruiz* (Jovene 1964) 792.

[15] See also the observations in David Daube, 'On the Use of the Term *Damnum*' in *Studi in onore di Siro Solazzi* (Jovene 1948) 142.

[16] See Grosso (n 14) 792. The *fil rouge* that connects the three chapters is an elimination: Zimmermann shares the opinion: Zimmermann (n 11) 957.

[17] For other deeper reflections on the theme, see Daube (n 15) 140.

[18] Lawson (n 13) 74. See also, in a quite similar way, Crook (n 7) 73; as well as Herbert F Jolowicz, 'The Original Scope of the *Lex Aquilia* and the Question of Damages' (1922) 38 LQR 220 and Antonio Guarino, *Diritto privato romano* (Jovene 2001) 996 n 89, 2. In the same way, also Max Kaser, *Quanti ea res est* (Beck 1935) and *Das römische Privatrecht* vol 2 (Beck 1971) then Alan Prichard, *Leage's Roman Private Law* (Macmillan 1964) 411; van Warmelo (n 6) 337; Fritz Schulz, *Classical Roman Law* (OUP 1951) 587; John Kelly, 'The Meaning of the *Lex Aquilia*' (1964) 80 LQR 80; Andrew Borkowski, *Textbook on Roman Law* (2nd edn, Blackstone 1997) 330 and Corbino (n 7) 43. The Roman-Dutch jurist Johannes Voet, in the seventeenth century, had reached such a conclusion already: Johannes Voet, *The Selective Voet – Commentary on the Pandects* (Buttterworths 1955) 589. For a procedural argument, see Peter Birks, 'A Point of Aquilian Pleading' (1985) 36 IURA 97. See also Ernest Metzger, 'Roman Judges, Case Law and Principles of Procedure' (2004) 22 Law and History Review 251, but also Paul Girard, *Manuel élémentaire de droit romain* (6th edn, Rousseau 1918) 424.

[19] See William Warwick Buckland, *A Text-Book of Roman Law from Augustus to Justinian* (CUP 1921) 580. See also van Warmelo (n 6) 338, and Valditara (n 8) 17. See also Gai.Inst.3.216 and Gai Inst.3.210. Other examples may be found in Gai.Inst.3.214, Gai.Inst.3.219 and Inst.4.3.16.

[20] See Gai.Inst.3.202, but also Cic., *Pro Tull.* 4.9; Cic., *Rosc. Com.* 32 and Cic., *Rosc. Com.* 54. See Kelly (n 18) 80.

The central importance of the concept of *damnum* is visible in the effort of the jurists to extend this concept as far as possible, to obtain a *condemnatio* under the action. Proof of this may be found in D.9.2.27.17, where Ulpian identifies as *damnum* the expenses undertaken to cure a wounded slave:

> *Rupisse eum utique accipiemus, qui vulneraverit, vel virgis vel loris vel pugnis cecidit, vel telo vel quo alio, ut scinderet alicui corpus, vel tumorem fecerit, sed ita demum, si damnum iniuria datum est: ceterum si nullo servum pretio viliorem deterioremve fecerit, Aquilia cessat iniuriarumque erit agendum dumtaxat: Aquilia enim eas ruptiones, quae damna dant, persequitur. Ergo etsi pretio quidem non sit deterior servus factus, verum sumptus in salutem eius et sanitatem facti sunt, in haec mihi videri damnum datum: atque ideoque lege Aquilia agi posse.*

Ulpian says that the *lex Aquilia* '*persequitur*' '*ea ruptiones, quae damna dant*', thereby demonstrating that *damnum*, the loss caused to the owner, was the essential element.[21] But if the central aspect of the third chapter was the occurrence of *damnum*, can it really be that, at the exact moment when the requirement was met, it suddenly disappeared? Such an interpretation of the sources would lead to a strange result worthy of a paraphrase of the Bible verse: 'the cornerstone has become the stone the builders rejected'.[22] This seems quite implausible. It would also be illogical to insist on the presence of both a wound and a *damnum*, but then to base the *condemnatio* solely on the value of the thing.[23] Since all the chapters required the existence of a loss, seeing that *condemnationes* under Chapters 1 and 2 gave rise to a mere reparation,[24] it seems rather implausible that a *condemnatio* under Chapter 3 had nothing to do with the real consequences of the fact.

The second argument concerns the relationship between the *lex Aquilia* and the 12 Tables. Before the *lex Aquilia* was enacted, wrongful damage to property was dealt with using fixed penalties. The 12 Tables provided for fines in the cases of *membrum ruptum*, *os fractum* and, maybe, also *adustio*. *Membrum ruptum* was objectively more serious than *os fractum*, thus 'we may conclude that the penalty was higher in this case', but Daube underlines that this may give rise to aberrant results, since the value of the thing could change, in which case, 'the *membrum ruptum* of a bad slave might often have caused less damage to his owner than the *os fractum* of a good one' and 'last

---

[21] The efforts by the jurists to also include the loss *re integra* within the notion of *damnum* is telling; see D.9.2.27.14.

[22] The text of the Psalm is: 'The stone the builders rejected has become the cornerstone' (Psalm 118 verse 22).

[23] It does not take much to appreciate that the traditional interpretation is irrational. See, for example, D.9.2.27.17.

[24] I find the reflections of de Robertis (n 6) 30, dealing with the first chapter, quite convincing. For the second chapter, see Giuseppe Valditara, 'Dall'*aestimatio rei* all'*id quod interest* nell'applicazione della *condemnatio aquiliana*' in Letizia Vacca (ed), *La responsabilità civile da atto illecito nella prospettiva storico-comparatistica* vol 1 (Giappichelli 1995) 76.

[but] not least it was certainly not uncommon that a *membrum ruptum*, though in itself a more severe wound than an *os fractum*, eventually turned out better and *vice versa*.[25] It was for this reason that the *lex Aquilia* was enacted, namely to achieve a result in law that was linked to the severity of the actual event.[26] Every rule betrays an underlying value of the system it belongs to. The Roman legal order established different rules for different events. This suggests not only a maturity of social conscience, but also one of juristic technique, an achievement from which it is implausible to return.[27]

According to the traditional interpretation, the legal consequence of killing and wounding was the same, since in both cases the wrongdoer had to compensate the owner on the basis of the highest value of the object involved. This means that, at least on some level, wounding was as grave as killing. Considering that wounding was objectively less severe than killing but that it was sanctioned in the same way as the more serious injury, one could make a case for saying that wounding was in fact legally worse. If, at a certain point, the wrongdoer also became liable for the expenses involved in curing the wounded slave, one might argue that an outright killing was in fact more advantageous than a wounding. The same argument could be made regarding 'spoiling' under Chapter 3.

The traditional interpretation states that 'the difference between *caps.* 1 and 3 would be reduced to no more than one of periods of retrospective valuation',[28] but

> the difference between wounding and killing would seem to call for a greater difference than that between taking the highest value in the past year and taking the highest value in the past thirty days, a difference which would in most cases be illusory

since the calculation of the value of the property made with reference to the month or year before the wrongful act would result in identical amounts, since it is implausible that the thing would change in value.[29]

We must also consider that the *lex Aquilia* had been extended to instances of wounding of free people.[30] According to these sources, the father of a free

---

[25] David Daube, 'On the Third Chapter of the *Lex Aquilia*' in David Cohen and Dieter Simon (eds), *Collected Studies in Roman Law* (Klostermann 1991) 6. See also Guillaume Cardascia, 'La portée privitive del la Loi Aquilia' in Alan Watson (ed), *Daube Noster: Essays in Legal History for David Daube* (Scottish Academic Press 1974) 55.

[26] Francis de Zulueta, *The Institutes of Gaius, part II, Commentary* (OUP 1953) 212.

[27] See Bernard (n 10) 452. See also de Zulueta (n 26) 212.

[28] De Zulueta (n 26) 212.

[29] Frederick Henry Lawson and Basil S Markesinis, *Tortious Liability for Unintentional Harm in the Common Law and the Civil Law* vol 1 (CUP 1982) 6. In the same manner, Cardascia (n 25) 55. See also Pasquale Voci, *Risarcimento e pena privata nel diritto romano classico* (Giuffrè 1939) 68, although he is convinced that the traditional interpretation is correct.

[30] See D.9.2.5.3, D.9.2.6, D.9.2.7.pr and D.9.2.13.pr. Dealing with these sources, Schulz writes

son wounded by his apprentice master could claim the value of the expense incurred to cure him and the equivalent of the loss of utility of his future labour. In the case of the free son, the value of the boy is of course not assessed, because the body of a free man did not have any value according to Roman law (in contrast to the case of a slave boy) that could be taken into account. The question is how the jurists shifted from one case to the other. In all likelihood, a similarity between the two cases led to an extension of the first case by analogy to the second. Nonetheless, despite the ubiquity of analogy as a juristic tool for developing Roman law, the gap between the two cases seems rather wide.

The sources we have so far considered provide another argument that disproves the traditional interpretation. If this interpretation is correct, it would imply that the *lex Aquilia* represented another regression with respect to the 12 Tables, since in this compilation of laws an act committed against a free man was punished more severely than one committed against a slave. The *condemnatio* for an *os fractum* of a free man, for example, was double that of a slave. According to the traditional interpretation, the *lex Aquilia* dealt with the matter in the opposite way, since the *condemnatio* for a delict committed against a slave was much more severe than one committed against a free man. Socially, such an effect would have been considered unacceptable.

It bears reinforcing that a system like the one proposed by the traditional interpretation would have paralysed any activity in society, since there would have been too many risks involved in any action. It would also have encouraged people to deliberately expose their slaves and other property to danger, since they could make good money from any damage caused to them. This would, in turn, lead to the suppression of the principle of self-responsibility. Such a reaction of the law was 'obviously unfair that one cannot believe any legislator intended it'.[31] If the two chapters gave the same result, how could the absence of the word *plurimi* in the third chapter be explained? As Cardascia asked: 'Pourquoi le chapitre I comporte-t-il un *plurimi* qui renvoie à *la valeur la plus haute* atteinte par le bien au cours de l'année précédente, tandis que le chapitre III ne contient pas ce mot?'.[32] Of course, it cannot be that '*legis latorem contentum fuisse, quod prima parte eo uerbo usus esset*',[33] since 'la ripetitività stucchevole delle leggi repubblicane' was a common feature of Republican legislation.[34]

that 'it is, however, hardly credible that an *actio utilis* was ever granted in classical times when a free person had suffered injury': Schulz (n 18) 591.
[31] Jolowicz (n 18) 220.
[32] Cardascia (n 25) 56 (cursive text).
[33] Gai.Inst.3.218, also Inst.4.3.15.
[34] De Robertis (n 6) 45.

Another argument against the traditional interpretation of the *lex Aquilia* is that, if the *condemnatio* under Chapters 1 and 3 was fundamentally the same, the matter could have been dealt with in one and the same chapter.[35] The crux of it all is the meaning of the expression '*ea res*'. Those scholars who oppose the traditional view interpret this phrase as 'affair', being the meaning it has in the Edict of the praetor.[36] Lenel reconstructs the first chapter *formula* in the following terms:

> S. p. N^m N^m *illum seruum iniuria occidisse, quam ob rem, quanti is seruus in eo anno plurimi fuit, tantam pecuniam* N^m N^m A^o A^o *dare oportet, tantam pecuniam duplam, iudex,* N^m N^m A^o A^o c. s. n. p. a.[37]

The section from the Basilica, in other words the part corresponding to D.9.2.27.5, confirms that *ea res* has the meaning of 'affair'.[38] Other sources too show the use of the word *res* referring to the matter, and not to a physical thing.[39]

There is also an enrichment angle that undermines the traditional inter-pretation. An application of such an interpretation would give rise to an unjustified form of *locupletatio*. In D.9.2.27.23, the case of a mule that has been overloaded is reported. The overloading caused damage (a fracture) to one of the animal's limbs: '*Et si mulum plus iusto oneraverit et aliquid membri ruperit, Aquiliae locum fore.*'[40]

Such an injury does not deprive the thing of its value, nor is there an attempt by the jurists to assimilate such a case to an *occisio*.[41] If the only dif-ference between the two chapters was the time frame, one would expect an attempt by jurists to force the interpretation of the case into the mould of

---

[35] Reginald Dias, 'Obscurities in the Development of *Damnum*' (1958) Acta Juridica 203; Cardascia (n 25) 56; Corbino (n 7) 181.

[36] Daube (n 25) 7. See also Charles Henry Monro (ed), *Digest IX.2. lex Aquilia* (CUP 1928) 35 Voci (n 29) 54; Voci, *Risarcimento e pena privata nel diritto romano classico* (Giuffrè 1939) 24; Lee (n 6) 473; Kelly (n 18) 80; Constantin St. Tomulescu, 'Les trois chapitres de la *lex Aquilia*' (1970) 21 IURA 192; Tony Honoré, 'Linguistic and Social Context of the *Lex Aquilia*' (1972) 7 IJ 144; Crawford (n 7) 723; Zimmermann (n 11) 967. For a valuable overview of sources where the word *res* appears with meaning of 'affair' see Sebastiano Tafaro, *La interpretatio ai verba 'quanti ea res est' nella giurisprudenza romana – L'analisi di Ulpiano* (Jovene 1980).

[37] Otto Lenel, *Essai de reconstitution de l'édit perpetuel* vol 1 (Larose 1901) 229.

[38] See Bas.603.2 and Bas.603.5.

[39] Gai.Inst.3.215, dealing with the second chapter, but see also Gai.Inst.4.6 and Gai.Inst.4.7.

[40] Cannata, thinking that the wound refers to the hoof of the mule, believes that the action corresponds to the total destruction of the thing, 'poiché un mulo con una zampa rotta è un mulo da abbattere': Cannata (n 14) 119. I do not agree: such a mule could still be used in a mill. The expression '*et aliquid membri ruperit*', then, seems meaningful, since it shows the intention of the jurist to delimit the object of the *ruptio*. In my view, such an argument is supported by the use of the same expression of the 12 Tables, *membrum ruptum*. Supporters of this view include Sandro Schipani (ed), *Iustiniani Augusti Digesta seu Pandectae. Digesti o Pandette dell'Imperatore Giustiniano* (Giuffrè 2005) and Monro (n 36) 44.

[41] Grueber confirms that this is a case covered by Chapter 3: Grueber (n 6) 100.

Chapter 1. Apart from this, a *condemnatio* for the entire value would in fact lead to an increase in the owner's assets.

D.9.2.27.6 contains the case of a slave that has been singed by a torch. The same arguments expressed above could be applied to this case. The goods have not been destroyed completely,[42] therefore there would be an unjustified enrichment for the *dominus*, while, if the source presented cases of effective elimination of value of the thing involved, the fact that jurists do not attempt to establish an affinity with Chapter 1 seems particularly meaningful.[43]

D.9.2.45.1, a response by Paul, states that, if a slave is wounded and then recovers, there will be an action under the *lex Aquilia*: '*Lege Aquilia agi potest et sanato vulnerato servo*'.

Apart from the fact that, also in this case, there would be a *locupletatio*, the strongest argument against the traditional interpretation is the fact that, since the response was collected in the Digest, it must have been a problematic topic. What is so peculiar that it deserves to be canonised in the Pandects? If the traditional interpretation is followed, such a statement would be meaningless, but it becomes meaningful if we consider that it deals with the *condemnatio* designed to compensate the loss, that is the expenses undertaken in curing the sick slave and the *lucrum cessans*.

De Robertis has convincingly demonstrated that the *condemnatio* to the highest value of the object in the previous year was designed to achieve total reparation, since slaves and *pecudes* fluctuated in price during the year. Agriculture was and still is: 'dalla lunga stasi nel periodo invernale (*feriae sementivae*) durante il quale – anche per prescrizioni religiose – erano astretti al riposo uomini e bestie che però, anche in questo periodo, dovevano essere pur sempre alimentati ed accuditi'.[44] That the first chapter protects only an animal which can be utilised during a specific season is telling (Gai 3.271 and Inst. 4.3.1). The fact that the *condemnatio* was for the highest value of the previous year suggests that the action had a reipersecutory function as can be seen, for example, in D. 9.2.21.pr: '*Ait lex: 'Quanti is homo in eo anno plurimi fuisset'. Quae clausula aestimationem habet damni, quod datum est*'.

---

[42] Corbino (n 7) 98 defines the slave as only '*ustionato*'. This is also clearly demonstrated by the source, since the jurist writes that if you have not killed the slave or the *pecus*, but caused damage by *ustio*, *fractio* or *ruptio*, then you will be considered liable under Chapter 3.

[43] There are other sources where the thing does not perish: D.9.2.27.30, which deals with the piercing of pearls, or D.9.2.27.18, which deals with tearing or soiling clothes. We may also consider D.9.2.27.14, which reports the case of the sowing of weeds in someone else's field. See also D.9.2.49.

[44] De Robertis (n 6) 32; Valditara (n 8) 43; Grant McLeod, 'Pigs, Boars and Livestock Under the *Lex Aquilia*' in John Cairns and Olivia Robinson (eds) *Critical Studies in Ancient Law, Comparative Law and Legal History* (Hart 2004) 87; Daube (n 15) 9; Grueber (n 6) 265; Cardascia (n 25) 57 and Cannata (n 14) 141. *Contra*, Ben Beinart, 'Once More on the Origin of the *Lex Aquilia*' (1956) BSALR 74. For deeper reflections, Lorusso (n 1) 156, n 218. See also Virg., *Georg.*, 1.43–46, 1.208–11 and 1.299.

The jurist explicitly affirms that the *plurimi* clause is what permits the quantification of the damage: there is clearly a link between this element of the text of the law and the prejudice suffered by the *dominus rei*.[45]

Scholars who support the traditional interpretation generally justify their belief that the *condemnatio* was for a sum higher than the value of the loss in terms of the penal nature of the *lex Aquilia*,[46] but this has in the past led to confusion. It is a myth that a penal action necessarily implied a *condemnatio* for a sum higher than the actual loss suffered. De Zulueta, for example, observed that in classical law the plaintiff, through a penal action, would not have obtained 'more than what would make good his loss, and in contrast to *furtum* there was no concurrent compensatory action', therefore he believes that the *actio ex lege Aquilia* was qualified as penal, while reipersecutory in results.[47] Zimmermann underlines that in the *lex Aquilia* 'what was penalized by doubling the amount of damages was the defendant's reluctance to confess, not the Aquilian delict as such', clarifying that the fact that an action is qualified as penal does not necessarily imply that the plaintiff will be awarded a sum higher than the loss suffered, because 'one and the same sum could have a dual function: it could be *poena* in the guise of compensation'.[48] Lawson explains that a *poena* remained a *poena* even if, in concrete terms, it only gave rise to a reparation.[49] The fact that an action was qualified as *poenalis* gave rise to many consequences, but did not imply that there was a *condemnatio* to a value higher than the effective loss suffered by the plaintiff. When the purpose was to punish, the legal order established a fixed penalty or a *condemnatio* to pay a multiple of the value of the thing, a fact that shows that *poenalis* clearly means something else.[50] In the majority of cases, the only effect of the action under the *lex Aquilia* was to obtain a reparation, since the modification in value of the thing in the time prior to the wrongful act was an implausible event. In most cases, therefore, the system may have operated like a lottery with a few losing numbers.[51]

The same Gaius in his *Institutes*, a source that cannot be suspected as altered by the compilers, says that, through the *lex Aquilia*, the plaintiff could get both a penalty and reparation only when the action was promoted

---

[45]   Grueber (n 6) 57.
[46]   Valditara (n 8) 18; Geoffrey MacCormack, 'On the Third Chapter of the *Lex Aquilia*' (1970) 5 IJ 174; du Plessis (n 5) 322.
[47]   De Zulueta (n 26) 210, but see also Cuq (n 14) 556; Schulz (n 18) 589. Referring only to the *lex Aquilia*, Grueber (n 6) 274. See also Monro (n 36) 15 and Buckland (n 19) 586.
[48]   Zimmermann (n 11) 974.
[49]   Frederick Henry Lawson, *Negligence in the Civil Law* (Clarendon Press 1950) 8. This scholar, referring to D.9.2.27.30 and D.9.2.56, underlines that since 'in general penal actions were not permitted between husband and wife', this proves that the aim of such an action was to produce a reparation and not a punishment.
[50]   For a critical approach to the theme see Beinart (n 44) 73 and Cardascia (n 25) 65, who writes: 'au temps d'Aquilius, n'existait pas de doctrine: l'instigateur de la loi eût été bien surpris si on lui avait demandé : votre action sera-t-elle pénale, réipersécutoire ou mixte?'.
[51]   Cardascia (n 25) 58.

in duplum contra infitiantem.[52] Gaius, discussing the second chapter, specifies that there was no need for it, because the *actio mandati* was sufficient, apart from instances when the action was against someone who had denied liability. Leaving aside the peculiar hypothesis of the *infitiatio*, Gaius clearly shows that there was a fundamental correspondence between the contractual action and the action *ex lege Aquilia*. This means that, although penal, the latter had a reipersecutory function.

We may derive the same principle from D.19.2.30.2: the case is that of a man who rented mules and overloaded them, thereby injuring them. As Thomas underlined: 'Alfenus presents the contractual and Aquilian actions as alternative, not cumulative (*vel* ... *vel*), whether the view be his own or the reported opinion of his master, Servius Sulpicius'.[53] What is noteworthy is the fact that 'having different *causae* and different *res*', the two actions were not incompatible under the *ius civile* and could be brought in a cumulative way, but the jurists dealt with the Aquilian remedy in this way.

Many sources provide proof that there was no cumulation between the *actio ex lege Aquilia* and others. Among these, we may list D.9.2.18: *'Sed et si is qui pignori servum accepit occidit eum vel vulneravit, lege Aquilia et pigneraticia conveniri potest, sed alterutra contentus esse debebit actor'.*

The source establishes that if somebody kills or wounds a slave received in pledge, there would be only one action.[54] Since there is no doubt that under the contractual action the plaintiff could obtain no more than mere reparation, the freedom to choose between the Aquilian and contractual action provides evidence that the traditional interpretation is wrong.[55]

In addition to all of these, it seems meaningful that jurists emphasise the fact that sometimes there may be a *condemnatio* to a value higher than the actual loss. One example will suffice, from D.9.2.23.3:

[52] Gai.Inst.3.216. See also Lawson and Markesinis (n 29) 4. For deeper reflections on the development of the concept of penalty in the *lex Aquilia*, see Lorusso (n 1) 172.

[53] Tony Thomas, '*Actiones ex locato/conducto* and Aquilian Liability' in Wouter de Vos (ed), *Essays in Honour of Ben Beinart* vol 3 (Juta 1979) 127.

[54] Other sources exclude the cumulation of actions: D.19.2.57, D.19.2.25.5, D.19.2.25.5 read together with D.19.2.25.3 and 4. See for more examples Thomas (n 53) 127. About the concurrence of actions both contractual and Aquilian, see Prichard (n 18) 416 and also Corbino (n 7) 10.

[55] Some scholars hold that the adverb *plurimi* was concerned with the problem of proof: Zimmermann (n 11) 961. For a slightly different approach, see Fritz Pringsheim, 'The Origin of the *Lex Aquilia*' in *Droits de l'Antiquité et Sociologie Juridique : Mélanges Henri Lévy-Bruhl* (Sirey 1959) 240. Recently, Corbino (n 7) at 77 has suggested another explanation for the presence of the adverb *plurimi*: slaves were goods 'di specialissimo pregio' and, their 'sfruttamento economico è legato non solo all'addestramento, ma alle loro specifiche ed irripetibili abilità'; similarly, animals received 'dall'organizzazione economica nella quale l'uomo li inserisce un valore aggiunto', being 'oggetto (con riferimento all'economia del tempo della legge) di una disciplina che tiene conto dello speciale pregiudizio che può derivare dallo loro uccisione'. The consideration of the highest value permitted the recovery for the loss of the unique features of the object destroyed. See also Valditara (n 8) 15, 34.

Idem Iulianus scribit aestimationem hominis occisi ad id tempus referri, quo plurimi in eo anno fuit: et ideo et si pretioso pictori pollex fuerit praecisus et intra annum, quo praecideretur, fuerit occisus, posse eum Aquilia agere pretioque eo aestimandum, quanti fuit priusquam artem cum pollice amisisset.

This is the case of the slave who used to be a good painter, but had been injured before eventually being killed. Ulpian notes that Julian quantified the *damnum* on the basis of his price as a painter, not as a man with a handicap. The record of this case attests that such an event was considered as noteworthy.

The sources show that, at least by the second century,[56] the remedy provided by the *lex Aquilia* was extended also to cases involving the wounding of a free man.[57] If the *corpus* is the ineliminable basis for the calculation of reparation, how could the jurists achieve the extension of the action to cases in which the body of a free man, in other words an object *extra-commercium*, thus ontologically valueless, was involved? Can we really imagine that jurists could have imagined the extension of the remedy to a case which could not imply the first and most immediate element of estimation?

According to traditional doctrine, consequential losses were added to the *corpus* but did not replace it, at least initially.[58] If the jurists suggested an extension of the remedy to such a case, it was because they could identify more common elements than differences. The same can be said of D.9.2.13. pr, the case of the wounding of a free man: '*Liber homo suo nomine utilem Aquiliae habet actionem: directam enim non habet, quoniam dominus membrorum suorum nemo videtur*'.

The only difference that is highlighted by the jurist is that the action would be indirect rather than direct. No consideration is given to the body. In both sources, the jurists, once they have identified the presence of a loss, a *damnum*, immediately assert that an action is available, but they do not spend time on the macroscopic aspect, that is, that contrary to what would have been expected, there is no valuation of the body.

3. TEXTUAL EVIDENCE AGAINST TRADITIONAL INTERPRETATION

Until now, my analysis has relied chiefly on arguments of juristic logic in order to refute the tradition interpretation of the quantification of *damnum* under Chapter 3. In this section, I wish to raise a number of textual matters that, in my view, also undermine said interpretation. As already pointed out

---

[56] Bear in mind that in D.9.2.5.3 and D.9.2.7.pr. Ulpian reports the opinion of Julian.

[57] See D.9.2.5.3, D.9.2.6, D.9.2.7.pr. For a useful dissertation on the reason why this could happen, see Lawson (n 49) 21.

[58] Valditara is convinced that evolution occurred in three steps. See Giuseppe Valditara, *Dall'aestimatio rei all'id quod interest* (CEDAM 1995) 239. See then de Zulueta (n 26) 211.

by Bernard, there is no trace of a *condemnatio* for the highest value of the thing in the texts themselves: 'les écrits dont se sont inspirés les jurisconsultes n'ont pas conservé la trace d'un pareil état de choses parce qu'il n'a, sans doute, jamais existé'.[59] Let us examine each of the cases in turn. In D.9.2.24, Paul discusses the case of a false confession relating to the wounding of a slave. '*Hoc apertius est circa vulneratum hominem: nam si confessus sit vulnerasse nec sit vulneratus, aestimationem cuius vulneris faciemus? Vel ad quod tempus recurramus?*'.[60]

The compilers of Justinian's Digest inserted this text after D.9.2.23.11, where Ulpian discussed the case of a false confession relating to the killing of a slave:

> *Si quis hominem vivum falso confiteatur occidisse et postea paratus sit ostendere hominem vivum esse, Iulianus scribit cessare Aquiliam, quamvis confessus sit se occidisse: hoc enim solum remittere actori confessoriam actionem, ne necesse habeat docere eum occidisse: ceterum occisum esse hominem a quocumque oportet.*

In this latter case, Ulpian explained that, if somebody confessed to killing a slave, but it was then discovered that the slave was alive, there could not be a *condemnatio* under Chapter 1 of the *lex Aquilia*. Although not immediately obvious, D.4.3.7.7, where Ulpian discusses the case of a chained slave that is freed unlawfully by a third party, should also be added here:

> *Idem Labeo quaerit, si compeditum servum meum ut fugeret solveris, an de dolo actio danda sit? Et ait Quintus apud eum notans: si non misericordia ductus fecisti, furti teneris: si misericordia, in factum actionem dari debere.*[61]

When taken together, the cases described in these three texts are basically threefold: the confession of a killing, that of a wounding and the release of a chained slave. If we read D.9.2.23.11 in a counterfactual manner, we must assume that, if the confession had been true, the wrongdoer would have been held liable under Chapter 1 of the *lex Aquilia*. The same can be said of D.4.3.7.7, since the freeing of a chained slave of another without his consent has the same effect as an unlawful killing in terms of Chapter 1, namely the total loss of the asset.

By contrast, D.9.2.24[62] reveals that, if the same reasoning were to be applied to the wounding, it leads to an intellectual cul-de-sac. In the other

[59] Bernard (n 10) 455.

[60] Watson holds this source is genuine, since 'any alteration would have necessitated the complete fabrication of the text': Alan Watson, *The Law of Obligations in the Later Roman Republic* (OUP 1965) 235. I do not agree, since there seems to be a bad connection between the two halves of the text: for further reflections, see Lorusso (n 1) 202 n 278.

[61] The case appears also in Inst.4.3.16. On this, see Daube (n 15) 110.

[62] Monro used this source as proof of the fact that, in the case of a wound, the *condemnatio* could not be based on the value of the body: Monro (n 36) 35. See also Bernard (n 10) 55 and n 1, and Watson (n 60) 235.

two sources, the problem faced by the jurists was one of proof: Ulpian, quoting Julian, specifies the effect of the confession. The *confessio* only exempted the plaintiff from proving that the act had been committed by the defendant. It did not discharge him from proving all the other elements of liability. The cases reported in D.9.2.23.11 and D.9.2.24 both imply the absence of the *corpus* and a confession by somebody who maintains that he has killed or wounded a slave that had disappeared. If the quantification of *damnum* under the first and the third chapter of the *lex Aquilia* was the same, how can this approach be justified? In my view, the answer lies in the wording of Paul: '*aestimationem cuius vulneris faciemus?*'; these words clearly reveal the working of the action, namely that an estimation of the real prejudice had to be made.

The second case involves the release of a boar. In D.41.1.55, Proculus discusses the case of a wild boar:

> *In laqueum, quem venandi causa posueras, aper incidit: cum eo haereret, exemptum eum abstuli: num tibi videor tuum aprum abstulisse? Et si tuum putas fuisse, si solutum eum in silvam dimisissem, eo casu tuus esse desisset an maneret? Et quam actionem mecum haberes, si desisset tuus esse, num in factum dari oportet, quaero. Respondit: laqueum videamus ne intersit in publico an in privato posuerim et, si in privato posui, utrum in meo an in alieno, et, si in alieno, utrum permissu eius cuius fundus erat an non permissu eius posuerim: praeterea utrum in eo ita haeserit aper, ut expedire se non possit ipse, an diutius luctando expediturus se fuerit. Summam tamen hanc puto esse, ut, si in meam potestatem pervenit, meus factus sit. Sin autem aprum meum ferum in suam naturalem laxitatem dimisisses et eo facto meus esse desisset, actionem mihi in factum dari oportere, veluti responsum est, cum quidam poculum alterius ex nave eiecisset.*[63]

The case is a complex one. A hunter set a trap in order to catch a wild boar. The boar was caught in the trap, but a third party came across the trapped boar, released it and took it. The question raised is whether the hunter acquired ownership of the animal while in the trap, since ownership of a wild animal (a *res nullius*) could be obtained by *occupatio*,[64] and, furthermore, whether the hunter would have any claim to wrongful damage to property against the person who made off with the boar. The jurist establishes that an *actio in factum* (*ex lege Aquiliae*) is available to the hunter against the person who took the trapped boar. Such a situation, clearly falling under Chapter

---

[63] Barton holds that 'the earlier portion of the text deals with the conditions which must be fulfilled before I can be taken to have acquired property in a trapped boar. The compilers have unfortunately shortened it, and shortened it to such purpose as to render it incomprehensible': John Barton, 'The *Lex Aquilia* and the Decretal Actions' in Alan Watson (ed), *Daube Noster: Essays in Legal History for David Daube* (Scottish Academic Press 1974) 18. The case is very close to that proposed in D.4.3.7.7, as Noodt noticed: G Noodt, *Opera omnia* (Luzac 1755) 140.

[64] See Gai.Inst.2.66–67.

3 of the *lex*,[65] demonstrates that *damnum* could be quantified also where the object was not present.

The third case is from D.19.5.23, where Alfenus reports the case of the ring that falls into the river: '*Duo secundum Tiberim cum ambularent, alter eorum ei, qui secum ambulabat, rogatus anulum ostendit, ut respiceret [respicerit]: illi excidit anulus et in Tiberim devolutus est. Respondit posse agi cum eo in factum actione*'.[66]

As has already been established in D.9.2.23.11 and D.4.3.7.7, Chapter 1 can function in absence of the body: the same applies to Chapter 3, when dealing with the suppression of the *dominium* (D.41.1.55 and D.19.5.23), but not when there is a case of simple wounding (D.9.2.24). This necessarily implies that Chapter 3 is conceptually different. All of these cases show that the third chapter of the *lex Aquilia*, when dealing with cases of the killing of a thing, or its destruction or similar, can also function if the thing is not available, whereas it cannot offer any solution in the case of mere deterioration.

The fourth case concerns the premature harvesting of crops in D.9.2.27.25:

Si olivam immaturam decerpserit vel segetem desecuerit immaturam vel vineas crudas, Aquilia tenebitur: quod si iam maturas, cessat Aquilia: nulla enim iniuria est, cum tibi etiam impensas donaverit, quae in collectionem huiusmodi fructuum impenduntur: sed si collecta haec interceperit, furti tenetur. Octavenus in uvis adicit, nisi inquit, in terram uvas proiecit, ut effunderentur.[67]

In the text, Ulpian examines the case of a person who, without the consent of the *dominus*, harvested unripe olives, corn or grapes, and assesses whether they could be held liable *ex lege Aquilia*.[68] What would the highest value of unripe fruit have been in the previous thirty days?[69] In D.9.2.33.pr, Paul reveals that prices were fixed by market: '*Sextus quoque Pedius ait pretia rerum non ex affectione nec utilitate singulorum, sed communiter fungi*'.

The question, therefore, is whether unripe fruit had any value. Was there a market for it? In these cases, if we consider the fruit that was harvested as the basis for the calculation of the *damnum*, it is clear that there was no real

---

[65] According to D.9.2.29.6 a boar is not a *pecus*.

[66] For an analysis of a case of dispersion, see Bernardo Albanese, 'Studi sulla legge Aquilia' in *Annali del seminario giuridico dell'Università di Palermo*, XXI (Giappichelli 1950).

[67] Similarly, D.9.2.27.26–27.

[68] According to Valditara's theory, by the time of Ulpian and Paul, *interesse* had become the central element for the valuation whereas it had previously been that of the mere *corpus* and then that of the *corpus* and *causae corpori cohaerentes*. In this source, Octavenus, a jurist who lived between the first and second centuries CE is mentioned: this element seems to disprove such a reconstruction.

[69] Riccardo Cardilli, *La nozione giuridica di fructus* (Jovene 2000) 185 n 131. If we considered the plants, instead of the fruits themselves, as the object of the *actio*, then we would arrive at the absurd result that the entire field had been damaged, with the consequence that the wrongdoer had to pay its highest value.

compensation for the owner, since in his view unripe fruit had no value or, at least, had less value than it would have been expected to have.

On the other hand, if we consider the land as the basis for the *condemnatio*, pursuant to the principle of *accessio*, the wrongdoer had to pay the highest value of the land. Daube, with no small hint of irony, reminds us that there is no child in the world

> that does not at some time or other scratch a letter or two, or even four, on the wall of a house. At Rome, on the basis of the prevalent view, the father would have to pay for the entire estate – not just the house, but the ground as well.[70]

The final text that contradicts the traditional view is D.9.2.40, where Paul discusses the destruction of a *chirographum*. If someone destroyed a document that contained proof that I was owed money subject to a condition and, through a trial in which witnesses were produced, I could provide evidence of this, I would have a claim under the *lex Aquilia* against the person who destroyed it, subject to the same condition listed in the original document. In all likelihood, given the nature and make-up of *chirographa* discovered in the archaeological record, the case in question concerned the destruction of a reusable surface (a waxed tablet with a wooden backing). Since an action under the *lex Aquilia* was granted, there was clearly a *damnum*: the *jus* represented by the credit had disappeared and had to be reconstructed through witness testimony in front of a judge.

4. INDICATIONS IN THE SOURCES REGARDING THE QUANTIFICATION OF *DAMNUM*

The quasi-delict *effusum vel deiectum* is particularly revealing. It constitutes

> l'ipotesi di versamento di liquidi o di getto di solidi dall'alto delle case nelle strade o nei luoghi di pubblico accesso sottostanti. Se dal fatto conseguiva un danno ad una *res* altrui (schiavi compresi), al proprietario dell'oggetto danneggiato il pretore concedeva un'*actio in duplum*, contro l'abitante dell'edificio (*habitator*); se da esso conseguiva una lesione personale ad un uomo libero (fosse o non fosse soggetto giuridico privato), all'offeso (o all'avente potestà su di lui) il pretore concedeva contro l'abitante un'actio *in quantum aequum*, come nel caso di *iniuria*.[71]

The difference between *effusum vel deiectum* and *damnum iniuria datum*, therefore, is reduced to the manner in which *damnum* has been caused. Phrased differently, it can be considered a *lex specialis* in relation to the *lex Aquilia*.

In D.9.3.1.pr, concerning this quasi-delict, Ulpian recounts the following case:

[70] David Daube, *Roman Law: Linguistic, Social and Philosophical Aspects* (EUP 1969) 67.
[71] Guarino (n 18) 1005.

Praetor ait de his, qui deiecerint vel effuderint: 'Unde in eum locum, quo volgo iter fiet vel in quo consistetur, deiectum vel effusum quid erit, quantum ex ea re damnum datum factumve erit, in eum, qui ibi habitaverit, in duplum iudicium dabo. Si eo ictu homo liber perisse dicetur, quinquaginta aureorum iudicium dabo. Si vivet nocitumque ei esse dicetur, quantum ob eam rem aequum iudici videbitur eum cum quo agetur condemnari, tanti iudicium dabo …'. [my emphasis]

Apart from the *condemnatio* itself, the expressions used in the Edict must be noted: referring to the throwing down or pouring out, the Magistrate speaks of '*ea res*' and then repeats this phrase at the end of the source. This phrase clearly refers to the event: '*ea res*' never refers to an object but always to an event.

Another piece of evidence against the traditional view may be found in D.9.3.7:

Cum liberi hominis corpus ex eo, quod deiectum effusumve quid erit, laesum fuerit, iudex computat mercedes medicis praestitas ceteraque impendia, quae in curatione facta sunt, praeterea operarum, quibus caruit aut cariturus est ob id, quod inutilis factus est. Cicatricium autem aut deformitatis nulla fit aestimatio, quia liberum corpus nullam recipit aestimationem.

In the context of *effusum vel deiectum*, Gaius discusses the case of a free man who has been injured by things thrown down or poured out. In his view, both the medical expenses incurred and the *lucrum cessans* (such as by taking time off from employment to recover) must be taken into account in arriving at a *quantum*. In arriving at a sum, account will not be taken of scars or deformities, since '*liberum corpus nullam recipit aestimationem*'. This explanation seems to me both important and meaningful, because Gaius (if we read this text in a counterfactual way) reveals how a quantification of *damnum* would have been made when dealing with a slave.

The *actio de pauperie* also provides some information regarding the quantification of *damnum*. D.9.1.3 states:

Ex hac lege iam non dubitatur etiam liberarum personarum nomine agi posse, forte si patrem familias aut filium familias vulneraverit quadrupes: scilicet ut non deformitatis ratio habeatur, cum liberum corpus aestimationem non recipiat, sed impensarum in curationem factarum et operarum amissarum quasque amissurus quis esset inutilis factus.

This source deals with the *actio de pauperie*, an action established in the 12 Tables, and it deals with damage caused by a *pecus*. To understand the scope of application of this action, D.9.1.1.3 must also be cited: '*Ait praetor "pauperiem fecisse". Pauperies est damnum sine iniuria facientis datum: nec enim potest animal iniuria fecisse, quod sensu caret*'.

Ulpian explains that *pauperies* is identical to the wrongful act punished by the *lex Aquilia*, apart from the absence of the element of *iniuria*, since the animal has no capacity to form a mental intention. In D.9.1.3, Gaius analyses the content of the *condemnatio*, in the case of an action made against a free man, and expresses a rule identical to that already indicated for *effusum vel deiectum*. It is revealing that the jurist, while dealing with the case of a free man, does not mention that there is no *condemnatio* based on the value of the body, yet highlighted that it was impossible to take the deformities into account, which would have been the case if the object of the act had been a slave.

5. WHEN MODIFICATION IN THE VALUE IS NEEDED

In D.9.2.46 (Ulpian) and D.9.2.47 (Julian), we find further evidence against the traditional interpretation of Chapter 3 of the *lex Aquilia*:

> *Si vulnerato servo lege Aquilia actum sit, postea mortuo ex eo vulnere agi lege Aquilia nihilo minus potest;*

> *Sed si priore iudicio aestimatione facta, postea mortuo servo, de occiso agere dominus instituerit, exceptione doli mali opposita compelletur, ut ex utroque iudicio nihil amplius consequatur, quam consequi deberet, si initio de occiso homine egisset.*

The case discussed in both texts is one of a mortal wound inflicted upon a slave. Ulpian explains that if you wounded a slave and he perished *ex eo vulnere*, although the action under Chapter 3 has already been started, there will be room for suing under Chapter 1 for killing. Julian,[72] in the second text, clarifies that if the *quantum* of the *damnum* had already been assessed in the first action, this fact must be taken into account in the second action in order to avoid the *dominus* receiving more than he would have, if he had brought the action for killing in the first place.[73] This clearly shows that two actions give rise to different *condemnationes*. If both actions ended in a *condemnatio* for at least the entire value of the body, why did Julian not simply affirm that the second action could not be started? There would not be room for such a matter, if the first and the third chapter amounted to the same thing. The only possible way to justify such an interpretation is to assume that the thing suffered a change in its value at least thirty days before the death.[74] Discussing these texts, Corbino observes:

> il possibile concorso tra azioni aquiliane (*ex capite primo* ed *ex capite tertio*) in tanto poteva essere possibile in quanto – con riferimento alla stessa cosa (schiavo ed

---

[72] Otto Lenel, *Palingenesia iuris civilis* vol 1 (Graz 1960) col 482: Lenel could not reconstruct the context from which the text by Julian has been extrapolated and therefore inserted it into texts by Ulpian. These two sources appear as expressive of a unique thought by Voet: Johannes Voet, *The Selective Voet – Commentary on the Pandects* (Durban 1955) 555.

[73] Grueber (n 6) 159.

[74] A rather odd fact, indeed, as underlined by Bernard (n 10) 452 n 2. Discussing the case of the painter who lost his finger that appears in D.9.2.23.3, Birks openly defines it as a 'freak' event (n 18) 100.

animale) – esse prevedessero un diverso '*damnum*'. Cosa che non sarebbe stata se l'*aestimatio ex capite tertio* avesse avuto ad oggetto la valutazione del medesimo interesse dell'attore (l'intero valore economico della cosa danneggiata) che veniva in considerazione *ex capite primo*.[75]

6. LIMITS EXPRESSED IN THE SOURCES

Certain sources contain indications of limits in the quantification of *damnum*. One of these is D.9.2.22.1:

> *Item causae corpori cohaerentes aestimantur, si quis ex comoedis aut symphoniacis aut gemellis aut quadriga aut ex pari mularum unum vel unam occiderit: non solum enim perempti corporis aestimatio facienda est, sed et eius ratio haberi debet, quo cetera corpora depretiata sunt.*

Dealing with the case of the killing of a member of a group (of actors or musicians, or of a team of chariot horses, or of a pair of mules), Paul observes that the quantification of *damnum* cannot be limited to the value of the body of the member who has been killed, since the depreciation of those that remain must also be taken into account. A similar case is raised in Gaius[76], in Justinian[77] and in Theophilus's *Paraphrasis*:[78] in all these cases, there are multiple acts, thus the immediate act affects others that are linked to it. The majority of scholars agree that these sources impose a limit upon the *condemnatio*: 'the valuation must cover not only the one who has been killed but also the depreciation in the value of the survivors',[79] since 'si dovrà fare il calcolo di quanto gli altri corpi (a quello connessi) sono diminuiti di valore'.[80] These texts show that there is a *damnum* with respect to the remaining members, and, at the same time, clearly reveal that the wrongdoer is not obliged to pay their entire value, but only 'how the other bodies are lowered in value'.[81] The rule that comes out of these sources is that 'not only must a valuation be made of the object destroyed but it must also be borne in mind how much the value of the others has be lessened'.[82]

---

[75] Corbino (n 7) 184. The same arguments can be used for D.9.2.51.pr, concerning which Valditara observes that 'nonostante i numerosi tentativi di individuare la presenza in D.9,2,51 di alcune più tarde alterazioni di natura sostanziale, la maggior parte della critica più recente è orientata ad affermare la complessiva classicità delle soluzioni ivi contenute': Valditara (n 58) 25, but also concerning D.9.2.11.2, D.9.2.11.3, D.9.2.15.1 and D.9.2.30.4. For more on these, see Lorusso (n 1), ch 6.

[76] Gai.Inst.3.212.

[77] Inst.4.3.10.

[78] *Theoph.*4.3.10.

[79] William Gordon and Olivia Robinson (eds), *The Institutes of Gaius* (Duckworth 1988).

[80] Schipani (n 40).

[81] Bruce Frier, *A Casebook on the Roman Law of Delict* (Scholars Press 1989) 65.

[82] Alan Watson (ed), *The Digest of Justinian* (University of Pennsylvania Press 1985). See also du Plessis (n 5) 323; Grueber (n 6) 61; Valditara (n 58) 62. There are very interesting, although

The price of the *causa corpori cohaerens* is not considered, when *damnum* is quantified.

Paul provides us with another example in D.9.2.33.pr–1:

> *Si servum meum occidisti, non affectiones aestimandas esse puto, veluti si filium tuum naturalem quis occiderit quem tu magno emptum velles, sed quanti omnibus valeret. Sextus quoque Pedius ait pretia rerum non ex affectione nec utilitate singulorum, sed communiter fungi: itaque eum, qui filium naturalem possidet, non eo locupletiorem esse, quod eum plurimo, si alius possideret, redempturus fuit, nec illum, qui filium alienum possideat, tantum habere, quanti eum patri vendere posset. In lege enim Aquilia damnum consequimur: et amisisse dicemur, quod aut consequi potuimus aut erogare cogimur. 1. In damnis, quae lege Aquilia non tenentur, in factum datur actio.*

The expression '*In lege enim Aquilia damnum consequimur*' is translated in Italian as '*in base alla* lex Aquilia *conseguiamo il valore del danno*'.[83] The translation of the final part of the *principium* may be, more or less: 'we can recover damages, and we will be considered to have lost either what we could have obtained, or what we were compelled to pay out'. In the words of Paul, *damnum* not only constitutes the reason for remedy under the *lex Aquilia*, but also its limit. Paul, in fact, underlines that the Aquilian remedy is designed for the recovery of *damnum*, that is both the function and the reason for its existence.

There is further proof of my position in the first paragraph of the text cited above, where Paul affirms that an *actio in factum* is given '*in damnis, quae lege Aquilia non tenentur*'. Schipani translates this passage as '*Per i danni per i quali non si è tenuti in base alla legge Aquilia, si può dare l'azione modellata sul fatto*'.[84] The expression used by Paul suggests a correspondence between *damnum* and *condemnatio*. The existence of the preposition *in* together with the ablative *damnis* must be underlined, since it shows that the action will be granted for those cases of *damnum*. In fact, I wish to suggest that the expression is not a simple ablative, but a fact characterised by a certain importance. While the mere ablative of *damna* in the absence of the word *in* would have permitted an interpretation that considered the damage exclusively as the reason for the reaction, being a complement of cause, this construction, also on the basis of what Paul has discussed in the preceding paragraph, represents a limit to the *condemnatio*. The fact that the sentence is not '*damnis, quae lege Aquilia non tenentur, in factum datur actio*', but is preceded by the preposition *in*, indicates not only the reason for the *condemnatio*, but also its limits. The concept of *damnum* thus inspires and also supports the entire system.

---

inconclusive, reflections in Alan Rodger, 'Body Language – Translating Some Elementary Texts on the *Lex Aquilia*' in *Festschrift für Rolf Knütel zum 70. Geburtstag* (Müller 2009) 961.

[83] Schipani (n 40).

[84] ibid.

Another source from which we can obtain a further support against the traditional interpretation is D.6.1.13:

Non solum autem rem restitui, verum et si deterior res sit facta, rationem iudex habere debebit: finge enim debilitatum hominem vel verberatum vel vulneratum restitui: utique ratio per iudicem habebitur, quanto deterior sit factus. Quamquam et legis Aquiliae actione conveniri possessor possit: unde quaeritur an non alias iudex aestimare damnum debeat, quam si remittatur actio legis Aquiliae. Et Labeo putat cavere petitorem oportere lege Aquilia non acturum, quae sententia vera est.

The theme of the text is the *rei vindicatio*. Ulpian says that if the thing taken has been damaged, through the *rei vindicatio*, the judge must also take into account any deterioration that occurred. The jurist clarifies that if a slave has been wounded '*utique ratio per iudicem habebitur, quanto deterior sit factus*' and specifies that, in any case, the *lex Aquilia* can also be used against the *possessor*.

A question arises from this text: should the judge quantify the *damnum*, or should he wait until the right of action under the *lex Aquilia* has been renounced? According to the passage, Labeo believed that the plaintiff was obliged to give security that he would not bring suit under the plebiscite (i.e. the *lex Aquilia*) and, defining his opinion as '*sententia vera*', Ulpian indicates that he shares this idea.

This passage contains phrases of primary relevance: while talking about the *rei vindicatio*, Ulpian says that what the judge may do is '*aestimare damnum*'. In the text, we read that when one action is brought, the other cannot be brought, therefore one is an alternative to the other. Thus, if one action can be promoted to the exclusion of the other, it means that they achieve the same result. This passage demonstrates, then, that the action brought under the *lex Aquilia* was not only justified by the *damnum*, but also delimited by it.

7. A RECONSTRUCTIVE HYPOTHESIS

The third chapter did not function in the manner proposed by the supporters of the traditional view. The evolution in the interpretation of the *lex Aquilia* occurred in two phases: originally, the plaintiff could only be compensated for the immediate *damnum*, that is, according to the third chapter, the difference in value of the thing before and after the event. The second phase consisted in the extension of the action to cover consequential loss too.[85] The end point of this evolution occurred, in the words of Bernard,

en cas de blessure, ce que demande le propriétaire, c'est la réparation du *damnum*, c'est-à-dire la différence entre l'ancienne valeur et la valeur actuelle de l'esclave

---

[85] This expression belongs to de Zulueta (n 26) 211.

blessée et le remboursement des frais engagés pour obtenir la guérison de l'esclave (ou de l'animal blessée).[86]

The basic idea is that the *'ea res'* clause dealt with the matter in general and not with the object damaged. Such an idea seems in contradiction to D.9.2.29.8, the passage about the addition of the word *plurimi* to the third chapter: *'Haec verba: "quanti in triginta diebus proximis fuit", etsi non habent "plurimi", sic tamen esse accipienda constat'.*
Gaius reveals that this addition was due to Sabinus (Gai.Inst.3.218):

> *Hoc tamen capite non quanti in eo anno, sed quanti in diebus* XXX *proximis ea res fuerit, damnatur is, qui damnum dederit. Ac ne 'plurimi' quidem uerbum adicitur; et ideo quidam putauerunt liberum esse iudici ad id tempus ex diebus* XXX *aestimationem redigere, quo plurimi res fuit, uel ad id, quo minoris fuit. Sed Sabino placuit proinde habendum ac si etiam hac parte 'plurimi' uerbum adiectum esset; nam legis latorem contentum fuisse, quod prima parte eo uerbo usus esset.*[87]

This latter text led Daube to adopt his position on the working of Chapter 3, namely that originally it used to cover only the wounding of property protected by the first chapter, then later it was expanded to cover *res quae anima carent* and that this, therefore, led on the one hand to the change in the time of quantification, from the future to the past, and on the other to a different interpretation of the expression *'ea res'* which from then on indicated the object that had been damaged. As Daube observed:

> so understood the rule was embarrassing indeed. For whilst the first chapter speaks of the highest value in the last year the third does not contain the word *plurimi*. Thus any moment of the last month might come into question – an absurd possibility.[88]

This was the reason for the Sabinian addition.

One final issue that needs to be addressed is the meaning of the phrase 'the highest value of the affair'. In my view, Chapter 3 never allowed a claim for the highest value of the thing involved. So how, then, was the claim quantified? Scholars agree that, in time, consequential losses were also included in the quantification owing to the enlargement of the concept of *damnum*.[89] Watson observed that 'there seems to be no evidence that Republican jurists

---

[86] Bernard (n 10) 454.

[87] Justinian preserved this information: *'Ac ne "plurimi" quidem verbum adicitur. Sed Sabino recte placuit, perinde habendam aestimationem ac si etiam hac parte 'plurimi' verbum adiectum fuisset: nam plebem Romanam, quae Aquilio tribuno rogante hanc legem tulit, contentam fuisse, quod prima parte eo verbo usa est.'* (Inst.4.3.15).

[88] Daube (n 25) 12.

[89] It is impossible to list all scholars. Among the many are Biondo Biondi, *Istituzioni di diritto romano* (Giuffrè 1956) 513 and Valditara (see elsewhere in this volume, 224).

allowed the plaintiff his *interesse* where this was greater than the market value'.[90] According to Valditara:

ciò che si puniva era sempre soltanto una azione mirante a distruggere o a lesionare un certo bene; era dunque la proprietà e non, più genericamente, il patrimonio ad essere tutelata. Inoltre, e per conseguenza, la clausola condemnatoria contemplata nella legge intendeva liquidare il solo valore della res danneggiata e cioè del *corpus* distrutto o lesionato. Solo successivamente si iniziò a tener conto dell'incidenza complessiva dell'illecito sul patrimonio del danneggiato, considerando quel dato bene inserito in una dinamica di rapporti e di situazioni soggettive. *Damnum* finì con il ricomprendere la perdita di quelle entità ulteriori che il possesso di quel bene nella sua integrità avrebbe garantito o quelle spese necessarie per ripristinarlo nelle sue originarie condizioni, venendo a coincidere sostanzialmente con il concetto moderno di danno emergente e lucro cessante.[91]

With the passing of time, the original mode of quantification, through a widening of the sense of the word *damnum*, came to include the consideration of the entire prejudice suffered by the owner of the object. Phrased differently, the loss was globally considered. Roman jurisprudence could thus 'collegare l'estensione della clausola condemnatoria della azione aquiliana nel senso della considerazione con funzione risarcitoria di entità ulteriori rispetto al *pretium corporis* e più in generale la liquidazione dell'*id quod interest*'.[92]

Daube reconstructed the evolution in the quantification of *damnum* in the following terms: 'it was gradually realized that, even in the case of chapter I, the one concrete result might not be all'. Consider, so Daube wrote, the case of the slave appointed as somebody's heir that passed away with the consequential loss of that asset. He wrote: 'Considerations like these, *i.e.*, the gradual adoption of the principle of *interesse* instead of that of the mere value of the object inevitably led to the conclusion that «Si quis servum occiderit» was not exhaustive enough', that here too, as in Chapter 3, 'the essential element was nothing less abstract than *damnum*; and that something like «Si quis alteri damnum faxit quod servum occiderit» had to be substituted, in sense if not in so many words'.

According to Daube, the evolution was complete by the end of the Republic: 'By this time, the entire statute, not only the third chapter, is declared to be about *damnum*, «loss»'.[93] But, if an enlargement took place, what permitted it? Legal doctrine suggests that the word *plurimi* is the key. Prichard highlights that 'the notion of the highest value came to be adopted

---

[90] Watson (n 60) 234 n 2.
[91] Valditara (n 8) 18 and (n 58). Similarly, Corbino (n 7).
[92] Giuseppe Valditara, *Sulle origini del concetto di damnum* (Laterza 1998) 3 and also Grueber (n 6) 58.
[93] Daube (n 15) 144. See further Lorusso (n 1) ch 8.

to include also certain consequential losses due to the defendant's act'.[94]
Once it is clear which element permitted the first chapter to be extended to
also include parallel losses, is there any reason why we should not justify
Sabinus' suggestion also with reference to Chapter 3?

When Sabinus suggested the inclusion of the word *plurimi*, he was merely
giving formal justification to a practical solution that was required by the
legal order. What was needed was to legitimate a process that had already
started, but could not go on, because of the lack of an element. The insertion of this word also permitted the solving of another problem, that of the
plurality of actions.

Three sources, D.9.2.27.35, D.9.2.29.3–5 and D.9.2.27.24, all by Ulpian,
but recounting the opinions of earlier jurists, must be examined in this
regard. The first text is the following: '*Item si tectori locaveris laccum vino
plenum curandum et ille eum pertudit, ut vinum sit effusum, Labeo scribit in factum
agendum*'.

Ulpian quotes Labeo, a jurist of the first century BCE/CE, thus prior to
Sabinus. The case is that of a plasterer who, having worked on a barrel filled
with wine, punctured it, so that the wine drained away.[95] As Ulpian states
that Labeo granted two actions for the reparation of the whole loss, a direct
one must have been given for the loss due to the damage to the barrel, and
a praetorian one for the wine that was lost.[96] The other source that deserves
attention is D.9.2.29.3–5:

> *Item Labeo scribit, si, cum vi ventorum navis impulsa esset in funes anchorarum alterius
> et nautae funes praecidissent, si nullo alio modo nisi praecisis funibus explicare se potuit,
> nullam actionem dandam. Idemque Labeo et Proculus et circa retia piscatorum, in quae
> navis piscatorum inciderat, aestimarunt. Plane si culpa nautarum id factum esset, lege
> Aquilia agendum. Sed ubi damni iniuria agitur ob retia, non piscium, qui ideo capti non
> sunt, fieri aestimationem, cum incertum fuerit, an caperentur. Idemque et in venatoribus
> et in aucupibus probandum. 4. Si navis alteram contra se venientem obruisset, aut in
> gubernatorem aut in ducatorem actionem competere damni iniuriae Alfenus ait: sed si
> tanta vis navi facta sit, quae temperari non potuit, nullam in dominum dandam actio-
> nem: sin autem culpa nautarum id factum sit, puto Aquiliae sufficere. 5. Si funem quis,
> quo religata navis erat, praeciderit, de nave quae periit in factum agendum.*[97]

In D.9.2.29.3, it is established that in the case of a ship that gets entangled in
your nets by the force of the wind, forcing you to cut them, there will be no

[94] See Cannata (n 14) 143.
[95] For another interpretation of the fact, see Robert Pothier, *Pandectes de Justinien mises dans un
      nouvel ordre* (Donde-Dupré 1820) 411 n 4.
[96] Paola Ziliotto, *L'imputazione del danno aquiliano. Tra iniuria e damnum coropore datum*
      (CEDAM 2000) 186 and Valditara (n 8) 28.
[97] For a reconstruction of the debate over the authenticity of this source, Carla Brunet, 'Alcune
      aperture prospettiche di Labeone nella valutazione del danno *ex lege Aquilia*' (2010) 58 IURA
      270.

condemnation, since there is no *iniuria*. Ulpian then adds that, according to Labeo and Proculus, in cases where nets are involved, the rule is the same; he goes on to say that no assessment should be made of the fish which were not caught, since it is uncertain whether any would have been caught. The same rule applies if nets to catch birds are involved.[98] It is clear that the conclusion, that the catch in the nets cannot be taken into account, belongs to Ulpian, since Labeo elsewhere stated that there was a need for two actions in cases like this.[99] This source attests the transcending of the Labeonian dichotomy and the confirmation of the unitary vision of the concept of *damnum*.[100]

In D.9.2.29.5, we once more deal with plurality of actions. It is to be noted that the sentence depends on the principal one, '*Alfenus ait*', that appears in D.9.2.29.4.[101] It is here established that, if you cut the ropes of a ship that drifts out to sea, you will be liable *in factum* for the loss of the ship, and you will be liable under a direct action for the loss of the mooring ropes.[102] Alfenus is a jurist who lived in the first century BCE and, indeed, grants two actions for one event: one is given for the cutting of the ropes and the other for the loss of the vessel.

In my view, there is confirmation in D.9.2.27.24 of the fact that, after the insertion of the term *plurimi* by Sabinus, things had changed: '*Si navem venaliciarum mercium perforasset, Aquiliae actionem esse, quasi ruperit, Vivianus scribit*'.

According to Ulpian, Vivianus, a jurist living in the first century CE,[103] held that if somebody pierced the hull of a ship loaded with goods, he was responsible *quasi ruperit*.[104] What this short text reveals is that one action is enough to recover the entire *damnum*, the loss of both the boat and the goods.

This passage seems to be at the halfway point of the maturative process since it uses the expression '*quasi ruperit*', which sounds rather odd, since the vessel has clearly been wrecked. It seems to me that in this passage we find the evidence of a hesitation on the part of Vivianus, who had to describe a legal situation that had not yet settled. Perhaps it is meaningful that he describes the ship as '*venaliciarum mercium*', literally as 'of goods to be sold'.

---

[98] This part is suspected of being a later addition: Peter Bremer, *Iurisprudentiae Antehadrianae quae supersunt* 2.2 (Teubner 1901) 137 and Alan Rodger, 'Labeo, Proculus and the Ones that Got Away' (1972) 88 LQR 410.

[99] Rodger (n 98) 409.

[100] The same Gaius considered one action in the case of killing of a member of a group as sufficient (Gai.Inst.3.212).

[101] *Contra* Rodger (n 98) 408.

[102] Frier highlighted the closeness of this case with that presented in D.9.2.27.35 (n 81) 19.

[103] Very little is known about this jurist.

[104] Pothier was convinced that the case dealt with 'un trou au vaisseau d'un marchand d'esclaves': Pothier (n 95) 401. Albanese calls this source interpolated and meant two actions: Albanese (n 66) 69 n 1.

It seems that there is an attempt to convey the idea that it is the vessel, with all its fixtures, that is the object of the illegal activity.

It may be that jurisprudence made the effort to force the concept, by presenting the boat as the passive object of the action, as if goods were part of the vessel. This, to me, seems quite likely, given the fact that the action is granted *quasi ruperit*,[105] even when the boat was *perforatum* and there was clearly a *ruptio*. The fact that the jurist speaks of *quasi ruptio* nonetheless may be justified by the fact that jurisprudence was trying to expand the borders, also considering things that had not been involved *corpore corpori*.

This source thus represents the link that joins the Labeonian position of two actions and the unitary approach of the mature classical era. So, by the end of the Republic, Labeo used to grant two actions. Alfenus in the first century CE proposed two actions while, at the same time, Vivianus proposed only one action. How is this possible? The answer must lie in the person of Masurius Sabinus, from Verona, the first jurist with the *jus publicae respondendi ex auctoritate Principis*, and who lived during the same time as Alfenus and Vivianus. It was he who, according to Gaius, suggested the inclusion of the word *plurimi* in the third chapter.

If the presence of this word *plurimi* allowed the jurists to also consider the lost inheritance (D.9.2.23.pr), the penalty for not having delivered the slave (D.9.2.22.pr), the damage to the survivors (D.9.2.22.1), then it is rather plausible that the word has also been the tool that permitted the whole prejudice to be considered through one action only.[106]

I believe that we may find a further confirmation of what I have suggested up to now in D.9.2.23.4:

> *Sed et si servus, qui magnas fraudes in meis rationibus commiserat, fuerit occisus, de quo quaestionem habere destinaveram, ut fraudium participes eruerentur, rectissime Labeo scribit tanti aestimandum, quanti mea intererat fraudes servi per eum commissas detegi, non quanti noxa eius servi valeat.*[107]

Ulpian mentions that Labeo discussed the case of the killing of the slave set to be tortured by his master in order to extract from him the names of his accomplices in the frauds he committed against his owner. Labeo says that account must be taken of the interest of the *dominus* to obtain the information he wanted. One aspect must be underlined: the jurist here grants a single

---

105 MacCormack holds that this solution is due to the fact that the vessel was not wrecked, but only pierced: 'Conceivably the boring of holes in a ship in order to sink it could be described as *rumpere*. Yet because the ship was not actually broken up or taken apart, Vivianus held that the case did not fall under *rumpere*. The fact that holes were bored precluded the treatment of the case as an example of *corrumpere*': Geoffrey MacCormack, 'Aquilian Studies' (1975) 41 SDHI 5.

106 For a different reconstruction, see Rodger (n 98) 409.

107 The authenticity of this source has been variously doubted. For an overall analysis of the matter, see Brunet (n 97) 254.

action, while he gave two actions for the case of the wine poured out. Why so? This was a case that fell under the first chapter, where the word *plurimi* was present. Is it that implausible that it is this element that permitted Labeo to consider how much that information was worth to the owner?[108]

Such a source allows us to understand that Labeo, when dealing with cases belonging to the third chapter, could not take a further step, because Sabinus' suggestion had not yet been made. We have in this text the proof that the jurisprudence in the time of Labeo, when dealing with cases that belong to the first chapter, could overcome obstacles and expand the borders beyond the value of the mere *corpus*, by virtue of the *plurimi* clause. This text seems to me particularly meaningful, because it shows that the same jurists could not consider a case belonging to the third chapter in the same way. A little push was required. It was found in the *fictio* suggested by Sabinus of considering the word *plurimi* as part of the third chapter too. With such an evolution, the legal order could also solve the problem of the plurality of actions, an outcome that Romans did not usually tolerate.[109]

8. CONCLUSION

I do not agree with those scholars who believe that the evolution occurred in three stages, the first based on the *pretium rei*, the second essentially consisting of *pretium rei* and *causae rei*[110] and the final one founded on the concept of *interesse*. In my view, the process moved from the 'market value of the thing damaged or destroyed' to a position where the 'entire loss which the injured person had sustained through the damage to his property' was taken into account, so that the condemnation was based on the difference 'in the plaintiff's property, as it was after the damaging act and as it would have been if the act had not been committed'. Thus, apart from the direct damage, the *damnum indirectum* was also taken into account, ultimately ending up in the concept of the *interesse*.[111] The evolution consisted in the expansion of

---

108 Brunet also notices that it is the consideration of the highest value of the *res* that permitted a *condemnatio* 'che si estende oltre il mero valore oggettivo della *res* danneggiata' and observes that the information the slave will never reveal represents an 'elemento aggiuntivo ed accrescitivo del valore del servo': Brunet (n 97) 268.

109 Gaius tells us that it is the reason why the earliest form of civil procedure was superseded: '*Sed istae omnes legis actiones paulatim in odium venerunt: namque ex nimia subtilitate veterum, qui tunc iura condiderunt, eo res perducta est, ut vel qui minimum errasset litem perderet. Itaque per legem Aebutiam et duas Iulias sublatae sunt istae legis actiones, effectumque est, ut per concepta verba, id est per formulas, litigaremus.*' (Gai.Inst.4.30).

110 Valditara calls this second era the time of the 'prezzo formale' and describes it in the following terms: 'il prezzo del *corpus* veniva sempre computato come entità base della condanna; ad esso veniva aggiunta una entità che già le fonti classiche indicavano con il nome di *causa rei*': Valditara (n 58) 229.

111 Grueber (n 6) 59, 265. See also Lawson (n 49) 59, who admits that 'how this came about is not entirely clear'.

the concept of *damnum* that, in the third chapter, could happen through a *fictio*, whereby the word *plurimi* was interpreted as belonging to the text of the law. Roman law arrived at the concept of *interesse*, but this represented the last phase of a linear run along a unique trajectory. The expression '*quanti ea res erit*' that appears in the third chapter always referred to 'the affair' and, through an expansion of its boundaries, it allowed 'l'*utilitas* del danneggiato come un elemento decisivo per la definizione della *summa condemnationis*'.[112] A progressive enlargement of the concept of *damnum* permitted an assessment of the entire prejudice caused to the victim.

---

[112] Valditara (n 8) 48. Corbino, after an analysis of the evolution of the first chapter that to include the plaintiff's *id quod interest*, writes that 'l'*aestimatio ex capite tertio* non pose mai alcun problema. Essa riguardò sempre il *damnum* e non la cosa. Segno dunque che è ad esso che i *verba legis* facevano nel terzo capitolo (al contrario che nel primo) espresso riferimento': Corbino (n 7) 188.

Chapter 7

Causation and Remoteness: British Steps on a Roman Path

David Johnston

1. INTRODUCTION

This chapter examines some well-known texts on causation and remoteness of damage in relation to the *lex Aquilia*. It asks whether there is a distinctive British approach to the discussion of these texts and, if so, what it is. In doing so, it aims to contribute to the broad theme of this volume of identifying what is (or has over the last century or so been) characteristic of the British way of studying Roman law.

First impressions suggest that it is very difficult to isolate a distinctive British approach, and that the lines followed by British scholars are many and various. Take, by way of example, the work of the following five British Romanists.[1] The work of David Daube is characterised by close analysis of the grammar, form and structure of legal utterances, and the palingenesia of juristic texts.[2] Tony Honoré focuses on the linguistic usage of individual jurists and what that can tell us about when they composed their works.[3] Peter Stein concentrated on the influence of grammar and rhetoric on the jurists' analysis and development of legal institutions, as well as the characteristics of the two schools of classical jurists.[4] Peter Birks emphasised the importance of procedure; and his work is also marked by frequent comparisons with the development of the common law.[5] Alan Rodger's approach was similar to

---

[1] This expression is used loosely to include those who are not British by birth but have lived and worked in Britain for an extended period.

[2] See e.g. David Daube, 'Zur Palingenesie einiger Digestenfragmente' (1959) 76 ZSS (RA) 149; 'On the Use of the Term *Damnum*' in *Studi in onore di Siro Solazzi* (Jovene 1948); and 'On the Third Chapter of the *Lex Aquilia*' (1936) 52 LQR 253.

[3] See e.g. Tony Honoré, 'Some Suggestions for the Study of Interpolations' (1981) 49 TvR 225; and *Ulpian: Pioneer of Human Rights* (2nd edn, OUP 2002).

[4] See e.g. Peter Stein, 'The Two Schools of Jurists in the Early Roman Principate' (1972) 31 CLJ 8; 'The Place of Servius Sulpicius Rufus in the Development of Roman Legal Science' in Okko Behrends and others (eds), *Festschrift für Franz Wieacker zum 70. Geburtstag* (Vandenhoeck & Rupprecht 1978).

[5] See e.g. Peter Birks, 'Cooking the Meat: Aquilian Liability for Hearths and Ovens' (1985) 20 IJ 352; 'Doing and Causing to be Done' in Andrew Lewis and David Ibbetson (eds), *The Roman Law Tradition* (CUP 1994).

that of Daube, with particular emphasis on the palingenesia of juristic texts.[6]

It therefore seems that the search for something distinctive or characteristic of the British Romanist must be at a different level. This chapter will look briefly at four topics within the general area of causation or remoteness of damage, focusing in each on one or more scholars and their approach.

2. BUCKLAND, *CULPA* COMPENSATION AND CONTRIBUTORY NEGLIGENCE

Both in his *Text-book of Roman Law* and in *Roman Law and Common Law* (and indeed in more or less the same words),[7] Buckland attacked the notion of *culpa* compensation advanced among others by Alfred Pernice in his *Zur Lehre von den Sachbeschädigungen nach römischen Rechte*.[8] Buckland described it as an invention into which these authors 'have attempted to force the Roman texts'.

The issue is clearly illustrated in Ulpian's well-known text about javelin throwing.[9] There he mentions three different situations: an Aquilian action for *occidere* against a person who struck a slave with a javelin; the lack of such an action if the slave chose an inopportune time to walk through an area in which javelins were being thrown; and an Aquilian action if a person took deliberate aim at the slave. It is especially the second of these that raises questions about the respective culpability of the javelin thrower and the slave.

Buckland pointed out that *culpa* compensation 'is an unsuitable name in any case, since it suggests set off (*compensatio*), a quantitative estimate of the negligence on each side or, at best, our Admiralty rule rather than the common-law rule recently discarded'.[10] To paraphrase: what Buckland appears to be suggesting is that Pernice's theory is neither that of the pre-1945 law in England and Scotland, whereby a claimant who contributed materially to his own loss had no claim, nor that of the Admiralty rule, whereby the parties shared the loss. Instead, it is (he suggests) an apportionment of the degree of negligence on either side. Buckland adds that the theory 'completely falsifies the Roman view. They seem to have applied here a theory of causation, no doubt a theory of causation which is not satisfactory, but that is not exceptional in theories of causation'.[11]

---

[6]   See e.g. Alan Rodger, 'Labeo, Proculus and the Ones that Got Away' (1972) 88 LQR 402; 'The Palingenesia of the Commentaries Relating to the *Lex Aquilia*' (2007) 124 ZSS (RA) 145.

[7]   William Warwick Buckland, *A Text-book of Roman Law from Augustus to Justininan* (Peter Stein ed, 3rd revised edn, CUP 1963) 587; William Warwick Buckland and Arnold McNair, *Roman Law and Common Law* (Frederick Henry Lawson ed, 2nd edn, CUP 1952) 370.

[8]   Alfred Pernice, *Zur Lehre von den Sachbeschädigungen nach römischem Rechte* (Böhlau 1867).

[9]   D.9.2.9.4.

[10] Buckland and McNair (n 7) 370.

[11] ibid 370–71.

Is the theory of *culpa* compensation intrinsically unsatisfactory? The fact that the 'name' is said to be unsuitable seems, although perhaps correct, to be of no real significance. The true question is whether the theory, under whatever name it goes, is satisfactory or not. Lawson for one was not satisfied that Buckland's strictures were justified.[12] Neither am I: the expression *culpa* compensation need not imply a quantitative estimate of the negligence of each party, certainly not in the terms of the Law Reform (Contributory Negligence) Act 1945, where damages may be reduced 'to such an extent as the court thinks just and equitable having regard to the claimant's share in the responsibility for the damage'.[13] Indeed, Pernice explains that his argument is that the negligence of the claimant makes the causal connection between the *culpa* of the defendant and the loss doubtful.[14] There is nothing here about quantification of the parties' respective contributions to the loss. It is true that from time to time Pernice speaks of compensation: in particular, he explains that *dolus* cannot be set off against *culpa*, because they are unlike.[15] But this does not imply that the notion of 'set off' that Pernice advocates is concerned with quantification: it remains entirely consistent with his view quoted above, that the claimant's fault may cast doubt on the causative potency of the defendant's act.

From Pernice's summary of the doctrine some thirty years later, it emerges reasonably clearly that the notion underlying *culpa* compensation is the simple one that, in considering the liability of the defendant, it is relevant to take account of the conduct of the claimant in bringing about the end result.[16] As Pernice says, this is a 'praktische-juristische Verwertung der natürlichen Empfindung: *quis tulerit Gracchos de seditione querentes*'.[17]

What can we take from this? At the most general level, we can identify an extreme caution on Buckland's part about accepting that fully worked-out theories can properly be identified in the Roman texts. No doubt it is important to be critically alert to whether a theory is legitimately attributable to the Roman jurists or is instead the result of later systematisation, for instance by the Pandectists. In this particular case, however, one might be forgiven for thinking that the criticism of forcing the texts into a theory is overdone.[18]

---

[12] Frederick Henry Lawson, *Negligence in the Civil Law* (CUP 1950) 55.

[13] 1945 Act s 1(1). In referring to the 'common-law rule recently discarded', Buckland is referring to this provision.

[14] Pernice (n 8) 60.

[15] ibid 62; see esp §9.4.

[16] Alfred Pernice, *Labeo* II.i (Niemeyer 1895) 89–102.

[17] Pernice (n 8) 90. Note the reference to *compensatio* in D.2.10.33: '*Si et stipulator dolo promissoris et promissor dolo stipulatoris impeditus fuerit quo minus ad iudicium veniret, neutri eorum praetor succurrere debebit, ab utraque parte dolo compensando*'.

[18] The same might be said of Buckland's attack on the notion of duty of care in common law. It first appeared in 'The Duty to Take Care' (1935) 51 LQR 637. It is also to be found in Buckland and McNair (n 7) 363. The excursus by Lawson in the 2nd edition explains

So far as the general theme of this volume is concerned, this example seems to illustrate a British concern to let the texts and the jurists speak for themselves; a probably understandable reaction against the ahistorical treatment of the Roman texts by the Pandectists, as well as a good old-fashioned British scepticism in the face of abstract theory.

3. SUPERVENING CAUSES: PUGSLEY, NÖRR, MACCORMACK

It is perhaps surprising, in light of what has just been said, that in the passage quoted above Buckland and McNair expressed the view that the Roman jurists applied 'a theory of causation'. Did they? Buckland and McNair do not spell out the theory in any detail but describe it in this way: 'The Roman view was that the negligent or intending person was liable for the harm if he caused it but not if some intervening agency prevented his act from producing its effect'.[19]

Well-known Roman texts discuss intervening acts. The texts that deal with the issue where two different people have inflicted mortal wounds on the same victim have generated an immense literature. Those who had not previously encountered these texts but have read Lord Rodger's speech in *Fairchild v Glenhaven Funeral Services*[20] have now been introduced to them too. This chapter will add only a few words to the literature. Since the concern here is whether any distinctively British contribution can be identified, no attempt is made to engage closely with the latest (non-British) analysis of these texts.[21]

Buckland and McNair criticise the treatment of causation in the texts of the Roman jurists. They say that 'difficult as the question is with us, difficult as it is to reconcile the various decisions and dicta on the matter, it must be admitted that the Roman authorities are still more unsatisfactory'.[22] The Roman jurists, they say, never really faced the question of remoteness except in what they (rather oddly) describe as 'simple' cases, one being where a man

---

at 367–70 that he regards the attack as ill-founded but did not feel that he could delete it without 'impiety'.

[19] Buckland and McNair (n 7) 371.

[20] [2003] 1 AC 32 at [157]–[160].

[21] See, in particular, Adriaan Johan Boudewijn Sirks, 'The Slave who was Slain Twice: Causality and the Lex Aquilia (Iulian. 86 dig. D. 9, 2, 51)' (2011) 79 TvR 313 (arguing that the text should be understood in the light of Stoic theories of causation, in which the notion of a *causa superveniens* did not feature); Jeroen Kortmann, '*Ab alio ictu(s)*. Misconceptions about Julian's View on Causation' (1999) 20 J Legal Hist 95; Jean-François Gerkens, '*Aeque perituris* …'. *Une approche de la causalité dépassante en droit romain classique* (Faculté de Droit de Liège 1997); Hans Ankum, 'Das Problem der "überholenden Kausalität" bei der Anwendung der lex Aquilia im klassischen römischen Recht' in Manfred Harder and Georg Thielmann (eds), *De iustitia et iure. Festschrift für Ulrich von Lübtow zum 80. Geburtstag* (Duncker & Humblot 1980).

[22] Buckland and McNair (n 7) 378.

is mortally wounded but is actually killed by a second wound inflicted by another person.

For present purposes the object of looking very briefly at this difficult issue is to see what place there is for theories of causation in the analysis of the texts. It will be enough to paraphrase the main texts:

(1) In the first, Ulpian cites Celsus: if one person inflicts a mortal wound (*mortiferum vulnus*) on a slave, and another later kills him, the first is liable for wounding and not for killing, because the slave died from a different wound; while the second is liable for killing. Marcellus and Ulpian say the same.[23]

(2) Here Ulpian recounts the case where a slave is mortally wounded and later dies owing to the collapse of a building or a shipwreck or from another blow.[24] Here the action is for wounding and not for killing; but, if the slave later dies from the wound, the action for killing can be brought. In that second case, the slave can be said to have been killed when he was wounded, but this came to light only when he died; whereas in the first case the collapse of the building did not allow it to be known whether he was killed.

(3) The third text is from Julian:[25] his view is that if one person inflicts a mortal wound on a slave, and another person wounds the slave later so that he dies sooner than he would have from the first wound, both are liable for killing.[26]

(4) A final text is interesting because it explains the basis on which Julian and Celsus respectively approached the question of quantification of damages: if a slave was mortally wounded and died some time later, according to Julian the year for quantifying Aquilian damages was to be counted back from the date of the wound. Celsus took the opposite view, so the year would be counted back from the date of death.[27]

As Pugsley explains, if the slave was wounded by A on Monday and died from that wound on Wednesday, Celsus would say that he was killed on Wednesday, when he actually died. Julian, on the other hand, would say (once the slave's death on Wednesday had actually taken place) that he had been killed on the Monday. If one adds the further complication of a mortal wound inflicted by a different person, B, on Tuesday, then B would

---

[23] D.9.2.11.3.

[24] D.9.2.15.1.

[25] D.9.2.51.pr.

[26] William Warwick Buckland, *The Roman Law of Slavery* (CUP 1908) 30 explains an apparent contradiction by pointing to the difference in language: in particular, in 51.pr it is not clear that the second wound is fatal; and in 51.1 Julian's argument is based on a case where it was doubtful whether both injuries were fatal.

[27] D.9.2.21.1.

be liable for killing. A would be liable for wounding. For Julian, the killing by B would mean that it did not become clear that A had killed the slave on Monday. For Celsus, it would not be possible to say that A had killed the slave on Wednesday because B had done so on Tuesday.[28]

What does seem clear from the texts mentioned is that there is an appreciation of the fact that the issue of responsibility for the death is complex. Julian expressly says that it cannot readily be decided which of the wrongdoers ought rather to be liable under the *lex* (*nec facile constitui possit uter potius lege teneatur*).[29] But this does not lead the jurists into any developed reasoning about causation, let alone analysing causation in terms of *causa sine qua non*, proximate cause, and so forth. Instead, the concern seems to be a pragmatic one, of identifying on a particular set of facts whether a particular defendant can be said *occidisse*. That seems to be particularly clear from the last of the four texts mentioned above: one cannot say with Julian, in an ordinary use of language, that the slave was killed any earlier than the day on which he died. But one can, in juristic interpretation of the word *occidere*, say that that is how the word is to be construed.[30]

Pugsley suggests that the differences between Celsus and Julian should not be overemphasised: 'Classical Roman law was a practical system of case law'. He points out that, while the jurists undoubtedly did differ on points of substance, it is likely that more often they reached the same conclusion by different routes, just as English appellate courts do.[31]

Yet a cautious assessment of the role of a theory of causation in the jurists is not confined to Britain. Dieter Nörr, in a series of studies culminating in *Causa mortis*,[32] has explored the contribution that rhetorical and philosophical discourse may have made to the development of the jurists' ideas about causation. It is fair to say that his conclusions about such influence are for the most part quite negative. So, for example, the expression *causa mortis* is found to have played a modest role in juristic discussion of the *lex Aquilia*; and most of what is said about causation is of an 'everyday' rather than philosophically sophisticated nature. For the particular issue in the texts dealing with what we might describe as supervening cause, Nörr comes to the conclusion that there is no reason to believe that in developing their thinking the jurists made use of tools drawn from philosophy or rhetoric.[33]

---

[28]   D Pugsley, 'Causation and Confessions in the *Lex Aquilia*' (1970) 38 TvR 163, 165–66.

[29]   D.9.2.51.2.

[30]   D.9.2.21.1.

[31]   Pugsley (n 28) 166.

[32]   Dieter Nörr, *Causa mortis* (Beck 1986). Among his earlier studies, see 'Kausalitätsprobleme im klassischen römischen Recht: ein theoretischer Versuch Labeos' in Okko Behrends and others (eds), *Festschrift für Franz Wieacker zum 70. Geburtstag* (Vandenhoeck & Rupprecht 1978); and '*Causam mortis praebere*' in Neil MacCormick and Peter Birks (eds), *The Legal Mind* (OUP 1986).

[33]   Nörr (n 32) 190.

That is very much in accordance with the conclusions reached by Geoffrey MacCormack after an extended discussion of these and other cases.[34] MacCormack points out that these texts had hitherto mostly been discussed in terms of causation, and that from that perspective the question would be whether the chain of causation which began with the first wound had been interrupted. But his conclusion is that the focus for the jurists was not causation: it was instead interpretation of the operative words of the *lex Aquilia*, and, in particular, whether the conduct of a particular defendant could properly be described as *occidere*. While drawing a very sharp line between that approach and asking what caused a death is not easily done, nonetheless there is an evident difference in approach between a focus on cause and a focus on whether a particular act falls within the scope of the words of a *lex*.

4. CAUSATION IN GENERAL: MACCORMACK AND NÖRR

The next question is the jurists' general approach to issues about causation of loss. Here the focus is on the views of Geoffrey MacCormack and Dieter Nörr.

In a well-known and apparently straightforward text, Proculus allowed a statutory action against a person who, although not holding a dog on a leash, incited it and caused it to bite someone.[35] Julian, on the other hand, restricted the statutory action to the case where the defendant was holding the dog; otherwise the appropriate action was an *actio in factum*. As ever, there are difficulties lurking beneath the surface. The first is that the precise issue is not quite clear. The text, according to Lenel,[36] comes from Ulpian's commentary on Chapter 1, so the starting point is whether there is an *occidere* or not. That requires one to assume that the bite caused death, although death is not mentioned. The second is that Proculus' rather liberal view on the availability of the direct action is unexpected. Elsewhere he appears to take a narrower view: in another text he held that, if one person pushed a second person causing the death of a slave, neither was liable: neither the person who pushed, as *non occidit*, nor the one who was pushed, as he did not wrongfully cause loss.[37] In the present text, however, at least where the defendant is not holding or controlling the dog, the harm done to the victim is no more direct than in the case of pushing: in each case there is an independent agent.

---

[34] Geoffrey MacCormack, 'Juristic Interpretation of the *Lex Aquilia*' in *Studi Sanfilippo* vol 1 (Giuffrè 1982) 255, 282; see also his 'Aquilian Studies' (1975) 41 SDHI 1.

[35] D.9.2.11.5.

[36] Otto Lenel, *Palingenesia iuris civilis* (Tauchnitz 1889), Ulpian no 614; also Rodger (n 6) 147, 195.

[37] D.9.2.7.3.

MacCormack suggests that it is possible to account for Proculus' (at first sight puzzling) direct statutory action on the ground that incitement of the dog was deliberate (*irritaverat*). That contrasts with the pushing case, where nothing is said about a deliberate act. If that is correct, the question of whether to grant a direct action is not treated (at least not by Proculus) in narrow terms of cause and effect. Instead it is a broader issue which may involve taking account of the presence of fault or intent on the part of the defendant.[38] That approach can be understood if we bear in mind that the key question for the jurist in Chapter 1 was whether there was an *occidere*. A deliberate incitement of a dog to attack, leading to an *occidere*, might well not require a theory of causation at all, but simply an acceptance that what the defendant did brought about the death.

MacCormack's detailed studies of many of the texts cover such matters as causation, *iniuria* and damages. They proceed jurist by jurist and so seek to recognise the development and refinement of juristic opinion. These studies have done much to demonstrate the very limited role played by grand theory in juristic interpretation of the *lex Aquilia*. MacCormack attempts to iden-tify why one decision is reached in one case but a different one is reached in another. The discussion reads very much like the approach of the common lawyer trying to reconcile conflicting case law: for example, in relation to the two texts just mentioned, he observes: 'If one does not resort to interpola-tion, one has to try and find some relevant difference in the facts of the two cases'.[39] Of course, this kind of approach cannot be claimed as the peculiar preserve of the common lawyer. What German lawyers call 'Subsumption' is precisely the process of identifying whether the particular requirements of an article of the *BGB* are met in any given case. The interpretative process involved in deciding whether for the purposes of the *lex Aquilia* the facts disclose *occidere* or *iniuria* or *damnum* is similar.

Another text on this general theme refers to a decision of Labeo.[40] Its main interest for present purposes is what to make of the reference to *causa*: is Labeo's decision most readily explicable on the basis of a philosophical approach to causation? The facts of the case are that the owner of a house leased an adjoining area of land to his neighbour; in the course of building work the neighbour piled up a mound of earth next to the owner's wall; the wall was damaged by penetrating damp; and the cause of the loss was identi-fied as being not the mound of earth itself, but damp which had penetrated from it once it had been inundated by rain. Labeo held that there was no Aquilian action against the person who had built the mound of earth. The reason given is that the action for loss wrongfully caused is available for cases in which loss was sustained without the intervention of an external cause

---

[38] MacCormack (n 34) 16, 277.
[39] ibid 15.
[40] D.19.2.57.

(*damni autem iniuriae actio ob ea ipsa sit per quae non extrinsecus alia causa oblata damno quis adfectus est*). Javolenus agreed.

This is one case where Nörr regards Labeo's reasoning as deriving from or influenced by philosophical argument about causation and in particular the distinction between *causae sua vi efficientes* and *causae sine quibus effici non potest*; and *causae proximae* and *causae antecedentes*.[41] MacCormack, on the other hand, prefers the view that the jurist is taking not a philosophical but a 'natural' or 'common-sense' approach to what it was that caused the loss. He argues that the neighbour is not liable, because it was not his act that caused the loss: that was instead something external, something over which he had no control. MacCormack recognises that Labeo could have employed philosophical distinctions in the way suggested by Nörr, but he is not persuaded that he actually did.[42]

One might think that Nörr's point is a sound one: after all, Labeo does not restrict himself to saying that it was the damp rather than the piling of the earth that caused the loss. He adds the general words '*damni autem iniuriae actio ob ea ipsa sit per quae non extrinsecus alia causa oblata damno quis adfectus est*'. This general, somewhat theoretical coda to the operative decision that there is no Aquilian liability seems to come closer than any other text to suggesting an awareness that there may be different kinds of causes; and that to draw distinctions between them is helpful to the legal analysis.

Nonetheless it is true that one can convincingly interpret the text as involving no philosophy but instead simply a conclusion on the applicability of the words of the *lex Aquilia*. In other words the critical question is whether a wrongful *rumpere* or *corrumpere* is present. If there is in itself nothing wrongful about piling the earth in the place that it was piled, then there is no basis for liability. The same would be true on the view that the piling of the earth was not itself an act giving rise to loss. On either approach one could conclude, without raising issues about causation, that there was an absence of *iniuria* or an absence of a *rumpere* or *corrumpere*.

5. ACTIONES IN FACTUM: RODGER; BIRKS

A final variation on this general theme of causation concerns actions *in factum*.

The first text is well known. It deals with the damaged nets of fishermen and their consequent inability to catch fish.[43] It has typically been discussed in the context of the measure of damages, in particular when addressing the question of whether the claimant fishermen could, in an action directed at damage to their nets, claim the value of (supposedly) lost catch. Lawson, for

---

[41] Nörr (n 32) 132.
[42] MacCormack (n 34) 265.
[43] D.9.2.29.3. See also D Pugsley, 'The *Lex Aquilia*' (1972) 89 BSALR 489.

example, in his note on the text, approved the view 'that here it is not the extent but the existence of the damage that is in question'; he went on to ask 'is it not also true that the chance of a catch was *prima facie* too speculative to be taken into account?'[44]

In a well-known article from 1972 Alan Rodger explained the text in a quite different way.[45] He regarded the issue as being one of procedure and pleading. The fishermen had a direct action for the damage to their nets. But the loss of fish could not be included in that action, since it had not been caused directly. To recover it, the fishermen would therefore need to bring a separate action *in factum*. Rodger regarded the reference to lost profit in the form of lost fish (*lucrum cessans*) as attributable to the compilers and so held the words referring to the uncertainty of the catch (*cum incertum fuerit an caperentur*) to be interpolated. He thought that was simply the compilers' explanation for why there was no action, whereas Labeo and Proculus were ruling out only the direct action in respect of loss not caused directly.

In 1972 Rodger took the view that the text came from Ulpian's commentary on *iniuria* in Chapter 3: the question was whether loss had been caused wrongfully. In particular, the jurists were concerned with necessity as a defence against an allegation of loss caused *iniuria*. When Rodger returned to this question about thirty-five years later, he suggested that this and the texts in D.9.2.27 immediately preceding and following it might in fact have come from a discussion about direct actions and actions *in factum*.[46] But the only one of these texts that raises the question of which action is appropriate is §29.2; §§29.3 and 29.4 contemplate only a direct action or no action at all. If Rodger is right about the compilers' addition of the reference to the uncertainty of the catch – that is, because they did not understand why the classical jurists had refused damages for the fish[47] – it seems rather unlikely that the whole passage was in fact focused on the difference between the direct action and the action *in factum*. If it had been, it would have been fairly clear why the catch was being left out of account.

More generally, however, Rodger's discussion of this text is another illustration of a broad theme: the questioning of the existence of a grand rule of damages for consequential loss in classical law; and a preference for explaining a text based on its specific facts and in light of its procedural context.

To conclude with a more general observation about procedure in general and actions *in factum* in particular: in an essay on Chapter 1 of the *lex Aquilia*, Peter Birks emphasised the fact that Chapter 1 was framed in terms of a verb in the active voice, *occidere*.[48] He suggested that it was this that led

---

[44] Lawson (n 12) 113–14.
[45] Rodger (n 6).
[46] ibid 187–89, 196.
[47] ibid 407.
[48] Birks (n 5).

the jurists, for the purposes of bringing the statutory action, to require a direct rather than an indirect killing. But the narrow scope of the statutory action necessarily entailed that there would be need for a supplementary remedy. That was the *actio in factum*, which was introduced for cases in which the defendant had caused something to be done rather than doing it directly himself. Birks therefore took issue with at least part of Nörr's theory in *Causa mortis*, namely the explanation of the narrow scope of Chapter 1 as deriving from the specific, narrow meaning of *occidere*, which is cognate with the verb *caedere*. Birks' view was that the explanation was not this narrow meaning but the use of a verb in the active voice which connoted a direct rather than indirect act.[49]

If one asks how Birks came to this view, the answer seems to be that it was very largely by considering the respective scope in the common law of the actions of trespass on the one hand and case on the other. It may even be (this is not entirely clear) that Birks' whole train of thought was set in motion by the case of *Williams v Holland*,[50] in which it was held that a claimant could bring an action on the case even if the injury to the defendant had been inflicted directly (and so the action of trespass was itself available). It seems to be this that led Birks to ask the question of whether the Romans too would have allowed an action *in factum* when the statutory action was available anyway because injury had been inflicted directly.[51] Unfortunately the Roman texts do not make the answer to that question clear.

The general point, however, is that this is just one example of a recurring theme in the work of Birks: the importance of the role played by procedure in the development of the law. Procedure is crucial, because even small differences in how claims can be advanced or formulated may offer important tactical advantages to one party or the other.[52]

6. CONCLUSION

These various examples of British studies on some of the Roman texts have a number of strands in common.

The first is an emphasis on analysis of the texts not in order to generate a grand theory but to understand the development of the law and its nuances.

The second is a tendency (at least in some writers) to focus on the procedural context, in order to see how the issues discussed in the text actually

---

[49] ibid 42–44.

[50] (1833) 10 Bing 112.

[51] Birks (n 5) 37.

[52] Cf his discussion of the supersession of the *legis actio* by formulary procedure: 'From *legis actio* to *formula*', (1969) 4 IJ 356. On the issue of trespass and case, see further David Ibbetson, *A Historical Introduction to the Law of Obligations* (CUP 1999) 155–57, noting that what seem at first sight quite minor differences in rules of procedure could become extremely important either on technical or tactical grounds.

emerged in practice and what significance they are likely to have had for the outcome of a case.

The third is a somewhat sceptical attitude towards grand theory and a preference for explaining texts not on the basis of an overarching theory but through an incremental accumulation of juristic opinion formed in the course of advising in individual cases (although some of the more extrava-gant cases with their causal *aporiai* may be meant for teaching).

The fourth is that, in spite of their reference to the Roman jurists' 'theory' of causation, ultimately the view to which Buckland and McNair (and indeed later writers) subscribe is that there is no such thing. Their final conclusion is that 'It seems that the Romans reached a result very like our own without any conscious analysis'.[53] With this reference to a lack of conscious analysis and the similarity of result between the Roman approach and that of the common law, we are back to the *topos* of the inner relationship between Roman law and the common law.

This *topos* goes back a long way. It featured in the title of an essay by Fritz Pringsheim in 1935.[54] In *Roman Law and Common Law* Buckland and McNair also said something of the sort.[55] And in the second edition Lawson spoke of a general resemblance in the methods followed by Roman and English law: neither is a general, coherent intellectual system; both are ways of doing the legal business of society, observed and developed more or less instinctively by relatively small groups of men trained by their predecessors in traditional procedures and habits of decision: 'Roman law never reached a state at all comparable to that reached by the pandectists of the nineteenth century, nor has English law yet reached it, if it ever will'.[56]

More specifically, Buckland and McNair noted that (with the exception of institutional works) it was unusual for a Roman jurist to enter on abstract general statements of the law; instead he would put the matter as a concrete case.[57] Rarely would the jurist go back to first principles: he would instead argue from cases; rules would gradually emerge from those cases; and the law and the rules were built up from case to case.[58]

So far as there is something distinctive about the British approach to Roman law in general and the *lex Aquilia* in particular, this notion of an inner relationship may have some value. It is true that in the course of discussion of the texts in D.9.2 we do not find explicit appeal to it (Birks' essay comes closest). But if one attempts to characterise generally the approach to the

---

[53] Buckland and McNair (n 7) 372.

[54] Fritz Pringsheim, 'The Inner Relationship Between English and Roman Law' (1935) 5 CLJ 347–65; see also Peter Stein, '"Equitable" Remedies for the Protection of Property' in Peter Birks (ed), *New Perspectives in the Roman Law of Property* (OUP 1989) 185.

[55] Buckland and McNair (n 7) 9–10, 21.

[56] ibid 21.

[57] ibid 9.

[58] Cf Peter Stein, *Regulae iuris: from juristic rules to legal maxims* (EUP 1966).

texts mentioned in this paper, it seems to have some explanatory force. In certain instances, there is even a suggestion that, for the purposes of under-standing the casuistic approach of the Roman jurists, the common lawyer is in a better position than the Continental theorist. That position is defensible (whether or not it is right) because there is a great difference between the Roman jurist and the Continental theorist. Austin famously observed in a lecture that 'Turning from the study of the English to the study of Roman law, you escape from the empire of chaos and darkness to a world which seems by comparison the region of order and light'.[59] But when we look at texts from the Digest we are reminded that, while the intellectual energy which powers the system of Roman law derives from the classical jurists, the order and light so admired by Austin result mainly from the institutional scheme and from Justinian as systematised in particular by the Pandectists.

This is the broadest of possible characterisations of what seems typical of British scholarship on the *lex Aquilia*. What it has not supplied is an explana-tion as to why so many British Romanists have written about the *lex Aquilia*. Here is one thought: when our concern is with creating a picture of Roman law in Britain in the last century or so, there are naturally some pivotal figures. Foremost among these is David Daube, not just because of what he published himself, but because he taught so many of the next generation of British Romanists: Stein; Watson; Rodger. At the beginning of Rodger's paper in *Daube Noster* he describes the *lex Aquilia* as Daube's 'favourite statute'.[60] Much British writing on the *lex Aquilia* might perhaps be seen as a response or reaction to Daube, and in particular to his views on the scope of Chapter 3 and the meaning of *damnum*. His essays raise large and challenging issues in a provocative manner: they are surely at least part of the explana-tion for British interest in Aquilian affairs.

Another explanation for the enduring fascination of the *lex Aquilia* which has nothing to do with Daube is this: for not one of the texts mentioned in this paper can it be said that there is now a certain, unequivocal and defini-tive interpretation. There still remains much work to be done to understand the *lex Aquilia* – and not just by British Romanists.

---

[59] John Austin, *Lectures on Jurisprudence* vol 1 (5th edn, Murray 1911) 58.

[60] Alan Rodger, 'Damages for the Loss of an Inheritance' in Alan Watson (ed), *Daube Noster: Essays in Legal History for David Daube* (Scottish Academic Press 1974) 289.

Chapter 8

Roman Law and Civil Law Reflections upon the Meaning of Iniuria in Damnum Iniuria Datum

Giuseppe Valditara

There are, in my view, four main issues concerning Aquilian *damnum* that are of interest to those studying Roman law, namely: the meaning of *iniuria*; the meaning of *plurimi*, which suggests a relationship – more and more relevant nowadays – between restitution and private punishment; the extension of the scope of the *actio legis Aquiliae* to include damage to a free person and to the *creditor* by a third party; and, finally, the *clausula condemnatoria* and the content of the *condemnatio*. In this chapter I will examine only the original meaning of *iniuria* in the phrase *damnum iniuria datum* and the extent to which such original meaning was confirmed in Continental law, starting from the rise of natural-law thinking in European legal thought.

Let us first consider the meaning of *iniuria* in the phrase *damnum iniuria datum*. The majority of modern Roman law scholars understand *iniuria* as 'unjustified behaviour'. This view has its origins with von Jhering, who examined *iniuria* in its historical context and who maintained that such a concept was born at a very early point in the history of Roman law when guilty and innocent wrongs were not distinguished. According to this interpretation, liability was objective and unlawfulness existed regardless of the presence of *culpa*.[1] Following von Jhering, Pernice[2] set a definite distinction between *iniuria* and *culpa*, highlighting the objectiveness of *iniuria* as a type of unlawful behaviour. Ferrini[3] highlighted the etymological meaning of the word and translated *iniuria* as 'mancanza di diritto dell'agente' and 'obiettività del torto'. Rotondi[4] reckoned that *iniuria* was originally disconnected from *culpa*, and saw it as an unlawful action. For Beinart,[5] Aquilian liability

---

[1] Rudolf von Jhering, *Das Schuldmoment im römischen Privatrecht. Eine Festschrift* (Bruhl'sche Univ.-Druckerei 1867) 5.

[2] Alfred Pernice, *Zur Lehre von den Sachbeschädigungen nach römischem Rechte* (Böhlau 1867) 26.

[3] Contardo Ferrini, *Danni (azione di)*, in *Enc. Giur. It.* vol 4 (Società editrice libreria 1911) 16; see also, more generally, Contardo Ferrini, *Diritto penale romano. Teorie generali* (Hoepli 1899) 73.

[4] Giovanni Rotondi, 'Dalla lex Aquilia all'art.1151 cod.civ. Ricerche storico-dogmatiche' (1917) 15 Riv Dir Comm 236, now in Giovanni Rotondi, *Scritti giuridici* vol 2 (Hoepli 1922) 479. Here I am quoting, for convenience, the text as in *Rivista di Diritto Commerciale*.

[5] Ben Beinart, 'The Relationship of *Iniuria* and *Culpa* in the *Lex Aquilia*' in *Studi in onore di V. Arangio Ruiz* vol 1 (Jovene 1953) 279. See also, more recently, Herbert Hausmaninger, *Das*

was at its origin objective, while *culpa* emerged because of 'gradual and cautious modifications of existing principles'. Daube[6] went as far as to suppose that the passage from the objective standard of *iniuria* to the subjective standard of *culpa* has to be dated to the beginning of the first century BCE with Aquilius Gallus. More recently, Cannata[7] and Schipani[8] considered the phrase *damnum iniuria datum* as damage caused without justification, that is, as unlawful detrimental behaviour.[9] From this perspective, the intention of the person who, physically and directly, made contact with the property of others was not relevant.[10] In a similar way, MacCormack[11] described *iniuria* as behaviour damaging others and done by someone with no right to do it. Lawson,[12] summarising the debate, considered *iniuria datum* to refer to the damage done in the absence of conditions that can justify the damaging act.

Lastly, Galeotti[13] supported the idea that *iniuria* (in the ablative case) had the same value as *sine iure* in the meaning of 'senza una ragione giuridica giustificativa'.[14]

In another direction, for some British scholars – I am thinking of Kelly[15] but also Pugsley[16] – there seemed to be a close connection between *iniuria* as a delict and *damnum iniuria datum*, to the extent that the latter could be an 'offshoot' of the former. This could lead to an interpretation of *iniuria* in the

Schadenersatzrecht der lex Aquilia (5. durchgesehene und erganzte Auflage, Manzsche 1996) 20 and n 61.

[6]   David Daube, *Roman Law: Linguistic, Social and Philosophical Aspects* (EUP 1969) 153.

[7]   Carlo Augusto Cannata, *Per lo studio della responsabilità per colpa nel diritto romano classico* (La Goliardica 1969) 307; *Genesi e vicende della colpa aquiliana* (1971) 17 Labeo 65; and 'Sul testo della *lex Aquilia* e la sua portata originaria' in Letizia Vacca (ed), *La responsabilità civile da atto illecito nella prospettiva storico-comparatistica* vol 1 (Giappichelli 1995) 40.

[8]   Sandro Schipani, *Responsabilità ex lege Aquilia. Criteri di imputazione e problema della culpa* (Giappichelli 1969) 83; 'Pluralità di prospettive e ruolo della *culpa* come criterio elaborato dalla scienza del diritto nell'interpretazione della *lex Aquilia*', now in *Contributi romanistici al sistema della responsabilità extracontrattuale* (Giappichelli 2009) 41; and '*Lex Aquilia, Culpa.* Responsabilità', now in *Contributi romanistici* (see above) 68.

[9]   In the same direction see also Giuseppe Valditara, *Damnum iniuria datum* (2nd edn, Giappichelli 2005) 33 and 'Dalla *iniuria* alla *culpa*. Su una dibattuta questione' (2009) 75 SDHI 131.

[10]   So affirms Schipani (n 8 1969) 89.

[11]   Geoffrey MacCormack, 'Aquilian *Culpa*' in Alan Watson (ed), *Daube Noster. Essays in Legal History for David Daube* (Scottish Academic Press 1974) 201.

[12]   Frederick Henry Lawson and Basil S Markesinis, *Tortious Liability for Unintentional Harm in the Common Law and the Civil Law* vol 1 (CUP 1982) 20 and, more generally, 19.

[13]   Sara Galeotti, *Ricerche sulla nozione di damnum* vol 2 (Jovene 2016) 76.

[14]   ibid 259.

[15]   John Kelly, 'The Meaning of the *Lex Aquilia*' (1964) 80 LQR 80; see also John Kelly, 'Further Reflections on the *Lex Aquilia*' in Luigi Aru (ed), *Studi in Onore di Edoardo Volterra* vol 1 (Giuffrè 1971) 239.

[16]   David Pugsley, '*Damni iniuria*' (1968) 36 TvR 378 and 'The Origins of the *Lex Aquilia*' (1969) 85 LQR 58.

sense of malicious behaviour. Kaser[17] was already in favour of the interpretation of Aquilian *iniuria* as 'typisierter *dolus*', though without pointing out any evidence of it.[18]

Cursi and Corbino have, instead, proposed a different explanation. For Cursi,[19] the distinction between 'wrongfulness' and *culpa* dates from natural-law thinking, though such division was also influenced by the thought of Saint Thomas Aquinas, for whom the notion of *iniuria* resembled the concept of injustice.[20] But no evidence of this interpretation emerges – according to Cursi – from the Roman sources. Therefore, the interpretation of *iniuria* in the sense of objective wrongfulness is the outcome of the projection of a modern category on a Roman concept.[21] So, the *iniuria* of the *lex Aquilia* is not objective wrongfulness but 'come nel delitto omonimo, indice di dolo', a sign of *dolus*.[22] According to Corbino,[23] it is impossible to speak about *iniuria* in reference to the Romans (of all times) 'senza tenere conto degli aspetti soggettivi (psicologici) del comportamento', considered as *culpa*, as the whole matter of justifications seems to show. Besides, for Corbino, evidence of the subjective characterisation of *iniuria* can be found in the fact that the Roman jurists reasoned using cases with constant reference to *culpa*.

---

[17]   Max Kaser, 'Typisierter *dolus* im altrömischen Recht' (1962) 65 BIDR 79. See Karl Binding, *Die Normen und ihre Übertretung. Eine Untersuchung über die rechtsmässige Handlung und die Arten des Delikts* (Meiner 1919) 46.

[18]   This is affirmed by Maria Floriana Cursi, *Iniuria cum damno. Antigiuridicità e colpevolezza nella storia del danno aquiliano* (Giuffrè 2002) 276.

[19]   ibid 271.

[20]   ibid 272.

[21]   ibid 271.

[22]   ibid 275; Maria Floriana Cursi, *Danno e responsabilitá extracontrattuale nella storia del diritto privato* (Jovene 2010) 31.

[23]   Alessandro Corbino, *Il danno qualificato e la lex Aquilia* (2nd edn, CEDAM 2008) 171; see also Alessandro Corbino, *Antigiuridicità e colpevolezza nella previsione del plebiscito aquiliano* (2009) 75 SDHI 77. However, we can observe how no arguments can be found in D.9.2.27.22 in favour of a relevance, already existing in the time of the jurist Brutus, of the 'aspetto soggettivo del comportamento' in the meaning of its 'intenzionalità' (Corbino (2009) 81 thinks so). As the same author admits (ibid 79), the problem of the induced abortion is seen by Brutus and by Quintus Mucius in D.9.2.39.pr 'da punti di vista diversi'. Brutus 'se ne occupa per valutare se la condotta in oggetto possa considerarsi o meno causa di un danno "aquiliano" (è un *rumpere?*)', while Quintus Mucius '(per il quale questo aspetto deve considerarsi acquisito) se ne occupa per valutare invece se di essa possano essere esimenti le circostanze nelle quali si è verificata', that is, the exercise of a right. We have no evidence on whose basis we can affirm that Brutus was referring to the exercise of a faculty of the owner; on the contrary it is meaningful that here the case consists in the beating of a slave woman and therefore is quite different from the one concerning the mare driven out of the field where she came to graze. It is, if anything, relevant that, once more, Brutus considers the concrete, typical act provided by the law as sufficient. The need for violence – thus, 'le modalità della condotta' (at 81) – is not in the reasoning of Brutus, but in the reasoning of the law. Here Brutus merely reasons on the existence of a *ruptio* of the unborn child, that is, of the woman.

One thing is certain: *iniuria* means first of all *non iure*, that is, *sine iure*, so 'in absence of the law'. This is perfectly explained in Ulpian, D.9.2.5.1: *'Iniuriam autem hic accipere nos oportet non quemadmodum circa iniuriarum actionem contumeliam quandam, sed quod non iure factum est, hoc est contra ius, id est si culpa quis occiderit'*; in D.47.10.1.pr: *'Iniuria ex eo dicta est quod non iure fiat: omne enim, quod non iure fit, iniuria fieri dicitur. hoc generaliter'*; and Paul in D.50.17.151: *'Nemo damnum facit, nisi qui id fecit, quod facere ius non habet'*.

So, *iniuria* means behaving in a way one has no right to. In this sense we also have to consider the reference to the delict of *iniuria* in the 12 Tables. In this regard, Gellius *NA* 20.1.32 is important:

> *Iniurias factas quinque et viginti assibus sanxerunt. Non omnino omnes, mi Favorine, iniurias aere isto pauco diluerunt, tametsi haec ipsa paucitas assium grave pondus aeris fuit; nam librariis assibus in ea tempestate populus usus est. Sed iniurias atrociores, ut de osse fracto, non liberis modo, verum etiam servis factas inpensiore damno vindicaverunt, quibusdam autem iniuriis talionem quoque adposuerunt.*

Such a passage says that all kinds of unjustified aggression to a person are *iniuriae*, some of them are *iniuriae atrociores*, and they have a proper name and identity. Apart from these there are unjustified minor kinds of aggression that, while being unspecific delicts, are generically called *iniuriae*, that is, examples of unlawful behaviour (behaviour that, it is implied, is also detrimental).[24]

The history of the word *iniuria* recalls other fables, for instance about the origins of the word praetor: this generally means 'commander': the *magister populi*, the *magister equitum* and the *praefectus urbi* were praetors.[25] The consuls were praetors, so all magistrates with *imperium* were praetors, that is, they had the power to command. Praetor, then, focuses on a specific magistrate with *imperium*, that is, one staying in Rome to exercise *iurisdictio*.

The element characterising *iniuria* cannot be *dolus*, as it was affirmed,[26]

---

[24] Tab.8.4 in *FIRA* 1.54. For the meaning of *iniuria* in Tab.8.4 see, among many authors holding different points of view, Paul Huvelin, 'La notion de l'*iniuria* dans le très ancien droit romain' in *Mélanges Ch. Appleton* (Rey–Rousseau 1903) 377; Giovanni Pugliese, *Studi sull'*iniuria, vol 1 (Giuffrè 1941); Dieter Simon, 'Begriff und Tatbestand der *iniuria* im altrömischen Recht' (1965) 82 *ZSS* (RA) 160, who highlights in *iniuria* the absence of a right to a damaging behaviour; Peter Birks, 'The Early History of *iniuria*' (1969) 37 *TvR* 179; Schipani (n 8 2009) 59; Roland Wittmann, *Die Körperverletzung an Freien im klassischen römischen Recht* (Beck 1972) 3; Arrigo Manfredini, *Contributi allo studio dell'*iniuria *in età repubblicana* (Giuffrè 1977), 15; Bernardo Albanese, 'Una congettura sul significato di *iniuria* in XII Tab.8.4' in Bernardo Albanese, *Scritti giuridici* vol 2 (Palumbo 1991) 21; Artur Völkl, *Die Verfolgung der Körperverletzung im frühen römischen Recht. Studien zum Verhältnis von Tötungsverbrechen und Injuriendelikt* (Böhlau 1984) 40; Cursi (n 18) 223; Cursi (n 22) 7; Antonino Milazzo, *Alle Origini della offesa morale come categoria giuridica* (Aracne 2011) 23; Galeotti (n 13) 73.

[25] Giuseppe Valditara, *Studi sul magister populi. Dagli ausiliari militari del rex ai primi magistrati repubblicani* (Giuffrè 1989) 336.

[26] Cursi (n 18) 271.

because the evaluation of the subjective element, as we will see, is explicitly excluded for *iniuriae atrociores* in Roman sources.[27]

Gai.Inst.4.16 should be understood in the same sense: *quando tu iniuria vindicavisti*,[28] that is, when a *rei vindicatio* is exercised *sine iure*, without any basis.[29] The meaning of *iniuria* as *sine iure* in the text of the *legis actio sacramento in rem* appears highly relevant if we examine the two reciprocal *vindicationes*: firstly, one litigant asks the other on what juridical reason he is claiming the property by means of the *vindicatio*; secondly, the other litigant answers '*ius feci*', that is, I had a right to do it. Then the first litigant replies '*iniuria vindicavisti*', you exercised '*rei vindicatio sine iure*', without any right. I believe there are no reasons to think of a different explanation.

Then, in a relevant rule belonging to the 12 Tables, a verb occurs which typically expresses one of the ways to cause the *damnum*, that is *occidere*. This is Tab.8.12: '*Si nox furtum faxsit, si im occisit, iure caesus esto*'.[30] It is the case of the killing of the thief at night. This killing occurs in the same way mentioned by the *lex Aquilia*: thus, *occidere* includes the *caedes*, the death blow. The ancient decemviral rule states '*iure caesus esto*', which means that this was considered a case of self-defence, as the rule seems to imply that there could be a *non iure*, *sine iure caedere*, that is, a *caedere/occidere iniuria*

---

[27] See Gell. NA 20.1.34: '*Verum est, mi Favorine, talionem parissimam fieri difficillime. Sed decemviri minuere atque exstinguere volentes huiuscemodi violentiam pulsandi atque laedendi talione, eo quoque metu coercendos esse homines putaverunt neque eius, qui membrum alteri rupisset et pacisci tamen de talione redimenda nollet, tantam esse habendam rationem arbitrati sunt, ut, an prudens inprudensne rupisset, spectandum putarent aut talionem in eo vel ad amussim aequiperarent vel in librili perpenderent; sed potius eundem animum eundemque impetum in eadem parte corporis rumpenda, non eundem quoque casum exigi voluerunt, quoniam modus voluntatis praestari posset, casus ictus non posset.*'

[28] Gai.Inst.4.16: '*Si in rem agebatur, mobilia quidem et mouentia, quae modo in ius adferri adduciue possent, in iure uindicabantur ad hunc modum: qui uindicabat, festucam tenebat; deinde ipsam rem adprehendebat, uelut hominem, et ita dicebat: HVNC EGO HOMINEM EX IVRE QVIRITIVM MEVM ESSE AIO SECVNDVM SVAM CAVSAM; SICVT DIXI, ECCE TIBI, VINDICTAM INPOSVI, et simul homini festucam inponebat. aduersarius eadem similiter dicebat et faciebat. cum uterque uindicasset, praetor dicebat: MITTITE AMBO HOMINEM, illi mittebant. qui prior uindicauerat, ita alterum interrogabat: POSTVLO, ANNE DICAS, QVA EX CAVSA VINDICAVERIS? ille respondebat: IVS FECI, SICVT VINDICTAM INPOSVI. deinde qui prior uindicauerat, dicebat: QVANDO TV INIVRIA VINDICAVISTI, QVINGENTIS ASSIBVS SACRAMENTO TE PROVOCO; aduersarius quoque dicebat similiter: ET EGO TE ...*'.

[29] For a different opinion, see Cursi (n 18) 22. For the meaning of *iniuria* in Gai.Inst.4.16 see, among others, Schipani (n 8 2009) 52, 58, specifically Schipani, *Contributi romanistici* 43; Max Kaser, *Das römische Privatrecht* vol 1 (2nd edn, Beck 1971) 26, 128 and n 15; 157 and n 17; Elemér Polay, *Iniuria Types in Roman Law* (Akademiai Kiado 1986) 75; Valditara (n 9 2009) 138; lastly Galeotti (n 13) 74; see also Carlo Augusto Cannata, '*Qui prior vindicaverat*: la posizione delle parti nella *legis actio sacramento in rem*' in Carlo Augusto Cannata, *Scritti scelti di diritto romano* vol 2 (Giappichelli 2012) 79.

[30] FIRA 1.57. For this decemviral line, see, recently, Marco A Fenocchio, *Sulle tracce del delitto di furtum. Genesi, sviluppi, vicende* (Jovene 2008) 26.

and thus, if the victim was a slave, a *damnum iniuria dare* on the facts. It is no accident that the decemviral rule is recalled by Gaius[31] in order to justify the absence of liability in the paradigmatic case of self-defence and consequently the absence of *iniuria*.

This meaning of *iniuria* is clearly used by Cicero in his *Oratio pro Tullio*,[32] where he says in conclusion: '*Si quis furem occiderit, iniuria occiderit. Quam ob rem? Quia ius constitutum nullum est. Quid, si se telo defenderit? Non iniuria. Quid ita? quia constitutum est*'. The difference between *iure* and *non iure* behaviour, which was crucial in order to define what could be considered as a delict deserving punishment, was not in the intention, because the *occisio* was in any case voluntary; the difference was rather in the justification of the maliciously detrimental behaviour, in the right to act that way, that is, in the presence or absence of self-defence.

To explain the original meaning of the Aquilian *iniuria*, several (with reference to the others quoted before) texts of Cicero belonging to *Pro Tullio* must be examined.[33]

Cicero defended a certain Tullius, whose servants were killed at night by the servants of Fabius. The defence counsel of Fabius argued that, in the provisions of Lucullus' edict, which specifically included a delict of violent damage, a reference to *iniuria* was implied, similarly to what the *lex Aquilia* stated in the case of the *occisio* of the slave; Cicero, however, replied that the substitution, in the edictal text, of *iniuria* with *dolo malo* was not casual and that this should be emphasised, as only *dolo malo* was mentioned.[34] Cicero said that this was to avoid a loophole (*latebra*) to those who used violence to take the law into their own hands. That is the crucial point: the defence counsel of Fabius asserted that the slaves were killed in order to free a plot of land unjustly occupied by the same slaves.

This echoes the case of Quintus Mucius[35] recorded in the Digest about the mare violently driven out of someone's land. If the Edict had implied a reference to *iniuria*, the behaviour of the killers would have been justified: the exercise of a right would have implied that the *damnum* was done *iure*. *Dolus*, instead, here implies conscious and violent conduct with the use of arms, not allowed by the Edict. Armed violence, regardless of the reason for it, was forbidden, so it was considered as behaving with *dolus*. *Iniuria*, clearly compared to *dolus malus*, here undoubtedly means *sine iure*, that is, without justification.

---

[31] See D.9.2.4.1.

[32] Cic. *Pro Tull.* 5.13. For more on this see Schipani (n 8 2009) 63; Schipani (n 8), *Contributi romanistici* 43; see also Letizia Vacca, *Ricerche in tema di actio vi bonorum raptorum* (Giuffrè 1972) 41 n 76. For a different opinion, see Cursi (n 18) 23.

[33] Cic. *Pro Tull.* 5.10.

[34] ibid 5.12.

[35] D.9.2.39.pr.

In this regard, it is sufficient to read this crucial passage of Cicero's oration:[36]

non ergo praetores a lege Aquilia recesserunt, quae de damno est, sed de vi et armis severum iudicium constituerunt, nec ius et iniuriam quaeri nusquam putarunt oportere, sed eos qui armis quam iure agere maluissent de iure et iniuria disputare noluerunt. Neque ideo de iniuria non addiderunt quod in aliis rebus non adderent, sed ne ipsi iudicarent posse homines servos iure arma capere et manum cogere, neque quod putarent, si additum esset, posse hoc talibus viris persuaderi non iniuria factum, sed ne quod tamen scutum dare in iudicio viderentur eis quos propter haec arma in iudicium vocavissent.

Iniuria here means the opposite of *ius*. The praetor did not want discussions about *ius* or *iniuria*, that is, justified or unjustified behaviour, because he did not want to give any protection to those who preferred to use arms to defend their rights, instead of going before the judge.

These words to me also seem crucial: '*cum iudicium ita daret ut hoc solum in iudicium veniret, videreturne vi hominibus coactis armatisve damnum dolo malo familiae datum, neque illud adderet "iniuria", putavit se audaciam improborum sustulisse, cum spem defensionis nullam reliquisset*'. The praetor, having excluded the reference to *iniuria* and inserted the phrase *dolo malo*, left the wrongdoers with no hope to defend themselves. It is evident that *iniuria* here did not mean either *dolus* or *culpa*, but, rather, unjustified behaviour. If *iniuria* were synonymous with *dolus*, Cicero's entire argument, which focused on the malicious aspect of the conduct of the killers and on the impossibility to justify it as exercise of a right, would be nonsense.

Cursi's[37] objection to this line of reasoning is that *iniuria* included psychological aspects that already existed in the time of Quintus Mucius, but this does not seem to me a relevant argument because, as we will see, Quintus Mucius, while building up the concept of *culpa*, assumed that *iniuria* meant the absence or the abuse of a justification. From this point of view, *culpa* seems to be conceived of as an improper use of a justification. It could be added that Lucullus' edict was not far removed in time from the observations of Quintus Mucius.

It is also interesting how in the 12 Tables[38] *iniuria* is mentioned with reference to the *actio de arboribus succisis*. This mention has traditionally been given less weight,[39] and it has been said that Pliny is not credible enough, all

---

[36] Cic. *Pro Tull.* 5.10.

[37] Cursi (n 18) 24.

[38] Tab.8.11, *FIRA* 1.57 = Plin. *HN* 17.1.7: '*cautum est XII tabulis, ut qui iniuria cecidisset alienas (arbores), lueret in singulas aeris XXV*'.

[39] Cf André Fliniaux, 'L'action *de arboribus succisis*' in *Studi in onore di Pietro Bonfante* vol 1 (Treves 1930) 528, 537; Schipani (n 8 2009) 63; Cursi (n 18) 274, n 6; see also Lucetta de Santi, '*Caedere est non solum succidere*: taglio di alberi, XII Tavole e D.47,7,5 pr (Paul.9 ad Sab.)' in *Per il 70. compleanno di Pierpaolo Zamorani. Scritti offerti dagli amici e dai colleghi di facoltà* (Giuffrè 2009) 147 and n 2.

the more so because *iniuria* is not mentioned in the other sources that refer to this *actio*. There is already evidence in favour of Pliny in the fact that the word *iniuria* is used in the 12 Tables with regard to delicts and that such word is still used in the *lex Aquilia*. But let us proceed in an orderly fashion.

The majority of scholars, though with different approaches, think that the civil *actio* provided by the 12 Tables was replaced by a pretorian *actio* known as the *actio arborum furtim caesarum*.[40] It is credible that this change was of a more substantive nature than merely in regard to the substitution of the *poena* of twenty-five asses with the *poena* of double the damage done. This seems similar to what happened to the *actio iniuriarum*, when the update of the *clausula condemnatoria* (that was also of twenty-five asses at its origins), owing to the currency devaluation, presented an opportunity for a more profound change of the other relevant aspects of the same action.[41] According to the majority of scholars,[42] the Edict provided more examples of delictal conduct for both the *actio arborum furtim caesarum* and the *actio iniuriarum*, so that the *actio arborum furtim caesarum* was reformed in order to punish other cases of tree cutting.[43] Furthermore, it now became relevant how the act had been carried out, that is, it was relevant if the tree had been cut secretly, but not if the tree had been cut with the specific aim of stealing it (in other words the psychological element characterising the event was irrelevant), as we can understand from Pedius and Ulpian in D.47.7.71.

The '*furtim*' cutting is the evolution of the unjustified cutting. If the cutting is done furtively, it means that it is not authorised and thus it means that one has no right to do it; it is, therefore, *iniuria*. In this way, the decemviral *actio* already became obsolete in the first century of the classical age.[44] The adverb *furtim* mentioned in the new praetorian *actio* must be the reason why rather few sources focus their attention on the way the wrong is committed. Furthermore, the replacement of '*furtim*' with '*iniuria*' explains why the sources mention '*furtim*' and no longer '*iniuria*'. To all this we have to add, in favour of the credibility of Pliny, that a similar process of overcoming the reference to *iniuria* occurred in Aquilian damage, where, towards the end of the Republican age, we can see that the phrase *damnum culpa datum* replaces the more ancient *damnum iniuria datum*. And this is actually the interesting point: we can understand, from the replacement of *iniuria* with *furtim*, that

---

[40] See, among many others, Fliniaux (n 39) 525; Odoardo Carrelli, 'I delitti di taglio di alberi e di danneggiamento alle piantagioni nel diritto romano' (1939) 5 SDHI 327; Emil Kiessling, 'Die *actio de arboribus succisis* im Lichte des PSI XI 1182' (1950) 4 JJP 317; Ugo Brasiello, 'Actio de arboribus succisis' *NNDI* vol 1 (Utet 1957) 259.

[41] Reinhard Zimmermann, *The Law of Obligations. Roman Foundations of the Civilian Tradition* (Juta 1990) 1052; more specifically see, among many others, Wittmann (n 24) 34.

[42] See de Santi (n 39) 148.

[43] Cf ibid 164.

[44] Ernst Levy, *Die Konkurrenz der Aktionen und Personen im klassischen römischen Recht* vol 2.1 (Aalen 1922) 204.

iniuria was no longer an adequate means to express the element of secrecy that the praetorian provisions specifically required, provisions that were more focused on the conduct (*clam*, secretly) than on the fixing of a kind of subjective liability.[45]

Therefore, it seems credible, from this initial examination of the word *iniuria*, that its original meaning was that of unlawfulness, that is, the absence of the right to act in a certain way, and did not refer to specific standards of liability. After all, if this were not so, the only, not to mention original reference in the *lex Aquilia* to the malicious (that is, with *dolus*) killing of a slave would be surprising, because the distinction between killing *dolo malo* and killing *imprudens* was already well known in the regal period.

Thus, *iniuria* seems a general word, widely used in the ancient age to define every unjustified behaviour that, as such, whenever it caused damage to somebody, could entitle the victim to private vengeance or to compensation for the damages suffered.

It is also interesting to observe that there is no original mention of the distinction between *dolus* and *culpa* not only with regard to cases of civil wrongs as *damnum*, but also as *membrum ruptum*, *os fractum*, *iniuriae*, or tree cutting – delicts for which, before the structures of the *civitas* established themselves, the immediate vengeance of the victim of the wrong was probably allowed. Even in the case of *pauperies*, that is, the case of damage done by skittish animals, no investigation of the culpability of the *dominus* occurred. He was liable only because of the damage done by his animal. In the case of *furtum*, this distinction was impossible because of the characterisation itself (*invito domino*) of the theft.

At this point, it is worth recalling what Aulus Gellius[46] reports that Caecilius Africanus says about *rumpere* in the case of *membrum ruptum*, that is certainly a precursor of the Aquilian provisions and is also called *iniuria atrocior*, that is, the most serious of the '*iniuriae*'. Africanus highlights that no distinction was made between *rumpere prudens* and *imprudens* and that this was intentional: the *decemviri* decided that it should not be investigated if the person who caused the *ruptio* acted with or without due diligence, that is, if the *ruptio* was voluntary or not. It is noteworthy that the distinction here is not between *dolus* and *culpa*, but between *prudens* and *imprudens*, and this implies that one could be considered liable even in the case of damage done with no intention to cause it and without any fault.

Why so? Because, Africanus would have answered, one should react to the unjustified aggression with the same attitude and the same violence of the aggression itself. The fact that talion was originally the punishment even in the case of *os fractum* – another precursor of the Aquilian provisions – as

---

[45] For a comparison, see the discussion of the provisions of the *lex Spoletina* regarding the cutting of a sacred wood, where the phrase *dolo sciens* is mentioned, later in the chapter.

[46] Gell. NA 20.1.34.

Cato[47] asserts, seems to exclude, analogously to what has been said about *ruptio*, that in cases of *frangere* also any distinction between *dolus* and *culpa* could be made. Since the dawn of time, an immediate defence followed the offence: the subsequent intervention of the *civitas* only aimed to offer a number of legal remedies in order to avoid (possible) reactions that were arbitrary, excessive and thus socially unacceptable, mostly if the offence was justified. In this context, it is normal that the only reference was to the justification of the behaviour, that is, to the right to act in that (detrimental) way. It is quite evident that the presence of a justification made the behaviour that was otherwise punished lawful.

It is, from another point of view, interesting how in all cases of public crime there is a reference to the subjective element, in order to determine if the act should be punished or not: that is in the case of murder[48] and in the case of fire,[49] but also in the case of tree cutting in the sacred wood dedicated to Jupiter, as we can infer from the *lex Spoletina*.[50] In the *lex* of the Spoletian colony, contrary to what the law provided in Rome for the cutting of private trees, there is an explicit reference to *dolus malus* ('*scies ... dolo malo*'), using, incidentally, a phrase typical of the archaic Roman juridical language ('*dolo sciens*' is also mentioned in a case of murder in the well-known *lex* of Numa).[51] Here it was essential to ascertain whether the behaviour was with *dolus* or not, in order to understand if there had been an offence to the god.[52] Some light in this sense comes from a *rogatio de vere sacro vovendo* (217 BCE), to which Livy[53] refers: if a person injured (*rumpere*) or killed

---

[47] See Cato Orig. 81 Peter (*ap. Priscian. gramm.* 6.13.69): '*si quis membrum rupit aut os fregit, talione proximus cognatus ulciscitur.*'

[48] Cf Fest. (Paul.) *s.v. Parrici <di> quaestores*, 247 L.

[49] Cf Tab.8.10 in *FIRA* vol 1.56 = D.47.9.9.

[50] See the text and the discussion about it in Silvio Panciera, 'La *lex luci* Spoletina e la legislazione sui boschi sacri in età romana' in Silvio Panciera, *Epigrafi, epigrafia, epigrafisti. Scritti vari editi e inediti (1956–2005) con note e complementi e indici* vol 1 (Quasar 2006) 905; see also de Santi (n 39) 155. Moreover, the inscription is included in *CIL*, XI-2, 698 n 4766 (cf 1374); I-2, 877 n 366; and 878 n 366.2872 (cf 720, 831).

[51] See Fest. (Paul.) *s.v. Parrici <di> quaestores*, 247 L.

[52] John Scheid makes an interesting observation in 'Le délit religieux dans la Rome tardo-républicaine', in *Le délit religieux dans la cité antique* (Table ronde, Rome, 6–7 avril 1978) (École française de Rome 1981) 140: whoever acted *dolo malo* was judged and punished because of the violation of the rules of public law.

[53] Liv. 22.10.5: '*Rogatus in haec verba populus: "Velitis iubeatisne haec sic fieri? Si res publica populi Romani Quiritium ad quinquennium proximum, sicut velim [vou]eamque, salva servata erit hisce duellis, quod duellum populo Romano cum Carthaginiensi est quaeque duella cum Gallis sunt qui cis Alpes sunt, tum donum duit populus Romanus Quiritium quod ver attulerit ex suillo ovillo caprino bovillo grege quaeque profana erunt Iovi fieri, ex qua die senatus populusque iusserit. Qui faciet, quando volet quaque lege volet facito; quo modo faxit probe factum esto. Si id moritur quod fieri oportebit, profanum esto, neque scelus esto. Si quis rumpet occidetve insciens, ne fraus esto. Si quis clepsit, ne populo scelus esto neve cui cleptum erit. Si atro die faxit insciens, probe factum esto. Si nocte sive luce, si servus sive liber faxit, probe factum esto. Si antidea senatus populusque iusserit fieri ac faxitur, eo populus solutus liber esto"'*.

(*occidere*) *insciens* a consecrated animal, there is no *scelus*, thus there is no offence.

Because of the intervention of the *civitas*, new provisions were put in place for cases of illicit behaviour with a wide social relevance: here the point is not only to limit the reaction of the offended party into forms that the community could accept, a reaction whose nature was, at its origin, a kind of vengeance,[54] but to sanction a behaviour considered intolerable by the whole community with very severe public penalties.[55]

With more specific regard to Aquilian damage, it seems to me meaningful that, in the provisions of the first and third *capita* of the law, there is no reference to *dolus* or *culpa*, which were concepts already well known (*dolus*), or almost presumed (*culpa*), for the case of murder and of arson involving a house – but there is reference to the more 'impersonal' *iniuria*. It is likewise meaningful that, dating perhaps as far back as Labeo,[56] the phrase *damnum iniuria datum* was replaced in the language of the jurists with *damnum culpa datum*, where *culpa* seems to imply the culpability, that is, the subjective fault of the offender, as a necessary condition, together with the *damnum*, for using the *actio legis Aquiliae*.[57] This seems much more surprising if we think that in the second *caput*, according to Gai.Inst.3.215, there was an explicit reference to the *fraus* of the *adstipulator*.[58]

We can suspect that a change was made in the meantime. If there had been a favourable attitude to culpability when the law was first established, the fact that the law does not talk of *damnum culpa datum* would be quite odd. On the other hand, we can observe that from the regal period, the law provided a sanction for the killing *imprudens* of a free man, where the killing of a ram replaced the original vengeance against the offender: therefore, it is not credible that, in case of the killing *imprudens* of a slave in the third century BCE, no penalty was provided by the law for the guilty killer.

In reflections made by Ulpian in D.9.2.5.1, *culpa* seems rather to be an end point. The historical evolution of the notion of *iniuria* appears to be reflected in the logic-semantic connections of the argument of the jurist. We can follow the steps by which Ulpian expresses the meaning of *iniuria*: (1) *damnum non iure datum*, that is, damage done with no right; (2) *hoc est damnum*

---

[54] Giuseppe Valditara, *Riflessioni sulla pena nella Roma repubblicana* (Giappichelli 2015) 14.

[55] Corbino (n 23 2009) 91 examines some cases of public *occisio* and *ustio* together with the cases of private law provided by the *lex Aquilia*, but does not seem to give relevance to the difference of rules, most of all with reference to the different considerations of the subjective element, between public and private wrongs.

[56] Labeo is at least the most ancient quoted jurist who is presumed to have used the syntagma *damnum culpa datum*. See Valditara (n 9 2009) 132.

[57] Valditara (n 9 2005) 36.

[58] Therefore, Corbino's reasoning (n 23 2009) 99, in favour of the original emerging of *culpa* as a standard for the *damnum* provided in the first and third *capita* of the law, is reversed *a contrario*.

contra ius, that is, damage done 'unlawfully' (this is the aspect called 'objective unlawfulness'); (3) *id est culpa*, that is, damage done with fault (this is the aspect of the 'reproachability' of the behaviour). *Culpa* seems to be not accidentally the end point.[59]

A further note: the *dolus* or *culpa* of the behaviour do not influence, in *damnum iniuria datum* and in all other private wrongs, and contrary to what happens in public crimes (murder, setting fire to a house, cutting of the sacred wood), the degree of the penalty. This seems in itself to suggest that originally the distinction between deliberate intention to damage and negligence was not relevant.

Besides, verification is ordinarily needed, in order to determine whether the offender acted *imprudens* or *dolo sciens*. It is interesting to note that in *damnum iniuria datum* we have a case of *manus iniectio pro iudicato*, that is, without verification and judgment about the liability of the offender, if he does not challenge the claim of the offended. The wrong is punished, directly in an execution phase, without verifying the *dolus* or *culpa* of the offender.

But was the *manus iniectio* originally implied? It was an iconic representation of a more ancient, immediate and direct reaction, that is, of laying hands on the offender. Thus, without evaluating the intention, the maliciousness or the *imprudentia* of the offender, the offended laid hands on him. The sources show clear evidence of it.[60]

At this point, the choice of the words that defines the Aquilian damage appears meaningful. The Romans already used *necare* in a wide sense,[61] and yet they used *occidere* in the *lex Aquilia*. These (*occidere*) are acts consisting of violent actions that, in themselves, imply an intrusion *non iure* into someone else's personal sphere, regardless, apparently, of any evaluation of the psychological element. As was highlighted by Schipani, these are examples of behaviour '*a forma vincolata*', that can be committed only in a specific manner.[62] So the reference to a material offence, a clearly unrefined principle of immediate and direct causation, suggests the original absence of reasoning about the psychological element. As I happened to notice,[63] jurists had a tendency '*a confondere la interpretazione del criterio della materialità della lesione con riferimenti alla esistenza o meno della culpa*', by showing the strict connection between the evolution of causation between act and damage and the relevance of the subjective element. This connection is well represented by the comment made by Ulpian to the word *occisum* in the seventeenth

---

[59] Paola Ziliotto, *L'imputazione del danno aquiliano. Tra iniuria e damnum corpore datum* (CEDAM 2000) 40, with regard to D.9.2.5.1, rightly observes 'un salto logico tra la spiegazione del termine *iniuria* rispettivamente come *non iure* e come *culpa*'.
[60] Gai.Inst. 4.21. is, in this sense, an example.
[61] Valditara (n 9 2005) 19, specifically 20.
[62] Schipani (n 8 2009) 46.
[63] Valditara (n 9 2009) 137.

book *ad edictum*, where the mixing of the two notions of *damnum corpore datum* and *damnum culpa datum* is evident. It was Pernice[64] who, with great clarity, observed that the *culpa*, as a standard of liability in Aquilian damage, had as its premise the overcoming of the physicality of the damage (*damnum corpore datum*) as a requirement, because the violence (required by the law) of the conduct would be inconsistent with an investigation about culpability.

The fact that acts of omission are irrelevant for Aquilian damage[65] can be explained with the need to have an immediately evident causation between the act of the wrongdoer and the damage, so as to make the liability of the wrongdoer certain and incontestable. It is evident that such an idea is incompatible with the notion that culpability is relevant for determining whether an act is punishable.

This standard that does not require any evaluation of the psychological element seems to apply very well to a context such as the age of the *decemviri* when the concept of *iniuria* emerged, where legal formalism made *voluntas* irrelevant. As legal consequences, obligations and liability derived from pronouncing *certa verba* and doing *certa gesta*, so being subject to punishment was born from the immediate and direct connection between the act of the wrongdoer and the damage. In the same way we cannot forget that, until the age of Aquilius Gallus, that is, just a few decades after Quintus Mucius, *dolus* was completely irrelevant in the ancient acts and contracts of *ius civile*. And we cannot avoid considering how a wider notion of killing, as *causam mortis praestare*, which is no longer connected to the material damaging and to the direct and immediate causation of the damage, began to spread only after the concept of *culpa* emerged.

In Roman sources, damage done in the presence of a justification is considered *iure*; more precisely, the exercise of a right makes *iure* the damage done. So *iniuria* suggests the absence of a justification.

It is likewise interesting that the jurists, commenting on the word *iniuria* in the field of Aquilian damage, considered the absence of justification of the behaviour separately from the aspect of the *culpa*. Ulpian and probably Gaius[66] examined, before the problem of culpability, the presence of a justification, which is self-defence in the case in question, as a cause that excludes *iniuria*. Today it is not so, because justifications are conceived of as excluding the subjective element, that is, so as to exclude *culpa*.

The later emergence of the phrase *damnum culpa datum* and the fact that, in the comment on the word *iniuria*, justifications were examined before culpability, provide good evidence that the starting point was unlawfulness (*non*

---

[64] Alfred Pernice, *Labeo* II.2.1 ([1873], reprint Scientia 1963) 60.

[65] For the irrelevance of omissions with regard to Aquilian damage, see, recently, Corbino (n 23) 145. For the meaning of such irrelevance, see Valditara (n 9 2009) 142.

[66] Otto Lenel, *Palingenesia iuris civilis* vol 2 (Tauchnitz 1889) 613 col 522, about Ulpian, and Otto Lenel, *Palingenesia iuris civilis* vol 1 183–87 cols 205–06, about Gaius.

iure datum) and not culpability (*culpa datum*). It is also relevant that the most ancient cases about *iniuria* are based on a discussion on whether the behaviour can or cannot be considered as justified: this is the case in D.9.2.31,[67] which contains a text from Quintus Mucius; again in D.9.2.39.pr[68] a text, also from Quintus Mucius, about the exercise of a right; D.9.2.52.1,[69] which concerns self-defence; D.9.2.52.4,[70] which comes from Alfenus and concerns sport; and D.43.24.7.4, which concerns the state of necessity and the act of the magistrate as justifications, and quotes the opinions of Aquilius Gallus and Servius.[71]

Culpa seems to emerge as a reflection on the 'malfunctioning' of a justification, the exercise of a right in D.9.2.31 and D.9.2.39.pr; self-defence in the case examined by Alfenus Varus in D.9.2.52.1; sport, which is also a justification if there is no *culpa*, in D.9.2.52.4.[72] Besides, it is interesting to note

---

[67] '*Si putator ex arbore ramum cum deiceret vel machinarius hominem praetereuntem occidit, ita tenetur, si is in publicum decidat nec ille proclamavit, ut casus eius evitari possit. Sed Mucius etiam dixit, si in privato idem accidisset, posse de culpa agi: culpam autem esse, quod cum a diligente provideri poterit, non esset provisum aut tum denuntiatum esset, cum periculum evitari non possit. Secundum quam rationem non multum refert, per publicum an per privatum iter fieret, cum plerumque per privata loca vulgo iter fiat. Quod si nullum iter erit, dolum dumtaxat praestare debet, ne immittat in eum, quem viderit transeuntem: nam culpa ab eo exigenda non est, cum divinare non potuerit, an per eum locum aliquis transiturus sit.*'

[68] '*Quintus Mucius scribit: equa cum in alieno pasceretur, in cogendo quod praegnas erat eiecit: quaerebatur, dominus eius possetne cum eo qui coegisset lege Aquilia agere, quia equam in iciendo ruperat. Si percussisset aut consulto vehementius egisset, visum est agere posse.*'

[69] '*Tabernarius in semita noctu supra lapidem lucernam posuerat: quidam praeteriens eam sustulerat: tabernarius eum consecutus lucernam reposcebat et fugientem retinebat: ille flagello, quod in manu habebat, in quo dolor inerat, verberare tabernarium coeperat, ut se mitteret: ex eo maiore rixa facta tabernarius ei, qui lucernam sustulerat, oculum effoderat: consulebat, num damnum iniuria non videtur dedisse, quoniam prior flagello percussus esset. Respondi, nisi data opera effodisset oculum, non videri damnum iniuria fecisse, culpam enim penes eum, qui prior flagello percussit, residere: sed si ab eo non prior vapulasset, sed cum ei lucernam eripere vellet, rixatus esset, tabernarii culpa factum videri.*'

[70] '*Cum pila complures luderent, quidam ex his servulum, cum pilam percipere conaretur, impulit, servus cecidit et crus fregit: quaerebatur, an dominus servuli lege Aquilia cum eo, cuius impulsu ceciderat, agere potest. Respondi non posse, cum casu magis quam culpa videretur factum.*'

[71] '*Est et alia exceptio, de qua Celsus dubitat, an sit obicienda: ut puta si incendii arcendi causa vicini aedes intercidi et quod vi aut clam mecum agatur aut damni iniuria. Gallus enim dubitat, an excipi oporteret: 'quod incendii defendendi causa factum non sit?' Servius autem ait, si id magistratus fecisset, dandam esse, privato non esse idem concedendum: si tamen quid vi aut clam factum sit neque ignis usque eo pervenisset, simpli litem aestimandam: si pervenisset, absolvi eum oportere. idem ait esse, si damni iniuria actum foret, quoniam nullam iniuriam aut damnum dare videtur aeque perituris aedibus. quod si nullo incendio id feceris, deinde postea incendium ortum fuerit, non idem erit dicendum, quia non ex post facto, sed ex praesenti statu, damnum factum sit nec ne, aestimari oportere labeo ait.*'

[72] See also D.9.2.7.4: '*Si quis in colluctatione vel in pancratio, vel pugiles dum inter se exercentur alius alium occiderit, si quidem in publico certamine alius alium occiderit, cessat Aquilia, quia gloriae causa et virtutis, non iniuriae gratia videtur damnum datum. Hoc autem in servo non procedit, quoniam ingenui solent certare: in filio familias vulnerato procedit. Plane si cedentem*

that in D.9.2.31 Paul refers specifically to the opinion of Quintus Mucius of a case of *occisio in privato*, that is, to a case where the *actio legis Aquiliae* follows from the (negligent) exercise of a right.[73]

In this context we can suppose that the investigation of the psychological element was needed in order to state once again the liability of the wrong-doer, while limiting the justification required by the word *iniuria* (in the sense of *non iure*).

Besides, it is paradigmatic that the whole subject of *iniuria* and, conse-quentially, of *culpa* is introduced by Ulpian[74] with an instance of a justifica-tion *par exellence*, as self-defence.

It was the need to deny the liability, even while risking a sentence in *duplum*, that gave room, in the Aquilian discipline, to justifications. Thus, justifications were in fact the way to deny liability in applying the *lex Aquilia*.

If all this is true, it means that one was originally considered liable without any evaluation of the subjective element: the damage to the property of others was sufficient and so today we could define that kind of liability as objective. This should not surprise us as it is similar to what happened in ancient German law, for instance: in the Edict of the Langobardic Rothar,[75] casual murder was punished with the payment of *weregild*, that is, with com-pensation, even if such murder excluded the feud because it was committed with no intention; also in the *Speculum Saxone*[76] objective liability occurs, as well as the liability of the underage and of the insane.

So, why could one, at the beginning, be liable for *damnum iniuria datum* every time there was no justification without the need to evaluate the sub-jective element? The answer can be found, on the one hand, in Caecilius Africanus' reasoning about the absence of the evaluation of the psychologi-

---

vulneraverit, erit Aquiliae locus, aut si non in certamine servum occidit, nisi si domino committente hoc factum sit: tunc enim Aquilia cessat.'

[73] Thus, the authenticity of the mention of *culpa*, for the *occisio in privato*, in Quintus Mucius seems to be confirmed, though the later definition of *culpa* cannot apparently refer to the republican jurist: on this point see Schipani (n 8 2009) 133, specifically 148; see, more recently, for the different opinions on this matter, Luis Rodriguez-Ennes, 'Contribución a una nueva hipotesis interpretativa de D.9.2.31' in *Estudios en homenaje al Profesor Juan Iglesias* vol 2 (Artes Graficas Benzal 1988) 1055.

[74] *'Sed et si quemcumque alium ferro se petentem quis occiderit, non videbitur iniuria occidisse: et si metu quis mortis furem occiderit, non dubitabitur, quin lege Aquilia non teneatur. Sin autem cum posset adprehendere, maluit occidere, magis est ut iniuria fecisse videatur: ergo et Cornelia tenebi-tur.'* This case was already examined by Gaius in D.9.2.4 pr.: *'Itaque si servum tuum latronem insidiantem mihi occidero, securus ero: nam adversus periculum naturalis ratio permittit se defen-dere'*; see also D.9.2.4.1: *'Lex duodecim tabularum furem noctu deprehensum occidere permittit, ut tamen id ipsum cum clamore testificetur: interdiu autem deprehensum ita permittit occidere, si is se telo defendat, ut tamen aeque cum clamore testificetur'.*

[75] Edict. Roth. 387 (Bluhme ed, *Monumenta Germaniae Historica*, Hahn 1868).

[76] Spec. Sax. 2.65.3 (Sachse ed, Winter 1848).

cal element in the case of *ruptio* (and of *fractio*) provided by the 12 Tables, and on the other, in the direct enforceability of the *manus iniectio pro iudicato*, that is, enforceability without any trial. There was an unjustified intrusion in the private sphere of the *dominus*: there was a damage *sine iure* to his property, which was the cornerstone of the absolute power of the *pater*,[77] the true lord of a sovereign community, the *familia*.[78] Property could not be damaged in any way. No intrusion *sine iure* in the sphere of the owner could be tolerated. From the damage, even if done with no *culpa*, to his property, the victim acquired a symmetrical power to redress the balance: this idea derives from *vindicta*, which was the original rule that governed conflicts among private citizens[79] and which, because of its nature, went beyond the evaluation of the psychological element. Here we can see an analogy with the reaction of the citizens' community against an aggression towards their territory.

Then, many new factors occurred: justifications were classified, intention emerged as a relevant element and prevailed as such according to the ancient strict formalism, commerce developed and property was considered in a dynamic of movement of goods and trade, acts against *bona fides* were specifically forbidden (the *exceptio doli* appeared not long after the reflections of Quintus Mucius about the abuse of a justification), a penal characterisation was recognised for the *actio legis Aquiliae* (and *poena* requires *culpa*). So it became insufficient as the cause of an unjustified damage to be liable for *damnum iniuria datum*; it was necessary to examine whether there was intention and/or negligence.

This perspective about Aquilian damage (but not about *effusum vel deiectum*, where relevant social matters were at stake) was constant for 1,700 years among commentators and writers of treatises of the *ius commune*. Rotondi summarised this well:[80] among the scholars, commentators and writers of treatises of the *ius commune* '*la colpa è requisito imprescindibile e la colpa va qui intesa come* culpa levissima, *nella nota antitesi colla* c.lata *e colla* c.levis'. To this regard, it is sufficient to recall Samuel Stryk: '*amplissimus (usus tituli) est, cum omnium damnorum reparatio ex hoc petatur, si modo ulla alterius culpa doceri possit*'[81] or Hugo Grotius: '*Maleficium hic appellamus culpam omnem, sive in faciendo, sive in non faciendo, pugnantem cum eo quod aut homines communiter, aut pro ratione certae qualitatis facere debent. Ex tali culpa obligatio naturaliter*

---

[77] For the characteristic relevance of property in archaic Roman society and the role of the *dominus/erus*, see the eternally relevant observations of Luigi Capogrossi Colognesi, *La struttura della proprietà e la formazione dei iura praediorum nell'età repubblicana* vol 1 (Giuffrè 1969) 417.

[78] For the political role of the *pater* and the *familia* as a political community, see Giuseppe Valditara, *Lo stato nell'antica Roma* (Soveria Mannelli 2008) 3.

[79] Valditara (n 54) 9.

[80] Rotondi (n 4) 245.

[81] See Samuel Stryk, *Usus modernus pandectarum*, in Samuel Stryk, *Opera omnia* (J Celli 1837) Lib.IX Tit.II para 1.

oritur, si damnum datum est, nempe ut id resarciatur'.[82] Such crucial relevance of the *culpa* inspired firstly the 'code Napoléon'[83], which was the model for some codes of the nineteenth century in the non-German area.[84]

Nonetheless, in 1700 a German jurist and philosopher, Christian Thomasius, introduced a different position into the scientific debate. His main work, *Larva legis Aquiliae*, has been republished with an English translation[85] and with a very accurate commentary by Zimmermann, but Rotondi[86] had already highlighted the revolutionary aspect of Thomasius' perspective.

What are its relevant points? To understand them better, we have to start with some reflections from Samuel Pufendorf who had a strong influence on Thomasius' thinking.[87] It was Pufendorf who highlighted the general principle of *neminem laedere*, which came from Ulpian.[88] The aim of such a principle, as Pufendorf pointed out, is crucial: '*Ut ne quis alterum laedat, utque si quod damnum alteri dederit, id reparet*'[89] which has also, at its base, a deep ethical need: 'Do as you would be done by'.[90] It is also interesting to observe how, for Pufendorf, objective liability appears whenever the wrongdoer derives an advantage from the damage he has caused to others.[91]

Thus, Thomasius, even in his first work, the *Institutiones*, does not start casually from the general prohibition *neminem laedere*. From this prohibition,

---

[82] Hugo Grotius, *De jure belli ac pacis libri tres* (G Blaeuw 1631) Lib.II Cap.XVII para I.

[83] Cf art 1382: 'Tout fait quelconque de l'homme, qui cause à autrui un dommage, oblige celui par la faute duquel il est arrivé, à le réparer'; and art 1383: 'Chacun est responsable du dommage qu'il a causé non seulement par son fait, mais encore par sa négligence ou par son imprudence'.

[84] See, for instance, arts 1131 and 1132 of the Italian civil code, which are a literal translation; similarly, see for instance art 1902 of the Spanish civil code of 1889.

[85] *Larva legis Aquiliae. The Mask of the Lex Aquilia Torn off the Action for Damage Done. A Legal Treatise by Christian Thomasius (1655–1728)*, edited and translated by Margaret Hewett, with an essay 'Christian Thomasius, the Reception of Roman Law and the History of the Lex Aquilia' by Reinhard Zimmermann (Hart 2000).

[86] Cf Rotondi (n 4) 261.

[87] See Frank Grunert, 'The Reception of Hugo Grotius's *De Jure belli ac pacis* in the Early German Enlightenment' in T Hochstrasser and P Schröder (eds), *Early Modern Natural Law Theories: Contexts and Strategies in the Early Enlightenment* (Kluwer 2003) 96. For the relationship between Thomasius and Pufendorf, see Gioele Solari, *L'idea individuale e l'idea sociale nel diritto privato: l'idea individuale* vol 1 (Fratelli Bocca 1911) 74. See also Thomas Kiefer, *Die Aquilische Haftung im 'Allgemeinen Landrecht für die Preussischen Staaten' von 1794* (Centaurus 1989) 106.

[88] Cf D.1.1.10.1.

[89] Cf Samuel Pufendorf, *De jure naturae et gentium libri octo* vol 3 ([1672], new edn Knochius-Wustius 1694) I I. See Berthold Kupisch, *La responsabilità da atto illecito nel diritto naturale*, in *La responsabilità civile da atto illecito nella prospettiva storico-comparatistica* vol 1: Congresso internazionale, ARISTEC, Madrid, 7–10 ottobre 1993 (Giappichelli 1995) 125; Kiefer (n 87) 83; Cursi (n 18) 52.

[90] See Zimmermann (n 85) 65.

[91] Cf Pufendorf (n 89) III I VI, on which see Kupisch (n 89) 130.

it is argued that one must indemnify the owner for the damage done to his property.[92] It is not relevant whether the damage was done intentionally, negligently or simply by accident.[93] In Thomasius' view, it would be fair and equal to indemnify the owner for damage that was done by accident: not only because the balance is, by such restitution, redressed (*aequum*), but also because this is according to morals (*justum*).[94] On the other side, Thomasius asserts that the owner who has suffered damage must not have contributed to cause the damage.[95]

In this regard, it is interesting that Thomasius refers[96] to a wider duty of moral solidarity (*pium et humanum est*) that compels us to help those who suffered an economic loss, although we did not damage them in any way. Even more importantly, we should give a *solatium* (consolation) to those who incurred a damage because of us.

Thomasius then presents the following case:[97] I am holding in my hand a glass belonging to someone else; suddenly something happens that startles not only me but also the owner of the glass. I am so startled that the glass falls from my hand and breaks. Certainly I had no intention of breaking the glass and I cannot be blamed for any negligence, but who is to suffer the loss? Should the restitution be divided in two? No, Thomasius answers, I have to pay it all, because I took the glass in my hand, and if I had not taken it, it would not have broken. This is the same standard that is the basis of the common saying 'if you break it, you have to pay for it', that is, you have to bear the cost of it, mostly in the context of small shopkeepers, with no evaluation of your responsibility. The mention of *aequitas* refers to the need to redress the balance. For the same reason, it is more equitable that my negligence damages me and not somebody else. And besides, according to Thomasius,[98] as many favourable events are an advantage to me even if no credit is to be given to me for them, it is also fair that I endure the mishaps that happen that are not my fault.

Thomasius adds a further remark:[99] I took the glass because I was curious, I took it for my pleasure or for my interest, so it is right that I have to suffer the consequences of my innocent curiosity. This reason for my liability recalls the principle of *cuius commoda eius et incommoda*. However, we should argue from it that, for instance, the doctor who caused damage to

---

[92] Cf Christian Thomasius, *Institutiones iurisprudentiae divinae* (Weidmannus 1688) II V 6; 11; 20; 21; 34.

[93] On which see also Thomasius (n 85) IV.

[94] Cf Thomasius (n 85) IV.

[95] Cf ibid IV: '*Nam quicquid sit de imputatione ex dolo et negligentia, sufficit, quod ego damnum dederim, dominus vero ad illud nec physice nec moraliter concurrerit.*'

[96] Cf ibid IV.

[97] Cf ibid IV.

[98] Cf ibid III.

[99] Cf ibid IV: '*Quam innocens igitur sit curiositas mea, mea tamen est, non domini vitri.*'

his patient by accident is not liable, because he entered the patient's sphere in the interest of the patient himself.

So, at the root of Thomasius' position, we can see four principles which are explicitly mentioned or implicitly inferable: (1) a general standard of *neminem laedere*, which compels us to indemnify the offended party for any damage to his property; (2) a principle of solidarity that compels us to support economically those who are in need; (3) a principle on whose basis the interests at stake must be compared, so that the *incommoda* are distributed depending on the benefits involved; (4) the need to respect equity as a value, redressing the balance.

So, this *actio* that Thomasius has in mind and that 'the Germans have hitherto used in court' derives from *ius naturae* or from *ius gentium*, and its function is only the restitution, because it does not punish a morally reproachable conduct.[100] Only the delicts committed with intention require a punishment, and a minor one if there is only negligence.[101] This *actio* defends the property and so, as I only ask, when somebody possesses a good of mine, the '*vindicatio substantiam rei eiusque fructus*', so in the same way if my property is damaged or my profit is prevented, I can only ask for the value of the goods or the estimate of the lost profit.[102] No sum as punishment of a misdeed is due to me, because no misdeed must be punished. Thus, this makes evident the difference between this restitutive action that derives from equity and is according to *ius gentium*, and the *actio legis Aquiliae*, which punishes a *maleficium*.[103] The former is an *actio ex aequitate*, the latter a penal action that deliberately allows a sum greater than the real damages to be paid, because of the *plurimi*, whereas the *actio ex aequitate* allows only what the offended actually suffered to be paid. In conclusion, the *actio ex aequitate* for delictual liability does not provide penalties for examples of morally reproachable conduct, but it provides a fair and equal distribution of the loss caused.[104] This implies the irrelevance of the subjective element.

This is the reason why, for Thomasius, restitution has also to be paid whenever the damage was done by an insane person or by an underage person for whom nobody is responsible.[105] The argument for this is as

---

[100] Cf Thomasius (n 85) I; XII.

[101] Cf Thomasius, ibid: '*poenam vero sola delicta dolo data requirunt, certe negligentia minimi gradus, qualis tamen ab hac actione non excusat, omnem poenam respuit: qua ex ratione Dominus damnum patiens posset poenam ab altero exigere?*'

[102] Cf Thomasius, ibid.

[103] See on this point Kupisch (n 89) 140. The Aquilian *actio* is intended as a *larva*, a mask that covers the true face of the action for compensation.

[104] Cf Zimmermann (n 85) 67.

[105] Cf Thomasius (n 85) LXII. For the distinctive influence of this solution of Thomasius on the Austrian legislation, see Hans Peter Benöhr, 'Ausservertragliche Schadensersatzpflicht ohne Verschulden? Die Argumente der Naturrechtslehren und Kodifikationen' (1976) 93 ZSS (RA) 208, 233, 237.

follows: if it is true that the *actio* for damage is given *iure gentium* when damage is done *iniuria*, it is the same word, '*iniuria*', that justifies such extension, because it means '*quod non iure fit*', that is, the absence of a right to cause damage, and certainly an insane person or an underage person had no right to cause damage.[106]

Kant and Zeiler also admitted this *actio* for damages against legally incompetent people.[107] This position somehow complies with the ancient German law where insane and underage persons are exempted from any penalty, but not from restitution.[108] In this context, Thomasius, though taking into account that in the *leges gentium* – that is, in the positive law – an action for compensation is given only against the one who acted guiltily, states that the victim must only prove the causation between the act of the wrongdoer and the damage: '*Porro Jure Gentium in actione de damno dato nihil probandum est ulterius, quam quod reus damnum dederit*'.[109] This is the root of the idea that it is up to the defendant to prove that he caused the damage without fault[110] and is the historical precedent of the presumption of fault that many modern laws provide for specific cases.[111]

This is evident in the following statement:[112]

> Il grandioso movimento di codificazione che si inizia nella seconda metà del secolo XVIII e che culmina nei tre codici – Prussiano, Austriaco e Francese – ha le sue immediate radici nel giusnaturalismo che dominava allora in tutte le scuole e informava di sè tutta la elaborazione dogmatica e la applicazione pratica del diritto comune.

But, while the French code is influenced by Grotius[113] and is still well connected to the standard of liability by fault (a perfect instance is art 1383 of the 'code Napoléon'), the Prussian and Austrian codes owe something to the ideas of Thomasius.[114] It is sufficient to say that Prussian legal science

---

[106] Cf Thomasius (n 85) IX. See, on this point, Gian Paolo Massetto, 'Responsabilità extracontrattuale (diritto intermedio)' in *Enciclopedia del Diritto* vol 39 (Giuffrè 1988) 1165.

[107] Cf Rotondi (n 4) 264; Massetto (n 106) 1165. Franz von Zeiller, *Das natürliche Privatrecht* (Beck 1819) para 179, specifically, highlights a comparison with the right to defend oneself and to prevent those who act unwillingly from doing harm: as it is licit to defend oneself even against the aggressions of the insane and the underage and as the offence to my property is lasting till the property is restored, so I have a right to be indemnified. See also n 119.

[108] In this sense, the edict of the Langobardic King Rothar (c 387) provided an obligation to pay the *weregild* even in the case of casual murder.

[109] Cf Thomasius (n 85) VIII.

[110] Cf Kupisch (n 89) 141.

[111] Cf, for example, BGB, para 831; CC arts 2048.3; 2050; 2051; 2052; 2053; 2054.1 and 2054.2.

[112] Rotondi (n 4) 267.

[113] Rotondi (n 4) 272; Massetto (n 106) 1165.

[114] Rotondi (n 4) 268; see, for all of this, Michael J Rainer, *Das römische Recht in Europa: Von Justinian zum BGB* (Manzsche 2012) *passim*, specifically 223.

focused on the University of Halle, where Thomasius taught from 1694 'esercitandovi una influenza profondissima e duratura'.[115]

Likewise, Zeiler, who had a meaningful role in the writing of the civil code of Austria, the *Allgemeines bürgerliches Gesetzbuch (ABGB)*,[116] was a follower of objective liability (*Erfolghaftung*) asserted by natural law, according to which the right to restitution was not based on the reproachability of the wrongdoer's conduct, but on the right of the victim to be indemnified,[117] that is, to see his position re-established, or 'restored'.

Thus, it comes as little surprise that in the *ABGB* of 1811, the title of section 30 refers to the right to restitution, whereas in the prior project of a code, approved by Maria Theresa of Austria, the title referred to 'culpability'. Similarly, if liability by fault is still the standard, paragraph 1310 provides restitution for damage done by legally incompetent people[118] and the reform of 1916 provides restitution even for cases in which damage is done by necessity.[119] It is also interesting to note that paragraph 1306 of the *ABGB* highlights how 'in der Regel' a person is not obliged to indemnify the damage if he caused it without fault. The expression 'in der Regel' allows exceptions.[120] Likewise, the Prussian code provided for the liability of insane and underage people, as long as it was not possible to have restitution from people who were obliged to take care of them. Similar provisions are included in the Swiss code of 1911.[121]

---

[115] As affirmed in Rotondi (n 4) 268. The Prussian ALR was conceived under the influence of natural law: 'Un monumento legislativo, frutto di quasi un secolo di lavoro ... iniziato nel 1713, prima sotto la direzione di Ch. Thomasius e, dal 1738, di Samuel Cocceius', according to Carlo Augusto Cannata, *Scritti scelti di diritto romano* (Giappichelli 2012) 282.

[116] Von Zeiller (n 107) paras 178–79. See on this point Rotondi (n 4) 271; Massetto (n 106) 1165; Rainer (n 114) 238.

[117] See also Franz Wieacker, *Storia del diritto privato moderno* vol 1 ([1952], Italian tr Giuffrè 1980) 512; Theo Mayer Maly, 'Zeiller, das ABGB und wir' in Walter Selb-Herbert Hofmeister (ed), *Forschungsband Franz von Zeiller (1751–1828). Beiträge zur Gesetzgebungs und Wissenschafsgeschichte* (Böhlau 1980) 8; Massetto (n 106) 1170; Valditara (n 9) 143.

[118] In this regard, see the interesting and articulate comments of Franz Xaver Nippel von Weyerheim, *Commento sul codice civile generale austriaco con ispeciale riguardo alla pratica* ([1830], Italian tr Fusi 1836) 130.

[119] With reference to the case of the liability of the legally incompetent person, Zeiller justifies the objective characterisation of it, affirming that, as the right of defence and prevention is legitimate even against those who act with no guilty will – such as children, insane people or sleepwalkers – in the same way, while the offence to the property of the victim is lasting and until such property is not restored as it was in its pristine state, the victim has the right to be indemnified with the goods of the wrongdoer: see Zeiller (n 107) para 179; on this point, see, recently, Cursi (n 18) 173 n 33.

[120] See Cursi (n 18) 172.

[121] Cf *Legge federale di complemento del Codice civile svizzero. Libro quinto: Diritto delle obbligazioni*, art 52.2 (I quote the Italian text): 'Chi mette mano alla cosa altrui per sottrarre sé od altri ad un danno o pericolo imminente, è obbligato a risarcire il danno secondo il prudente criterio del giudice. Art. 54.1: Per motivi di equità il giudice può condannare anche una persona incapace di discernimento al risarcimento parziale o totale del danno da essa cagionato'.

In the same vein, the BGB provides in paragraph 829 a restitution 'for equity reasons' if damage is done by legally incompetent people. The influence of the *actio ex aequitate* of Thomasius is clear.[122] Besides, the preparatory works show an intention to extend the rule of the restitution to all those cases where a liability for damage done could be found even without fault: thus, this was a kind of objective liability that was, in the end, discarded.[123]

In Italy, Giacomo Venezian,[124] arriving at consequences that could be potentially even more relevant, though developing his thoughts exclusively inside the Romanistic tradition, went so far as to consider 'il punto di vista della responsabilità oggettiva' as not extraneous to the Roman sources.[125] As was clearly observed,[126] in 'un momento in cui il processo di industrializzazione si sviluppa in Italia, e si moltiplicano le occasioni di danno, si avvia un dibattito per il superamento del principio della responsabilità per colpa'. Actually, it is starting from such arguments that Nicola Coviello, in his work *La responsabilità senza colpa*, wrote:[127] 'Qual meraviglia se per il prodigioso moltiplicarsi di ardite industrie, per l'impiego di macchine ognor crescente, per l'uso delle cieche ma possenti forze naturali, assoggettate all'uomo, sono oggi così frequenti i grandi danni', thus, as in the perspective of some part of the German doctrine of natural law, there was such a tendency that 'nella società attuale' the cost of the damage should be divided 'tra più'.[128]

---

[122] See, recently, on the influence of natural law and of Thomasius on the history of the German codification, Ina Ebert, *Pönale Elemente im deutschen Privatrecht. Von der Renaissance der Privatstrafe im deutschen Recht* (Mohr Siebeck 2004) *passim*, 99.

[123] The intention of the second commission for the drafting of the BGB was to extend the rule (see para 829) about the duty of the legally incompetent person to indemnify the victim whenever equity required it: this extension would have included all cases where liability for damage done could be found even without fault. The *Bundesrat* decided to limit such objective liability to the case of legally incompetent people; the attempt to replace the principle of fault with the 'Veranlassungsprinzip' was rejected; it was observed that this latter was not at all a peculiarity of German law, as the supporters of some natural-law traditions stated, but a characteristic of all laws of a lower level: see, on this point, Rotondi (n 4) 281, including references to other authors. Moreover, it is interesting to observe that the BGB does not express a general principle of liability by fault, though it provides a number of specific provisions referring to such a principle.

[124] Cf Giacomo Venezian, *Danno e risarcimento fuori dei contratti*, 1884–86 in Giacomo Venezian, *Opere Giuridiche* vol 1 (Athenaeum 1919) 1, 76, specifically.

[125] On this point, see Sandro Schipani, 'Pluralità di prospettive e ruolo della *culpa* come criterio elaborato dalla scienza del diritto nell'interpretazione della *lex Aquilia*', now in *Contributi romanistici al sistema della responsabilità extracontrattuale* (Giappichelli 2009) 32.

[126] ibid 32; Carlo Castronovo, *La nuova responsabilità civile* (3rd edn, Giuffrè 2006) 276. Roman jurisprudence was, however, already inclined towards a standard of reduced liability in case the wrongdoer had been inserted into the economic sphere of the victim for the benefit of the latter: see D.41.1.54.2, about which see Giuseppe Valditara, *Superamento della* aestimatio rei *nella valutazione del danno aquiliano ed estensione della tutela ai* non domini (Giuffrè 1992) 414; Valditara (n 9 2005) 39.

[127] Nicola Coviello, 'La responsabilità senza colpa' (1897) 23 Riv.it.sc.giur. 202.

[128] So writes Coviello, ibid.

Therefore, liability without fault must exist beside liability by fault, 'non in rapporto di subordinazione, come d'eccezione a regola, ma coordinate fra loro' and 'indipendenti'.[129] But the problem was how to reconcile the general standard expressed in art 1151 of the 1865 Italian code, which undoubtedly favoured liability by fault, with this new need, possibly by interpreting in the sense of the objective responsibility the various cases of responsibility for acts done by a third party provided by arts 1153 *ff*.[130]

Venezian's point of view is summarised well in the following words:[131]

> le applicazioni della responsabilità nel diritto romano non sono solidamente appoggiate sul principio della responsabilità oggettiva. Ma tanto meno appariscono informate al principio della imputabilità

and again:

> Il principio della responsabilità oggettiva non ha avuto nel diritto romano tutto lo sviluppo di cui è capace, principalmente perché le condizioni economiche e politiche ne rendevano inutile o impossibile l'applicazione a tutti quei casi per i quali oggi importa di più affermarlo fortemente.

While re-reading the Roman sources and looking for an interpretative evolution that could follow from them, Venezian proposed a new standard for liability founded on the principle of 'causation'.[132]

We now come to the provisions of the modern Italian civil code. To fully understand them, we need to keep the project of the Italian-French code of obligations of 1927 in mind.[133] There, the principle of liability for fault[134] was expressly weakened by taking from the BGB[135] the restitu-

---

[129] Coviello (n 127) 206.

[130] Lodovico Barassi, 'Contributo alla teoria della responsabilità per fatto non proprio, in special modo a mezzo di animali' (1897) 24 Riv.it.sc.giur. 175.

[131] Venezian (n 124) 93.

[132] ibid 86.

[133] Cf *Il progetto italo francese delle obbligazioni (1927). Un modello di armonizzazione nell'epoca della codificazione* (Giovanni Chiodi ed, Giuffrè 2007) 228, the *Relazione sul progetto di codice delle obbligazioni e dei contratti, comune all'Italia ed alla Francia*, 364, and the articles.

[134] The discussion about the standard for liability ended with the preservation of the general principle of fault, as it can clearly be deduced from Roberto de Ruggiero, *Istituzioni di diritto civile* vol III (Principato 1934) 65, 494 n 1, 498: '… sebbene in casi particolari e in materie speciali la responsabilità oggettiva sia stata riconosciuta nel diritto civile nostro, questo resta tuttora assiso sul principio tradizionale, tramandato dal diritto romano, della imputabilità del fatto: un principio generale nuovo ed opposto non può dirsi ancora ad esso sostituito'. The preservation of the general principle of fault and the liberal structure of Italian society, the demands coming from our capitalist economy, occured, owing to the influence of Roman law.

[135] See the *Relazione sul progetto* in *Il progetto italo francese* (n 133) 230: 'Anche da noi però si è consentito a fare qualche strappo al rigido principio che non v'ha responsabilità senza colpa'. In art 77.2 of the same text – referring to the case of the equal indemnity due from the person who caused damage to others to save himself or others from another imminent and much more serious damage – is commented on as follows: 'E con questa un'altra dispo-

tion for damage done by a legally incompetent or insane person,[136] when it was impossible to obtain restitution from the people who had to look after such people and when the economic circumstances of the wrongdoer and the victim would suggest a restitution for equitable reasons. This liability of the legally incompetent was expressly defined as objective.[137] It is rooted in a need for solidarity in the distribution of loss when this is the outcome of conduct *sine iure*.[138] In addition, the liability of masters and mandators was considered as a kind of liability without fault and treated separately from the liability of parents, tutors, teachers and craftsmen: article 80 of the project, after pointing out that it was a liability without fault, associated it with the liability of the incompetent people.[139]

Here we seem to find an echo of Thomasius' reflections: the damage was done because of an activity in the interest of the wrongdoer, who created an objective risk to his own advantage. It seems here that the basis of such provisions is in the following (implicit) premise: the risk is here created for an economic advantage, and because of that advantage society bears (potential) costs; risk generates profit. The person who created the risk for his own economic advantage must always be liable. It would not be fair,

---

sizione nuova s'è pur introdotta, che come la precedente, si trova già nel codice germanico, il cui fondamento di equità sociale è innegabile'. The terminology used in the *Relazione sul progetto di codice* (in *Il progetto italo francese* (n 133) 230) is interesting, as it expressly talks of 'qualche strappo' to the general principle of fault: see in this sense also Alfredo Ascoli, *Istituzioni di diritto civile: corso dettato nella regia università di Roma* (3rd edn, Dante Alighieri 1934) 280, who highlights the influence of the BGB on the insertion of this objective liability.

The 1919 Commission held a different opinion and in the *Relazione* considered the liability of the legally incompetent person as opposite to equity: 'Ma questa regola non sembra davvero preferibile all'opposta che è fondata su un principio di logica e di giustizia molto più saldo di questa *equità del tutto arbitraria*. Il danno causato da un pazzo o da un bambino, se non si può attribuire ad alcuna responsabilità per difetto di sorveglianza, è un caso fortuito; e se si fa sopportare all'autore che manca di discernimento, non si applica un principio di equità, ma solo si trasporta il danno da uno all'altro'.

The BGB, the 'Novellierungen' of the ABGB and the Swiss code of obligations of 1911 were expressly models for the project of the code of obligations of 1927: see *Relazione*, in *Il progetto italo francese* (n 133) 186. On this point see Chiodi (n 133) 61.

[136] Cf *Il progetto italo francese* (n 133) art 76.

[137] Affirmed in *Il progetto italo francese* (n 133) 230–32, where a 'responsabilità puramente oggettiva' is mentioned.

[138] Affirmed explicitly and in more than one occurrence in *Relazione sul progetto di codice*, in *Il progetto italo francese* (n 133) 232: the deviations from the rigid principle of liability by fault can be justified 'da un alto principio di equità sociale'.

[139] See the *Relazione sul progetto di codice* in *Il progetto italo francese*, 230. René Savatier, 'La responsabilità da delitto nel Diritto francese e nel Progetto italo-francese di un Codice delle Obbligazioni' (1930) 3 Annuario di diritto comparato 271, pointed out in the project three cases of objective liability: (1) the liability of the person who caused damage in a state of necessity; (2) the liability of the legally incompetent person as a wrongdoer, if the victim could not have obtained compensation from the person who should look after him; (3) the liability of masters and clients for what was done by people put in charge by them.

just as Thomasius thought while elaborating the *actio ex aequitate*, that the person who only undertook the risk without deriving any profit from it must endure the consequences.[140] This position was revoked in the code of 1942.

The change of the section title is already meaningful: from 'atti illeciti' (illicit acts) to 'fatti illeciti' (illicit facts). As the 'Relazione Ministeriale' explains,[141] such a change was necessary because 'in altra parte' of the code the word 'atti' was used to define the 'negozi giuridici', that is, facts characterised by the element of will. Such terminology was already used in the BGB[142] and in the Swiss code (section II).[143]

A second, crucial variation consists in the addiction of the adjective 'ingiusto' (unjust) that here refers to the damage and no longer to the fact. As can be seen in the 'Relazione Ministeriale',[144] 'Si precisa così, conferendo maggior chiarezza alla norma dell'art.1151 cod.civ. del 1865, che la *culpa* e l'*iniuria* sono concetti distinti'. Here we have an evident split with a very old tradition that identified *iniuria* with *culpa*. By contrast, it is explained that *iniuria* is an unlawful behaviour, that is, the *iniuria* implies that a fact or an omission harmed the juridical sphere of others. In this manner, we revert to the perspective of the original Aquilian *iniuria*. Thus, the famous sentence no 500/1999 of the Italian Supreme Court summarises it perfectly:[145] 'Non può negarsi che nella disposizione in esame risulta netta la centralità del danno'. Also in this sentence we can read: 'la normativa sulla responsabilità aquiliana ha funzione di riparazione del danno ingiusto' and it is defined 'ingiusto il danno che l'ordinamento non può tollerare che rimanga a carico della vittima, ma che va trasferito sull'autore del fatto, in quanto lesivo di interessi giuridicamente rilevanti'.

Culpability moves somehow to the background. It is not accidental that in the 'Relazione Ministeriale',[146] liability with no fault is examined immediately after the paragraph that explains the novelty of the 'unjust damage' and not, as it would have been more logical and consistent with tradition, in connection with the paragraphs where the problem of fault was discussed. This is treading on the same path as Thomasius and Zeiler, where the liability of incompetent people and the resulting right to restitution was connected

---

[140] It is not accidental that here the *Relazione* recalls a need for 'equità sociale' that leads to distribute the negative consequences 'dei casi fortuiti' among those who are 'più vicini all'evento dannoso': cf *Relazione sul progetto di codice* in *Il progetto italo francese* (n 133) 232–34.

[141] Cf *Relazione Ministeriale al codice civile* (Istituto Poligrafico dello Stato 1943) 179 para 793.

[142] See *BGB* XXV book II.

[143] See *Legge federale di complemento del codice civile svizzero* V book II.

[144] *Relazione Ministeriale al codice civile* 181 para 797.

[145] Cf Cass. Sez. unite civili 22 luglio 1999 n 500 in (sept. 1999) 124–29 *Foro it.* part 1 col 2487. For the sentence 500/1999 see, among many authors, Giovanna Visintini, *Danno ingiusto e lesione di interessi legittimi*, (2001) 17 *Contratto e impresa* vol 1, 16; Guido Alpa, *La responsabilità civile. Parte generale* (Utet 2010) 598.

[146] See *Relazione Ministeriale al codice civile* 181 paras 797, 798, 799.

to the need to restore in any case the position of the victim. It is also no accident that, in line with this tendency towards an objective liability, a proposal was presented to accept the reversal of the burden of proof from the victim to the wrongdoer as a general principle.[147]

This solution was not approved, but the principle – which had already been applied in the code of 1865 regarding the liability of parents, tutors, teachers and craftsmen (where the reversal was founded on the *culpa* and on the major diligence required to those who had a duty to look after somebody) because of the influence of the 'code Napoléon' – was extended. The reversal of the burden of proof has now been extended to people who have a duty to look after an incompetent person (2047.1), to dangerous activities (2050),[148] to damage done by things in safekeeping (2051), to damage done by animals (2052), to the collapse of a building (2053) and to the circulation of vehicles (2054.1).[149]

It is meaningful how, in the Report to the King, such cases of reversal of the burden of proof are considered as intermediate with regard to the 'extreme' objective liability.[150] Thus, the reversal of the burden of proof was conceived by the legislator as a bridge between subjective and objective liability.[151] Furthermore, it is meaningful that, in the interpretative evolution, the cases of liability provided by arts 2050 *ff.* are now conceived of as cases of objective liability,[152] with the partial exception of art 2054 where we can find a particularly strong presumption of fault and where the liability *in solidum* of the owner or of the usufructuary of the vehicle is certainly a case of objective liability.[153] Similarly, the case of art 2049, which refers to the liability of masters and mandators, seems, more than a presumption of liability *iuris et de iure* that is founded on a *culpa in eligendo* and *in vigilando*, a case of objective liability.[154]

---

[147] Cf *Relazione Ministeriale al codice civile* 180 para 794.

[148] In this regard, the *Relazione* is extremely clear when it examines the liability *ex* art 2050 referring to the case of dangerous activities: 'Sulla materia non si è creduto di adottare alcuna delle soluzioni estreme: nè quella che annetterebbe a tali attività una responsabilità oggettiva, nè quella che vi ricollegherebbe l'ordinaria responsabilità per colpa. Si è adottata invece una soluzione intermedia per la quale, sempre mantenendo la colpa a base della responsabilità, non solo si è posta a carico del danneggiante la prova liberatoria, ma si è ampliato il dovere di diligenza che è posto a suo carico'.

[149] Moreover, with reference to liability for damage done by the circulation of vehicles, I believe that the legislator actually thought of objective liability, so it has already been affirmed by Stefano Rodotà, *Il problema della responsabilità civile* (Giuffrè 1964) 163.

[150] Cf, for all this, Francesco Caringella, *Corso di diritto civile II. La responsabilità extracontrattuale* (Dike 2013) 4.

[151] See also Pier Giuseppe Monateri, *La responsabilità civile* (Utet 2006) 88.

[152] See Guido Alpa, 'La responsabilità oggettiva' (2005) 21 *Contratto e impresa* vol 2, 968.

[153] On this point, see Pier Giuseppe Monateri, '*Illecito e responsabilità civile* II' in Mario Bessone (ed), *Trattato di diritto privato* vol 10 (Giappichelli 2005) 173.

[154] See Alpa (n 145) 101; 718; Alpa, in (2005) 21 *Contratto e impresa* vol 2, 965. In this direction goes also the jurisprudence: see Cass. civ. 5957/2000 and Cass. civ. 11241/2003.

In short, as Visintini[155] effectively summarised, 'la colpevolezza non è più l'unico criterio di imputazione della responsabilità', and Busnelli asserted: 'la convinzione del definitivo superamento del principio tradizionale "nessuna responsabilità senza colpa" è incontrovertibile e perfino ovvia'.[156] Thus, it was rightly observed that 'è lo sviluppo della responsabilità oggettiva a ridisegnare la responsabilità civile nei suoi profili strutturali'.[157] This is actually the evolution of a 'world debate' that involved jurists from the different legal systems.[158]

The orientation is towards the victim and not towards the wrongdoer, the provisions focus on the victim of the damage instead of on the person who caused it.[159] Thus, to judge if the victim deserves the restitution is more crucial than to judge if the conduct of the wrongdoer deserves to be punished. The fact that an 'absolute' right, as the right to property is defined in Roman law systems, is infringed upon, is no longer relevant. Even the damage done to credit rights by a third party, or of a legitimate interest (that is, a legal position that a private citizen can claim against the state administration), legitimate expectations, chances and even the interest to keep something in one's custody can lead to a restitution. Art 2043 c.c. becomes a primary rule that determines 'il divieto di ingerirsi senza autorizzazione nella sfera giuridica altrui e il conseguente obbligo di risarcire il danno derivante dalla eventuale interferenza'.[160]

---

[155] See Giovanna Visintini, *I fatti illeciti*, vol 1 (CEDAM 2004) 28 and more generally 2; Visintini, 'Il danno ingiusto' (1987) 5 Rivista critica del diritto privato, 177, where it is highlighted (at 179) that 'apparve manifesto, con la rivoluzione industriale e lo sviluppo dell'assicurazione contro la responsabilità civile, che la colpa non poteva più essere posta al centro del sistema della responsabilità civile', and thus 'si cominciò ad avvertire che la problematica in esame doveva essere scomposta a vari livelli e in particolare dovevano essere tenuti separati il discorso sulla valutazione degli interessi meritevoli di tutela (danno ingiusto) e il discorso sulla imputabilità della responsabilità (colpa e altro)'. Again Visintini, (above) 28, correctly emphasises: 'Quando si comprende che il criterio di imputazione della responsabilità può essere diverso dalla colpa, la tecnica delle responsabilità civile viene studiata a due livelli e vengono tenuti separati il discorso sulla valutazione degli interessi meritevoli di tutela (danno ingiusto) e il discorso sulla imputabilità della responsabilità (colpa o altro criterio di imputazione)'. Visintini concludes by writing: 'Dunque la inserzione nell'art. 2043 della qualificazione in termini di ingiustizia del danno rivela l'opzione per una concezione non tipizzante del fatto illecito ma tale da lasciare libero il giudice di apprezzare le modalità delle fattispecie concrete e di svolgere un ruolo nella costruzione di una serie aperta di fatti illeciti'.

[156] So writes Francesco Donato Busnelli, 'Nuove frontiere della responsabilità civile' (1976) 23 Ius 42.

[157] Cf Castronovo (n 126) 275. For more about the development of the principle of objective liability in general, see Alpa (n 145) 305; Alpa (n 152) 959.

[158] For an initial brief list see Monateri (151) 84 n 3 and Alpa (n 152) 959 and the book references included.

[159] Cf Caringella (n 150) 3. On this point see, more widely, Castronovo (n 126) 278.

[160] Cf Caringella (n 150) 4.

If we pay attention, we can note that this was exactly the sense, with reference only to the interference with *dominium*, of the original Aquilian provisions. The Italian code of 1942 – with some interesting analogies with the original Aquilian perspective,[161] though for different reasons – put in first place, as a foundation of the action for damage, the damage itself done to the legal position of the victim, more than the wrongdoer's fault.

We can catch a glimpse of the decline of the age of *culpa*[162] which was functional to a certain kind of society where freedom and autonomy were privileged.[163] The breakthrough of the civilisation of machines, which at the same time is a civilisation of masses, gradually highlighted the idea of an individual who, for better or worse, is the only centre of liability of his life history.[164] Mostly work accidents elicited a reaction in jurists against the old dogmas that, most of the time, caused areas of true irresponsibility.[165]

We now consider solidarity as central, as the 'Relazione Ministeriale' somehow made explicit. We can examine point 799, about the liability of someone who causes damage because of a state of necessity: here 'l'incidenza del danno' is transferred

> da una sfera a un'altra, indice evidente di un dovere di mutua comprensione da parte dei consociati. Questo dovere può essere posto perché l'ordinamento corporativo non isola l'interesse del singolo, distaccandolo dalla vita di relazione, ma pone l'utilità generale nel crogiuolo che fonde ogni egoismo, per comporne viva materia di sano equilibrio, di armonia e di coordinazione per gli interessi di tutti'.

Here, from the perspective of a stronger social solidarity, and moreover considering the collective interest as superior, the ideas already recalled in the Italian-French code project – caused by a 'high principle of social equity', which in its turn recalled the 'natural equity' that was the foundation for the

---

[161] This is affirmed in Valditara (n 9 2009) 145.

[162] For the decline of *culpa* see, among many authors, Paolo Franceschetti, 'La categoria della colpevolezza' in Giovanna Sebastio (ed), *La colpa nella responsabilità civile* 1 (Utet 2006) 76, including many references to other authors; Castronovo (n 126) 276. Further, see Massimo Franzoni, *L'illecito* (Giuffrè 2010) 179 who, after highlighting how art 2043 is still in any case focused on the principle of *culpa*, observes that we should not 'incoraggiare le opinioni formatesi soprattutto durante gli anni sessanta, secondo le quali la colpa come criterio per amministrare il costo del danno sarebbe superata o sarebbe sempre oggetto di una presunzione'. We should rather consider 'i diversi criteri di imputazione in ragione della funzione legislativamente loro attribuita', without blocking out the role of *culpa*: this is also affirmed by Franzoni (above) 180.

[163] The centrality of *culpa*, as the only standard for liability, mirrors the idea 'che ha posto al centro dell'ondata codificante di primo ottocento il soggetto di diritto, signore assoluto del proprio destino in quanto padrone della propria scienza e della propria volontà', so writes Castronovo (n 126) 276. Such centrality was, in other words, consistent with the triumph of the individualistic philosophy of liberalism 'e dell'idea soggettiva che ne sta alla base', ibid 276.

[164] Castronovo (n 126) 276.

[165] Franzoni (n 162) 176.

principle of objective responsibility stated by Thomasius – are followed and made stronger.

Four points are now highlighted: the novelty of the corporate legal system that has somehow overcome the liberal system; the crucial role of the general usefulness; the rejection of selfishness; the balance, coordination and harmony among the different interests.

The scholars, independently from the intention of the legislator, but in a perspective partially consistent with it, highlighted the standard of solidarity as foundation for a lessening of the principle of *culpa*, and for the stating of a civil responsibility always in the objective way. What Paolo Franceschetti writes is a summarising instance of such attitude:[166]

> si è rilevato che attualmente un posto sempre più importante nel diritto civile è assegnato all'uomo, allo sviluppo della sua personalità e alla rimozione delle disuguaglianze economiche e giuridiche. Se ciò è vero, non può disconoscersi che il principio della colpa, in determinati casi, è più immorale di un principio di responsabilità che tenga conto di altri criteri: si deve ritenere moralmente accettabile che dei cittadini, danneggiati da un'industria chimica (o da una fabbrica che utilizza sostanze inquinanti), non vengano risarciti perché il proprietario non è il colpevole, oppure è più morale stabilire a priori che il proprietario dell'industria debba risarcire tutti i danni arrecati, cercando di evitarli e preventivando in anticipo il loro costo?[167]

In civil law, a more and more important place is given to the person. Therefore, in certain cases, the principle of fault seems, for Franceschetti, more immoral than a principle of liability that takes due account of the different social and economical conditions of wrongdoer and victim.

The development of the concept of objective liability is characterised by the theory of 'risk-profit',[168] according to which whoever creates the risk for his profit must be liable for it. In the Roman sources, the relevance of the 'risk-profit' principle about the standards of Aquilian liability was already present,[169] though such relevance concerned the different case of the person

---

[166] Cf Franceschetti (n 162) 77.

[167] Moreover, it can be noted that, in positive law, if we exclude some specific statute, liability without fault does not seem to have gone very far beyond the cases emphasised by the authors of the last century. Excepting the German legal system, where we can count fewer than a dozen laws focused on objective liability, the legislation of European countries, specifically that of Italy, did not receive the inputs already included in the civil code, cf Castronovo (n 126) 284. Objective liability was essentially provided for such specific cases as the law regarding the pacific use of nuclear energy (1860/1962) and the law regarding the falling of space objects (23/1983). More relevant are the law regarding damage done by defective products (206/2005) and the law regarding producers of toys and cosmetics. For the special cases of objective liability in our legal system see some initial information at Alpa (n 152) 978.

[168] Pietro Trimarchi, *Rischio e responsabilità oggettiva* (Giuffrè 1961), and in general Alpa (n 145) 293.

[169] See D.41.1.54.1, on which see Valditara (n 126) 414, and more recently Valditara (n 9) 39.

who was appointed by the victim, and in the interest of the latter, to be a member of his economic organisation.

As was clearly observed, the wrongdoer is held liable by reason of the principle of objective liability, 'indipendentemente dal livello dei suoi investimenti in prevenzione'[170] and thus 'non vi è alcun livello di prevenzione che possa salvare il danneggiante dalla responsabilità'.[171]

In light of this standard, the fact that every measure was taken to avoid damage can only operate on the kind of liability, because such a fact excludes only criminal liability, which must always and necessarily be founded on fault[172] whenever no negligence can be ascribed to the wrongdoer.

Obviously, someone who caused damage with justification cannot be liable. Particularly relevant is art 2044, which excludes all liability if damage was caused because of self-defence or the defence of others. As was highlighted:

> La legittima difesa è una norma di nuova introduzione: infatti, non esisteva nel c.c. del 1865 e neppure nel code Napoléon. Insieme allo stato di necessità, costituisce una causa di giustificazione nel sistema dell'illecito civile: esclude che il danno sia ingiusto, poiché la lesione prodotta, ancorché *contra ius*, è *iure*: manca cioè uno degli elementi dell'*iniuria*.[173]

This innovation of the Italian civil code keeps pace with the evolution of the concept of *iniuria*/unjust damage, which is now detached from culpability. We come full circle and we return, at least as a trend, to the starting point, that is, we tend to punish every damage caused without justification. In the case of the state of necessity, a fair restitution is however provided.[174] Thus, we see the return of the idea of *iniuria* as '*contra ius*', that is, '*sine iure*' – without justification.

Furthermore, the explicitly solidaristic vision that the courts (and the scholars) developed in the last decades marks a deep difference from the original Aquilian scheme, where the need to protect property without conditions was central and where the interest of the *paterfamilias* to the integrity of his goods was considered crucial and was defended. It was this need to defend the property unconditionally to determine the penal characterisation of the *actio legis Aquiliae* that was probably the reason for the following emerging relevance of the subjective element.

Today, the centrality of property as a value is replaced with the central-

---

[170]   See Monateri (n 151) 40.

[171]   ibid 41.

[172]   Along these lines, see art 27 of the Italian Constitution. On this point, see Bricola, 'Teoria generale del reato' *NNDI* vol 19 (Utet 1973) 53.

[173]   See Massimo Franzoni, 'Dei fatti illeciti' in Antonio Scialoja and Giuseppe Branca (eds), *Commentario al codice civile* (Zanichelli 1993) on arts 2043–59, 289.

[174]   See art 2045 of the civil code.

ity of the person:[175] looking at this point more closely, the return to *iniuria* as unlawfulness, that is, as an infringement of legally relevant interests, is functional to the idea of an action for damages that defends the human being in all their possible aspects, against every kind of unjustified damage to their sphere of interests. The *ABGB* (para 1293) and the *BGB* (para 823) tended, not casually, towards this perspective: in the former, it states that damage is every loss caused to someone's the assets, rights or person; in the latter, damage can follow a violation of someone's life, body, health, freedom, property or any other right. At this point, we cannot fail to highlight a curious consonance with the most ancient Roman law, where the unjustified act *par excellence* – the delict of *iniuria* of the 12 Tables – was against the human person.[176] But that is another story.

---

[175] Cf Nicola Rescigno, *Introduzione al Codice civile* (7th edn, Laterza 2001) 159 where, highlighting the difference from the preceding code, the author emphasised the 'accresciuta sfera di protezione del singolo, soprattutto con riguardo alle esplicazioni della persona, laddove nella passata esperienza la responsabilità aquiliana poteva esaurire quasi interamente la sua azione nella difesa dei beni e nella tutela dell'integrità fisica dell'individuo'.

[176] Cf Valditara (n 9) 106.

Chapter 9

Lord Atkin, Donoghue v Stevenson *and the* Lex Aquilia: *Civilian Roots of the 'Neighbour' Principle*

Robin Evans-Jones and Helen Scott

1. INTRODUCTION

Scotland was an independent kingdom until the union of the crowns of Scotland and England in 1603 with the accession of James VI of Scotland to the English crown. Scotland ceased to be a separate state only in 1707 when, by the Acts of Union, it combined with England (and Wales) as constituents of the single state of Great Britain. This union later came to include Ireland; hence Scotland is now part of the union state of the United Kingdom of Great Britain and Northern Ireland (UK). Under the terms of the union the Scottish Parliament in Edinburgh was dissolved and in its place a single parliament was based at the Palace of Westminster in London which hitherto had been the seat of the English Parliament. The Parliament of the UK comprises two chambers, the House of Commons and the House of Lords. In a referendum in 1997 the Scots voted in favour of devolution from Westminster and in 1999 a new devolved Scottish Parliament met for the first time in Edinburgh (Holyrood). Private law matters fall within the competence of the Scottish Parliament. In 2014 a referendum was held on whether Scotland should become an independent state once more (Indyref1). By a margin of 55 per cent to 45 per cent the Scots voted to maintain the union. One issue of some influence on the result was the doubt, strongly encouraged by the European Union (EU) itself, that Scotland could remain within the EU if it became independent from the UK. In June 2016 a referendum on whether the UK should leave the EU was held (Brexit). By a margin of 51.9 per cent to 48.1 per cent the UK voted to leave. In Scotland 62 per cent of the electorate voted to remain. The Scottish First Minister has now announced (March 2017) that she will ask the Scottish Parliament to support an application to Westminster to give the Scottish Government the power to hold a second referendum on independence (Indyref2). If the Scottish people were to vote for independence it is hoped by the present Scottish Government that this would enable Scotland to remain within the European Union. As things stand (September 2017) there may be a second referendum, but only once the details of Brexit are known.

This brief overview of the constitutional relations between Scotland and England highlights a commonality and equivocation that is also found in the relationship between their legal systems. The Scottish legal system was recognised as separate from that of England by the Acts of Union of 1707; however, in private law disputes the judicial committee of the House of Lords (being the Monarch in Parliament) came to be recognised as the final court of appeal, not only for England but, in non-criminal matters, also for Scotland. Since 2009 this role has been performed by the UK Supreme Court sitting in London.

Commonly the modern Scottish legal system is described as 'mixed', showing in its private law significant and relatively unintegrated blocks drawn from the civilian (Roman law) tradition and the English common law. How Scots private law came to be 'mixed' and whether it was a good thing is a matter which over the years has given rise to considerable debate, the positions taken depending largely upon the cultural and political outlooks of those involved. Notable extremes are represented by Thomas (T B) Smith and Alan Rodger, Lord Rodger of Earlsferry. Smith revered the early modern Scots law as pure because it was civilian. Its later mixture with English law, in his view, was unnatural and often functionally dissonant as represented by his metaphor of the 'common-law cuckoo'.[1] Rodger, a staunch unionist, poured scorn on what he saw to be Smith's misplaced romanticism.[2] He did not deny that Scottish law had had a civilian past but suggested that Scots lawyers in the nineteenth century, like those in the rest of Europe, rightly turned away from the old books of the *ius commune* which had increasingly become unfathomable to them. While Europe chose to modernise by codification, Scots law was brought up to date by judges who, in the practice of the English common law, over time built up bodies of precedent based on long exposure to, and understanding of, the real-life practical and commercial needs of modern society. In Rodger's opinion, statements of broad legal principle – usually a product of civilian university-based learning – were properly regarded with scepticism by judges of the common law as too abstract and remote from reality to be workable in the practical legal world. In addition, UK judges were consistently aware of the need to provide a lead in establishing sound workable rules of law for use throughout the worldwide British Empire.

As regards the quality of the Scottish 'mixed' legal system, opinions have differed. Some have viewed it as the end product of a process of critical choosing by lawyers over many years of what was best in the civilian and common-law traditions.[3] *Ex facie*, then, Scots law is therefore better than

---

[1]   Eg Thomas Broun Smith, 'The Common-Law Cuckoo: Problems of "Mixed" Legal Systems with Special Reference to Restrictive Interpretations in the Scots Law of Obligations' (1956) Scottish Law Review 147; *Studies Critical and Comparative* (W Green 1962) 89.

[2]   'Thinking about Scots Law' (1996) 1 Edin LR 3; '"Say Not the Struggle Naught Availeth": The Costs and Benefits of Mixed Legal Systems' (2003) 78 Tulane Law Review 419.

[3]   Eg Lord Cooper of Culross, 'The Scottish Legal Tradition' reprinted in *The Scottish Legal Tradition* (Saltire and Stair Society 1991) 65.

all others. A modality on the 'better' idea is that its past eclecticism at least now offers contemporary lawyers wider choices when seeking solutions to the problems before them.[4] In this it has been argued that there is an unusually ancient and unbroken Scottish legal tradition on which to draw.[5] Smith, on the other hand, regarded Scots private law as worse for the influence of English law since it diluted the integrity of the civilian laws and system, while Rodger regarded the reception of English law and the common-law method as positive modernising developments. Robin Evans-Jones has argued that 'reception' is at the root of the 'mixed' nature of the Scottish legal system.[6] Reception is normally a non-deliberative process which comes about when lawyers form a preference for, and therefore take over on a large scale, laws which are not their own. Some might now say that it results from a 'colonisation' of their minds.[7] In the special circumstances in which a 'reception' occurs it is irresistible, and for that reason there is little point in regarding it as either good or bad: it simply 'is' or 'has been'. The law of Scotland has experienced two receptions brought about by powerful cultural and political forces which it has been unable to resist. These receptions were the natural outcome of the circumstances in which Scotland found itself at particular times in its history.

The first reception was brought about by education. From the earliest of times a legal training in Scotland was acquired at university. The example of the University of Aberdeen is instructive. It was founded in 1495 partly as a law school. Bishop Elphinstone, its founder, instructed that Roman law was to be taught according to the model of the University of Orléans and canon law according to the model of the University of Paris. Elphinstone was typical of Scottish students of the time in having acquired his training as a lawyer on the European Continent, in his case at these two great French universities. However, even after the founding of law schools in the Scottish universities like that in Aberdeen, for a considerable time the teaching of law in Scotland proved to be unsuccessful and, following the Reformation, Scots in the sixteenth, seventeenth and eighteenth centuries went mainly to the universities of the Netherlands for their legal education. The curriculum in the universities was the *Corpus Iuris Civilis*. When they returned home,

---

[4] Cf Kenneth Reid, 'The Idea of Mixed Legal Systems' (2003) 78 Tulane Law Review 5.

[5] Cf W David H Sellar, 'Scots Law: Mixed from the Very Beginning? A Tale of Two Receptions' (2000) 4 Edin LR 3.

[6] 'Unjust Enrichment, Contract and the Third Reception of Roman Law in Scotland' (1993) 109 LQR 663; 'Receptions of Law, Mixed Legal Systems and the Myth of the Genius of Scots Private Law' (1998) 114 LQR 228; 'Roman Law in Scotland and England and the Development of One Law for Britain' (1999) 115 LQR 605; 'Mixed Legal Systems, Scotland, and the Unification of Private Law in Europe' in J Smits (ed), *The Contribution of Mixed Legal Systems to European Private Law* (Intersentia 2001) 39.

[7] Cf Ngũgĩ wa Thiong'o, *Decolonising the Mind: The Politics of Language in African Literature* (Heinemann 1986).

unsurprisingly the lawyers were inclined to apply Roman law in the cases
that came before them because this is what they had been trained in. Thereby
indigenous Scottish laws were sometimes supplanted by Roman law. Roman
law was useful also because, as a gap filler in the indigenous laws, it enabled
complete systematic statements of Scots law to be made. In Scotland there
was a reception of Roman law but because it came relatively late, it was not
in complexu as in Germany.

During the nineteenth century, however, the Scots came to view themselves increasingly as British.[8] With the English they were now members of
the same state, they shared the same language, the same monarch, the same
parliament, the same religion and the same enemies, and the Scots were
enthusiastic beneficiaries of British colonisation. To many it must also have
seemed odd that the mother nation of a worldwide empire had two quite
distinct legal systems. There was a clear perception that a lead had to be given
to the Empire in legal matters and inevitably there were pressures for unification of laws within the UK on the basis of the immensely more powerful
English law. The current population of England is 54.3 million and that of
Scotland 5.3 million. The disparity is very considerable in terms of overall
impact. In time the USA came also to be regarded as a close legal friend
of the UK, not as a member of the Empire but as a particularly significant
partner within the worldwide, eclectic family of the common law. Scotland
was, and remains, a constituent part of the UK, of the mother nation of the
British Empire and of the family of the common law.

This shift in the prevailing political culture had a huge effect on how
Scottish lawyers came to regard both the content and methodology of
Scottish law. Court practice, practical judicial reasoning and precedent inevitably gained in stature in the minds of the lawyers over the intellectualised
'text'-driven doctrine of the civil law drawn from the *Corpus Iuris Civilis* and
widely expressed in Latin. A pressing problem of an uncodified civilian legal
system is that it does not have a clear mechanism by which to determine
what is authoritative in the (too) many texts of which it is composed. As
Rodger makes clear, the uncodified civilian tradition and its 'old books'
must have appeared not only anachronistic but unmanageable to the modern
British Scots lawyers. Due to these factors, the second reception of laws in
Scotland was of English law and the doctrine of *stare decisis*, with the result
that significant parts of the Scottish civilian heritage were either forgotten or
actively suppressed. From one perspective this reception was as brutal as the
first: when viewed from afar, receptions are inevitably disruptive, and only
major events, political or cultural, can explain them. However, in practice
they happen largely unconsciously and over a long period of time: one set
of legal rules and ways of doing things is replaced with another according to

---

[8] See Linda Colley, *Britons: Forging the Nation 1707–1837* (Yale University Press 2009).

the preference of the lawyers who bring them about. Those Scots lawyers who were involved in the changes that 'reception' brought about of course regarded it as a positive development.

It is against the backdrop of Scottish legal culture during the first half of the twentieth century that we propose to examine *Donoghue v Stevenson*.[9] This case forms part of the essential iconography of Scots law. It appears in all the books and many commentaries have been devoted to it.[10] A substantial plaque has been erected on the site in Paisley of the Wellmeadow café (since demolished) where May (McAllister) Donoghue ingested a decomposed snail. Although the events took place in Scotland, the final decision as to relevancy was made by the House of Lords on the basis of English law alone. Therefore, why the case should be regarded as so important for Scots law is not immediately clear. One possibility is that it decided an issue of great importance on the basis of 'general' jurisprudence common to both jurisdictions. *Ex facie*, the two Scottish judges on the side of the majority in the House of Lords discovered a long-standing principle in English law which two of the dissenting English judges themselves failed to recognise in their own law. However, the pivotal, inspirational figure in the decision was Lord Atkin, who was not a Scot but Welsh, Australian born. Reinhard Zimmermann records that his famous *dictum* in the case[11] has variously been hailed as 'a seed of an oak tree, a source of inspiration, a beacon of hope, a fountain of sparkling wisdom, a skyrocket in the midnight sky'.[12] Rodger describes it as 'probably the most famous case in the whole Commonwealth world of the common law'.[13] Clearly something very important was going on. Lord Buckmaster, who dissented, has fallen into relative obscurity, yet he gave a superb judgment that eschewed abstractions and founded on what

---

[9] *Donoghue v Stevenson* [1932] SC (HL) 31.

[10] See esp Matthew Chapman, *The Snail and the Ginger Beer, The Singular Case of Donoghue v Stevenson* (Wildy, Simmonds & Hill 2010).

[11] 'The liability for negligence, whether you style it such or treat it as in other systems as a species of "culpa," is no doubt based upon a general public sentiment of moral wrongdoing for which the offender must pay. But acts or omissions which any moral code would censure cannot, in a practical world, be treated so as to give a right to every person injured by them to demand relief. In this way rules of law arise which limit the range of complainants and the extent of their remedy. The rule that you are to love your neighbour becomes in law, you must not injure your neighbour; and the lawyer's question, Who is my neighbour? receives a restricted reply. You must take reasonable care to avoid acts or omissions which you can reasonably foresee would be likely to injure your neighbour. Who, then, in law, is my neighbour? The answer seems to be – persons who are so closely and directly affected by my act that I ought reasonably to have them in contemplation as being so affected when I am directing my mind to the acts or omissions which are called in question ...' [44].

[12] Reinhard Zimmermann, *The Law of Obligations: Roman Foundations of the Civilian Tradition* (Juta 1990) 1039 n 264, citing A M Linden, 'The Good Neighbour on Trial: A Fountain of Sparkling Wisdom' (1983) 17 University of British Columbia Law Review 67.

[13] Alan Rodger, 'Mrs Donoghue and Alfenus Varus' (1988) 41 Current Legal Problems 1, 2.

he saw to be the established precedents of English law. By contrast, Lord Atkin, on the basis of his judgment in favour of Mrs Donoghue, quickly became a, if not *the*, leading celebrity of the common law. Drawing from his personal religiosity,[14] he expressed a broad principle of law founded upon the idea of 'neighbourhood'. He then limited the principle, seeking thereby to make it workable in the real world. His expressions of the principle and its limitations were both superbly elegant and effective to revolutionise the understanding of the English tort of negligence. It is therefore not surprising that Scots lawyers like to take some gratification from the decision whose events in Paisley, at least, were theirs.

The purpose of this chapter is to examine some of the puzzles that remain after *Donoghue v Stevenson*. Mrs Donoghue was a pauper who successfully carried her claim through to the House of Lords notwithstanding its rejection by the Scottish Court of Session on the basis of English law authority that had very recently been followed by the Scottish Court.[15] She cannot have done so alone. It is possible that powerful members of the English establish-ment supported her because they thought that the restrictive understanding of 'duty of care' in contemporary English law, which had been received into Scots law, was ill-suited to the demands of a modern consumer society and out of step with 'general' jurisprudence. They saw Mrs Donoghue's claim as the opportunity to change English law and to provide a lead to the British Empire. This support is likely to have been essential to the progress of her case to the House of Lords.

A second puzzle pertains to the nature of Lord Atkin's role in the for-mulation of the general principle for which *Donoghue* is famous. The status which Lord Atkin has assumed in the common law on the basis of his judgment was attributed to him even by his contemporaries and has been sustained by later generations. The 'neighbourhood' principle is now univer-sally regarded as his own creation. But that is not the case. There can be no doubt that the principle was drawn from the civilian tradition, in particular from the teachings of the natural lawyers. On the other hand, the restrictions placed upon it by Lord Atkin appear to have been drawn from the humanist tradition, and perhaps specifically from Donellus. These – both the princi-ple and the restrictions – were expressions of general civilian jurisprudence which had been well known to English lawyers for hundreds of years. Any idea that English lawyers of the time were not fully conversant with the doc-trines of the civilian tradition is untrue, as a brief reference to the works of Sir Frederick Pollock makes perfectly clear. Atkin was nevertheless creative

---

[14] See e.g. Elspeth Reid, 'The Snail in the Ginger Beer Float, *Donoghue v Stevenson*' in John Grant and Elaine Sutherland (eds) *Scots Law Tales* (Dundee University Press 2010) 83, 90–91.

[15] In *Mullen v Barr* 1929 SC 461. See, further, William McBryde, '*Donoghue v Stevenson*: The Story of the "Snail in a Bottle Case"', in Alan Gamble (ed), *Obligations in Context: Essays in Honour of Professor D M Walker* (W Green 1990) 13, 22.

in bringing together these two strands of civilian jurisprudence in his famous summation in favour of Mrs Donoghue.

Lord Macmillan, one of the Scottish judges in the House of Lords, did, in the end, support Mrs Donoghue's claim on his reading of English law, but only the second time round.[16] In the first version of his speech he was doubtful whether English law supported her claim but was of the view that Scots law did. The first judgment was never delivered and was later changed. The hearing of the appeal before the House of Lords had to be delayed because of his *volte face*. In the final event the decision of the House of Lords went in favour of Mrs Donoghue on the basis of English law, but only by a majority of three to two: the two Scottish judges on the bench of five, Lords Macmillan and Thankerton, combined with Australian-born Lord Atkin, in a statement of what was English law against the dissenting English judges, Lords Buckmaster and Tomlin. It is clear from the language of the latter two that they were angry at the result. This, too, merits some further examination.

In fact, *Donoghue* is closely connected with another Scottish case that some years earlier (1923) had ended up on appeal from Scotland to the House of Lords: *Cantiere San Rocco SA v Clyde Shipbuilding and Engineering Co Ltd*.[17] The subject matters of the cases were very different, but the strategic factors at play as regards law reform in each were inter-related.[18] They both show how derivative of English law Scots law had become, since in both the pursuers' claim was rejected by the Scottish Court of Session on the basis of English law authority. The English law in question had been decided only at the level of the Court of Appeal and was disapproved of by contemporary leading English lawyers who wanted it changed. The appeals from Scotland to the House of Lords in both cases were seen to be the opportunity to change English law. Normally the direction of the 'reception' in Scotland was towards English law, as the decisions of the Court of Session in both *Cantiere* and *Donoghue* show. Yet in both appeals to the House of Lords, Scots law doctrine drawn from its civilian tradition was the bridge over which the English law that was in force was led in order to change it. In *Cantiere* the intended change of English law by the House of Lords was unsuccessful because Lord Shaw founded too expressly upon Scottish law drawn from the civil law which could not be treated as authoritative in England.

The lack of success in *Cantiere* was precisely the reason why Lord Macmillan amended his first judgment in *Donoghue*. In fact, the neighbourhood principle identified by Lord Atkin was clearly expressed by one of the Scottish Institutional writers, Erskine, in a passage referred to by Lord

---

[16] See Alan Rodger, 'Lord Macmillan's Speech in Donoghue v Stevenson' (1992) 108 LQR 236.

[17] 1923 SC (HL) 105.

[18] For a more detailed treatment of the issues, see Robin Evans-Jones (1999) 115 LQR 605.

Macmillan in his first judgment. Lord Atkin must have been fully conversant with this first judgment. Lord Macmillan removed this reference to Erskine from the second version of his judgment in order to suppress the Scottish sources upon which he had relied in finding for Mrs Donoghue. As will be shown, the debt to the civilian tradition in *Donoghue* is beyond question, but it had to be hidden in order to ensure that the decision of the House of Lords changed English law. This was a lesson which had been learned from the unhappy experience of the over-reliance by Lord Shaw in the House of Lords on civilian doctrine drawn from Scots law in *Cantiere*.

2. DONOGHUE V STEVENSON IN CONTEXT: THE LESSON FROM CANTIERE

In 1928 May Donoghue travelled with a friend from Glasgow to Paisley, just outside Glasgow. In the Wellmeadow café the friend ordered her some ice cream and ginger beer (ginger beer float) from the café owner, Mr Minchella. He poured out some of the ginger beer which Mrs Donoghue drank. When her friend poured the remainder, out of the bottle popped a partly decomposed snail. At the sight of it Mrs Donoghue suffered immediate nervous shock and subsequent severe gastroenteritis.

Could Mrs Donoghue raise a claim in the Scots law of delict against the manufacturer? In the English tort of negligence a wrongdoer is not liable for harm negligently caused unless he or she owes a duty of care to the victim and that duty is breached. In *Mullen v Barr*[19] the Scots law on the matter as it related to the manufacture of defective goods had very recently (1929) been stated to be the same as English law. Two children had suffered injury from drinking a bottle of ginger beer, bought for them by their father, which contained the body of a dead mouse. The Court of Session held, *inter alia*, that a manufacturer owed no duty of care to the consumer unless the goods were dangerous *per se* and no warning had been given or, if the goods were not dangerous *per se*, the manufacturer knew of the danger and had failed to give due warning to the purchaser. The pursuers relied heavily on the contrary authority of *George v Skivington*,[20] to the effect that a duty of care was owed by the manufacturer, but it was doubted that this represented the law of England.[21] Since ginger beer is not inherently dangerous, the Court of Session rejected the claim.

The consumer who suffered loss from defective goods but who was not entitled to a claim in delict was expected to raise a claim in contract against the supplier who in turn could sue the manufacturer in contract if the manufacturer had been at fault. Thereby, it was thought, proper limits were

---

[19] 1929 SC 461.
[20] (1869) L.R. 5 Ex. 1.
[21] See esp Lord Justice-Clerk Alness [469]–[470].

placed on the potential liability of manufacturers who might otherwise be responsible to a huge number of consumers for the fault of others (such as suppliers to the consumer) over which they had no control. However, no claim in contract lay in the name of Mrs Donoghue against the café owner because she had not bought the ginger beer, and no assignment of rights on the contract could be made to her by her friend who had suffered no injury.

The wider background to the Scottish appeal to the House of Lords in *Donoghue* was the earlier Scottish appeal to the House of Lords in *Cantiere*. Behind *Cantiere* in turn stood the so-called 'Coronation' cases of English law, for example *Chandler v Webster* (1904).[22] In *Chandler* the plaintiff had hired, for the considerable sum at the time of £141 15s, a room on the Mall from which to view the coronation of Edward VII. The sum of £100 was paid in advance. The procession was postponed because the king had appendicitis; at issue was whether the money was recoverable. It was held not only that the £100 was not recoverable but that the balance of £41 15s was payable to the defendant. The rather odd result was reached due to complications regarding the meaning, according to context, of 'consideration'. 'Consideration' is a necessary requirement to form a contract in English law. In the law of restitution its failure also appears as an essential requirement of the claim on which the plaintiff in *Chandler* relied: claim to recover money given for a consideration that had totally failed. The king's illness did not avoid the contract for the hire of the rooms so, according to the reasoning of the Court of Appeal, since the contract required consideration and it was still in existence, there cannot by definition have been a total failure of consideration to found a claim in restitution because of the cancellation of the coronation. The matter was viewed by the court as an incidence of risk under the contract, which explains why the balance was also held to have been payable.

Cantiere concerned a valid contract for the manufacture of marine engines under the terms of which the pursuers made a payment up front to a Scottish company. The First World War broke out which rendered the contract, not void, but legally impossible to perform because the pursuers were now enemy aliens. At the end of the war they reclaimed the money that had been paid in advance. Before the Court of Session their claim was rejected on the authority of the Court of Appeal in *Chandler v Webster*. Thereafter the matter was taken on appeal to the House of Lords. The claim was presented as a *condictio causa data causa non secuta* which was drawn in origin from Roman law and which was now part of 'received' Scots law. As translated by the House of Lords it was treated as the claim to recover what was given for a consideration that had totally failed, that is, it was exactly the same as the claim of the English law of restitution. Its utility was that its formulation highlighted the error of the Court of Appeal in confusing the meaning of 'consideration' in

[22] [1904] 1KB 493.

contract with its meaning in the law of restitution. In the latter context the formulation showed that the failure of the consideration for the payment of money (*causa data*) lay in the failure of 'performance' (*causa non secuta*) not in the failure (invalidity) of the actual contract. Therefore, as applied to *Chandler v Webster*, it would mean that since the plaintiff did not get the room to view the coronation (performance) he was entitled to get his money back even though the contract itself had not been avoided.[23]

The wider intention was that the House of Lords in *Cantiere* should overrule the doctrine expressed by the Court of Appeal in the *Coronation* cases. Lord Shaw remarked in his judgment:[24]

> I am not surprised that there is in high legal quarters a feeling both of uneasiness and of disrelish as to the English rule, and that that feeling has found expression. I cite, for instance, the language of *Sir Frederick Pollock* (emphasis supplied) in his work on Contracts (8th ed.), p.440 ... Only the House of Lords can review these decisions, but they are not universally approved by the profession.

In the end result the appeal in *Cantiere* to the House of Lords was effective to change Scots law but not English law. Why did it have this limited effect if in the Court of Session, as was also to be the case in *Donoghue*, Scots law had just been held to be the same as English law?[25] In his judgment, at times in disparaging terms, Lord Shaw drew a clear distinction between the English approach as expressed by the *Coronation* cases and what he understood to be the current position in Scots law if that was properly understood. For example, he conjectured that had the pursuers paid the full price in advance:[26]

> The builder [of the engines according to the *Coronation* cases] would retain as his own the whole price of an article which he never supplied and would never supply. Counsel was right; the 'something for nothing' doctrine goes the whole length. This result under other systems of jurisprudence might be viewed as monstrous; but in England, it was contended, this is the law, and the principle is worthy of acceptance in Scotland – such is the argument.

In substantiating his understanding of Scots law Lord Shaw made copious reference to Roman jurists, the Digest of Justinian and to the Scottish institutional writers. The result was to establish a sufficient differentiation between Scots and English law to prevent the decision of the House of Lords allowing the pursuers to recover their pre-payment from being authoritative in English law. It overruled the *Coronation* cases only for Scots law. It was not

---

[23] For more detail, see Evans-Jones (n 18).

[24] *Cantiere San Rocco v Clyde Engineering and Shipbuilding Co Ltd* 1923 SC 725; 1923 SC (HL) 105 [121].

[25] As understood by the House of Lords, including Lord Shaw, the *condictio* claim was in substance exactly the same as the claim in the English law of restitution, the only difference being that it was expressed in Latin and highlighted the issue of failure of performance.

[26] [121].

until 1942 in *Fibrosa Spolka Akcyjna v Fairbairn Lawson Combe Barbour Ltd*[27] that the opportunity arose once more for the House of Lords to address the matter for English law, when, following the lead given in *Cantiere*, it held that the plaintiffs were entitled to recover what they had paid in advance. In *Fibrosa* Lord Shaw was strongly rebuked by Viscount Simon[28] for the tenor of his judgment in *Cantiere* and, as Lord Macmillan observed in his judgment in *Fibrosa* (on which Lord Atkin also sat), 'The mills of the law grind slowly'.[29] Shortly thereafter English law was given a statutory basis in the Law Reform (Frustrated Contracts) Act 1943. Scots law is still governed by its common law as stated by the House of Lords in *Cantiere*. Notwithstanding this difference between the two jurisdictions, in cases of 'frustration' both moved from a regime of allocation of risks under contract to one based on unjustified enrichment as that was expressed in *Cantiere*.

3. DONOGHUE V STEVENSON BEFORE THE HOUSE OF LORDS

In the light of *Mullen v Barr* the hearing in *Donoghue* proceeded on the reasonable understanding that English law was the same as Scots law. It was held by the House of Lords that English law does recognise that a duty of care is owed by a manufacturer to the consumer of its products because the consumer is a 'neighbour' to the manufacturer, who is therefore under an obligation to take reasonable care to ensure that the consumer is not harmed by its negligent production of, for example, ginger beer. The decision established a principled basis on which to determine whether a duty of care is owed which was a major change to the limited individualised circumstances in which a duty of care was recognised in most of the English case law that had been decided in the lower courts. It settled the uncertainty in the decisions of the lower courts and, as will be shown, it responded to pressures from influential English lawyers outwith the House of Lords who had been pushing for a more generalised approach to the duty of care. The decision was by majority on a split of three to two. The two dissenting English judges, Lords Buckmaster and Tomlin, argued very forcefully, indeed angrily, against the recognition of the broad principle which the other judges of the House of Lords discovered in English law.

Lords Buckmaster and Tomlin

Lord Buckmaster, referring to *Heaven v Pender*, said:[30] 'this ... has been used as a *tabula in naufragio* for many litigants struggling in the seas of adverse

---

[27] [1943] A.C. 32.
[28] [44].
[29] [57].
[30] [39].

authority'. Referring also to *George v Skivington* he said:[31] 'it is, in my opinion, better that they should be buried so securely that their perturbed spirits shall no longer vex the law'. And, 'If one step, why not fifty?'[32] He also approved the 'emphatic language' of Lord Anderson in *Mullen v Barr* who said that 'in a case like the present, where the goods of the defenders are widely distributed throughout Scotland, it would seem little short of outrageous to make them responsible to members of the public ...'.[33] Lord Tomlin referred to the 'alarming consequences'[34] of accepting the general proposition argued for by Mrs Donoghue.

Lord Macmillan

As already noted, Alan Rodger discovered that Lord Macmillan rewrote the speech that he had first intended to deliver and that the hearing of the appeal before the House of Lords was delayed for some months as a result. Rodger analyses in detail the differences between the first and second versions of the speech:[35]

> What Lord Macmillan has done ... is to excise the examination of Scots law which he originally placed at the forefront of his speech ... Not only did Lord Macmillan originally begin by looking at the Scots law: he actually professed to decide the case on the basis of Scots law ... Lord Macmillan concludes his survey of Scots law by saying that if English law had reached an unreasonable and unjust result: 'I see no reason why the law of Scotland should follow suit. In my opinion the native principles of Scots law are quite adequate for the disposal of the present case and there is certainly no decision of your Lordships on this branch of the law of Scotland which requires a Scottish Judge to offend his legal conscience by following it.[36]

Rodger noted:

> It is fair, I think, to say that Lord Macmillan is less than positive in his formulation of the English position ... Contrast that approach with what he says in his [second speech] where he takes a much more positive view on the relevant English law:[37] 'For myself, I am satisfied that there is no speciality of Scots law involved, and that the case may safely be decided on principles common to both systems ...'.

Rodger rightly surmised that Lord Atkin prevailed on Lord Macmillan to alter his speech because he wanted the House of Lords to deliver a decision

---

[31] [42].
[32] [42].
[33] [43].
[34] [57].
[35] Rodger (n 16) 238–39.
[36] ibid Appendix 252.
[37] [71]–[72].

in favour of the recognition of a duty of care for the common law as a whole. Lord Macmillan's first speech was very like that of Lord Shaw in *Cantiere* in both content (heavily reliant on purely Scottish authorities) and tone (jingoistic) and Lord Atkin knew that there was every likelihood that if it were not rewritten the decision of the House of Lords would not change English law.

As regards the Scottish content of the first speech Rodger observes that:[38]

> What we find is that Lord Macmillan cites some rather unhelpful passages from Stair, Erskine and Bell [Scottish Institutional writers] … [A]lthough Lord Macmillan visited what he called 'the fountain heads of Scots law' his trip was essentially a detour which achieved little even in purely Scottish terms. We lost nothing of significance for Scots law when he altered his speech …

It has already been noted that Rodger was a staunch unionist and a champion of the English common law. Whether he was right to dismiss the influence of the Scottish authorities so thoroughly may be doubted. One of the passages to which Lord Macmillan refers that was excised from the first speech was the following from Erskine, the eighteenth-century Scottish institutional writer:[39]

> *Alterum non laedere* is one of the three general precepts laid down by Justinian which it has been the chief purpose of all civil enactments to enforce. In consequence of this rule, everyone who has the exercise of reason, and so can distinguish between right and wrong, is naturally obliged to make up the damage befalling his neighbour from a wrong committed by himself … wrong may arise, not only from positive acts … but from blameable omission.

This is the expression of a general principle of delictual liability founded upon the Aquilian principle of *damnum iniuria datum* by the natural lawyers.[40] Nils Jansen has recently given an insightful overview of its importance to the understanding of liability for fault in the western legal tradition.[41] The principle has been received by a number of modern legal systems, *inter alia*, French law,[42] South African law[43] and the state law of Louisiana.[44]

---

[38] 241–42.

[39] *An Institute of the Law of Scotland* 3, 1, 13.

[40] See e.g. Hugo Grotius, *De Iure Belli Ac Pacis* II.17 (edn BJA de Kanter-van Hettinga Tromp 1939, reissued Scientia 1993)

[41] 'The Development of Legal Doctrine in Europe: Extracontractual Liability for Fault' in Niels Jansen (ed), *The Development and Making of Legal Doctrine* (CUP 2014).

[42] Civil Code art 1382: 'Any act whatever of man which causes damage to another obliges him by whose fault it occurred to make reparation'.

[43] See e.g. Johan Neethling, 'Tort Law in South Africa, The Mixing of the General and the Particular' in Jan Smits (ed), *The Contribution of Mixed Legal Systems to European Private Law* (Intersentia 2001); Johan Neethling and Jopie Potgieter, *Neethling – Potgieter – Visser: Law of Delict*, (7th edn, LexisNexis 2015).

[44] Civil Code art 2315:'Every act whatever of man that causes damage to another obliges him by whose fault it occurred to repair it'.

It represents the culmination of a process of generalisation which begins with the discussion of the *lex Aquilia* by the Roman jurists in Title 9.2 of Justinian's Digest.

Lord Atkin

The decision of the House of Lords in *Donoghue v Stevenson* has assumed iconic status in the common law mainly because of the judgment of Lord Atkin. It was underpinned by his disbelief that English law was 'so remote from the ordinary needs of civilized society and the ordinary claims it makes upon its members as to deny a legal remedy where there is so obviously a social wrong'.[45] Notwithstanding the breadth of his judgment, the focus here will be on the following famous passage:[46]

> In English law there must be, and is, some general conception of relations giving rise to a duty of care, of which the particular cases found in the books are but instances. The liability for negligence, whether you style it such or treat it as in other systems as a species of '*culpa*', is no doubt based upon a general public sentiment of moral wrongdoing for which the offender must pay. But acts of omissions which any moral code would censure cannot, in a practical world, be treated so as to give a right to every person injured by them to demand relief. In this way rules of law arise which limit the range of complainants and the extent of their remedy. The rule that you are to love your neighbour becomes in law, you must not injure your neighbour; and the lawyer's question, Who is my neighbour? receives a restricted reply. You must take reasonable care to avoid acts or omissions which you can reasonably foresee would be likely to injure your neighbour. Who then is my neighbour? The answer seems to be – persons who are so closely and directly affected by my act that I ought reasonably to have had them in contemplation as being so affected when I am directing my mind to the acts or omissions which are called in question. This appears to me to be the doctrine of *Heaven v Pender*... I think the judgment of Lord Esher [in *Heaven v Pender*] expresses the law of England.[47]

It is useful to compare parts of Lord Atkin's speech with the passage of Erskine quoted above. Lord Atkin said: 'you must not injure your neighbour ... You must take reasonable care to avoid acts or omissions which you can reasonably foresee would be likely to injure your neighbour'.

Like Erskine, he distinguishes between acts and omissions. He then, in effect, reproduces in English the admonition *alterum non laedere* and, where Erskine says that one must make good a loss caused wrongfully to one's neighbour, Atkin says that one must take reasonable care to avoid acts or omissions that one can reasonably foresee would injure one's neighbour. In

[45]   [46].
[46]   [44].
[47]   [44]–[45].

fact, the responsibility of a wrongdoer to the 'neighbour' found in Erskine has a long provenance also in English law. Francis Buller in his *Introduction to the Law of Trials at Nisi Prius* (first published anonymously in 1767) states:[48]

> Every man ought to take reasonable care that he does not injure his neighbour; therefore, wherever a man receives hurt thro' the default of another, tho' the same were not wilful, yet if it be occasioned by negligence or folly, the law gives him an action to recover damages for the injury so sustained.

Again, the similarities with Lord Atkin's speech are very clear. Both state that there is a duty to take reasonable care not to injure one's neighbour.

David Ibbetson has shown that in its pre-nineteenth-century history the English tort of negligence was profoundly influenced by the teaching of the natural lawyers.[49] The above extract from Buller, which dates from the time of Erskine,[50] may be an example.[51] In fact, it is possible that both Buller and Erskine were drawing directly on Samuel von Pufendorf's *De Iure Naturae et Gentium* (first published in 1672) in which the ancient formula *alterum non laedere*[52] was applied to the delict of *damnum iniuria* as the engine of its generalisation.[53] In this respect it may be significant that in an early English translation of Pufendorf's work by Basil Kennett the word *alterum* is translated as 'neighbour', albeit inconsistently.[54] The language of neighbourhood then recalls the lawyer's question[55] which features so prominently both in the preamble to the parable of the Good Samaritan and in Lord Atkin's famous

[48] Francis Buller, *An Introduction to the Law of Trials at Nisi Prius* (5th edn, H Gaine 1788) 25.

[49] David Ibbetson, *Historical Introduction to the Law of Obligations* (OUP 1999) ch 9; 'The Tort of Negligence in the Common Law in the Nineteenth and Twentieth Centuries' in Eltjo Schrage (ed), *The Comparative Legal History of the Law of Torts: Negligence* (Duncker & Humblot 2001); 'The Tort of Negligence in England' in Niels Jansen (ed), *The Development and Making of Legal Doctrine* (CUP 2014) 46. Cf David Ibbetson, 'Natural Law and Common Law' (2001) 5 Edin LR 4.

[50] Erskine's *Institute of the Law of Scotland* appeared posthumously in 1773: see Kenneth Reid, 'John Erskine and the Institute of the Law of Scotland', Edinburgh School of Law Research Paper No 2015/26.

[51] Ibbetson (n 49) 165.

[52] Cf Ulpian's famous *dictum* in D.1.1.10.1: '*Iuris praecepta sunt haec: honeste vivere, alterum non laedere, suum cuique tribuere.*'

[53] Chapter 1 of Book 3 is entitled, 'That no man be hurt, and if a damage be done to any man, that reparation be made' (*Ut nemo laedatur, et si quod damnum fuit datum reparetur*), and fragment 1 begins with a statement of the first among the absolute duties imposed by natural law in respect of others, namely 'that no man hurt another, and that in case of any hurt or damage done by him, he fail not to make reparation' (*Ut ne quis alterum laedat, utque, si quod damnum alteri dederit, id reparet*). All translations are taken from the 4th edn of Basil Kennett's translation into English of *De Jure Naturae et Gentium*, entitled *Of the Law of Nature and Nations*, published together with English translations of Barbeyrac's commentary in 1729. Pufendorf refers heavily to Digest 9.2 throughout this title.

[54] For example, in the context of Book III.1.4. See the 4th edition of Kennett's translation (1729) 216.

[55] The 'lawyer' of the KJV is in the Vulgate *legisperitus* and in the original Greek *nomikos*.

dictum.[56] The parallel with Erskine's 'do not harm your neighbour (*alterum non laedere*)' would have been clearly apparent to Lord Atkin.[57]

This strongly suggests that the application of the 'neighbour' principle in the context of the law of delict/tort for which *Donoghue v Stevenson* is famous was not Lord Atkin's creation but rather that it was drawn from the teachings of the natural lawyers, probably by way of Erskine. What we do not find in Erskine is Lord Atkin's reference to a test of 'reasonable foreseeability'. At this point in his judgment Lord Atkin provides the 'restricted reply' to the lawyer's question posed in the parable of the Good Samaritan to which Jesus had given a purely moral answer. David Ibbetson[58] has argued that foreseeability first entered English law as a criterion for remoteness[59] and was derived from the work of the natural lawyers, especially Jean-Jacques Burlamaqui, concerning the imputability of harm to the defendant.[60] Here again, there is some evidence for its reception into English law in Buller's *Nisi Prius*.[61] According to Ibbetson, from here it spread to breach of duty – *Blyth v Birmingham Waterworks*[62] – and, ultimately, to duty of care itself,

---

[56]   The Latin of the Vulgate asks, '*Quis est meus proximus?*' which the English King James version of the Bible translates as 'Who is my neighbour?' The parable in full reads as follows (again in the original King James Bible):

> 25 And, behold, a certain lawyer stood up, and tempted him, saying, Master, what shall I do to inherit eternal life? 26 He said unto him, What is written in the law? how readest thou? 27 And he answering said, Thou shalt love the Lord thy God with all thy heart, and with all thy soul, and with all thy strength, and with all thy mind; and thy neighbour as thyself. 28 And he said unto him, Thou hast answered right: this do, and thou shalt live. 29 But he, willing to justify himself, said unto Jesus, And who is my neighbour? 30 And Jesus answering said, A certain *man* went down from Jerusalem to Jericho, and fell among thieves, which stripped him of his raiment, and wounded *him*, and departed, leaving *him* half dead. 31 And by chance there came down a certain priest that way: and when he saw him, he passed by on the other side. 32 And likewise a Levite, when he was at the place, came and looked *on him*, and passed by on the other side. 33 But a certain Samaritan, as he journeyed, came where he was: and when he saw him, he had compassion *on him*, 34 And went to *him*, and bound up his wounds, pouring in oil and wine, and set him on his own beast, and brought him to an inn, and took care of him. 35 And on the morrow when he departed, he took out two pence, and gave *them* to the host, and said unto him, Take care of him; and whatsoever thou spendest more, when I come again, I will repay thee. 36 Which now of these three, thinkest thou, was neighbour unto him that fell among the thieves? 37 And he said, He that shewed mercy on him. Then said Jesus unto him, Go, and do thou likewise.

[57]   See e.g. Richard Castle, 'Lord Atkin and the Neighbour Test: Origins of the Principles of Negligence in *Donoghue v Stevenson*' (2003) 7(33) Ecclesiastical Law Journal 210.

[58]   Ibbetson (n 49 1999) 174–77; (n 49 2001) 245–48, 263, 265.

[59]   See e.g. *Rigby v Hewitt* (1850) 5 Ex 240.

[60]   Jean-Jacques Burlamaqui, *The Principles of Natural and Politic Law* (Thomas Nugent tr, W Green 1817) 241–42.

[61]   See the 5th edn 26.

[62]   (1856) 11 Ex 781, 784.

as in *Donoghue*, and *Heaven v Pender*.[63] However, it is possible that Atkin's foreseeability principle has its origin rather in the well-known passage in Justinian's *Digest* on the liability of the pruner:

> *Si putator ex arbore ramum cum deiecerit vel machinarius hominem praetereuntem occidit, ita tenetur si is in publicum decidat nec ille proclamavit, ut casus evitari possit. Sed Mucius dixit, etiam si in privato idem accidisset posse de culpa agi: culpam autem esse quod cum a diligente provideri poterit, not esset provisum ...*[64]
>
> If a pruner threw down a branch from a tree and killed a slave passing underneath (the same applies to a man working on a scaffold), he is liable only if it falls down in a public place and he failed to shout a warning so that the accident could be avoided. But Mucius says that even if the accident occurred in a private place, an action can be brought on account of his *culpa*; and he thinks there is *culpa* when what could have been foreseen by a diligent man was not foreseen ...[65]

It is generally thought that Mucius did not give a generalised definition of *culpa* for Roman law[66] but this was to change: for example, Donellus in his *Commentary on the Civil Law* at XV.27.II elevates what he found in D.9.2.31 into a general definition of *culpa*:

> *Ea autem culpa hoc verbo intelligenda est, cum quod a diligente provideri potuit, ne quid damni ex re aliqua accideret, non est provisum. Exstat definitio in L. si putator D. ad leg. Aquil...*
>
> *Culpa* must be understood as follows, when what could have been foreseen by a diligent person, that some loss might come about from a particular event, was not foreseen. This definition is found in D.9.2.31 ...[67]

Thus it appears that just as Buller and Erskine, drawing on the natural-law tradition, anticipated Lord Atkin's neighbourhood principle by several centuries, so 'reasonable foreseeability' was used by Humanist writers as a general criterion to determine the circumstances in which a duty of care was owed more than three centuries before *Donoghue*. In this respect it is instructive to compare the speech of Lord Atkin with the judgment of Chief Justice Innes of the South African Appellate Division in 1921 in *Union Government v National Bank of South Africa*:

> Legal negligence consists in a failure to exercise that degree of care which, under the circumstances, it was the duty of the person concerned to use towards another. It involves therefore the existence of a duty to take care owed to the complainant ... [Whether there was a duty] must be looked for in the circumstances of the case.

---

[63] (1883) 11 QBD 503.

[64] D.9.2.31.

[65] This is an adapted version of the Watson translation.

[66] See e.g. Geoffrey MacCormack, 'Aquilian *Culpa*' in Alan Watson (ed), *Daube Noster: Essays in Legal History for David Daube* (Scottish Academic Press 1974) 201; 'Aquilian Studies' (1975) 41 SDHI 45.

[67] Authors' translation.

Every man has a right that others shall not injure him in his person or property by their actions or conduct, but that involves a duty to exercise proper care. The test as to the existence of the duty is, by our law, the judgment of the reasonable man. Could the infliction of injury to others have been reasonably foreseen? If so, the person whose conduct is in question must be regarded having owed a duty to others ... whoever they might be ... to take due and reasonable care to avoid such injury. There are innumerable cases in which South African Courts have dealt with these questions by an application of the extended principles of the Aquilian Law. [68]

More than ten years before *Donoghue* was handed down, Chief Justice Innes had no difficulty in recognising the existence of a general legal duty to act without negligence in respect of all those persons whom one could reasonably foresee would suffer loss as the result of one's act. This suggests a much closer link between the *lex Aquilia* and Lord Atkin's test of reasonable foreseeability than is usually acknowledged.

Sir Frederick Pollock

At the beginning of Lord Buckmaster's dissenting speech in *Donoghue* he mentions that the works of living authors are not authoritative on the matter before the committee. He says:[69]

Now the common law must be sought in law books by writers of authority and in judgments of the judges entrusted with its administration. The law books give no assistance, because the works of living authors, however deservedly eminent, cannot be used as authority, though the opinions they express may demand attention; and the ancient books do not assist. I turn, therefore, to the decided cases to see if they can be construed so as to support the appellant's case.

Lord Shaw in *Cantiere* referred to Pollock's work on *Contracts* to highlight the disapproval of members of the English legal establishment of the understanding of failure of consideration as it was applied by the Court of Appeal to the law of restitution. Lord Macmillan referred to Pollock twice in his judgment in *Donoghue*.[70] In all probability Lord Buckmaster was also referring to Pollock in the passage quoted above. Pollock's opinion on the shortcomings of the narrow conception of the duty of care as expressed in most of the English case law was stated in the following terms shortly before *Donoghue*:[71]

The whole modern law of negligence with its many developments, enforces the duty of fellow-citizens to observe ... an appropriate measure of prudence to avoid

---

[68] 1921 AD 121, 128–29.
[69] [35].
[70] [64] and [66].
[71] Frederick Pollock, *Law of Torts* (13th edn, Stevens & Sons Ltd 1929) 21–22.

causing harm to others ... As our law of contract has been generalised ... so has our law of civil wrongs ... it is submitted that any attempt, at this day, to maintain a narrower conception of civil duty can lead only to interminable difficulties.

Pollock's disapproval helps to explain why Mrs Donoghue's claim gained momentum in the face of clear contrary authority like *Mullen v Barr*. It had the backing of powerful members of the English legal establishment who wanted the law changed, and they saw the opportunity in this claim being taken to the House of Lords.

4. CONCLUSION

Lord Atkin spoke of liability for both negligence and *culpa* in seeking 'some general conception of relations giving rise to a duty of care' in order to give expression in English law to what he regarded to be common (that is, worldwide?) moral and social values. There was a minority testimony in the English case law that supported a broad understanding of duty of care. In an exercise of its 'declaratory' power, the majority in the House of Lords stated that these cases expressed the law of England and Scotland. Lord Buckmaster called them 'perturbed spirits'. In identifying the circumstances in which a duty of care was owed, however, Lord Atkin gave a far more prominent role to principle than precedent. He elegantly crystallised the essential elements of the 'general' approach as represented by these minority cases in the terms *alterum non laedere* (you must not injure others), my 'neighbour' and 'reasonable foreseeability'. On the one hand, the pivotal idea of a general duty of care owed to one's neighbour appears to have had deep roots in the natural-law tradition. This is evident from its use by Scottish Institutional writers such as Erskine, reliance on whose work by Lord Macmillan had been suppressed in the final version of his judgment in *Donoghue*.

On the other hand, in a tradition distinct from that of the natural lawyers, 'reasonable foreseeability' had been elevated (by Donellus, for example) into the essential element in the definition of *culpa*. The *dictum* of Chief Justice Innes in South Africa in 1921 suggests that in this regard there was a tradition of standing within the common law well before *Donoghue*. Lord Atkin certainly elaborated upon it by combining it with the idea of my 'neighbour' to whom a general duty of care is owed, but he was not its originator.

Out of the conflicting testimony in the lower courts of England the House of Lords drew on 'general jurisprudence' to identify the true markers of the tort of negligence. These yielded a result to which, in the view of the majority, the common law was turning as an evolutionary imperative. Lord Macmillan said:[72]

---

[72] [56].

It is always a satisfaction to an English lawyer to be able to test his application of fundamental principles of the common law by the development of the same doctrines by the lawyers of the Courts of the United States ... I must not ... do more than refer to the illuminating judgment of Cardozo J. in *MacPherson v Buick Motor Company* in the New York Court of Appeals, in which he states the principles of the law as I should desire to state them ...

However, 'negligence' as it was formulated by the House of Lords in *Donoghue* proved to be an evolutionary cul-de-sac. Although *Anns v Merton BC*[73] seemed to recommit English law to Lord Atkin's neighbourhood principle, the decision of the House of Lords in *Caparo v Dickman*[74] has narrowly circumscribed it; in particular, the additional requirement of proximity detracts from the generality of Lord Atkin's original proposition. Just as Lord Atkin's reply to the lawyer's question was more restricted than that given in the Gospel itself, so 'neighbourhood' as English lawyers now understand it describes a more narrowly drawn class than that which Lord Atkin himself envisaged.[75]

---

[73] *Anns v Merton London Borough Council* [1978] AC 728.
[74] *Caparo Industries Plc v Dickman* [1990] 2 AC 605.
[75] We are grateful to John Ford and Geoffrey MacCormack for their comments.

Chapter 10

Conclusions

Paul J du Plessis

Roman legal texts on the *lex Aquilia* teem with life. This is no doubt one of the reasons why the topic of wrongful damage to property has had such a profound impact upon the legal landscape of Roman law in the United Kingdom.[1] Students and teachers like cases and the Roman legal texts provide ample fodder for detailed analytical discussions of the elements of a civil wrong. But it is not merely the attractiveness of the cases that has cemented the place of the *lex Aquilia* in the legal landscape of Roman law in the United Kingdom. This association goes far deeper than that. In fact, the *lex Aquilia* reveals the very DNA of Roman law studies in the United Kingdom.

In this volume, a group of established and younger scholars of Roman law were asked to reflect upon this topic. Their task was to examine the impact which the teaching of and research into this area of the Roman law of delict has had on the discipline of Roman law in the United Kingdom during the course of the twentieth century. The aim of this investigation has been to assess the extent to which the *lex Aquilia* may be used to draw larger conclusions about the nature of Roman law in the United Kingdom as an academic discipline.

The chapters by Cairns, Ibbetson, Mitchell and Spagnolo provide the contexts in which the *lex Aquilia* in Britain should be viewed. As Cairns shows, the teaching of this aspect of the Roman law of delict must be seen

---

[1] It is not my intention to engage with the debate about the merits of teaching Roman law as part of a law degree in the United Kingdom. I take this as a given and refer the reader to the following discussions of the subject with specific reference to England and Scotland. On the topic, generally, see Andrew Lewis and David Ibbetson (eds), *The Roman Law Tradition* (CUP 2011) and the chapters collected therein. On the teaching of Roman law in the United Kingdom more generally, see Peter Birks 'Roman Law in Twentieth-Century Britain' in Jack Beatson and Reinhard Zimmermann (eds), *Jurists Uprooted: German-Speaking Émigré Lawyers in Twentieth-Century Britain* (OUP 2007). While the courts' use of Roman law in Scotland is somewhat different to that of England, there are sufficient similarities to warrant a broad perspective that encompasses the entire United Kingdom. For a survey of this debate, see the chapters by Birks, Cairns and Rodger in David L Carey-Miller and Reinhard Zimmermann (eds), *The Civilian Tradition and Scots Law: Aberdeen Quincentenary Essays* (Duncker & Humblot 1997).

against the backdrop of changes to university education during the course of the nineteenth century. Furthermore, the relationship between the exegetical mode of teaching (using Roman law texts) and a desire by university authorities to equip students with a knowledge of juristic reasoning and intellectual techniques are vital to our understanding of this topic. To this must be added the availability of teaching material such as the translations and commentaries of Monro. Cairns' comments about the relationships between the British methods of teaching this topic and their engagement with the Pandectist exposition of settled doctrine is well worth noting (a point to which I will return later). In fact, it is a leitmotiv that recurs in many of the chapters in this volume.

Ibbetson's account of Buckland's lectures provides important additional context. Given the importance of Buckland for the development of Roman law scholarship in the United Kingdom, the transcription of his lectures on the *lex Aquilia* provides valuable insights, not only about the nature of his teaching, but also about the topics that he regarded as important. Even if Buckland had a systemic view of Roman law, which was not at all uncommon for the period, it is clear that he was not teaching the topic in a Pandectist fashion (as doctrine). Rather, much like the insights by Cairns confirm, the teaching of Roman law was concerned with textual interpretation and juristic techniques rather than an exposition of settled doctrine. Buckland's lectures show that very clearly.

Mitchell provides insights into another seminal work in the history of British scholarship on the *lex Aquilia*, namely Lawson's *Negligence* (1950). This curious work, part Roman law and part comparative law, represents an important moment in Roman law scholarship in Britain on this topic. In many ways, it was the reason why the topic became so popular in the teaching of Roman law subsequently, but as a work of Roman and comparative law, it also demonstrates much about Lawson's own views on Roman law. It would of course be wrong to deny that this work was also important for the development of comparative law in the United Kingdom, but whether it was successful in the longer term is a matter for another book.[2] More importantly, though, is the method employed in this work, its didactic aims and the reactions provoked from Continental scholars of Roman law.

The final chapter in this section, by Spagnolo, provides an overview of the teaching of the *lex Aquilia* at Oxford during the course of the twentieth century. In many ways, it completes the narrative begun by Cairns and rounds off the context part of this volume. There are many great insights in this chapter, but above all it shows that the teaching of Roman law has never been static (a common, if lazy criticism often levelled against the subject).

---

[2]   See on this point John Cairns, 'The Development of Comparative Law in Great Britain' in Mathias Reimann and Reinhard Zimmermann (eds), *The Oxford Handbook of Comparative Law* (OUP 2006).

It has adapted itself constantly, while at the same time remaining true to its original purpose, namely to provide students with the juristic tools, methods and grammar to undertake the study of law.

The second part of this volume is devoted to a number of case studies. Here, scholars of Roman law (from the United Kingdom and the Continent) have been asked to reflect upon the extent to which there can be said to be a British method in its own right. The results of this investigation have shown that there are definitely certain unifying elements visible in Roman law scholarship in Britain and that these are connected to the didactic aims of the subject as set out above. Sampson has argued that British scholars of Roman law are not necessarily interested in finding one single answer to a problem raised in Roman legal doctrine. To this extent, their method deviates considerably from that of Continental scholarship. Rather, scholars in the United Kingdom seem to be more willing to entertain a range of answers using a variety of source material (often also including historical contextual facts). The same conclusion is reached by Lorusso who has shown that an awareness of historical fact and juristic technique can do much to inform modern scholarship when attempting to solve unresolved issues in the Roman law of wrongful damage to property. Johnston's contribution takes this one step further. As he has argued, one should not merely look at method alone. It is also important to appreciate that the *translatio studii* that has taken place in the United Kingdom as a result of scholars such as David Daube and Fritz Schulz have done much to shape the modern British method of Roman law scholarship. With that said, Johnston makes a clear case for a method which, while informed by Continental scholarship, is not dominated by it.

The final two contributions by Valditara and Evans-Jones/Scott round off the volume. The contribution by Valditara, the leading scholar on this topic in the world, shows that an appreciation of Roman juristic techniques on their own terms can be very useful when investigating the rationale behind later incarnations of Roman legal rules found in the codifications of Europe, while Evans-Jones/Scott demonstrate the practical importance of Roman legal texts in the creation of modern law.

This is by no means the last word on this topic. There is still much work to be done on the teaching of Roman law in the United Kingdom, especially in relation to the relationship between Roman law and prevailing legal theory during the course of the twentieth century. Much work also remains to be done on the relationship between the juristic discussions in Roman legal texts on the *lex Aquilia* and Roman legal practice. Thus, for example, few scholars have studied Cicero's oration for Quintus Roscius the comedian, a case which is squarely based on an instance of wrongful damage to property arising from the death of a co-owned slave. One thing is certain, however. The teaching of and research into Roman law in the United Kingdom has its own didactic and conceptual logic, and, while it is undoubtedly aware of and willing to engage with Continental scholarship on Roman law, it is not dominated by it. In this respect, it may well be said that the teaching of Roman law is firmly rooted in the 'legal culture' of the United Kingdom where it has a specific role and a unique didactic function.

Index